# German

Phrasebook

LAROUSSE

*Editors*
Helen Galloway, Sigrid Koehler

*with*
Valerie Grundy, Kathrin Hadeler, Christy Johnson, Donald Watt

*Supplement on German language and culture*
Helen Galloway

*Publishing manager*
Janice McNeillie

*Design and typesetting*
Sharon McTeir

© Larousse 2006
21, rue du Montparnasse
75283 Paris Cedex 06

ISBN: 2-03-542151-9

Sales: Houghton Mifflin Company, Boston

Achevé d'imprimer en Mai 2006 sur les presses de « La Tipografica Varese S.p.A. » à Varese (Italie)

# Introduction

This phrasebook is the ideal companion for your trip. It gets straight to the point, helping you to understand and make yourself understood so that you don't miss a thing. Use it like a dictionary to find the exact word you're looking for right away. And at each word we've provided a selection of key phrases that will help you in any situation, no matter how tricky things may have gotten.

The English–German section contains all those essential expressions that you'll need to get by in Germany. And because you need to be able to pronounce the words you see on the page properly, we've provided a simple and straightforward phonetic transcription that will enable you to make yourself understood with ease.

The German–English section provides all the most important words and expressions that you might read or hear while on vacation.

And that's not all: we've added practical and cultural tips for getting by, a supplement on German language, life and culture – everything, in fact, to make your trip go as smoothly as possible.

*Gute Reise!*

# Pronunciation

So that you can say what you want to say in German without running any risk of being misunderstood, we have devised a simple and straightforward phonetic transcription to show how every German word or phrase used in this phrasebook is pronounced. This phonetic transcription, which is shown in brackets after each German word or phrase, uses as many standard English sounds as possible, so that it is virtually self-explanatory. The following list provides further clarification:

| | |
|---|---|
| [a] | as in m**a**t |
| [aa] | as in b**a**r |
| [ay] | as in w**ay** |
| [e] | as in th**e** |
| [ee] | as in f**ee** |
| [eh] | as in g**e**t |
| [eu] | as in chauff**eur** |
| [ey] | as in **eye** |
| [i] | as in s**i**t |
| [kh] | as in lo**ch** |
| [o] | as in h**o**t |
| [oh] | as in c**oa**t |
| [oo] | as in p**oo**l |
| [ow] | as in h**ow** |
| [oy] | as in b**oy** |
| [sh] | as in **sh**op |
| [tsh] | as in ca**tch** |
| [u] | as in p**u**sh |
| [uu] | as in the French word r**u**e |
| [zh] | as in plea**s**ure |

# Abbreviations

| | |
|---|---|
| *abbr* | abbreviation |
| *adj* | adjective |
| *adv* | adverb |
| *art* | article |
| *conj* | conjunction |
| *das* | neuter noun |
| *der* | masculine noun |
| *die* | feminine noun |
| *excl* | exclamation |
| *num* | numeral |
| *pl* | plural |
| *prep* | preposition |
| *pron* | pronoun |
| *v* | verb |

# English–German phrasebook

**able**
- to be able to können [keunen]
- I'm not able to come tonight ich kann heute Abend nicht kommen [ish kan hoy-te aabent nisht kom-en]

**about** etwa [ehtva]
- I think I'll stay for about an hour ich glaube, ich bleibe etwa eine Stunde [ish glow-be ish bley-be ehtva ey-ne shtun-de]

**abroad** *(live)* im Ausland [im owslant]; *(travel)* ins Ausland [ins owslant]
- I've never been abroad before ich war noch nie im Ausland [ish vaar nokh nee im owslant]

**absolutely** völlig [feulish]
- you're absolutely right Sie haben völlig Recht [zee haaben feulish rehsht]

**accept** annehmen [an-naymen]
- do you accept traveler's checks? nehmen Sie Reiseschecks an? [naymen zee reyzeshehks an]

**access** der Zugang [tsoogang]
- is there disabled access? gibt es einen behindertengerechten Zugang? [gipt ehs eynen behindertengerehshten tsoogang]

**accident** der Unfall [unfal]
- there's been an accident es hat einen Unfall gegeben [ehs hat eynen unfal gegayben]

**according to** laut [lowt]
- it's well worth seeing, according to the guidebook laut Reiseführer ist es sehr sehenswert [lowt reyzefuurer ist ehs zehr zayenzvehrt]

**address** die Adresse [adreh-se] ◆ *(speak to)* anreden [anrayden]
- could you write down the address for me? könnten Sie die Adresse für mich aufschreiben? [keunten zee dee adreh-se fuur mish owfshreyben]
- here is my address and phone number hier sind meine Adresse und Telefonnummer [heer zint mey-ne adreh-se unt tehlehfohn-numer] ▶ see box on p. 2

**adult** der, die Erwachsene [ehrvakse-ne]
- two adults and one student, please zwei Erwachsene und ein Student, bitte [tsvey ehrvakse-ne unt eyn shtoodehnt bi-te]

**advance** *(money)* der Vorschuss [forshus]
- do you have to book in advance? muss man im Voraus buchen? [mus man im forows bookhen]

**after** nach [nakh]

### addressing people

When you're meeting another adult for the first time, you shake hands and give your last name. Use the polite *Sie* form of the verb when talking to them, e.g. *wo kommen Sie her?* (where are you from?). Once you are on first-name terms you can use the familiar *du* form of the verb, e.g. *was machst du heute Abend?* (what are you doing tonight?). If you're on business, you should address your colleagues as *Herr* or *Frau* (Mr. or Mrs./Ms.), followed by their last name. Since so many people use the title *Doktor* (teachers, businessmen, etc.), it's just as well to use this title too, so say *Herr Doktor* or *Frau Doktor* to be on the safe side.

▸ it's twenty after eight **es ist zwanzig nach acht** [ehs ist tsvantsish nakh akht]
▸ the stadium is just after the traffic lights **das Stadium kommt gleich nach der Ampel** [das shtaadium komt gleysh nakh dehr ampel]

**afternoon** der Nachmittag [nakhmitaak]
▸ is the museum open in the afternoons? **ist das Museum nachmittags geöffnet?** [ist das muzayum nakhmitaaks ge-eufnet]

**aftershave** das Aftershave [ehfteshayv]
▸ a bottle of aftershave **eine Flasche Aftershave** [ey-ne flash-e ehfteshayv]

**afterwards** danach [daanakh]
▸ join us afterwards **komm danach zu uns** [kom daanakh tsoo uns]

**again** wieder [veeder]
▸ the train is late again **der Zug hat wieder Verspätung** [dehr tsook hat veeder fehrshpaytung]

**age** das Alter [alter]
▸ what ages are your children? **in welchem Alter sind Ihre Kinder?** [in vehlshem alter zint ee-re kin-der]
▸ we've been waiting for ages! **wir warten schon ewig!** [veer varten shohn ayvig]

### agreement/disagreement

▸ absolutely! **stimmt genau!** [shtimt genow]
▸ that's fine by me **einverstanden** [eynfehrshtanden]
▸ you're right **du hast Recht** [doo hast rehsht]
▸ go on, then **also gut** [alzoh goot]
▸ I'm not at all convinced **ich bin ganz und gar nicht überzeugt davon** [ish bin gants unt gar nisht uuber-tsoykt daafon]
▸ I disagree **da bin ich anderer Meinung** [daa bin ish anderer meynung]

**agency** die Agentur [aagehntoor]
> what is the contact number for the agency? wie lautet die Kontaktnummer der Agentur? [vee lowtet dee kontaktnumer dehr aagehntoor]

**ago** vor [for]
> I've been before, several years ago ich war schon einmal vor mehreren Jahren da [ish vaar shohn eynmal for mehreren yaaren daa]

**ahead** vorne [forn-e]
> is the road ahead clear? ist die Straße vorne frei? [ist dee shtraa-se forn-e frey]

**air** die Luft [luft]
> the air is much fresher in the mountains die Luft ist in den Bergen viel frischer [dee luft ist in dayn behrgen feel frisher]

**air-conditioning** die Klimaanlage [kleema-anlaa-ge]
> do you have air-conditioning? haben Sie Klimaanlage? [haaben zee kleema-anlaa-ge]

**airline** die Fluggesellschaft [flookgezehlshaft]
> no, we're traveling with a different airline nein, wir fliegen mit einer anderen Fluggesellschaft [neyn veer fleegen mit eyner anderen flookgezehlshaft]

**airmail** die Luftpost [luftpost]
> I'd like to send it airmail ich möchte es per Luftpost schicken [ish meush-te ehs per luftpost shiken]

**airport** der Flughafen [flookhaafen]
> how long does it take to get to the airport? wie weit ist es bis zum Flughafen? [vee veyt ist ehs bis tsum flookhaafen]

**airport shuttle** der Flughafenshuttle [flookhaafen-shut-el]
> is there an airport shuttle? gibt es einen Flughafenshuttle? [gipt ehs eynen flookhaafen-shut-el]

---

### at the airport

> where is gate number 2? wo ist Flugsteig Nummer 2? [voh ist flookshteyk numer tsvey]
> where is the check-in desk? wo ist der Check-in-Schalter? [voh ist dehr tshekinshalter]
> I'd like an aisle seat ich möchte gerne einen Sitz am Gang [ish meush-te gehrn-e eynen zits am gang]
> where is the baggage claim? wo ist die Gepäckausgabe? [voh ist dee gepehk-owsgaa-be]

## alcohol

Before or after a meal you might fancy drinking a *Schnaps* (a type of strong spirit). Distilled from Black Forest fruits (cherries, raspberries, plums, etc.), *schnapps* in Westphalia is white, but in Mainz where it's known as *Weinbrand* it's very much like cognac, and in the North it comes in the shape of the absolutely explosive *Ratzeputz*, which is made from ginger. This is great drunk with a beer to keep out the cold!

**air pressure** der Luftdruck [luftdruk]
- could you check the air pressure in the tires? könnten Sie den Reifendruck prüfen? [keunten zee dayn reyfendruk pruufen]

**airsick** flugkrank [flook-krank]
- can I have an airsick bag? kann ich eine Spucktüte haben? [kan ish ey-ne shpuktuute haaben]

**aisle** *(between plane seats)* der Gang [gang]; *(plane seat)* der Sitz am Gang [zits am gang]
- two seats, please: one window and one aisle zwei Sitze, bitte, einen Fensterplatz und einen Sitz am Gang [tsvey zit-se bi-te, eynen fehnsterplats unt eynen zits am gang]

**aisle seat** der Sitz am Gang [zits am gang]
- I'd like an aisle seat ich hätte gerne einen Sitz am Gang [ish heh-te gehrn-e eynen zits am gang]

**alarm (clock)** der Wecker [vehker]
- I set the alarm for nine o'clock ich habe den Wecker für neun Uhr gestellt [ish haa-be dayn vehker fuur noyn oor geshtehlt]

**alcohol** der Alkohol [alkoh-hohl]
- I don't drink alcohol ich trinke keinen Alkohol [ish trin-ke keynen alkoh-hohl]

**alcohol-free** alkoholfrei [alkoh-hohlfrey]
- what kind of alcohol-free drinks do you have? was für alkoholfreie Getränke haben Sie? [vas fuur alkoh-hohlfrey-e getrehn-ke haaben zee]

**all** alle [al-e] ✦ *(the whole amount)* alles [al-es]; *(everybody)* alle [al-e]
- all the time die ganze Zeit [dee gant-se tseyt]
- all English people alle Engländer [al-e ehnglehnder]
- will that be all? ist das alles? [ist das al-es]

**allergic** allergisch [alehrgish]
- I'm allergic to aspirin/nuts/wheat/dairy products ich bin allergisch gegen Aspirin/Nüsse/Weizen/Milchprodukte [ish bin alehrgish gaygen aspireen/nuus-e/veytsen/milshprohdukt-e]

**allow** erlauben [ehrlowben]
- how much luggage are you allowed? wie viele Gepäckstücke sind erlaubt? [vee fee-le gepehkshtuu-ke zint ehrlowbt]
- are you allowed to smoke here? darf man hier rauchen? [darf man heer rowkhen]

**almost** fast [fast]
- it's almost one o'clock es ist fast ein Uhr [ehs ist fast eyn oor]

**alone** alleine [aley-ne]
- leave us alone! lassen Sie uns in Ruhe! [las-en zee uns in roo-e]

**along** entlang [ehntlang]
- along the river am Fluss entlang [am flus ehntlang]

**altogether** *(in total)* insgesamt [insgezamt]
- how much does it cost altogether? wie viel kostet es insgesamt? [vee feel kostet ehs insgezamt]

**always** immer [im-er]
- it's always the same thing es ist immer das Gleiche [ehs ist im-er das gleysh-e]

**ambulance** der Krankenwagen [krankenvaagen]
- could you send an ambulance right away to...? könnten Sie sofort einen Krankenwagen zu ... schicken? [keunten zee zohfort eynen krankenvaagen tsoo shiken]

**ambulance service** der Rettungsdienst [rehtungzdeenst]
- what's the number for the ambulance service? was ist die Nummer für den Rettungsdienst? [vas ist dee nu-mer fuur dayn rehtungzdeenst]

**America** das Amerika [amehrika]
- I'm from America ich komme aus Amerika [ish kom-e ows amehrika]
- I live in America ich lebe in Amerika [ish layb-e in amehrika]
- have you ever been to America? waren Sie schon einmal in Amerika? [vaaren zee shohn eynmal in amehrika]

**American** amerikanisch [amehrikaanish] ◆ der Amerikaner [amehrikaaner], die Amerikanerin [amehrikaanerin]
- I'm American ich bin Amerikaner/Amerikanerin [ish bin amehrikaaner/amehrikaanerin]
- we're Americans wir sind Amerikaner [veer zint amehrikaaner]

**ankle** der Knöchel [kneushel]
- I've sprained my ankle ich habe mir den Knöchel verstaucht [ish haa-be meer dayn kneushel fehrshtowkht]

**announcement** die Ansage [anzaa-ge]
- was that an announcement about the Berlin train? war das eine Ansage zu dem Zug nach Berlin? [vaar das ey-ne anzaa-ge tsoo daym tsook nakh behrleen]

**another** *(additional)* noch ein [nokh eyn]; *(different)* ein anderer [eyn anderer]
- another coffee, please noch ein Kaffee, bitte [nokh eyn kafay bi-te]
- (would you like) another drink? noch etwas zu trinken? [nokh ehtvas tsoo trinken]

**answer** die Antwort [antvort] ♦ antworten [antvorten]
- there's no answer *(on telephone)* es nimmt keiner ab [ehs nimt keyner ap]
- I phoned earlier but nobody answered ich habe schon einmal angerufen, aber es hat keiner abgenommen [ish haa-be shohn eynmal angeroofen aber ehs hat keyner apgenomen]

**answering machine** der Anrufbeantworter [anroof-be-antvorter]
- I left a message on your answering machine ich habe eine Nachricht auf dem Anrufbeantworter hinterlassen [ish haa-be ey-ne nakh-risht owf daym anroof-be-antvorter hinterlas-en]

**anti-dandruff shampoo** das Antischuppenshampoo [antishupenshampoo]
- do you have anti-dandruff shampoo? haben Sie Antischuppenshampoo? [haaben zee antishupenshampoo]

**anybody, anyone** jemand [yaymant]
- is there anybody there? ist da jemand? [ist daa yaymant]

**anything** irgendetwas [irgentetvas]
- is there anything we can do? können wir irgendetwas tun? [keunen veer irgentetvas toon]

**anywhere** irgendwo [irgentvoh]
- I can't find my room key anywhere ich kann meinen Zimmerschlüssel nirgendwo finden [ish kan meynen tsimershluusel nirgentvoh finden]
- do you live anywhere near here? wohnen Sie hier irgendwo in der Nähe? [vohnen zee heer irgentvoh in dehr nay-e]

**apartment** die Wohnung [vohnung]
- we'd like to rent an apartment for one week wir möchten gerne eine Wohnung für eine Woche mieten [veer meushten gehrn-e ey-ne vohnung fuur ey-ne vokh-e meeten]

**apologize** sich entschuldigen [zish ehntshuldigen]
- there's no need to apologize Sie müssen sich nicht entschuldigen [zee meusen zish nisht ehntshuldigen]

**appetizer** die Vorspeise [forshpeyz-e]
- which of the appetizers would you recommend? welche Vorspeise würden Sie empfehlen? [vehlsh-e forshpeyz-e vuurden zee ehmpfaylen]

---

### apologizing

- excuse me! Entschuldigung! [ehntshuldigung]
- I'm sorry, I can't come on Saturday es tut mir Leid, aber ich kann am Samstag nicht kommen [ehs toot meer leyt aber ish kan am zamztaak nisht kom-en]
- that's OK das ist in Ordnung [das ist in ordnung]
- it doesn't matter es macht nichts [ehs makht nishts]
- don't mention it keine Ursache [key-ne oorzakh-e]

**apple** der Apfel [apfel]
▸ could I have a pound of apples, please? könnte ich bitte ein Pfund Äpfel haben? [keun-te ish bi-te eyn pfunt ehpfel haaben]

**apple juice** der Apfelsaft [apfelzaft]
▸ I'd like some apple juice ich hätte gerne etwas Apfelsaft [ish heh-te gehrn-e ehtvas apfelzaft]

**appointment** der Termin [tehrmeen]
▸ could I get an appointment for tomorrow morning? könnte ich einen Termin für morgen Früh ausmachen? [keun-te ish eynen tehrmeen fuur morgen fruu owsmakhen]
▸ I have an appointment with Doctor ... ich habe einen Termin bei Dr. ... [ish haa-be eynen tehrmeen bey doktor]

**April** der April [apreel]
▸ April 6th sechster April [zehkster apreel]

**area** *(region, locality)* die Gegend [gaygent]; *(small)* der Teil [teyl]; *(sector, subject)* der Bereich [bereysh]
▸ I'm visiting the area ich bin zu Besuch in der Gegend [ish bin tsoo bezookh in dehr gaygent]
▸ what walks can you recommend in the area? welche Spaziergänge können Sie in der Gegend empfehlen? [vehlshe shpatseergehng-e keunen zee in dehr gaygent ehmpfaylen]

**area code** die Vorwahl [forvaal]
▸ what's the area code for Frankfurt? was ist die Vorwahl für Frankfurt? [vas ist dee forvaal fuur frankfurt]

**arm** der Arm [arm]
▸ I can't move my arm ich kann meinen Arm nicht bewegen [ish kan meynen arm nisht bevaygen]

**around** herum [hehrum]; *(nearby)* in der Nähe [in dehr nay-e]; *(on every side)* überall [uuberal] ◆ *(encircling)* um [um], um ... herum [um hehrum]; *(through)* durch [dursh]; *(approximately)* etwa [ehtva]
▸ we've been traveling around Europe wir sind durch Europa gereist [veer zint dursh oyrohpa gereyzt]
▸ I don't know my way around yet ich kenne mich noch nicht aus [ish ken-e mish nokh nisht ows]
▸ I arrived around two o'clock ich bin etwa um zwei Uhr angekommen [ish bin ehtva um tsvey oor an-gekom-en]
▸ I'd like something for around 15 euros ich hätte gerne etwas um die fünfzehn Euro [ish heh-te gehrn-e ehtvas um dee fuunftsayn oyroh]

**arrive** ankommen [ankom-en]
▸ my luggage hasn't arrived mein Gepäck ist nicht angekommen [meyn gepehk ist nisht angekom-en]

## alternative arts

The alternative arts scene (*die alternative Szene*) is very strong in Germany. This is not only the case in Berlin but also in many of the main towns where local troupes put on their own shows. Plays, rock concerts and jazz shows are performed in dozens of bars, clubs and small venues.

- we arrived late *(by train, plane)* wir kamen mit Verspätung an [veer kaamen mit fehrshpaytung an]
- we just arrived wir sind gerade angekommen [veer zint geraa-de angekom-en]

**art** die Kunst [kunst]
- I'm not really interested in art ich interessiere mich nicht wirklich für Kunst [ish interehseer-e mish nisht virklish fuur kunst]

**as** *(while)* während [vehrent]; *(like)* wie [vee]; *(since)* da [daa] ◆ *(in comparisons)* wie [vee]
- the lights went out just as we were about to eat die Lichter gingen aus, als wir gerade anfangen wollten zu essen [dee lishter gingen ows als veer geraa-de anfangen volten tsoo ehsen]
- as I said before wie ich schon sagte [vee ish shohn zaag-te]
- leave it as it is lass es so wie es ist [las ehs zoh vee ehs ist]
- as ... as so ... wie [zoh vee]
- as much as so viel wie [zoh feel vee]
- as many as so viele wie [zoh feel-e vee]

**ashtray** der Aschenbecher [ashenbehsher]
- could you bring us an ashtray? könnten Sie uns einen Aschenbecher bringen? [keunten zee uns eynen ashenbehsher bringen]

**ask** *(question)* fragen [fraagen]; *(time)* fragen nach [fraagen nakh]
- can I ask you a question? kann ich Sie etwas fragen? [kan ish zee ehtvas fraagen]

## asking questions

- is this seat free? ist dieser Platz frei? [ist deezer plats frey]
- where is the station? wo ist der Bahnhof? [voh ist dehr baanhohf]
- could you help me get my suitcase down, please? könnten Sie mir bitte helfen meinen Koffer herunterzuholen? [keunten zee meer bi-te hehlfen meynen kof-er hehrunter-tsoo-hohlen]
- could you give me a hand? könnten Sie mir helfen? [keunten zee meer hehlfen]
- could you lend me ten euros? könnten Sie mir zehn Euro leihen? [keunten zee meer tsayn oyroh leyen]

### ATMs

ATMs are often indicated by the letters *EC*. Check that the logo of your particular card is shown on the machine, as Visa® is still less widely used than MasterCard®. Some small stores still won't accept payment by credit card.

**aspirin** das Aspirin [aspireen]
- I'd like some aspirin ich hätte gerne etwas Aspirin [ish heh-te gehrn-e ehtvas aspireen]

**asthma** das Asthma [astma]
- I have asthma ich habe Asthma [ish haa-be astma]

**at** *(indicating place, position)* an [an]; *(indicating time)* um [um]
- our bags are still at the airport unser Gepäck ist noch am Flughafen [unzer gepehk ist nokh am flookhaafen]
- we arrive at midnight wir kommen um Mitternacht an [veer kom-en um miternakht an]
- I'm at the hotel ich bin im Hotel [ish bin im hohtehl]

**ATM** der Geldautomat [gehlt-owtohmaat]
- I'm looking for an ATM ich suche einen Geldautomat [ish zookh-e eynen gehlt-owtohmaat]
- the ATM has eaten my card der Geldautomat hat meine Karte eingezogen [dehr gehlt-owtohmaat hat mey-ne kart-e eyngetsohgen]

**attack** *(of illness)* der Anfall [anfal] ◆ *(person)* angreifen [angreyfen]
- he had a heart attack er hatte einen Herzanfall [ehr ha-te eynen hehrtsanfal]
- I've been attacked ich bin angegriffen worden [ish bin angegrifen vorden]

**attention** die Aufmerksamkeit [owfmehrkzaamkeyt]
- may I have your attention for a moment? kann ich Ihre Aufmerksamkeit für einen Moment haben? [kan ish ee-re owfmehrkzaamkeyt fuur eynen mohmehnt haaben]

**attractive** attraktiv [atraktif]
- I find you very attractive ich finde Sie sehr attraktiv [ish fin-de zee zehr atraktif]

**August** der August [owgust]
- we're arriving on August 29th wir kommen am neunundzwanzigsten August an [veer kom-en am noyn-unt-tsvantsigsten owgust an]

**automatic** automatisch [owtohmaatish] ◆ *(car)* der Automatikwagen [owtohmaatikvaagen]
- I want a car with automatic transmission ich möchte einen Automatikwagen [ish meush-te eynen owtohmaatikvaagen]

- is it a manual or an automatic? ist es mit Gangschaltung oder Automatik? [ist ehs mit gang-shaltung ohder owtohmaatik]

**available** verfügbar [fehrfuugbar]
- you don't have a table available before then? haben Sie keinen Tisch davor frei? [haaben zee keynen tish daafor frey]

**average** durchschnittlich [dursh-shnitlish]
- what's the average price of a meal there? was kostet dort ein Essen im Durchschnitt? [vas kostet dort eyn ehsen im dursh-shnit]

**avoid** vermeiden [fehrmeyden]
- is there a route that would help us avoid the traffic? gibt es eine Strecke, durch die wir den Verkehr vermeiden können? [gipt ehs ey-ne shtreh-ke dursh dee veer dayn fehrkehr fehrmeyden keunen]

**away** *(indicating movement)* weg [vek]; *(indicating position)* entfernt [ehntfehrnt]
- the village is ten miles away das Dorf ist zehn Meilen entfernt [das dorf ist tsayn meylen ehntfehrnt]
- we're looking for a cottage far away from the town wir suchen ein Häuschen weit außerhalb der Stadt [veer zookhen eyn hoyzshen veyt owserhalp dehr shtat]
- do you have any rooms away from the main road? haben Sie Zimmer, die nach hinten heraus liegen? [haaben zee tsimer dee nakh hinten hehrows leegen]

**b**

**baby bottle** die Babyflasche [baybiflash-e]
- I need to sterilize a baby bottle ich muss eine Babyflasche sterilisieren [ish mus ey-ne baybiflash-e shtehrilizieren]

**back** zurück [tsuruuk] ◆ *(part of body)* der Rücken [ruuken]; *(of room)* der hintere Teil [hinter-e teyl]
- I'll be back in 5 minutes ich bin in fünf Minuten zurück [ish bin in fuunf minooten tsuruuk]
- I've got a bad back ich habe Rückenschmerzen [ish haa-be ruukenshmehrtsen]
- I prefer to sit at the back ich sitze lieber hinten [ish zit-se leeber hinten]

**backache** die Rückenschmerzen [ruukenshmehrtsen]
- I've got a backache ich habe Rückenschmerzen [ish haa-be ruukenshmehrtsen]

**backpack** der Rucksack [rukzak]
- my passport's in my backpack mein Pass ist in meinem Rucksack [meyn pas ist in meynem rukzak]

**back up** *(car)* zurücksetzen [tsuruukzehtsen]
- I think we have to back up and turn right ich glaube, wir müssen zurücksetzen und rechts abbiegen [ish glow-be veer meusen tsuruuk-zehtsen unt rehshts apbeegen]

**bad** schlecht [shlehsht]
- the weather's bad today das Wetter ist heute schlecht [das wehter ist hoy-te shlehsht]

**bag** die Tasche [tash-e]; *(suitcase)* der Koffer [kof-er]; *(purse)* die Handtasche [hant-tash-e]
- are these the bags from flight 502? sind das die Koffer von Flug 502? [zint das dee kof-er fon flook fuunf nul tsvey]
- can someone take our bags up to the room, please? kann bitte jemand unsere Koffer aufs Zimmer bringen? [kan bi-te yaymant unzer-e kof-er owfs tsimer bringen]

**baggage** das Gepäck [gepehk]
- my baggage hasn't arrived mein Gepäck ist noch nicht angekommen [meyn gepehk ist nokh nisht angekom-en]
- I'd like to report the loss of my baggage ich möchte den Verlust meines Gepäcks melden [ish meush-te dayn fehrlust meynez gepehks mehlden]

**baggage cart** der Gepäckwagen [gepehkvaagen]
- I'm looking for a baggage cart ich suche einen Gepäckwagen [ish zookh-e eynen gepehkvaagen]

**bakery** die Bäckerei [behkerey]
- is there a bakery nearby? ist hier in der Nähe eine Bäckerei? [ist heer in dehr nay-e ey-ne behkerey]

**balcony** der Balkon [balkon]
- do you have any rooms with a balcony? haben Sie Zimmer mit Balkon? [haaben zee tsimer mit balkon]

**banana** die Banane [banaan-e]
- a kilo of bananas, please ein Kilo Bananen, bitte [eyn keeloh banaanen bi-te]

**bandage** der Verband [fehrbant]
- I need a bandage for my ankle ich brauche einen Verband für meinen Knöchel [ish browkh-e eynen fehrbant fuur meynen kneushel]

**Band-Aid**® das Pflaster [pflaster]
- can I have a Band-Aid® for my cut? kann ich ein Pflaster für meine Schnittwunde haben? [kan ish eyn pflaster fuur mey-ne shnitvun-de haaben]

**bank** *(finance)* die Bank [bank]
- is there a bank nearby? gibt es eine Bank in der Nähe? [gipt es ey-ne bank in dehr nay-e]
- are banks open on Saturdays? sind Banken samstags geöffnet? [zint banken zamztaagz ge-eufnet] ▶ see box on p. 12

## at the bank

I'd like to change 200 dollars into euros **ich möchte bitte zweihundert Dollar in Euro umtauschen** [ish meush-te bi-te tsveyhundert dolar in oyroh umtowshen]

in small bills, please **bitte in kleinen Scheinen** [bi-te in kleynen sheynen]

what is the exchange rate for the euro? **was ist der Umtauschkurs für Euro?** [vas ist dehr umtowshkurs fuur oyroh]

how much is that in euros? **wie viel ist das in Euro?** [vee feel ist das in oyroh]

do you take traveler's checks? **nehmen Sie Reiseschecks?** [naymen zee reyzeshehks]

do you charge a commission? **berechnen Sie eine Gebühr?** [berehshnen zee ey-ne gebuur]

**bank card** die Scheckkarte [shehk-kart-e]

I've lost my bank card **ich habe meine Scheckkarte verloren** [ish haa-be mey-ne shehk-kart-e fehrloren]

**bar** *(place serving alcohol)* die Bar [bar]; *(counter)* die Theke [tay-ke]; *(of chocolate)* die Tafel [taafel]; *(of soap)* das Stück [shtuuk]

are there any good bars around here? **gibt es hier in der Gegend irgendwelche gute Bars?** [gipt ehs heer in dehr gaygent irgentvehlsh-e goo-te barz]

**base** *(of lamp)* der Fuß [foos]; *(for exploring)* der Ausgangspunkt [owsgangzpunkt]

the base of the lamp got broken **der Lampenfuß ist kaputtgegangen** [dehr lampenfoos ist kaputgegangen]

we're going to use the village as our base to explore the area **wir werden das Dorf als Ausgangspunkt nehmen, um die Gegend zu erkunden** [veer vehrden das dorf als owsgangzpunkt naymen um dee gaygent tsoo ehrkunden]

**basic** Grund- [grunt]

do the staff all have a basic knowledge of English? **haben alle Mitarbeiter Grundkenntnisse in Englisch?** [haaben al-e mitarbeyter gruntkehntni-se in ehnglish]

I know the basics, but no more than that **ich weiß das Wesentliche, aber nicht mehr** [ish veys das vayzentlish-e aber nisht mehr]

**basis** die Grundlage [gruntlaa-ge]

the price per night is on a double-occupancy basis **der Preis pro Nacht wird auf der Grundlage von Doppelbelegung berechnet** [dehr preys proh nakht virt owf dehr gruntlaa-ge fon dop-el-belaygung berehshnet]

**bat** *(for sport)* der Schläger [shlayger]

can you rent bats? **kann man Schläger mieten?** [kan man shlayger meeten]

**bath** das Bad [baat]

to take a bath **ein Bad nehmen** [eyn baat naymen]

**bathroom** *(with bathtub or shower)* das Badezimmer [baadetsimer]; *(toilet)* die Toilette [toyleh-te]
- where's the bathroom? wo ist die Toilette? [voh ist dee toyleh-te]

**bathtub** die Badewanne [baadeva-ne]
- there's no plug for the bathtub es gibt keinen Stöpsel für die Badewanne [ehs gipt keynen shteupsel fuur dee baadeva-ne]

**battery** die Batterie [bateree]
- I need new batteries ich brauche neue Batterien [ish browkh-e noy-e bateree-en]
- the battery needs to be recharged die Batterie muss aufgeladen werden [dee bateree mus owfgelaaden vehrden]
- the battery's dead die Batterie ist tot [dee bateree ist toht]

**be** sein [zeyn]; *(referring to prices)* kosten [kosten]
- where are you from? woher sind Sie? [voh-hehr zint zee]
- I'm a teacher ich bin Lehrer/Lehrerin [ish bin lehrer/lehrerin]
- I'm happy ich bin glücklich [ish bin gluuklish]
- what day is it? welcher Tag ist heute? [vehlsher taak ist hoy-te]
- it's eight o'clock es ist acht Uhr [ehs ist akht oor]
- how are you? wie geht es Ihnen? [vee gayt ehs eenen]
- I'm fine es geht mir gut [ehs gayt meer goot]
- where is terminal 1? wo ist Terminal 1? [voh ist tehrminal eyns]
- could you show me where I am on the map? können Sie mir auf der Karte zeigen, wo ich bin? [keunen zee meer owf dehr kart-e tseygen voh ish bin]
- have you ever been to the United States? waren Sie schon einmal in den Vereinigten Staaten? [vaaren zee shohn eynmal in dayn fehreynigten shtaaten]
- it's the first time I've been here ich bin zum ersten Mal hier [ish bin tsum ehrsten mal heer]
- how old are you? wie alt sind Sie? [vee alt zint zee]
- I'm 18 (years old) ich bin achtzehn (Jahre alt) [ish bin akht-tsayn (yaa-re alt)]
- it was over thirty-five degrees es waren über fünfunddreißig Grad [ehs vaaren uuber fuunfuntdreysish graat]
- it's cold in the evenings es ist abends kalt [ehs ist aabents kalt]
- how much is it? wie viel kostet es? [vee feel kostet ehs]
- I'm 1.68 meters tall ich bin einen Meter achtundsechzig groß [ish bin ey-ne mayter akhtunt-zesh-tsish grohs]

**beach** der Strand [shtrant]
- it's a sandy beach es ist ein Sandstrand [ehs ist eyn zant-shtrant]
- is it a quiet beach? ist es ein ruhiger Strand? [ist ehs eyn rooiger shtrant]

**beach umbrella** der Sonnenschirm [zo-nenshirm]
- can you rent beach umbrellas? kann man Sonnenschirme mieten? [kan man zo-nenshirm-e meeten]

**beautiful** schön [sheun]
- isn't the weather beautiful today? ist das Wetter heute nicht schön? [ist das vehter hoy-te nisht sheun]

**bed** das Bett [beht]
- is it possible to add an extra bed? ist es möglich, noch ein weiteres Bett ins Zimmer zu stellen? [ist ehs meuglish nokh eyn veyteres beht ins tsimer tsoo shtehlen]
- do you have a children's bed? haben Sie ein Kinderbett? [haaben zee eyn kin-der-beht]
- to go to bed ins Bett gehen [ins beht gayen]
- I went to bed late ich bin spät ins Bett gegangen [ish bin shpayt ins beht gegangen]
- I need to put my children to bed now ich muss jetzt meine Kinder ins Bett bringen [ish mus yehtst mey-ne kin-der ins beht bringen]

**bedroom** das Schlafzimmer [shlaaftsimer]
- how many bedrooms does the apartment have? wie viele Schlafzimmer hat die Wohnung? [vee feel-e shlaaftsimer hat dee vohnung]

**bedside lamp** die Nachttischlampe [nakht-tishlamp-e]
- the bedside lamp doesn't work die Nachttischlampe funktioniert nicht [dee nakht-tishlamp-e funktiohniert nisht]

**beef** das Rindfleisch [rintfleysh]
- I don't eat beef ich esse kein Rindfleisch [ish eh-se keyn rintfleysh]

**beer** das Bier [beer]
- two beers, please zwei Bier, bitte [tsvey beer bi-te]

**begin** anfangen [anfangen]
- when does the performance begin? wann fängt die Vorstellung an? [van fehnkt dee fohrshtehlung an]

**beginner** der Anfänger [anfehnger], die Anfängerin [anfehngerin]
- I'm a complete beginner ich bin ein totaler Anfänger/eine totale Anfängerin [ish bin eyn tohtaaler anfehnger/ey-ne tohtaal-e anfehngerin]

**behind** hinten [hinten]
- from behind von hinten [fon hinten]
- the rest of our party is in the car behind der Rest unserer Gruppe ist im Auto hinter uns [dehr rehst unzerer gru-pe ist im owtoh hinter uns]

**berth** *(on ship)* die Koje [koy-e]
- I'd prefer the upper berth ich hätte lieber die obere Koje [ish heh-te leeber dee ohber-e koy-e]

**beside** neben [nayben]
- is there anyone sitting beside you? sitzt jemand neben Ihnen? [zitst yaymant nayben eenen]

**best** beste [behst-e]
- what's the best restaurant in town? was ist das beste Restaurant in der Stadt? [vas ist das behst-e rehstoront in dehr shtat]

## bikes

It's a well-known fact that Germans care about the environment. So it stands to reason that every effort is made to make life as easy as possible for cyclists in towns. There are cycle paths, special road signs, bike-racks outside buildings, and even access to the *S-Bahn* (commuter trains). You'll find bikes for rent in all the big towns and even special cycle routes for visitors.

**better** besser [behser]
- I've been on antibiotics for a week and I'm not any better ich nehme seit einer Woche Antibiotika, und es geht mir kein bisschen besser [ish nay-me zeyt eyner vokh-e antibiohtika unt ehs gayt meer keyn bis-shen behser]
- the better situated of the two hotels das günstiger gelegene der beiden Hotels [das guunstiger gelehgen-e dehr beyden hohtehlz]

**between** zwischen [tsvishen]
- a bus runs between the airport and the hotel ein Bus verkehrt zwischen dem Flughafen und dem Hotel [eyn bus fehrkehrt tsvishen daym flookhaafen unt daym hohtehl]

**bicycle** das Fahrrad [faar-raat]
- is there a place to leave bicycles? kann man Fahrräder irgendwo abstellen? [kan man faar-rayder irgentvoh apshtehlen]

**bicycle lane** der Fahrradweg [faar-raat-vayk]
- are there any bicycle lanes? gibt es Fahrradwege? [gipt ehs faar-raat-vayg-e]

**bicycle pump** die Fahrradpumpe [faar-raat-pump-e]
- do you have a bicycle pump? haben Sie eine Fahrradpumpe? [haaben zee ey-ne faar-raat-pump-e]

**big** groß [grohs]
- do you have it in a bigger size? haben Sie es in einer größeren Größe? [haaben zee ehs in eyner greuseren greu-se]
- it's too big es ist zu groß [ehs ist tsoo grohs]

**bike** das Fahrrad [faar-raat]
- I'd like to rent a bike for an hour ich möchte gerne ein Fahrrad für eine Stunde mieten [ish meush-te gehrn-e eyn faar-raat fuur ey-ne shtun-de meeten]
- I'd like to do a bike tour ich möchte gerne eine Fahrradtour machen [ish meush-te gehrn-e ey-ne faar-raat-toor makhen]

**bill** *(in hotel, for goods)* die Rechnung [rehshnung]; *(paper money)* der Geldschein [gehltsheyn]

> I think there's a mistake with the bill ich glaube, bei der Rechnung stimmt etwas nicht [ish glow-be bey dehr rehshnung shtimt ehtvas nisht]

> put it on my bill setzen Sie es auf meine Rechnung [zehtsen zee ehs owf mey-ne rehshnung]

> can you write up my bill, please? können Sie bitte meine Rechnung fertig machen? [keunen zee bi-te mey-ne rehshnung fehrtish makhen]

**birthday** der Geburtstag [geburtstaak]

> happy birthday! herzlichen Glückwunsch zum Geburtstag! [hehrtslishen gluuk-vunsh tsum geburtstaak]

**bite** *(of animal)* der Biss [bis]; *(of insect)* der Stich [shtish] ♦ *(animal)* beißen [beysen]; *(insect)* stechen [shteshen]

> do you have a cream for mosquito bites? haben Sie eine Creme gegen Moskitostiche? [haaben zee ey-ne kray-me gaygen moskeetohshtish-e]

> I've been bitten by a mosquito ich bin von einem Moskito gestochen worden [ish bin fon eynem moskeetoh geshtokhen vorden]

**black** schwarz [shvarts]

> I'm looking for a little black dress ich suche ein kleines schwarzes Kleid [ish zookh-e eyn kleynez shvartsez kleyt]

**black-and-white** schwarz-weiß [shvartsveys]

> I like black-and-white movies ich mag Schwarz-Weiß-Filme [ish maak shvarts-veys-film-e]

**black ice** das Glatteis [glat-eys]

> there's black ice es ist Glatteis [ehs ist glat-eys]

**blanket** die Decke [deh-ke]

> I'd like an extra blanket ich hätte gerne eine extra Decke [ish heh-te gehrn-e ey-ne ehkstra deh-ke]

**bleed** bluten [blooten]

> it won't stop bleeding es hört nicht auf zu bluten [ehs heurt nisht owf tsoo blooten]

**blind** *(on window)* das Rollo [rol-oh]

> can we pull down the blinds? können wir die Rollos herunterlassen? [keunen veer dee rol-ohz hehrunterlas-en]

**blister** die Blase [blaaz-e]

> I got a blister ich habe eine Blase [ish haa-be ey-ne blaaz-e]

**block** *(pipe, sink)* verstopfen [fehrshtopfen]; *(road)* blockieren [blokieren]

> the toilet's blocked die Toilette ist verstopft [dee toyleh-te ist fehrshtopft]

> my ears are completely blocked meine Ohren sind völlig verstopft [mey-ne ohren zint feulish fehrshtopft]

**blond** blond [blont]

> I have blond hair ich habe blonde Haare [ish haa-be blond-e haar-e]

**blood** das Blut [bloot]
 ▸ traces of blood Blutspuren [bloot-shpooren]

**blood pressure** der Blutdruck [blootdruk]
 ▸ I have high blood pressure ich habe Bluthochdruck [ish haa-be bloot-hohkhdruk]

**blood type** die Blutgruppe [blootgrup-e]
 ▸ my blood type is A positive meine Blutgruppe ist A positiv [mey-ne blootgrup-e ist aa pohziteev]

**blue** blau [blow]
 ▸ the blue one der Blaue [dehr blow-e]

**board** (plane) an Bord gehen [an bohrt gayen]
 ▸ what time will the plane be boarding? um wie viel Uhr boardet das Flugzeug? [um vee feel oor bohrdet das flooktsoyk]
 ▸ where is the flight to Dublin boarding? an welchem Gate boardet das Flugzeug nach Dublin? [an vehlshem geyt bohrdet das flooktsoyk nakh dublin]

**boarding pass** der Boardingpass [bohrdingpas]
 ▸ I can't find my boarding pass ich kann meinen Boardingpass nicht finden [ish kan meynen bohrdingpas nisht finden]

**boat** das Boot [boht]
 ▸ can we get there by boat? können wir dort mit dem Boot hinkommen? [keunen veer dort mit daym boht hinkom-en]

**boat trip** die Bootfahrt [bohtfaart]
 ▸ are there boat trips on the river? kann man auf dem Fluss Bootfahrten machen? [kan man owf daym flus bohtfaarten makhen]

**book** (for reading) das Buch [bookh]; (of tickets, stamps) das Heft [hehft]; (of matches) das Heftchen [hehft-shen] ◆ (ticket, room) reservieren [rehzervieren] ◆ buchen [bookhen]
 ▸ do you sell English–language books? verkaufen Sie englische Bücher? [fehrkowfen zee ehnglish-e buukher]
 ▸ is it more economical to buy a book of tickets? ist es günstiger ein Fahrkartenheft zu kaufen? [ist ehs guunstiger eyn faarkartenhehft tsoo kowfen]
 ▸ I'd like to book a ticket ich möchte eine Fahrkarte reservieren [ish meush-te ey-ne faarkart-e rehzervieren]
 ▸ do you need to book in advance? muss man im Voraus buchen? [mus man im for-ows bookhen]

**born**
 ▸ to be born geboren sein [geboren zeyn]
 ▸ I was born on March 3rd, 1985 ich bin am dritten März neunzehnhundertfünfundachtzig geboren worden [ish bin am drit-en mehrts noyntsaynhundert-fuunfuntakhtsish geboren vorden]

**bottle** die Flasche [flash-e]
 ▸ a bottle of red wine, please eine Flasche Rotwein, bitte [ey-ne flash-e rohtveyn bi-te]

## bread

Germany might have about 200 different types of bread, each more tempting than the last, to offer you but bread is not served as a matter of course in restaurants. If you ask for it, you will be charged for it.

**bottle opener** der Flaschenöffner [flasheneufner]
▸ can you pass me the bottle opener? können Sie mir den Flaschenöffner reichen? [keunen zee meer dayn flasheneufner reyshen]

**bottom** *(of a box etc.)* der Boden [bohden]
▸ my passport's at the bottom of my suitcase mein Pass ist ganz unten in meinem Koffer [meyn pas ist gants unten in meynem kof-er]

**box** *(small)* die Schachtel [shakhtel]; *(large)* der Karton [kartohn]
▸ could I have a box of matches, please? könnte ich bitte eine Streichholz-schachtel haben? [keun-te ish bi-te ey-ne shtreysh-holts-shakhtel haaben]

**boy** der Junge [yung-e]; *(son)* der Sohn [zohn]
▸ he seems like a nice boy er scheint ein netter Junge zu sein [ehr sheynt eyn nehter yung-e tsoo zeyn]
▸ she has two boys sie hat zwei Söhne [zee hat tsvey zeun-e]

**boyfriend** der Freund [froynt]
▸ my boyfriend is a biologist mein Freund ist Biologe [meyn froynt ist bee-oh-loh-ge]

**brake** die Bremse [brehm-ze]
▸ the brakes aren't working properly die Bremsen funktionieren nicht richtig [dee brehmzen funktsiohnieren nisht rishtish]

**brake fluid** die Bremsflüssigkeit [brehmzfluusishkeyt]
▸ could you check the brake fluid? könnten Sie die Bremsflüssigkeit nachsehen? [keunten zee dee brehmzfluusishkeyt nakhzayen]

**branch** *(of bank)* die Zweigstelle [tsveyg-shtehl-e]
▸ which branch should I visit to get the replacement traveler's checks? zu welcher Zweigstelle sollte ich gehen, um die Ersatzreiseschecks zu bekommen? [tsoo vehlsher tsveyg-shtehl-e zol-te ish gayen um dee ehrzats-reyzeshehks tsoo bekom-en]

**bread** das Brot [broht]
▸ do you have any bread? haben Sie Brot? [haaben zee broht]
▸ could we have some more bread? könnten wir noch etwas Brot bekommen? [keunten veer nokh ehtvas broht bekom-en]

**break** *(pause)* die Pause [powz-e] ◆ *(make unusable)* kaputtmachen [kaputmakhen]; *(fracture)* sich brechen [zish brehshen]
▸ should we take a break? sollten wir eine Pause machen? [zolten veer ey-ne powz-e makhen]
▸ be careful you don't break it sei vorsichtig, dass du es nicht kaputtmachst [zey forzishtish das doo ehs nisht kaputmakhst]

## breakdowns

If you happen to break down, call the 'Yellow Angels' (*die Gelben Engel*) at the *ADAC* (the German Automobile Club). Although you'll have to pay for parts, labor is free to members of affiliated automobile associations such as the *AAA*. Call 0180/2222222 (you don't need to dial the 0180 from a cellphone).

‣ I think I've broken my ankle **ich glaube, ich habe mir den Knöchel gebrochen** [ish glow-be ish haa-be meer dayn kneushel gebrokhen]

**break down** *(car)* **eine Panne haben** [ey-ne pa-ne haaben]; *(person, theory)* **zusammenbrechen** [tsoozam-en-brehshen]

‣ my car has broken down **mein Auto hat eine Panne** [meyn owtoh hat ey-ne pa-ne]

**breakdown** *(of car)* **die Panne** [pa-ne]; *(of person, theory)* **der Zusammenbruch** [tsoozam-en-brukh]

‣ we had a breakdown on the freeway **wir hatten eine Panne auf der Autobahn** [veer hat-en ey-ne pa-ne owf dehr owtohbaan]

**breakfast** **das Frühstück** [fruushtuuk]

‣ to have breakfast **frühstücken** [fruushtuuken]

‣ what time is breakfast served? **um wie viel Uhr gibt es Frühstück?** [um vee feel oor gipt ehs fruushtuuk]

**bridge** *(over river, on ship)* **die Brücke** [bruuk-e]

‣ do you have to pay a toll to use the bridge? **muss man eine Gebühr für die Brücke bezahlen?** [mus man ey-ne gebuur fuur dee bruuk-e betsaalen]

**bring** **bringen** [bringen]

‣ what should we bring to drink? **was sollen wir zu trinken mitbringen?** [vas zol-en veer tsoo trinken mitbringen]

**bring down** *(bags, luggage)* **herunterbringen** [hehrunterbringen]

‣ could you get someone to bring down our luggage, please? **könnten Sie bitte jemanden unser Gepäck herunterbringen lassen?** [keunten zee bi-te yaymanden unzer gepehk hehrunterbringen las-en]

## breakfast

*Frühstück* is sometimes included in the price of your room and is a whole meal in itself. You can have the classic continental breakfast of coffee and a croissant or bread, but you will usually be offered cooked meats, cheese, fruits, cereals or dairy products too. It provides a great start to the day, and means you can cut down on lunch.

**bring in** *(bags, luggage)* hereinbringen [hehreynbringen]
- ▸ can you bring in my bags, please? können Sie bitte mein Gepäck hereinbringen? [keunen zee bi-te meyn gepehk hehreynbringen]

**broken** *(object)* kaputt [kaput]; *(leg)* gebrochen [gebrokhen]
- ▸ the lock is broken das Schloss ist kaputt [das shlos ist kaput]
- ▸ I think I've got a broken leg ich glaube, mein Bein ist gebrochen [ish glow-be meyn beyn ist gebrokhen]

**bronchitis** die Bronchitis [bronkeetis]
- ▸ do you have anything for bronchitis? haben Sie etwas gegen Bronchitis? [haaben zee ehtvas gaygen bronkeetis]

**brother** der Bruder [brooder]
- ▸ I don't have any brothers or sisters ich habe keine Geschwister [ish haa-be key-ne geshvister]

**brown** braun [brown]
- ▸ he has brown hair er hat braune Haare [ehr hat brown-e haar-e]
- ▸ I'm looking for a brown leather belt ich suche einen braunen Ledergürtel [ish zookh-e eynen brownen layderguurtel]

**brush** *(for hair, clothes)* die Bürste [buurst-e]; *(broom)* der Besen [bayzen]; *(with short handle)* der Handfeger [hantfayger] ♦ *(clothes)* bürsten [buursten]
- ▸ where are the brush and dustpan? wo sind der Handfeger und die Schaufel? [voh zint dehr hantfayger unt dee showfel]
- ▸ I am brushing my teeth ich bürste mir die Zähne [ish buurst-e meer dee tsayn-e]
- ▸ I am brushing my hair ich bürste mir die Haare [ish buurst-e meer dee haar-e]

**bulb** *(light)* die Glühbirne [gluubeer-ne]
- ▸ the bulb's out in the bathroom die Glühbirne im Badezimmer ist kaputt [dee gluubeer-ne im baadetsimer ist kaput]

**bunk beds** das Stockbett [shtokbeht]
- ▸ are there bunk beds for the children? gibt es Stockbetten für die Kinder? [gipt ehs shtokbehten fuur dee kin-der]

**burn** verbrennen [fehrbrehnen]
- ▸ the food's completely burnt das Essen ist total verbrannt [das ehsen ist tohtaal fehrbrant]
- ▸ I've burned my hand ich habe mir die Hand verbrannt [ish haa-be meer dee hant fehrbrant]

**burst** *(tire)* zum Platzen bringen [tsum platsen bringen] ♦ *(of tire)* platzen [platsen]
- ▸ one of my tires burst einer meiner Reifen ist geplatzt [eyner meyner reyfen ist geplatst]

**bus** der Bus [bus]
- ▸ does this bus go downtown? fährt dieser Bus in die Stadt? [fehrt deezer bus in dee shtat]

▸ which bus do I have to take to go to...? welchen Bus muss ich nehmen um in ... zu fahren? [vehlshen bus mus ish naymen um in tsoo faaren]

**bus driver** der Busfahrer [busfaarer]

▸ can you buy tickets from the bus driver? kann man beim Busfahrer Fahrkarten kaufen? [kan man beym busfaarer faarkarten kowfen]

**business** *(commerce)* das Geschäft [geshehft]; *(company)* das Unternehmen [unternaymen]; *(concern, affair, matter)* die Angelegenheit [an-gelaygenheyt]

▸ it's none of your business das geht dich nichts an [das gayt dish nishts an]

**business card** die Visitenkarte [vizeetenkar-te]

▸ here's my business card hier ist meine Visitenkarte [heer ist mey-ne vizeetenkar-te]

**business class** die Businessklasse [biznes-kla-se] ◆ Businessklasse [biznes-kla-se]

▸ are there any seats in business class? gibt es Sitze in der Businessklasse? [gipt ehs zit-se in dehr biznes-kla-se]

▸ I prefer to travel business class ich fliege lieber Businessklasse [ish flee-ge leeber biznes-kla-se]

**bus station** der Busbahnhof [busbaanhohf]

▸ I'm looking for the bus station ich suche den Busbahnhof [ish zookh-e dayn busbaanhohf]

**bus stop** die Bushaltestelle [bus-halteshtehle]

▸ where's the nearest bus stop? wo ist die nächste Bushaltestelle? [voh ist dee nehkst-e bus-halteshtehle]

**busy** *(person)* beschäftigt [beshehftisht]; *(town, beach, street)* belebt [belehbt]; *(phone line)* besetzt [bezehtst]

▸ I'm afraid I'm busy tomorrow es tut mir Leid, ich habe morgen viel zu tun [ehs toot meer leyt ish haa-be morgen feel tsoo toon]

▸ the line's busy es ist besetzt [ehs ist bezehtst]

**butter** die Butter [buter]

▸ could you pass the butter please? könnten Sie mir bitte die Butter reichen? [keunten zee meer bi-te dee buter reyshen]

**buy** kaufen [kowfen]

▸ where can I buy tickets? wo kann ich Karten kaufen? [voh kan ish karten kowfen]

▸ can I buy you a drink? kann ich Ihnen ein Getränk spendieren? [kan ish eenen eyn getrehnk shpehndieren]

**bye** tschüs(s) [tshuus]

▸ bye, see you tomorrow! tschüs(s), bis morgen! [tshuus bis morgen]

# C

**cab** das Taxi [taksi]
- can you order me a cab to the airport? können Sie mir ein Taxi zum Flughafen bestellen? [keunen zee meer eyn taksi tsum flookhaafen beshtehlen]

**cab driver** der Taxifahrer [taksifaarer]
- does the cab driver speak English? spricht der Taxifahrer Englisch? [shprisht dehr taksifaarer ehnglish]

**cabin** *(on boat)* die Kabine [kabee-ne]; *(on plane)* der Passagierraum [pasazhierowm]
- can I have breakfast in my cabin? kann ich in meiner Kabine frühstücken? [kan ish in meyner kabee-ne fruushtuuken]

**cable** das Kabel [kaabel]
- does the hotel have cable? hat das Hotel Kabelfernsehen? [hat das hohtehl kaabelfehrnzayen]

**café** das Café [ka-fay]
- is there a café near here? gibt es hier in der Nähe ein Café? [gipt ehs heer in dehr nay-e eyn ka-fay]

**cake** der Kuchen [kookhen]
- a piece of that cake, please ein Stück von diesem Kuchen, bitte [eyn shtuuk fon deezem kookhen bi-te]

**call** *(on phone)* der Anruf [anroof] ◆ *(name, describe)* nennen [nehnen]; *(on phone)* anrufen [anroofen]
- I have to make a call ich muss jemanden anrufen [ish mus yaymanden anroofen]
- what is this called? wie nennt man das? [vee nehnt man das]
- who's calling? wer spricht da? [vehr shprisht daa]

---

### in a café

- is this table/seat free? ist dieser Tisch/Platz frei? [ist deezer tish/plats frey]
- excuse me! Entschuldigung! [ehntshuldigung]
- two black coffees/coffees with cream, please zwei Kaffees/Kaffees mit Sahne, bitte [tsvey kafayz/kafayz mit zaa-ne bi-te]
- can I have another beer, please? kann ich bitte noch ein Bier haben? [kan ish bi-te nokh eyn beer haaben]

**call back** zurückrufen [tsuruukroofen]

> could you ask her to call me back? könnten Sie sie bitten mich zurückzurufen? [keunten zee zee bi-ten mish tsuruuktsooroofen]

> I'll call back (later) ich rufe (später) zurück [ish roo-fe (shpayter) tsuruuk]

**calm** ruhig [rooish]

> keep calm! bleib ruhig! [bleyp rooish]

**camera** die Kamera [kamehra]

> can I use my camera here? darf ich hier meine Kamera benutzen? [darf ish heer meyne kamehra benutsen]

**camper** das Wohnmobil [vohnmohbeel]

> do you have a space left for a camper? haben Sie noch einen Platz für ein Wohnmobil? [haaben zee nokh eynen plats fuur eyn vohnmohbeel]

> I'd like to book space for a camper for the night of August 15th ich möchte einen Platz für ein Wohnmobil für die Nacht vom fünfzehnten August buchen [ish meush-te eynen plats fuur eyn vohnmohbeel fuur dee nakht fom fuunftsaynten owgust bookhen]

**campground** der Campingplatz [kehmpingplats]

> I'm looking for a campground ich suche einen Campingplatz [ish zoo-khe eynen kehmpingplats]

**camping** das Zelten [tsehlten]

> I love going camping ich gehe gerne zelten [ish gay-e gehrn-e tsehlten]

**can** die Dose [doh-ze]

> a can of oil, please eine Dose Öl, bitte [ey-ne doh-ze eul bi-te]

**can** können [keunen]

> can I help you? kann ich Ihnen helfen? [kan ish eenen hehlfen]

> can you speak German? können Sie Deutsch sprechen? [keunen zee doytsh shprehshen]

**Canada** das Kanada [kanada]

> I'm from Canada ich komme aus Kanada [ish ko-me ows kanada]

> I live in Canada ich lebe in Kanada [ish layb-e in kanada]

> have you ever been to Canada? waren Sie schon einmal in Kanada? [vaaren zee shohn eynmal in kanada]

**Canadian** kanadisch [kanaadish] ◆ der Kanadier [kanaadier], die Kanadierin [kanaadierin]

> I'm Canadian ich bin Kanadier/Kanadierin [ish bin kanaadier/kanaadierin]

> we're Canadians wir sind Kanadier [veer zint kanaadier]

**cancel** *(meeting, concert)* absagen [apzaagen]; *(reservation, order)* stornieren [shtornieren]

> is it possible to cancel a reservation? ist es möglich, eine Reservation zu stornieren? [ist ehs meuglish ey-ne rehzervatsiohn tsoo shtornieren]

**canoeing** das Kanufahren [kanoofaaren]
- I was told we could go canoeing man hat mir gesagt, wir könnten Kanu fahren [man hat meer gezaakt veer keunten kanoo faaren]

**car** *(automobile)* das Auto [owtoh]; *(on train)* der Wagen [vaagen]
- I'd like to rent a car for a week ich möchte ein Auto für eine Woche mieten [ish meush-te eyn owtoh fuur ey-ne vokh-e meeten]
- I've just crashed my car ich habe gerade einen Autounfall gehabt [ish haa-be geraa-de eynen owtoh-unfal gehabt]
- can you help us push the car? können Sie uns helfen das Auto zu schieben? [keunen zee uns helfen das owtoh tsoo sheeben]
- my car's been towed away mein Auto ist abgeschleppt worden [meyn owtoh ist apgeshlehpt vorden]
- my car's broken down mein Auto hat eine Panne [meyn owtoh hat ey-ne pa-ne]

**carafe** die Karaffe [karaf-e]
- a large carafe of water, please eine große Karaffe Wasser, bitte [ey-ne groh-se karaf-e vas-er bi-te]
- a carafe of house wine eine Karaffe Hauswein [ey-ne karaf-e howsveyn]

**car crash** der Autounfall [owtohunfal]
- he's been killed in a car crash er ist bei einem Autounfall ums Leben gekommen [ehr ist bey eynem owtohunfal ums layben gekom-en]

**card** die Karte [kart-e]
- the waiter hasn't brought my card back der Ober hat meine Karte noch nicht zurückgebracht [dehr ohber hat mey-ne kart-e nokh nisht tsuruukgebrakht]
- I need to get a card for my parents for their anniversary ich muss eine Karte für meine Eltern zum Hochzeitstag besorgen [ish mus ey-ne kart-e fuur mey-ne ehltern tsum hohkh-tseyts-taak bezorgen]
- can I give you my card? kann ich Ihnen meine Karte geben? [kan ish eenen mey-ne kart-e gayben]

**cardigan** die Strickjacke [shtrik-ya-ke]
- should I take a cardigan for the evening? soll ich für den Abend eine Strickjacke mitnehmen? [zol ish fuur dayn aabehnt ey-ne shtrik-ya-ke mitnaymen]

---

### renting a car

- with comprehensive insurance mit Vollkaskoversicherung [mit folkaskohfehr-zisherung]
- can I leave the car at the airport? kann ich das Auto am Flughafen lassen? [kan ish das owtoh am flookhaafen las-en]
- can I see your driver's license, please? kann ich bitte Ihren Führerschein sehen? [kan ish bi-te eeren fuurersheyn zayen]

**carpet** der Teppich [tehpish]
▸ the carpet hasn't been vacuumed der Teppich ist nicht gesaugt worden [dehr tehpish ist nisht gezowkt vorden]

**car rental** die Autovermietung [owtohfehrmeetung]
▸ is car rental expensive? ist es teuer, ein Auto zu mieten? [ist ehs toyer eyn owtoh tsoo meeten]

**car rental agency** die Autovermietung [owtohfehrmeetung]
▸ do you know of any car rental agencies? kennen Sie irgendwelche Autovermietungen? [kehnen zee irgentvehlsh-e owtohfehrmeetungen]

**carry** tragen [traagen]
▸ could you help me carry something? könnten Sie mir helfen etwas zu tragen? [keunten zee meer hehlfen ehtvas tsoo traagen]

**carry-on bag** das Handgepäck [hantgepehk]
▸ am I only allowed one carry-on bag? ist nur ein Handgepäck erlaubt? [ist noor eyn hantgepehk ehrlowbt]

**cart** der Wagen [vaagen]
▸ where can I get a cart? wo bekomme ich einen Wagen? [voh bekom-e ish eynen vaagen]

**carton** (of cigarettes) die Stange [shtang-e]; (of milk) die Tüte [tuu-te]
▸ I'd like a carton of cigarettes ich hätte gerne eine Stange Zigaretten [ish heh-te gehrn-e ey-ne shtang-e tsigarehten]

**in case** für den Fall [fuur dayn fal]
▸ just in case für alle Fälle [fuur al-e fehl-e]

**cash** das Bargeld [bargehlt] ✦ (check) einlösen [eynleuzen]
▸ I'll pay cash ich bezahle bar [ish betsaal-e bar]
▸ I want to cash this traveler's check ich möchte diesen Reisescheck einlösen [ish meusht-e deezen reyzeshehk eynleuzen]

**castle** das Schloss [shlos]
▸ is the castle open to the public? ist das Schloss für die Öffentlichkeit zugänglich? [ist das shlos fuur dee eufentlishkeyt tsoogehnglish]

**catalog** der Katalog [katalohg]
▸ do you have a catalog? haben Sie einen Katalog? [haaben zee eynen katalohg]

**catch** (with hands) fangen [fangen]; (bus, train) nehmen [naymen]; (cold) sich holen [zish hohlen]; (hear clearly) verstehen [fehrshtayen]
▸ I've caught a cold ich habe mir eine Erkältung geholt [ish haa-be meer ey-ne ehrkehltung geholt]
▸ I'm sorry, I didn't quite catch your name es tut mir Leid, aber ich habe Ihren Namen nicht richtig verstanden [ehs toot meer leyt aber ish haa-be eeren naamen nisht rishtish fehrshtanden]

**Catholic** katholisch [katohlish] ✦ der Katholik [katohlik], die Katholikin [katohleekin]
▸ where is there a Catholic church? wo ist hier eine katholische Kirche? [voh ist heer ey-ne katohlish-e kirsh-e]

**CD** die CD [tsayday]
- how much does this CD cost? wie viel kostet diese CD? [vee feel kostet deez-e tsayday]

**cellphone** das Handy [hehndi]
- what's your cellphone number? was ist Ihre Handynummer? [vas ist eer-e hehndi-num-er]

**center** das Zentrum [tsehntrum]
- we want to be based near the center of the region wir möchten unseren Sitz in der Nähe des Zentrums der Gegend haben [veer meushten unzeren zits in dehr nay-e dehz tsehntrumz dehr gaygent haaben]

**chair** der Stuhl [shtool]
- could we have another chair in our room? könnten wir noch einen Stuhl für unser Zimmer bekommen? [keunten veer nokh eynen shtool fuur unzer tsim-er bekom-en]

**change** (gen) die Veränderung [fehrehnderung]; (money received back) das Wechselgeld [vehkselgehlt]; (coins) das Kleingeld [kleyngehlt] ♦ (gen) ändern [ehndern]; (baby) wickeln [vikeln] ♦ sich ändern [zish ehndern]
- do you have any change? haben Sie Kleingeld? [haaben zee kleyngehlt]
- keep the change der Rest ist für Sie [dehr rehst ist fuur zee]
- I don't have exact change ich habe es nicht passend [ish haa-be ehs nisht pas-ent]
- give me change for fifty euros geben Sie mir Wechselgeld für fünfzig Euro [gayben zee meer vehkselgehlt fuur fuunftsish oyroh]
- is it possible to change a reservation? ist es möglich eine Reservation zu ändern? [ist ehs meuglish ey-ne rehzervatsiohn tsoo ehndern]
- I'd like to change 200 dollars into euros ich möchte 200 Dollar in Euro umtauschen [ish meush-te tsveyhundert dolar in oyroh umtowshen]
- I'd like to change these traveler's checks ich möchte diese Reiseschecks umtauschen [ish meush-te dee-ze reyzeshehks umtowshen]
- could you change a 100 euro bill? könnten Sie einen Hunderteuroschein wechseln? [keunten zee eynen hundertoyrohsheyn vehkseln]
- can you help me change the tire? können Sie mir helfen den Reifen zu wechseln? [keunen zee meer hehlfen dayn reyfen tsoo vehkseln]
- the oil needs to be changed das Öl muss gewechselt werden [das eul mus gevehkselt vehrden]

**changing table** der Wickeltisch [vikeltish]
- is there a changing table? gibt es hier einen Wickeltisch? [gipt ehs heer eynen vikeltish]

**charge** (cost) die Gebühr [gebuur]
- is there a charge for the parking lot? ist der Parkplatz gebührenpflichtig? [ist dehr parkplats gebuurenpflishtish]
- is there a charge for using the facilities? kostet es etwas, wenn man die Einrichtungen nutzen will? [kostet ehs ehtvas vehn man dee eynrishtungen nutsen vil]

## the check

Sometimes in a café or a restaurant, you might feel the urge to say *stimmt so* (keep the change). If you want to pay for only your own share, and not for anyone else's, say *getrennt* (separately). Otherwise, you can say *zusammen* (all together).

▸ is there a charge for cancellations? sind Stornierungen gebührenpflichtig? [zint shtornierungen gebuurenpflishtish]

▸ I'd like to speak to the person in charge ich möchte mit der verantwortlichen Person sprechen [ish meush-te mit dehr fehrantvortlishen pehrsohn shprehshen]

**charter flight** der Charterflug [tsharterflook]

▸ where do we board the charter flight to Hamburg? wo ist das Gate für den Charterflug nach Hamburg? [voh ist das geyt fuur dayn tsharterflook nakh hamburk]

**cheap** billig [bilish]

▸ I'm trying to find a cheap flight home ich versuche einen billigen Flug nach Hause zu finden [ish fehrzoo-khe eynen bilishen flook nakh howz-e tsoo finden]

**check** (in restaurant) die Rechnung [rehshnung]; (for paying) der Scheck [shehk] ♦ (test, verify) nachprüfen [nakhpruufen]

▸ the check, please! die Rechnung, bitte! [dee rehshnung bi-te]

▸ can I pay by check? kann ich mit Scheck bezahlen? [kan ish mit shehk betsaalen]

▸ can you check the oil? können Sie das Öl nachprüfen? [keunen zee das eul nakhpruufen]

**checkbook** das Scheckbuch [shehkbookh]

▸ my checkbook's been stolen mein Scheckbuch ist gestohlen worden [meyn shehkbookh ist geshtohlen vorden]

## checking

▸ is it right and then left? ist es rechts und dann links? [ist ehs rehshts unt dan links]

▸ is this the train for Bremen? ist dies der Zug nach Bremen? [ist dees dehr tsook nakh braymen]

▸ could you tell me where to get off, please? könnten Sie mir bitte sagen, wo ich aussteigen muss? [keunten zee meer bi-te zaagen voh ish ows-shteygen mus]

▸ is this the right stop for ...? ist das die richtige Haltestelle für ...? [ist das dee rishtige halt-e-shtehl-e fuur]

▸ are you sure that he'll be able to come? sind Sie sicher, dass er kommen kann? [zint zee zisher das ehr kom-en kan]

## cheers!

If you're doing the rounds of the beer festivals, you really ought to learn how to make a toast in German. *Prost!* comes from the Latin *prosit*, meaning 'may you profit from that.' Or if you want to sound really classy, say *Zum Wohl!*

**check in** einchecken [eyntshehken]
- I'd like to check in both these bags, please ich möchte bitte diese beiden Koffer einchecken [ish meush-te bi-te deez-e beyden kof-er eyntshehken]
- what time do you have to be at the airport to check in? um wie viel Uhr müssen Sie am Flughafen sein um einzuchecken? [um vee feel oor muusen zee am flookhaafen zeyn um eyn-tsoo-tshehken]

**check-in desk** der Check-in-Schalter [tshehkinshalter]
- where is the United Airlines check-in desk? wo ist der Check-in-Schalter von United Airlines? [voh ist dehr tshehkinshalter fon juneyted ehrleynz]

**check out** *(from hotel)* auschecken [ows-tshehken]
- what time do you have to check out by? bis wann muss man ausgecheckt haben? [bis van mus man ows-ge-tshehkt haaben]

**cheers** prost [prohst]
- cheers and all the best! prost und alles Gute! [prohst unt al-es goot-e]

**cheese** der Käse [kayz-e]
- what are the best local cheeses? was sind die besten regionalen Käsesorten? [vas zint dee behsten rehgionaalen kayzezorten]

**chicken** das Huhn [hoon]; *(meat)* das Hähnchen [hehnshen]
- half a roast chicken, please ein halbes Brathähnchen, bitte [eyn halbez braathehnshen bi-te]
- a chicken sandwich and fries ein Geflügelsandwich und Pommes frites [eyn gefluugelsehntvitsh unt pom-ez frit-ez]

**child** das Kind [kint]
- do you have children? haben Sie Kinder? [haaben zee kin-der]
- two adults and two children, please zwei Erwachsene und zwei Kinder, bitte [tsvey ehrvaksene unt tsvey kin-der bi-te]
- do you have discounts for children? gibt es bei Ihnen Ermäßigungen für Kinder? [gipt ehs bey eenen ehrmasigungen fuur kin-der]

**children's menu** die Kinderkarte [kin-der-kart-e]
- do you have a children's menu? haben Sie eine Kinderkarte? [haaben zee ey-ne kin-der-kart-e]

**chilled** *(wine)* gekühlt [gekuult]
- this wine isn't chilled enough dieser Wein ist nicht lange genug gekühlt [deez-e veyn ist nisht lang-e genookh gekuult]

**chocolate** die Schokolade [shokohlaa-de]
  ▸ I'd like a bar of chocolate ich hätte gerne eine Tafel Schokolade [ish heh-te gehrn-e ey-ne taafel shokohlaa-de]

**choose** (aus)wählen [(ows)vaylen]
  ▸ I don't know which one to choose ich weiß nicht, welchen ich wählen soll [ish veys nisht vehlshen ish vaylen zol]

**Christmas** das Weihnachten [veynakhten]
  ▸ merry Christmas! frohe Weihnachten! [froh-e veynakhten]
  ▸ I wish you a very merry Christmas ich wünsche Ihnen ein ganz frohes Weihnachtsfest [ish vuunsh-e eenen eyn gants frohez veynakhtsfehst]

**Christmas Day** der erste Weihnachtstag [ehrst-e veynakhtstaak]
  ▸ we're closed on Christmas Day wir haben an Weihnachten geschlossen [veer haaben an veynakhten geshlos-en]

**church** die Kirche [kirsh-e]
  ▸ how old is the church? wie alt ist die Kirche? [vee alt ist dee kirsh-e]
  ▸ where can we find a Protestant church? wo können wir eine protestantische Kirche finden? [voh keunen veer ey-ne protestantish-e kirsh-e fin-den]
  ▸ where is there a Catholic church? wo gibt es hier eine katholische Kirche? [voh gipt ehs heer ey-ne katohlish-e kirsh-e]

**cigarette** die Zigarette [tsigareht-e]
  ▸ can I ask you for a cigarette? darf ich Sie um eine Zigarette bitten? [darf ish zee um ey-ne tsigareht-e bit-en]
  ▸ where can I buy cigarettes? wo kann ich Zigaretten kaufen? [voh kan ish tsigarehten kowfen]

**cigarette lighter** das Feuerzeug [foyertsoyk]
  ▸ do you have a cigarette lighter? haben Sie ein Feuerzeug? [haaben zee eyn foyertsoyk]

**city** die Stadt [shtat]
  ▸ what's the nearest big city? wo ist die nächste große Stadt? [voh ist dee nehkst-e grohs-e shtat]

**class** die Klasse [kla-se]
  ▸ which class are your seats in? in welcher Klasse sind Ihre Plätze? [in vehlsher kla-se zint eer-e plehts-e]

**clean** sauber [zowber] ◆ sauber machen [zowber makhen]
  ▸ the sheets aren't clean die Laken sind nicht sauber [dee laaken zint nisht zowber]
  ▸ do we have to clean the apartment before leaving? müssen wir die Wohnung sauber machen, bevor wir abreisen? [muusen veer dee vohnung zowber makhen befor veer ap-reyzen]
  ▸ could you clean the windshield? könnten Sie die Windschutzscheibe sauber machen? [keunten zee dee vintshuts-sheyb-e zowber makhen]

**cleaning** das Putzen [putsen]
  ▸ who does the cleaning? wer putzt hier? [vehr putst heer]

**clear** klar [klaar]; *(way, road)* frei [frey] ◆ *(road, path)* räumen [roymen]

▸ is that clear? ist das klar? [ist das klaar]

▸ is the road ahead clear? ist die Straße vorne frei? [ist dee shtraas-e forn-e frey]

▸ when will the road be cleared? wann wird die Straße geräumt? [van virt dee shtraas-e geroymt]

**climb** *(mountaineer)* bergsteigen [behrg-shteygen]; *(plane)* (auf)steigen [(owf) shteygen]; *(road)* ansteigen [an-shteygen]

▸ the road climbs steadily after you leave the village die Straße steigt ständig an, nachdem man das Dorf verlässt [dee shtraas-e shteygt shtehndish an nakhdaym man das dorf fehrlehst]

**climbing** das Bergsteigen [behrg-shteygen]

▸ can you go climbing here? kann man hier bergsteigen gehen? [kan man heer behrg-shteygen gayen]

**cloakroom** *(in a museum, a theater)* die Garderobe [garderohb-e]

▸ is there a charge for the cloakroom? kostet die Garderobe etwas? [kostet dee garderohb-e ehtvas]

▸ I'd like to leave my things in the cloakroom ich möchte meine Sachen in der Garderobe lassen [ish meush-te meyn-e zakhen in dehr garderohb-e las-en]

**close** zumachen [tsoomakhen]

▸ what time do the stores close? wann machen die Geschäfte zu? [van makhen dee geshehft-e tsoo]

▸ what time do you close? wann machen Sie zu? [van makhen zee tsoo]

▸ the door won't close die Tür geht nicht zu [dee tuur gayt nisht tsoo]

**closed** geschlossen [geshlos-en]

▸ are the stores closed on Sundays? sind die Läden sonntags geschlossen? [zint dee layden zontaaks geshlos-en]

**clothes** die Kleidung [kleydung]

▸ where can we wash our clothes? wo können wir unsere Wäsche waschen? [voh keunen veer unzer-e vehsh-e vashen]

**club** *(nightclub)* der Nachtklub [nakhtklub]

▸ we could go to a club afterwards wir könnten danach in einen Nachtklub gehen [veer keunten daanakh in eynen nakhtklub gayen]

**coach** *(vehicle)* der Bus [bus]

▸ what time does the coach leave? wann fährt der Bus ab? [van fehrt dehr bus ap]

**coast** die Küste [kuust-e]

▸ an island off the coast of Germany eine Insel vor der deutschen Küste [ey-ne inzel for dehr doytshen kuust-e]

**coffee** der Kaffee [kafay]

▸ coffee with milk or cream Kaffee mit Milch oder Sahne [kafay mit milsh ohder zaan-e]

▸ black coffee schwarzer Kaffee [shvartser kafay]

## coffee

Not to be missed is *Kaffee und Kuchen* time, when coffee is served with delicious cakes. You are usually given filtered coffee, served either by the cup or in a small French press (*Kännchen*) with a jug of (often concentrated) milk. If you prefer decaf, ask for *Kaffee Hag*, a very well-known brand.

▸ I'd like a coffee ich hätte gerne einen Kaffee [ish heh-te gehrn-e eynen kafay]
▸ would you like some coffee? möchten Sie Kaffee? [meushten zee kafay]

**coin** die Münze [muun-tse]
▸ the machine only takes coins die Maschine nimmt nur Münzen [dee masheen-e nimt noor muuntsen]

**cold** kalt [kalt] ◆ *(illness)* die Erkältung [ehrkehltung]; *(low temperature)* die Kälte [kehlt-e]
▸ it's cold today es ist kalt heute [ehs ist kalt hoy-te]
▸ I'm very cold mir ist sehr kalt [meer ist zehr kalt]
▸ to have a cold eine Erkältung haben [ey-ne ehrkehltung haaben]
▸ I've caught a cold ich habe mich erkältet [ish haa-be mish ehrkehltet]

**collect** per R-Gespräch [per ehr geshprehsh]
▸ I have to call my parents collect ich muss meine Eltern per R-Gespräch anrufen [ish mus mey-ne ehltehm per ehr geshprehsh anroofen]

**collect call** das R-Gespräch [ehr geshprehsh]
▸ to make a collect call ein R-Gespräch machen [eyn ehr geshprehsh makhen]

**color** die Farbe [farb-e]
▸ do you have it in another color? haben Sie es in einer anderen Farbe? [haaben zee ehs in eyner anderen farb-e]

**color film** der Farbfilm [farbfilm]
▸ I'd like a roll of color film ich hätte gerne einen Farbfilm [ish heh-te gehrn-e eynen farbfilm]

**come** kommen [kom-en]
▸ come here! kommen Sie her! [kom-en zee hehr]
▸ coming! ich komme! [ish kom-e]
▸ when does the bus come? wann kommt der Bus? [van komt dehr bus]

**come from** kommen aus [kom-en ows]
▸ where do you come from? woher kommen Sie? [vohehr kom-en zee]

**come in** *(enter)* hereinkommen [hehreyn-kom-en]; *(train)* ankommen [ankom-en]; *(tide)* kommen [kom-en]
▸ may I come in? darf ich hereinkommen? [darf ish hehreyn-kom-en]
▸ come in! kommen Sie herein! [kom-en zee hehreyn]
▸ the tide's coming in die Flut kommt [dee floot komt]

**come on** *(light, heating)* angehen [angayen]
- the heating hasn't come on die Heizung ist nicht angegangen [dee heytsung ist nisht angegangen]
- come on! komm schon! [kom shohn]

**come with** *(go with)* mitkommen [mitkom-en]; *(be served with)* serviert werden mit [zehrviert vehrden mit]
- could you come with me to ...? könnten Sie mit mir zu ... kommen? [keunten zee mit meer tsoo kom-en]
- what does it come with? womit wird es serviert? [vohmit virt ehs zehrviert]

**comfortable** *(person)* gemütlich [gemuutlish]; *(chair, bed)* bequem [bekvaym]
- we're very comfortable here wir haben es uns hier sehr gemütlich gemacht [veer haaben ehs uns heer zehr gemuutlish gemakht]

**commission** die Provision [proviziohn]
- what commission do you charge? was für eine Provision berechnen Sie? [vas fuur ey-ne proviziohn berehshnen zee]

**company** *(firm)* die Firma [firma]
- is it a big company? ist es eine große Firma? [ist ehs ey-ne grohs-e firma]

**compartment** *(on train)* das Abteil [apteyl]
- which compartment are our seats in? in welchem Abteil sind unsere Plätze? [in vehlshem apteyl zint unzere plehts-e]

**complain** sich beschweren [zish beshvehren]
- I will be writing to your headquarters to complain ich werde an Ihre Zentrale schreiben und mich beschweren [ish vehrd-e an eer-e tsehntraal-e shreyben unt mish beshvehren]

---

## complaints

- I'd like to see the manager, please ich möchte bitte den Geschäftsführer sprechen [ish meush-te bi-te dayn geshehfts-fuurer shprehshen]
- I have a complaint ich habe eine Beschwerde [ish haa-be ey-ne beshvehr-de]
- there's a problem with the heating es gibt ein Problem mit der Heizung [ehs gipt eyn problehm mit dehr heytsung]
- I am relying on you to sort this problem out ich verlasse mich darauf, dass Sie das Problem in Ordnung bringen [ish fehrlas-e mish daarowf dass zee das problehm in ordnung bringen]
- I expect the cost of the camera to be fully reimbursed ich erwarte, dass die Kosten für die Kamera voll erstattet werden [ish ehrwart-e das dee kosten fuur dee kamera fol ehrshtatet vehrden]

**complaint** die Beschwerde [beshvehr-de]
- I'd like to make a complaint ich möchte mich beschweren [ish meush-te mish beshvehren]

**complete** *(form)* ausfüllen [owsfuulen]
- here's the completed form hier ist das ausgefüllte Formular [heer ist das owsgefuult-e formular]

**comprehensive insurance** die Vollkaskoversicherung [fol-kaskoh-fehrzisherung]
- how much extra is the comprehensive insurance coverage? wie viel mehr kostet die Vollkaskoversicherung? [vee feel mehr kostet dee fol-kaskoh-fehrzisherung]

**computer** der Computer [kompyooter]
- is there a computer I could use? gibt es einen Computer, den ich benutzen kann? [gipt ehs eynen kompyooter dayn ish benutsen kan]

**concert** das Konzert [kontsehrt]
- did you like the concert? hat Ihnen das Konzert gefallen? [hat eenen das kontsehrt gefal-en]

**condom** das Kondom [kondohm]
- do you have any condoms? haben Sie Kondome? [haaben zee kondohm-e]

**confirm** bestätigen [beshtaytigen]
- I confirmed my reservation by phone ich habe meine Buchung am Telefon bestätigt [ish haa-be mey-ne bookhung am tehlehfohn beshtaytisht]
- I'd like to confirm my return flight ich möchte meinen Rückflug bestätigen [ish meush-te meynen ruukflook beshtaytigen]

**congratulations** die Glückwünsche [gluukvuunsh-e]
- congratulations! herzlichen Glückwunsch! [hehrtslishen gluukvunsh]

**connecting flight** der Anschlussflug [anshlusflook]
- does the connecting flight leave from the same terminal? fliegt der Anschlussflug vom selben Terminal ab? [fleekt dehr anshlusflook fom zehlben tehrminal ap]

**connection** *(on phone)* die Verbindung [fehrbindung]; *(transportation)* der Anschluss [anshlus]
- the connection is very bad: I can't hear very well die Verbindung ist sehr schlecht, ich kann Sie nicht sehr gut verstehen [dee fehrbindung ist zehr shlesht ish kan zee nisht zehr goot fehrshtayen]
- I've missed my connection ich habe meinen Anschluss verpasst [ish haa-be meynen anshlus fehrpast]

**consulate** das Konsulat [konzulaat]
- where is the American consulate? wo ist das amerikanische Konsulat? [voh ist das amehrikaanish-e konzulaat]

**contact** *(communication)* die Verbindung [fehrbindung] ✦ sich in Verbindung setzen mit [zish in fehrbindung zehtsen mit]
- I need to contact my family in the States ich muss mich mit meiner Familie in

den Staaten in Verbindung setzen [ish mus mish mit meyner fameeli-e in dayn shtaaten in fehrbindung zehtsen]

▸ do you know how to get in contact with him? wissen Sie, wie man sich mit ihm in Verbindung setzen kann? [vis-en zee vee man zish mit eem in fehrbindung zehtsen kan]

**contact lens** die Kontaktlinse [kontaktlin-ze]

▸ I've lost a contact (lens) ich habe eine Kontaktlinse verloren [ish haa-be ey-ne kontaktlin-ze fehrloren]

**cookie** *(food)* der Keks [kayks]

▸ a box of cookies, please eine Schachtel Kekse, bitte [ey-ne shakhtel kayks-e bi-te]

**cooking** *(activity)* das Kochen [kokhen]; *(type of food)* das Essen [ehsen]

▸ we prefer to do our own cooking wir kochen lieber selber [veer kokhen leeber zehlber]

▸ do you like German cooking? mögen Sie deutsches Essen? [meugen zee doytshes ehsen]

**cork** *(for a bottle)* der Korken [korken]

▸ where's the cork for the bottle? wo ist der Korken für die Flasche? [voh ist dee korken fuur dee flash-e]

**corked** nach Kork schmeckend [nakh kork shmekend]

▸ this wine is corked dieser Wein schmeckt nach Kork [deezer veyn shmehkt nakh kork]

**corner** die Ecke [ehk-e]

▸ stop at the corner halten Sie an der Ecke an [halten zee an dehr ehk-e an]

**coronary** der Herzinfarkt [hehrtsinfarkt]

▸ he's had a coronary er hatte einen Herzinfarkt [ehr hat-e eynen hehrtsinfarkt]

**correct** *(right)* richtig [rishtish]

▸ that's correct das ist richtig [das ist rishtish]

**cost** kosten [kosten]

▸ how much will it cost to go to the airport? wie viel kostet eine Fahrt zum Flughafen? [vee feel kostet ey-ne faart tsum flookhaafen]

▸ it cost us 150 euros es hat uns einhundertfünfzig Euro gekostet [ehs hat uns eynhundertfuunftsish oyroh gekostet]

**cot** das Klappbett [klapbeht]

▸ we can put a cot in the room for you wir können Ihnen ein Klappbett ins Zimmer stellen [veer keunen eenen eyn klapbeht ins tsim-er shtehlen]

**cough** der Husten [husten] ◆ husten [husten]

▸ I've got a cough ich habe Husten [ish haa-be husten]

▸ I need something for a cough ich brauche etwas gegen Husten [ish browkh-e ehtvas gaygen husten]

**could**

▸ could you help me? könnten Sie mir helfen? [keunten zee meer hehlfen]

**count** zählen [tsaylen]
- that doesn't count das zählt nicht [das tsaylt nisht]

**counter** *(in store)* die Theke [tayk-e]; *(in bank)* der Schalter [shalter]
- which counter do I have to go to? zu welchem Schalter muss ich gehen? [tsoo velshem shalter mus ish gayen]
- do you sell this medication over the counter? ist dieses Medikament rezeptfrei? [ist deezes mehdikamehnt rehtsehptfrey]

**country** das Land [lant]
- what country do you come from? aus welchem Land kommen Sie? [ows vehlshem lant kom-en zee]

**couple** das Paar [par]
- married couple Ehepaar [ay-e-par]
- it's for a couple and two children es ist für zwei Erwachsene und zwei Kinder [ehs ist fuur tsvey ehrvakzen-e unt tsvey kin-der]

**course** *(of a meal)* der Gang [gang]; *(for a race)* die Strecke [shtrehk-e]; *(in yoga, sailing)* der Kurs [kurs]
- is the set meal three courses? besteht das Menü aus drei Gängen? [beshtayt das mehnuu ows drey gehngen]
- how much does the sailing course cost? was kostet der Segelkurs? [vas kostet dehr zaygelkurs]
- of course natürlich [natuurlish]
- of course he'll come natürlich wird er kommen [natuurlish virt ehr kom-en]

**cream** *(for the skin)* die Creme [kraym-e]; *(on dessert)* die Sahne [zaan-e]
- I need some cream for my sunburn ich brauche eine Creme gegen meinen Sonnenbrand [ish browkh-e ey-ne kraym-e gaygen meynen zon-en-brant]

**credit card** die Kreditkarte [krehdeetkart-e]
- do you take credit cards? nehmen Sie Kreditkarten? [naymen zee krehdeetkarten]

**cross** überqueren [uuber-kvehren]; *(border)* passieren [paseeren]
- how do we cross this street? wo können wir diese Straße überqueren? [voh keunen veer deez-e shtraas-e uuber-kvehren]

**cross-country skiing** der Skilanglauf [shee-langlowf]
- where can I go cross-country skiing around here? wo kann ich hier Skilanglauf machen? [voh kan ish heer shee-langlowf makhen]

**crosswalk** der Fußgängerüberweg [foosgehngner-uubervayk]
- always cross at the crosswalk gehen Sie immer über den Fußgängerüberweg [gayen zee im-er uuber dayn foosgehngner-uubervayk]

**cruise** die Kreuzfahrt [kroytsfaart]
- how much does a cruise on the Rhine cost? was kostet eine Kreuzfahrt auf dem Rhein? [vas kostet ey-ne kroytsfaart owf daym reyn]

**cry** weinen [veynen]
> don't cry weine doch nicht [veyn-e dokh nisht]

**cup** die Tasse [tas-e]
> I'd like a cup of tea ich hätte gerne eine Tasse Tee [ish heh-te gehrn-e ey-ne tas-e tay]
> a coffee cup eine Kaffeetasse [ey-ne kafaytas-e]
> could we have an extra cup? könnten wir noch eine Tasse bekommen? [keunten veer nokh ey-ne tas-e bekom-en]

**currency** die Währung [vehrung]
> how much local currency do you have? wie viel Landeswährung haben Sie? [vee feel landezvehrung haaben zee]

**cut** schneiden [shneyden]
> I had my hair cut today ich habe mir heute die Haare schneiden lassen [ish haa-be meer hoy-te dee haar-e shneyden las-en]
> I cut my finger ich habe mir in den Finger geschnitten [ish haa-be meer in dayn fing-er geshnit-en]

**daily** täglich [tayglish] ◆ die Tageszeitung [taagez-tseytung]
> what's the name of the local daily newspaper? wie heißt die örtliche Tageszeitung? [vee heyst dee eurtlish-e taagez-tseytung]

**damage** beschädigen [beshaydigen]
> my suitcase was damaged in transit mein Koffer wurde beim Transport beschädigt [meyn kof-er vurd-e beym transport beshaydisht]

**damp** feucht [foysht]
> it's damp today heute ist es feucht [hoy-te ist ehs foysht]

**dance** tanzen [tantsen]
> shall we dance? wollen wir tanzen? [vol-en veer tantsen]
> I can't dance ich kann nicht tanzen [ish kan nisht tantsen]

**dancing** das Tanzen [tantsen]
> where can we go dancing? wo können wir tanzen gehen? [voh keunen veer tantsen gayen]
> will there be dancing? wird auch getanzt? [virt owkh getantst]

**dandruff** die Schuppen [shup-en]
> I have bad dandruff ich habe starke Schuppen [ish haa-be shtark-e shup-en]

**danger** die Gefahr [gefaar]
> hurry! someone's in danger! schnell! jemand ist in Gefahr! [shnehl yaymant ist in gefaar]

**dangerous** gefährlich [gefehrlish]
- this stretch of the river is quite dangerous an dieser Stelle ist der Fluss sehr gefährlich [an deezer stehl-e ist dehr flus zehr gefehrlish]

**dark** dunkel [dunkel]
- it's dark es ist dunkel [ehs ist dunkel]
- she has dark hair sie hat dunkles Haar [zee hat dunklez haar]

**dark chocolate** die dunkle Schokolade [dunkl-e shokohlaad-e]
- I prefer dark chocolate ich mag lieber dunkle Schokolade [ish maak leeber dunkl-e shokohlaad-e]

**date** *(in time)* das Datum [daatum]; *(appointment)* die Verabredung [fehr-apraydung]
- I've got a date tonight ich habe heute Abend eine Verabredung [ish haa-be hoy-te aabent ey-ne fehr-apraydung]

**date-stamp** abstempeln [apshtempeln]
- do I have to date-stamp this ticket? muss ich das Ticket abstempeln? [mus ish das tikit mit daym daatum apshtempeln]

**daughter** die Tochter [tokhter]
- this is my daughter das ist meine Tochter [das ist meyn-e tokhter]

**day** der Tag [taak]
- what day is it? welcher Tag ist heute? [vehlsh-e taak ist hoy-te]
- I arrived three days ago ich bin vor drei Tagen angekommen [ish bin for drey taagen an-gekom-en]
- I'd like to do a round trip in a day ich möchte an einem Tag hin- und zurückreisen [ish meusht-e an eynem taak hin unt tsuruukreyzen]
- how much is it per day? was kostet es pro Tag? [vas kostet ehs proh taak]

**dead** tot [toht]
- when the ambulance got there, he was already dead als der Krankenwagen kam, war er bereits tot [als dehr krankenvaagen kaam var ehr bereyts toht]
- the battery's dead die Batterie ist leer [dee bateree ist lehr]

**dead end** die Sackgasse [zakgas-e]
- it's a dead end das ist eine Sackgasse [das ist ey-ne zakgas-e]

**deal** *(business agreement)* das Geschäft [geshehft]
- I'll make a deal with you ich mache ein Geschäft mit Ihnen [ish makh-e eyn geshehft mit eenen]
- I got a good deal on the room ich habe das Zimmer zu einem günstigen Preis bekommen [ish haa-be das tsim-er tsoo eynem guunstigen preys bekom-en]

**death** *(state)* der Tod [tohd]; *(person)* der die Tote [toht-e]
- there were two deaths es gab zwei Tote [ehs gaap tsvey toht-e]

**decaf, decaffeinated** der koffeinfreie Kaffee [kofayeenfrey-e kafay] ◆ koffeinfrei [kofayeenfrey]

▸ a decaf/decaffeinated coffee, please einen koffeinfreien Kaffee, bitte [eynen kofayeenfreyen kafay bi-te]

**December** der Dezember [daytsehmber]
   ▸ December 10th zehnter Dezember [tsaynter daytsehmber]

**decide** sich entscheiden [zish ehntsheyden]
   ▸ we haven't decided yet wir haben uns noch nicht entschieden [veer haaben uns nokh nisht ehntsheeden]

**deck** *(of ship)* das Deck [dehk]; *(of cards)* das Spiel [shpeel]
   ▸ how do I get to the upper deck? wie komme ich zum Oberdeck? [vee kom-e ish tsum ohberdehk]

**deckchair** der Liegestuhl [leeg-e-shtool]
   ▸ I'd like to rent a deckchair ich würde gerne einen Liegestuhl mieten [ish vuurd-e gehrn-e eynen leeg-e-shtool meeten]

**declare** *(at customs)* verzollen [fehr-tsol-en]
   ▸ I have nothing to declare ich habe nichts zu verzollen [ish haa-be nishts tsoo fehr-tsol-en]
   ▸ I have a bottle of spirits to declare ich habe eine Flasche Spirituosen zu verzollen [ish haa-be ey-ne flash-e spirituohzen tsoo fehr-tsol-en]

**definitely** bestimmt [beshtimt]
   ▸ definitely not! ganz bestimmt nicht! [gants beshtimt nisht]
   ▸ we'll definitely come back here wir werden auf jeden Fall wiederkommen [veer vehrden owf yayden fal veederkom-en]

**degree** der Grad [graat]
   ▸ it's 5 degrees below freezing es ist fünf Grad unter null [ehs ist fuunf graat unter nul]

**delay** die Verspätung [fehrshpaytung]
   ▸ is there a delay for this flight? hat der Flug Verspätung? [hat dehr flook fehrshpaytung]

**delayed** verspätet [fehrshpaytet]
   ▸ how long will the flight be delayed? wie viel Verspätung hat der Flug? [vee feel fehrspaytung hat dehr flook]

**delighted** hocherfreut [hohkh-ehrfroyt]
   ▸ we're delighted you could make it wir sind hocherfreut, dass Sie kommen konnten [veer sint hohkh-ehrfroyt das zee kom-en konten]

**dentist** der Zahnarzt [tsaan-artst], die Zahnärztin [tsaan-ehrtstin]
   ▸ I need to see a dentist urgently ich muss dringend zum Zahnarzt [ish mus dringend tsum tsaan-artst]

**department** *(in store)* die Abteilung [apteylung]
   ▸ I'm looking for the menswear department ich suche die Herrenabteilung [ish zookh-e dee hehren-apteylung]

**department store** das Kaufhaus [kowfhows]
▶ where are the department stores? wo finde ich Kaufhäuser? [voh fin-de ish kowfhoyzer]

**departure** *(of person)* die Abreise [apreyz-e]; *(of bus, train)* die Abfahrt [apfart]; *(of plane)* die Abflug [apflook]
▶ 'departures' *(in airport)* 'Abflug' [apflook]

**departure lounge** *(in airport)* die Abflughalle [apflook-hal-e]
▶ where's the departure lounge? wo ist die Abflughalle? [voh ist dee apflook-hal-e]

**deposit** *(against loss or damage)* die Kaution [kowtsiohn]; *(down payment)* die Anzahlung [antsaalung]
▶ is there a deposit to pay on the equipment? muss für die Ausrüstung eine Kaution gezahlt werden? [mus fuur dee owsruustung ey-ne kowtsiohn getsaalt vehrden]
▶ how much is the deposit? wie hoch ist die Kaution? [vee hohkh ist dee kowtsiohn]

**desk** *(in office, home)* der Schreibtisch [shreybtish]; *(at hotel)* die Rezeption [rehtsehptsiohn]; *(in shop)* die Kasse [ka-se]; *(at airport, station)* der Schalter [shalter]
▶ where can I find the American Airlines desk? wo ist der Schalter von American Airlines? [voh ist dehr shalter fon american airlines]

**dessert** der Nachtisch [nakhtish]
▶ what desserts do you have? was haben Sie zum Nachtisch? [vas haaben zee tsum nakhtish]

**dessert wine** der Dessertwein [dehsehrtveyn]
▶ can you recommend a good dessert wine? können Sie einen Dessertwein empfehlen? [keunen zee eynen dehsehrtveyn ehmpfaylen]

**detour** die Umleitung [umleytung]
▶ is there a detour ahead? ist da vorne eine Umleitung? [ist daa forn-e ey-ne umleytung]

**develop** entwickeln [ehntvikeln]
▶ how much does it cost to develop a roll of 36 photos? was kostet es, einen 36er-Film entwickeln zu lassen? [vas kostet ehs eynen sehks-unt-dreysiger film ehntvikeln tsoo las-en]

**diabetic** zuckerkrank [tsukerkrank] ◆ der Diabetiker [deeabaytiker], die Diabetikerin [deeabaytikerin]
▶ I'm diabetic and I need a prescription for insulin ich bin zuckerkrank und benötige ein Insulin-Rezept [ish bin tsukerkrank unt beneutig-e eyn inzuleen rehtsehpt]

**diarrhea** der Durchfall [durshfal]
▶ I'd like something for diarrhea ich hätte gerne etwas gegen Durchfall [ish heh-te gehrn-e ehtvas gaygen durshfal]

**difference** der Unterschied [untersheed]; *(in price, cost)* die Differenz [diferehnts]
▶ will you pay the difference? zahlen Sie die Differenz? [tsaalen zee dee diferehnts]

## dinner

Germans tend to sit down for dinner (*Abendessen*) from about 6 p.m. and have a cold meal of bread, cooked meats and cheese. The restaurants start to fill up at about the same time.

**difficult** schwierig [shveerish]
> some sounds are difficult to pronounce **einige Laute sind schwierig auszusprechen** [eynig-e lowt-e zint shveerish ows-tsu-shprehshen]

**difficulty** *(trouble)* die Schwierigkeit [shveerishkeyt]; *(problem)* das Problem [problaym]
> I'm having difficulty finding my hotel **ich habe Schwierigkeiten, mein Hotel zu finden** [ish haa-be shveerishkeyten meyn hohtehl tsoo fin-den]

**digital camera** die Digitalkamera [digitaalkamera]
> my digital camera's been stolen **meine Digitalkamera ist gestohlen worden** [meyn-e digitaalkamera ist geshtohlen vorden]

**dining room** der Speisesaal [shpeyzezaal]
> do you have to have breakfast in the dining room? **gibt es das Frühstück nur im Speisesaal?** [gipt ehs das fruushtuuk noor im shpeyzezaal]

**dinner** das Abendessen [aabent-ehsen]
> up to what time do they serve dinner? **bis wann gibt es Abendessen?** [bis van gipt ehs aabent-ehsen]

**direct** direkt [deerehkt]
> is that train direct? **ist das ein Direktzug?** [ist das eyn deerehkt-tsook]

**direction** die Richtung [rikhtung]
> am I going in the right direction for the train station? **ist das die richtige Richtung zum Bahnhof?** [ist das dee rishtig-e rikhtung tsum baanhohf]

**directory assistance** die Auskunft [owskunft]
> what's the number for directory assistance? **welche Nummer hat die Auskunft?** [vehlsh-e num-er hat dee owskunft]

**dirty** *(room, tablecloth)* schmutzig [shmutsish]
> the sheets are dirty **die Laken sind schmutzig** [dee laaken zint shmutsish]

**disability** die Behinderung [behinderung]
> do you have facilities for people with disabilities? **sind Sie behindertengerecht ausgestattet?** [zint zee behinderten-gerehsht owsgeshtatet]

**disabled** behindert [behindert]
> where's the nearest disabled parking spot? **wo ist der nächste Behindertenparkplatz?** [voh ist dehr nehkst-e behindertenparkplats]

**disco** die Disko [diskoh]
> are there any discos around here? **gibt es hier Diskos?** [gipt ehs heer diskohz]

**discount** der Rabatt [rabat]

 ▶ is there any chance of a discount? **kann ich einen Rabatt bekommen?** [kan ish eynen rabat bekom-en]

**dish** *(plate)* der Teller [tehler]; *(food)* das Gericht [gerisht]

 ▶ what's the dish of the day? **was ist das Tagesgericht?** [vas ist das taagezgerisht]

 ▶ can I help you with the dishes? **kann ich Ihnen beim Geschirrspülen helfen?** [kan ish eenen beym gesheer-shpuulen hehlfen]

**disposable** Einweg- [eynvayg]

 ▶ I need some disposable razors **ich brauche Einwegrasierer** [ish browkh-e eynvayg-razeerer]

 ▶ do you sell disposable cameras? **haben Sie Einwegkameras?** [haaben zee eynvaygkameraz]

**distance** die Entfernung [ehntfehrnung]

 ▶ the hotel is only a short distance from here **das Hotel ist nicht weit von hier entfernt** [das hohtehl ist nisht veyt fon heer ehntfehrnt]

**district** *(of town)* der Stadtteil [shtat-teyl]; *(of country)* das Gebiet [gebeet]

 ▶ which district do you live in? **in welchem Stadtteil wohnen Sie?** [in vehlshem shtat-teyl vohnen zee]

**dive** *(under sea)* tauchen [towkhen]; *(into swimming pool)* einen Kopfsprung machen [eynen kopfshprung makhen] ◆ *(under sea)* der Tauchgang [towkhgang]; *(into swimming pool)* der Kopfsprung [kopfshprung]

 ▶ can we do a night dive? *(scuba diving)* **können wir einen Nachttauchgang machen?** [keunen veer eynen nakht-towkhgang makhen]

**diving** *(scuba diving)* das Tauchen [towkhen]

 ▶ what's the diving like around here? **kann man hier gut tauchen?** [kan man heer goot towkhen]

 ▶ I'd like to take diving lessons **ich möchte gerne einen Tauchkurs machen** [ish meusht-e gehrn-e eynen towkhkoors makhen]

 ▶ do you rent out diving equipment? **verleihen Sie Tauchausrüstungen?** [fehrleyen zee towkh-owsruustungen]

**diving board** das Sprungbrett [shprungbreht]

 ▶ is there a diving board? **gibt es ein Sprungbrett?** [gipt ehs eyn shprungbreht]

**dizzy spell** der Schwindelanfall [shvindelanfal]

 ▶ I've been having dizzy spells **ich hatte Schwindelanfälle** [ish hat-e shvindelanfehl-e]

**do** *(perform action)* machen [makhen], tun [toon]; *(cover distance)* zurücklegen [tsuruuklaygen]

 ▶ is there anything I can do (to help)? **kann ich irgendetwas machen?** [kan ish irgentehtvas makhen]

 ▶ what are you doing tonight? **was machen Sie heute Abend?** [vas makhen zee hoy-te aabent]

- ▸ what is there to do here on Sundays? was kann man hier sonntags machen? [vas kan man heer zontaaks makhen]
- ▸ what do you do for a living? was machen Sie beruflich? [vas makhen zee berooflish]

**doctor** der Arzt [artst], die Ärztin [ehrtstin]
- ▸ I have to see a doctor ich muss zum Arzt [ish mus tsum artst]

**dollar** der Dollar [dolar]
- ▸ I'd like to change some dollars into euros ich möchte gerne Dollar in Euro umtauschen [ish meusht-e gehrn-e dolar in oyroh umtowshen]

**door** die Tür [tuur]
- ▸ do you want me to answer the door? soll ich die Tür öffnen? [zol ish dee tuur eufnen]

**dormitory** (in youth hostel) der Schlafsaal [shlaafzaal]; (for students) das Studentenwohnheim [shtudehnten-vohnheym]
- ▸ are you living in the dormitory? wohnst du im Studentenwohnheim? [vohnst doo im shtudehnten-vohnheym]

**double** doppelt [dop-elt] ♦ verdoppeln [fehrdop-eln]
- ▸ it's spelled with a double 'l' es wird mit Doppel-L geschrieben [ehs virt mit dop-el ehl geshreeben]
- ▸ prices have doubled since last year die Preise haben sich seit dem letzten Jahr verdoppelt [dee preyz-e haaben zish zeyt daym lehtsten yaar fehrdop-elt]

**double bed** das Doppelbett [dop-el-beht]
- ▸ does the room have a double bed? ist das Zimmer mit Doppelbett? [ist das tsim-er mit dop-el-beht]

**double room** das Doppelzimmer [dop-el-tsim-er]
- ▸ I'd like a double room for 5 nights, please ich hätte gerne ein Doppelzimmer für fünf Nächte, bitte [ish heh-te gehrn-e eyn dop-el-tsim-er fuur fuunf nehkht-e bi-te]

**downtown** Innenstadt- [inen-shtat] ♦ (to be) im Zentrum [im tsehntrum], in der Innenstadt [in dehr inen-shtat]; (to go) ins Zentrum [ins tsehntrum], in die Innenstadt [in dee inen-shtat] ♦ das Zentrum [tsehntrum], die Innenstadt [inen-shtat]
- ▸ we're looking for a good downtown hotel wir suchen ein gutes Hotel im Zentrum [veer zookhen eyn gootez hohtehl im tsehntrum]
- ▸ does this bus go downtown? fährt dieser Bus in die Innenstadt? [fehrt deezer bus in dee inen-shtat]

**draft beer** das Fassbier [fasbeer]
- ▸ a draft beer, please ein Bier vom Fass, bitte [eyn beer fom fas bi-te]

**dream** der Traum [trowm] ♦ träumen [troymen]
- ▸ to have a dream träumen [troymen]
- ▸ I dreamt (that)... ich habe geträumt(, dass)... [ish haa-be getroymt (das)]

**drink** das Getränk [getrehnk] ◆ trinken [trinken]

▸ I'll have a cold drink ich werde etwas Kaltes trinken [ish vehrd-e ehtvas kaltes trinken]

▸ I could do with a drink ich würde gerne etwas trinken [ish vuurd-e gehrn-e ehtvas trinken]

▸ what kind of hot drinks do you have? was haben Sie an heißen Getränken? [vas haaben zee an heysen getrehnken]

▸ shall we go for a drink? wollen wir etwas trinken gehen? [vol-en veer ehtvas trinken gayen]

▸ can I buy you a drink? darf ich Sie zu einem Drink einladen? [darf ish zee tsoo eynem drink eynlaaden]

**drinking water** das Trinkwasser [trinkvas-er]

▸ I'm looking for bottled drinking water ich suche Trinkwasser in Flaschen [ish zookh-e trinkvas-er in flashen]

**drive** *(in vehicle)* die Fahrt [fart] ◆ fahren [faaren]

▸ is it a long drive? ist die Fahrt lang? [ist dee fart lang]

▸ could you drive me home? könnten Sie mich nach Hause fahren? [keunten zee mish naakh howz-e faaren]

**driver** der Fahrer [faarer], die Fahrerin [faarerin]

▸ the other driver wasn't looking where he was going der andere Fahrer hat nicht auf den Verkehr geachtet [dehr ander-e faarer hat nisht owf dayn fehrkehr ge-akhtet]

**driver's license** der Führerschein [fuurersheyn]

▸ can I see your driver's license? kann ich Ihren Führerschein sehen? [kan ish eeren fuurersheyn zayen]

**drop** *(of liquid)* der Tropfen [tropfen] ◆ *(let fall)* fallen lassen [fal-en las-en]; *(let out of vehicle)* herauslassen [hehrows-las-en]

▸ could I just have a drop of milk? könnte ich etwas Milch haben? [keunt-e ish ehtvas milsh haaben]

▸ I dropped my scarf ich habe meinen Schal fallen lassen [ish haa-be meynen shaal fal-en las-en]

▸ could you drop me off at the corner? können Sie mich an der Ecke herauslassen? [keunen zee mish an dehr ehk-e hehrowslas-en]

**drop off** *(let out of vehicle)* absetzen [apzehtsen]

▸ could you drop me off here? könnten Sie mich hier absetzen? [keunten zee mish heer apzehtsen]

**drown** ertrinken [ehrtrinken]

▸ he's drowning, somebody call for help er ertrinkt: holen Sie Hilfe [ehr ehrtrinkt hohlen zee hilf-e]

## drugstores

If you need beauty products or any of the usual things you buy from a drugstore, go to a *Drogerie* or *Drogeriemarkt*. You'll find them in all German-speaking countries.

**drugstore** die Drogerie [drogeree]
- where is the nearest drugstore? **wo ist die nächste Drogerie?** [voh ist dee nehkste drogeree]

**drunk** betrunken [betrunken]
- he's very drunk **er ist sehr betrunken** [ehr ist zehr betrunken]

**dry** trocken [trok-en] ♦ *(gen)* trocknen [troknen]; *(with a cloth, a towel)* abtrocknen [aptroknen]
- a small glass of dry white wine **ein kleines Glas trockenen Weißwein** [eyn kleynez glaas trokenen veysveyn]
- where can I put my towel to dry? **wo kann ich mein Handtuch zum Trocknen aufhängen?** [voh kan ish meyn hant-tookh tsum troknen owfhehngen]

**dry cleaner's** die Reinigung [reynigung]
- is there a dry cleaner's nearby? **gibt es in der Nähe eine Reinigung?** [gipt ehs in dehr nay-e ey-ne reynigung]

**dryer** *(for laundry)* der Trockner [trokner]
- is there a dryer? **gibt es einen Trockner?** [gipt ehs eynen trokner]

**dub** *(movie)* synchronisieren [zuunkrohnizeeren]
- do they always dub English-language movies? **werden englischsprachige Filme immer synchronisiert?** [vehrden ehnglish-shpraakhig-e film-e im-er zuunkrohnizeert]

**during** während [vayrent]
- is there restricted parking during the festival? **gibt es während des Festivals ein Parkverbot?** [gipt ehs vayrent dehz fehstivalz eyn parkfehrboht]

## at the drugstore

- I'd like something for a headache/a sore throat/diarrhea **ich hätte gerne etwas gegen Kopfschmerzen/Halsschmerzen/Durchfall** [ish heh-te gehrn-e ehtvas gaygen kopfshmehrtsen/hals-shmehrtsen/durshfal]
- I'd like some aspirin/some Band-Aids® **ich hätte gerne Aspirin/Pflaster** [ish heh-te gehrn-e aspireen/pflaster]
- could you recommend a doctor? **können Sie mir einen Arzt empfehlen?** [keunen zee meer eynen artst ehmpfaylen]

**duty** *(tax)* der Zoll [tsol]

▸ do I have to pay duty on this? muss ich darauf Zoll zahlen? [mus ish daarowf tsol tsaalen]

▸ I want to see the doctor on duty ich möchte den diensthabenden Arzt sehen [ish meusht-e dayn deenst-haabenden artst zayen]

**duty-free shop** der Duty-free-Shop [dooti-free-shop]

▸ where are the duty-free shops? wo sind die Duty-free-Shops? [voh zint dee dooti-free-shops]

**DVD** die DVD [day-fow-day]

▸ which region is this DVD coded for? welchen Regionalcode hat die DVD? [vehlshen rehgiohnaalkoht hat dee day-fow-day]

**ear** das Ohr [ohr]

▸ I have a ringing in my ears ich habe ein Klingeln in den Ohren [ish haa-be eyn klingeln in dayn ohren]

**earache** die Ohrenschmerzen [ohrenshmehrtsen]

▸ he has an earache er hat Ohrenschmerzen [ehr hat ohrenshmehrtsen]

**ear infection** die Ohrenentzündung [ohren-ehnt-tsuundung]

▸ I think I have an ear infection ich glaube, ich habe eine Ohrenentzündung [ish glowb-e ish haa-be ey-ne ohren-ehnt-tsuundung]

**early** früh [fruu] ♦ *(earlier than expected time)* früher [fruuer]; *(too early)* zu früh [tsoo fruu]

▸ is there an earlier flight? gibt es einen früheren Flug? [gipt ehs eynen fruueren flook]

▸ we arrived early wir sind früher angekommen [veer zint fruuer angekom-en]

▸ I'll be leaving early in the morning ich werde früh am Morgen abreisen [ish vehrd-e fruu am morgen apreyzen]

**Easter** das Ostern [ohstern]

▸ Happy Easter! frohe Ostern! [froh-e ohstern]

**easy** leicht [leysht]

▸ is it easy to use? ist es leicht zu bedienen? [ist ehs leysht tsoo bedeenen]

▸ I'd like something easy to carry ich suche etwas Leichtes [ish zookh-e ehtvas leishtez]

**eat** essen [ehsen]

▸ I'm afraid I don't eat meat ich esse leider kein Fleisch [ish ehs-e leyder keyn fleysh]

▸ where can we get something to eat? wo können wir etwas zu essen bekommen? [voh keunen veer ehtvas tsoo ehsen bekom-en]

**economy (class)** die Touristenklasse [tooristen-klas-e]

- are there any seats in economy class? gibt es noch Plätze in der Touristenklasse? [gipt ehs nokh plehts-e in dehr tooristen-klas-e]
- I'd prefer to go economy ich fliege lieber Touristenklasse [ish fleeg-e leeber tooristen-klas-e]

**egg** das Ei [ey]

- I'd prefer a fried egg ich hätte lieber ein Spiegelei [ish heh-te leeber eyn shpeegeley]

**eight** acht [akht]

- there are eight of us wir sind acht [veer zint akht]

**electric heater** der Heizstrahler [heyts-shtraaler]

- do you have an electric heater? haben Sie einen Heizstrahler? [haaben zee eynen heyts-shtraaler]

**electricity** der Strom [shtrohm]

- there's no electricity in the room im Zimmer gibt es keinen Strom [im tsim-er gipt ehs keynem shtrohm]

**electric razor, electric shaver** der Elektrorasierer [ehlehktroh-razeerer]

- where can I plug in my electric razor? wo kann ich meinen Elektrorasierer anschließen? [voh kan ish meynen ehlehktroh-razeerer anshleesen]

**elevator** der Fahrstuhl [faarshtool]

- is there an elevator? gibt es einen Fahrstuhl? [gipt ehs eynen faarshtool]
- the elevator is out of order der Fahrstuhl ist kaputt [dehr faarshtool ist kaput]

**eleven** elf [ehlf]

- there are eleven of us wir sind zu elft [veer zint tsoo ehlft]

**e-mail** die E-Mail [ee-mayl]

- I'd like to send an e-mail ich möchte eine E-Mail versenden [ish meusht-e ey-ne ee-mayl fehrzehnden]
- where can I check my e-mail? wo kann ich meine E-Mails checken? [voh kan ish meyn-e ee-maylz tshehken]

**e-mail address** die E-Mail-Adresse [ee-mayl-adrehs-e]

- do you have an e-mail address? haben Sie eine E-Mail-Adresse? [haaben zee ey-ne ee-mayl-adrehs-e]

**embarrassing** peinlich [peynlish]

- an embarrassing situation eine peinliche Situation [ey-ne peynlish-e zituatsiohn]

**emergency** der Notfall [nohtfal]

- it's an emergency! das ist ein Notfall! [das ist eyn nohtfal]
- what number do you call in an emergency? welche Nummer wählt man im Notfall? [vehlsh-e num-er vaylt man im nohtfal]

### enjoy your meal!     *(i)*

When you're tucking into a mountain of sausages at a beer festival, don't forget to wish the people sitting next to you *Guten Appetit!* or *Mahlzeit!* Their reply should be *Danke, gleichfalls!* In Switzerland they say *Guten Appetit!* or *En Guete!*

---

**emergency cord** die Notbremse [nohtbrehmz-e]
▸ someone's pulled the emergency cord jemand hat die Notbremse gezogen [yaymant hat dee nohtbrehmz-e ge-tsohgen]

**emergency exit** der Notausgang [noht-owsgang]
▸ remember that the nearest emergency exit may be behind you denken Sie daran, dass der nächste Notausgang hinter Ihnen sein könnte [dehnken zee daaran das dehr nehkst-e noht-owsgang hinter eenen zeyn keunt-e]

**emergency room** die Unfallstation [unfal-shtatsiohn]
▸ I need to go to the emergency room right away ich muss sofort zur Unfallstation [ish mus zohfort tsoor unfal-shtatsiohn]

**end** das Ende [ehnd-e]
▸ at the end of July Ende Juli [ehnd-e yooli]

**engine** der Motor [mohtor]
▸ the engine is making funny noises der Motor macht komische Geräusche [dehr mohtor makht kohmish-e geroysh-e]

**English** englisch [ehnglish] ◆ *(language)* das Englisch [ehnglish]
▸ the English die Engländer [dee ehnglehnder]
▸ I'm English ich komme aus England [ish kom-e ows ehnglant]
▸ that's not how you say it in English so sagt man das nicht auf Englisch [zoh zaakt man das nisht owf ehnglish]
▸ do you understand English? verstehen Sie Englisch? [fehrshtayen zee ehnglish]

**enjoy** genießen [geneesen]
▸ to enjoy life das Leben genießen [das layben geneesen]
▸ to enjoy oneself sich amüsieren [zish amuuzeeren]
▸ enjoy your meal! guten Appetit! [gooten apehteet]
▸ did you enjoy your meal? hat es Ihnen geschmeckt? [hat ehs eenen geshmehkt]

**enough** genügend [genuugent] ◆ genug [genookh]
▸ I don't have enough money ich habe nicht genügend Geld [ish haa-be nisht genuugent gehlt]
▸ that's enough! jetzt reicht es! [yehtst reysht ehs]
▸ no thanks, I've had quite enough nein danke, ich bin satt [neyn dank-e ish bin zat]

**enter** *(type in)* eingeben [eyngayben]
▶ do I enter my PIN number now? muss ich jetzt meine Geheimzahl eingeben? [mus ish yehtst meyn-e geheymtsaal eyngayben]

**entrance** der Eingang [eyngang]
▶ where's the entrance to the subway? wo ist der Eingang zur U-Bahn? [voh ist dehr eyngang tsoor oo-baan]

**entry** *(to place)* der Eintritt [eyntrit]
▶ entry to the exhibit is free der Eintritt zur Ausstellung ist frei [dehr eyntrit tsoor ows-shtehlung ist frey]

**envelope** der Umschlag [umshlaak]
▶ I'd like a pack of envelopes ich hätte gerne eine Packung Umschläge [ish heh-te gehr-e ey-ne pakung umshlayg-e]

**equipment** die Ausrüstung [owsruustung]
▶ do you provide the equipment? stellen Sie die Ausrüstung? [shtehlen zee dee owsruustung]

**escalator** die Rolltreppe [roltrehp-e]
▶ is there an escalator? gibt es eine Rolltreppe? [gipt ehs ey-ne roltrehp-e]

**euro** der Euro [oyroh]
▶ I'd like to change some dollars into euros ich möchte gerne Dollar in Euro umtauschen [ish meusht-e gehrn-e dolar in oyroh umtowshen]

**evening** der Abend [aabent]
▶ why don't we meet up this evening? wollen wir uns heute Abend treffen? [vol-en veer uns hoyt-e aabent trehfen]
▶ in the evening *(of every day)* abends [aabents]
▶ good evening! guten Abend! [gooten aabent]

**ever** *(at any time)* jemals [yaymals]; *(before now)* schon einmal [shohn eynmal]
▶ have you ever been to Boston? sind Sie schon einmal in Boston gewesen? [zint zee shohn eynmal in Boston gevayzen]

**everything** alles [al-es]
▶ that's everything, thanks das ist alles, danke [das ist al-es dank-e]
▶ we didn't have time to see everything wir hatten keine Zeit alles zu sehen [veer hat-en keyn-e zeyt al-es tsoo zayen]

**excess baggage** das Übergepäck [uubergepehk]
▶ what's your policy on excess baggage? wie sind Ihre Bestimmungen für Übergepäck? [vee zint eer-e beshtimmungen fuur uubergepehk]

**exchange** umtauschen [umtowshen]
▶ I'd like to exchange this T-shirt ich möchte dieses T-Shirt umtauschen [ish meusht-e deezez teeshert umtowshen]

**exchange rate** der Wechselkurs [vehkselkoors]
- what is today's exchange rate? wie ist der heutige Wechselkurs? [vee ist dehr hoytig-e vehkselkoors]

**excursion** der Ausflug [owsflook]
- I'd like to sign up for the excursion on Saturday ich möchte mich für den Ausflug am Samstag anmelden [ish meusht-e mish fuur dayn owsflook am zamztaak anmehlden]

**excuse** *(behavior, person)* entschuldigen [ehntshuldigen]
- excuse me? *(asking for repetition)* wie bitte? [vee bi-te]
- excuse me! *(to get attention, to apologize)* Entschuldigung! [ehntshuldigung]; *(when interrupting)* entschuldigen Sie! [ehntshuldigen zee]; *(expressing disagreement)* erlauben Sie mal! [ehrlowben zee mal]
- you'll have to excuse my (poor) German ich muss mich für mein (schlechtes) Deutsch entschuldigen [ish mus mish fuur meyn (shlehshtez) doytsh ehntshuldigen]

**exhaust** der Auspuff [owspuf]
- the exhaust is making strange noises der Auspuff macht merkwürdige Geräusche [dehr owspuf makht mehrkvuurdig-e geroysh-e]

**exhausted** *(tired)* erschöpft [ehrsheupft]
- I'm exhausted ich bin erschöpft [ish bin ehrsheupft]

**exhibit** die Ausstellung [ows-shtehlung]
- I'd like a ticket for the temporary exhibit ich hätte gerne eine Eintrittskarte für die Sonderausstellung [ish heh-te gehrn-e ey-ne eyntritskart-e fuur dee zonder-ows-shtehlung]
- is this ticket valid for the exhibit too? gilt diese Eintrittskarte auch für die Ausstellung? [gilt deez-e eyntritskart-e owkh fuur dee ows-shtehlung]

**exit** *(door)* der Ausgang [owsgang]; *(road)* die Ausfahrt [owsfart]
- where's the exit? wo ist der Ausgang? [voh ist dehr owsgang]

**expect** erwarten [ehrvarten]
- I'll be expecting you at eight o'clock ich erwarte Sie um acht Uhr [ish ehrvart-e zee um akht oor]
- when do you expect it to be ready? wann wird es fertig sein? [van virt ehs fehrtish zeyn]

**expensive** teuer [toyer]
- the hotel restaurant is very expensive das Hotelrestaurant ist sehr teuer [das hohtehlrehsteront ist zehr toyer]
- do you have anything less expensive? haben Sie etwas Günstigeres? [haaben zee ehtvas guunstigerez]

**expire** *(visa)* ablaufen [aplowfen]
- my passport has expired mein Reisepass ist abgelaufen [meyn reyzepas ist apgelowfen]

**explain** erklären [ehrklehren]

▸ please explain how to get to the airport können Sie mir bitte erklären, wie ich zum Flughafen komme? [keunen zee meer bi-te ehrklehren vee ish tsum flookhaafen kom-e]

▸ can you explain what this means? können Sie mir das erklären? [keunen zee meer das ehrklehren]

**express (train)** der Schnellzug [shnehltsook]

▸ how long does it take by express train? wie lange fährt man mit dem Schnellzug? [vee lang-e fehrt man mit daym shnehltsook]

**extension** *(phone line)* die Durchwahl [durshvaal]; *(cord)* die Verlängerung [fehrlehngerung]

▸ what's the extension? wie lautet die Durchwahl? [vee lowtet dee durshvaal]

▸ could I have extension 358, please? könnten Sie mich bitte mit Apparat 358 verbinden? [keunten zee mish bi-te mit aparaat drey fuunf akht fehrbinden]

**extra** zusätzlich [tsoo-zehts-lish]

▸ is it possible to add an extra bed? können wir noch ein zusätzliches Bett bekommen? [keunen veer nokh eyn tsoo-zehts-lishez beht bekom-en]

▸ would it be possible to stay an extra night? können wir eine zusätzliche Nacht bleiben? [keunen veer ey-ne tsoo-zehts-lish-e nakht bleyben]

**extra charge** der Aufpreis [owfpreys]

▸ at no extra charge ohne Aufpreis [ohn-e owfpreys]

**eye** das Auge [owg-e]

▸ she has blue eyes sie hat blaue Augen [zee hat blow-e owgen]

▸ can you keep an eye on my bag for a few minutes? können Sie kurz ein Auge auf meine Tasche werfen? [keunen zee kurts eyn owg-e owf meyn-e tash-e vehrfen]

**eye drops** die Augentropfen [owgentropfen]

▸ do you have any eye drops? haben Sie Augentropfen? [haaben zee owgentropfen]

**eye shadow** der Lidschatten [leet-shat-en]

▸ is this the only eye shadow you've got? ist das der einzige Lidschatten, den Sie haben? [ ist das dehr eyntsig-e leet-shat-en dayn zee haaben]

**eyesight** die Sehkraft [zaykraft]

▸ I don't have very good eyesight ich sehe nicht besonders gut [ish zay-e nisht bezonderz goot]

**face** *(of person)* das Gesicht [gezisht]

▸ the attacker had a broad face der Angreifer hatte ein breites Gesicht [dehr angreyfer hat-e eyn breytez gezisht]

**facilities** die Einrichtungen [eynrishtungen]

▸ do you have facilities for people with disabilities? haben Sie Einrichtungen für Behinderte? [haaben zee eynrishtungen fuur behindert-e]

▸ are there play facilities for children? gibt es Spielmöglichkeiten für Kinder? [gipt ehs shpeelmeuglishkeyten fuur kin-der]

▸ what kind of exercise facilities do you have here? welche Fitnesseinrichtungen bieten Sie an? [vehlsh-e fitnes-eynrishtungen beeten zee an]

**faint** ohnmächtig werden [ohnmehshtish vehrden]

▸ I fainted twice last week ich bin letzte Woche zweimal ohnmächtig geworden [ish bin lehtst-e vokh-e tsveymal ohnmehshtish gevorden]

**fair** *(person, situation)* gerecht [gerehsht]; *(price)* angemessen [angemes-en]; *(hair)* blond [blont]; *(skin, complexion)* hell [hehl]

▸ this isn't a fair price der Preis ist nicht angemessen [dehr preys ist nisht angemes-en]

▸ it's not fair! das ist nicht gerecht! [das ist nisht gerehsht]

**fall** fallen [fal-en]

▸ I fell on my back ich bin auf den Rücken gefallen [ish bin owf dayn ruuken gefal-en]

**family** die Familie [fameeli-e]

▸ do you have any family in the area? haben Sie Familie in der Umgebung? [haaben zee fameeli-e in dehr umgaybung]

**fan** der Ventilator [vehntilator]

▸ how does the fan work? wie funktioniert der Ventilator? [vee funktsiohneert dehr vehntilator]

**far** weit [veyt]

▸ am I far from the village? bin ich weit vom Dorf entfernt? [bin ish veyt fom dorf ehntfehrnt]

▸ is it far to walk? ist es weit zu laufen? [ist ehs veyt tsoo lowfen]

▸ is it far by car? ist es weit zu fahren? [ist ehs veyt tsoo faaren]

▸ how far is the market from here? wie weit ist es von hier zum Markt? [vee veyt ist ehs fon heer tsum markt]

▸ far away/off weit weg [veyt vehk]

▸ so far bisher [bis-hehr]

**fast** schnell [shnehl]
- ▸ please don't drive so fast fahr bitte nicht so schnell [faar bi-te nisht zoh shnehl]
- ▸ to be fast *(watch, clock)* vorgehen [forgayen]
- ▸ my watch is five minutes fast meine Uhr geht fünf Minuten vor [meyn-e oor gayt fuunf minooten for]

**fat** *(in diet)* das Fett [feht] ◆ *(person)* dick [dik]
- ▸ it's low in fat es ist fettarm [ehs ist fehtarm]

**father** der Vater [faater]
- ▸ this is my father das ist mein Vater [das ist meyn faater]

**fault** *(responsibility)* die Schuld [shult]
- ▸ it was my fault es war meine Schuld [ehs var meyn-e shult]

**favor** *(kind act)* der Gefallen [gefal-en]
- ▸ can I ask you a favor? darf ich Sie um einen Gefallen bitten? [darf ish zee um eynen gefal-en bit-en]

**favorite** Lieblings- [leeblingz]
- ▸ it's my favorite book das ist mein Lieblingsbuch [das ist meyn leeblingzbookh]
- ▸ that's my favorite das mag ich am liebsten [das maak ish am leebsten]

**feather** die Feder [fayder]
- ▸ are these feather pillows? sind das Federkissen? [zint das fayder-kis-en]

**February** der Februar [faybruar]
- ▸ February 8th achter Februar [akhter faybruar]

**feed** füttern [fuutern]
- ▸ where can I feed the baby? wo kann ich das Baby füttern? [voh kan ish das baybi fuutern]

**feel** *(touch)* fühlen [fuulen]; *(be aware of)* spüren [shpuuren] ◆ *(hard, happy, sleepy)* sein [zeyn]; *(ill, old)* sich fühlen [zish fuulen]
- ▸ I can't feel my feet ich spüre meine Füße nicht [ish shpuur-e meyn-e fuus-e nisht]
- ▸ I don't feel well ich fühle mich nicht gut [ish fuul-e mish nisht goot]
- ▸ I feel like going into town ich habe Lust, in die Stadt zu gehen [ish haab-e lust in dee shtat tsoo gayen]

**ferry** die Fähre [fehr-e]
- ▸ when does the next ferry leave? wann fährt die nächste Fähre? [van fehrt dee nehkst-e fehr-e]

**ferry terminal** der Fährhafen [fehrhaafen]
- ▸ which way is the ferry terminal? wo geht es zum Fährhafen? [voh gayt ehs tsum fehrhaafen]

**fever** das Fieber [feeber]
- ▸ the baby's got a fever das Baby hat Fieber [das baybi hat feeber]

**few** wenige [vaynig-e]
- ▸ there are few sights worth seeing around here es gibt hier nur wenige

interessante Sehenswürdigkeiten [ehs gipt heer noor vaynig-e interehsant-e zayenz-vuurdishkeyten]

 ▸ a few ein paar [eyn par]
 ▸ we're thinking of staying a few more days wir wollen vielleicht ein paar Tage länger bleiben [veer vol-en feeleysht eyn par taag-e lehnger bleyben]
 ▸ I spent a month in Germany a few years ago ich habe vor ein paar Jahren einen Monat in Deutschland verbracht [ish haa-be for eyn par yaar-e eynen mohnaat in doytshlant fehrbrakht]

**fifth** fünfter [fuunfter] ◆ *(gear)* der Fünfte [fuunft-e]
 ▸ I can't get it into fifth ich kann den Fünften nicht einlegen [ish kan dayn fuunften nisht eynlaygen]

**filling** die Füllung [fuulung]
 ▸ one of my fillings has come out mir ist eine Füllung herausgefallen [meer ist ey-ne fuulung hehrowsgefal-en]

**fill up** *(glass etc.)* voll füllen [fol fuulen]; *(car with gas)* voll tanken [fol tanken]
◆ sich füllen [zish fuulen]
 ▸ fill it up, please einmal voll tanken, bitte [eynmal voltanken bi-te]

**film** *(for camera)* der Film [film] ◆ filmen [filmen]
 ▸ I'd like to have this film developed ich möchte diesen Film entwickeln lassen [ish meushte-e deezen film ehntvikeln las-en]
 ▸ do you have black-and-white film? haben Sie Schwarzweißfilme? [haaben zee shvarts-veys-film-e]
 ▸ is filming allowed in the museum? darf man im Museum filmen? [darf man im moozayum filmen]

**find** finden [finden]
 ▸ where can I find a doctor on a Sunday? wo kann ich sonntags einen Arzt finden? [voh kan ish zontaaks eynen artst finden]
 ▸ has anyone found a watch? hat jemand eine Uhr gefunden? [hat yaymant ey-ne oor gefunden]

**find out** herausfinden [hehrowsfinden]
 ▸ I need to find out the times of trains to Berlin ich muss herausfinden, wann Züge nach Berlin fahren [ish mus hehrowsfinden van tsuug-e naakh behrleen faaren]

**fine** *(in health etc.)* gut [goot] ◆ die Geldstrafe [gehltshtraaf-e]
 ▸ fine thanks, and you? gut, danke, und Ihnen? [goot dank-e unt eenen]
 ▸ I feel fine es geht mir gut [ehs gayt meer goot]
 ▸ how much is the fine? wie hoch ist die Strafe? [vee hokh ist dee shtraaf-e]

**finger** der Finger [fing-er]
 ▸ I've cut my finger ich habe mir in den Finger geschnitten [ish haa-be meer in dayn fing-er geshnit-en]

**finish** fertig sein mit [fehrtish zeyn mit]
 ▸ can we leave as soon as we've finished our meal? können wir gehen, sobald wir

mit dem Essen fertig sind? [keunen veer gayen zohbalt veer mit daym ehsen fehrtish zint]

▸ the movie finishes at 10 o'clock der Film ist um 10 Uhr zu Ende [dehr film ist um tsayn oor tsoo ehnd-e]

**fire** das Feuer [foyer]; *(out of control)* der Brand [brant]

▸ to make a fire Feuer machen [foyer makhen]

▸ to be on fire *(forest, house)* brennen [brehnen]

**fire department** die Feuerwehr [foyervehr]

▸ call the fire department! rufen Sie die Feuerwehr! [roofen zee dee foyervehr]

**fireworks** das Feuerwerk [foyervehrk]

▸ what time do the fireworks start? wann fängt das Feuerwerk an? [van fehnkt das foyervehrk an]

**first** erster [ehrster] ◆ der die das Erste [ehrst-e]; *(gear)* der Erste [ehrst-e]; *(class)* die erste Klasse [ehrst-e klas-e]

▸ it's the first time I've been here ich bin zum ersten Mal hier [ish bin tsum ehrsten mal heer]

▸ you have to take the first left after the lights Sie müssen hinter der Ampel die Erste links fahren [zee muusen hinter dehr ampel dee ehrste links faaren]

▸ put it into first legen Sie den Ersten ein [laygen zee dayn ehrsten eyn]

**first-aid kit** der Verbandskasten [fehrbantskasten]

▸ do you have a first-aid kit? haben Sie einen Verbandskasten? [haaben zee eynen fehrbantskasten]

**first class** die erste Klasse [ehrst-e klas-e]

▸ are there any seats in first class? gibt es Plätze in der ersten Klasse? [gipt ehs plehts-e in dehr ehrsten klas-e]

▸ I prefer to travel first class ich reise lieber erster Klasse [ish reyz-e leeber ehrst-e klas-e]

**fish** der Fisch [fish]

▸ I don't eat fish ich esse keinen Fisch [ish ehs-e keynen fish]

**fishing permit** der Angelschein [ang-el-sheyn]

▸ do you need a fishing permit to fish here? braucht man hier zum Angeln einen Angelschein? [browkht man heer tsum ang-eln eynen ang-el-sheyn]

**fit** *(of coughing)* der Anfall [anfal] ◆ passen [pas-en]

▸ I think she's having some kind of fit ich glaube, sie hat einen Anfall [ish glowb-e zee hat eynen anfal]

▸ those pants fit you better diese Hose passt Ihnen besser [deez-e hohz-e past eenen behser]

▸ the key doesn't fit in the lock der Schlüssel passt nicht in das Schloss [dehr shluusel past nisht in das shlos]

▸ we won't all fit around the table wir passen nicht alle an den Tisch [veer pas-en nisht al-e an dayn tish]

**fit in** hineinpassen [hineynpas-en] ♦ passen in [pas-en in]
- ▸ I can't get everything to fit in my suitcase es passt nicht alles in meinen Koffer [ehs past nisht al-ez in meynem kof-er]
- ▸ how many people can you fit in this car? wie viele Personen passen in den Wagen? [vee feel-e pehrzohnen pas-en in dayn vaagen]

**fitting room** die Umkleidekabine [umkleyd-e-kabeen-e]
- ▸ where are the fitting rooms? wo sind die Umkleidekabinen? [voh zint dee umkleyd-e-kabeenen]

**five** fünf [fuunf]
- ▸ there are five of us wir sind fünf [veer zint fuunf]

**fix** reparieren [rehpareeren]
- ▸ where can I find someone to fix my bike? wo finde ich jemanden, der mir mein Fahrrad repariert? [voh find-e ish yaymanden dehr meer meyn faar-raat rehpareert]

**fixed price** der Festpreis [fehstpreys]
- ▸ do taxis to the airport charge a fixed price? bezahlt man in Taxis zum Flughafen einen Festpreis? [betsaalt man in takseez tsum flookhaafen eynen fehstpreys]

**flash** der Blitz [blits]
- ▸ I'd like some batteries for my flash ich hätte gerne Batterien für meinen Blitz [ish heh-te gehrn-e bateree-en fuur meynen blits]

**flash photography**
- ▸ is flash photography allowed here? kann man hier mit Blitz fotografieren? [kan man heer mit blits fohtohgrafeeren]

**flat** *(tire)* platt [plat]
- ▸ the tire's flat der Reifen ist platt [dehr reyfen ist plat]

**flavor** *(of food)* der Geschmack [geshmak]
- ▸ I'd like to try a different flavor of ice cream ich würde gerne eine andere Eissorte probieren [ish wuurd-e gehrn-e ey-ne ander-e eys-zort-e prohbeeren]

**flight** der Flug [flook]
- ▸ how many flights a day are there? wie viele Flüge gibt es täglich? [vee feel-e fluug-e gipt ehs tayglish]
- ▸ what time is the flight? wann geht der Flug? [van gayt dehr flook]

**flight of stairs** die Treppe [trehp-e]
- ▸ your room's up that flight of stairs Ihr Zimmer ist diese Treppe hoch [eer tsim-er ist deez-e trep-e hokh]

**floor** *(story)* die Etage [ehtaazh-e]
- ▸ which floor is it on? in welcher Etage ist es? [in vehlsh-e ehtaazh-e ist ehs]
- ▸ it's on the top floor es ist in der obersten Etage [ehs ist in dehr ohbersten ehtaazhe]

**flower** die Blume [bloom-e]
- ▸ do you sell flowers? verkaufen Sie Blumen? [fehrkowfen zee bloomen]

**flu** die Grippe [grip-e]
  ▸ I'd like something for the flu ich hätte gerne etwas gegen Grippe [ish heh-te gehrn-e ehtvas gaygen grip-e]

**flush** *(toilet)* spülen [shpuulen] ◆ *(person)* rot werden [roht vehrden]
  ▸ the toilet won't flush die Toilettenspülung funktioniert nicht [dee toylehten-shpuulung funktsiohneert nisht]

**fog** der Nebel [naybel]
  ▸ is there a lot of fog today? ist es heute sehr neblig? [ist ehs hoyt-e zehr nayblish]

**food** das Essen [ehsen]
  ▸ is there someplace to buy food nearby? kann man hier in der Nähe etwas zu Essen kaufen? [kan man heer in dehr nay-e ehtvas tsoo ehsen kowfen]
  ▸ the food here is excellent das Essen hier ist hervorragend [das ehsen heer ist hehrfor-raagent]

**food cart** *(on train, plane)* der Servierwagen [zehrveervaagen]
  ▸ is there food cart service on this train? gibt es im Zug einen Servierwagen? [gipt ehs im tsook eynen zehrveervaagen]

**food section** *(in store)* die Lebensmittelabteilung [laybenzmitel-apteylung]
  ▸ where's the food section? wo ist die Lebensmittelabteilung? [voh ist dee laybenzmitel-apteylung]

**foot** der Fuß [foos]
  ▸ on foot zu Fuß [tsoo foos]

**for** für [fuur]; *(indicating direction, destination)* nach [naakh]; *(since)* seit [zeyt]
  ▸ what's that for? wofür ist das? [vohfuur ist das]
  ▸ the flight for Frankfurt der Flug nach Frankfurt [dehr flook naakh frankfurt]
  ▸ is this the right train for Hamburg? ist das der Zug nach Hamburg? [ist das dehr tsook naakh hamburg]
  ▸ I'm staying for two months ich bleibe zwei Monate [ish bleyb-e tsvey mohnat-e]
  ▸ I've been here for a week ich bin seit einer Woche hier [ish bin zeyt eyner vokh-e heer]
  ▸ I need something for a cough ich brauche etwas gegen Husten [ish browkh-e ehtvas gaygen husten]

**foreign** fremd [frehmt]
  ▸ I don't speak any foreign languages ich spreche keine Fremdsprachen [ish shpresh-e keyn-e frehmt-shpraakhen]

**foreign currency** die Fremdwährung [frehmtvehrung]
  ▸ do you change foreign currency? tauschen Sie Fremdwährungen? [towshen zee frehmtvehrungen]

**foreigner** der Ausländer [owslehnder], die Ausländerin [owslehnderin]
  ▸ as a foreigner, this custom seems a bit strange to me für mich als Ausländer ist dieser Brauch ein bisschen merkwürdig [fuur mish als owslehnder ist deezer browkh eyn bis-shen mehrkvuurdish]

**forever** ewig [ayvish]
- our money won't last forever unser Geld wird nicht ewig reichen [unzer gehlt virt nisht ayvish reyshen]

**fork** *(for eating with)* die Gabel [gaabel]; *(in road)* die Gabelung [gaabelung]
- could I have a fork? kann ich eine Gabel haben? [kan ish ey-ne gaabel haaben]

**forward** weiterleiten [veyterleyten]
- can you forward my mail? können Sie meine Post weiterleiten? [keunen zee meyn-e post veyterleyten]

**four** vier [feer]
- there are four of us wir sind vier [veer zint feer]

**fourth** vierter [feerter] ♦ *(gear)* der Vierte [feert-e]
- it's hard to get it into fourth der Vierte lässt sich schwer einlegen [dehr feert-e lehst zish shvehr eynlaygen]

**four-wheel drive** *(vehicle)* der Wagen mit Allradantrieb [vaagen mit alraat-antreep]
- I'd like a four-wheel drive ich hätte gerne einen Wagen mit Allradantrieb [ish heh-te gehrn-e eynen vaagen mit alraat-antreep]

**fracture** der Bruch [brukh]
- she has a wrist fracture sie hat sich das Handgelenk gebrochen [zee hat zish das hantgelehnk gebrokhen]

**free** *(offered at no charge)* umsonst [umzonst]; *(not occupied)* frei [frey]
- is it free? ist es umsonst? [ist ehs umzonst]
- is this seat free? ist der Platz frei? [ist dehr plats frey]
- are you free on Thursday evening? haben Sie am Donnerstagabend Zeit? [haaben zee am donerztaak-aabent tseyt]

**freeway** die Autobahn [owtohbaan]
- what is the speed limit on freeways? welche Geschwindigkeitsbegrenzung gilt auf Autobahnen? [vehlsh-e geshvindishkeyts-begrehntsung gilt owf owtohbaanen]
- how do I get onto the freeway? wie komme ich zur Autobahn? [vee kom-e ish tsoor owtohbaan]

**freezing (cold)** *(room, day)* eiskalt [eyskalt]
- I'm freezing (cold) mir ist eiskalt [meer ist eyskalt]

**frequent** häufig [hoyfish]
- how frequent are the trains to the city? wie häufig fahren die Züge in die Stadt? [vee hoyfish faaren dee tsuug-e in dee shtat]

**fresh** *(food)* frisch [frish]
- I'd like some fresh orange juice ich hätte gerne einen frischen Orangensaft [ish heh-te gehrn-e eynen frishen orondzhenzaft]

**freshly** *(ironed)* frisch [frish]
- freshly squeezed orange juice frisch gepresster Orangensaft [frish geprehster orondzhenzaft]

**Friday** der Freitag [freytaak]
- we're arriving/leaving on Friday wir kommen am Freitag an/wir reisen am Freitag ab [veer kom-en am freytaak an/veer reyzen am freytaak ap]

**fried egg** das Spiegelei [shpeegeley]
- I'd prefer a fried egg ich hätte lieber ein Spiegelei [ish heh-te leeber eyn shpeegeley]

**friend** der Freund [froynt], die Freundin [froyndin]
- are you with friends? sind Sie mit Freunden? [zint zee mit froynden]
- I've come with a friend ich habe einen Freund/eine Freundin mitgebracht [ish haa-be eynen froynt/eyn-e froyndin mitgebrakht]
- I'm meeting some friends ich treffe ein paar Freunde [ish trehf-e eyn par froynd-e]

**from** von [fon]; *(town, country)* aus [ows]
- I'm from the United States ich komme aus den Vereinigten Staaten [ish kom-e ows dayn fehreynigten shtaaten]
- how many flights a day are there from Frankfurt to JFK? wie viele Flüge gibt es täglich von Frankfurt nach JFK? [vee feel-e fluug-e gipt ehs tayglish fon frankfurt naakh dzhay-ehf-kay]

**front** *(front side)* die Vorderseite [forderzeyt-e]; *(front portion)* das der Vorderteil [forderteyl] ◆ **in front** vorne [forn-e] ◆ **in front of** vor [for]
- I'd like a seat toward the front of the train ich hätte gerne einen Platz vorne im Zug [ish heh-te gehrn-e eynen plats forn-e im tsook]
- let's sit at the front sitzen wir vorne [zitsen veer forn-e]
- the car in front braked suddenly der Wagen vor uns hat plötzlich gebremst [dehr vaagen for uns hat pleutslish gebrehmzt]
- I'll wait for you in front of the museum ich warte vor dem Museum auf Sie [ish vart-e for daym moozayum owf zee]

**front door** *(of house)* die Haustür [howstuur]; *(of apartment)* die Wohnungstür [vohnungztuur]
- which is the key to the front door? welcher Schlüssel ist für die Haustür? [vehlsher shluusel ist fuur dee howstuur]
- the front door is closed die Wohnungstür ist geschlossen [dee vohnungztuur ist geshlos-en]

**frozen** *(person)* durchgefroren [durshgefroren]; *(pipes)* eingefroren [eyngefroren]; *(food)* tiefgekühlt [teefgekuult]
- I'm absolutely frozen ich bin völlig durchgefroren [ish bin feulish durshgefroren]
- the lock is frozen das Schloss ist eingefroren [das shlos ist eyngefroren]

**frozen food** die Tiefkühlkost [teefkuulkost]
- is that all the frozen food you have? haben Sie noch mehr Tiefkühlkost? [haaben zee nokh mehr teefkuulkost]

**fruit juice** der Saft [zaft]
- what types of fruit juice do you have? welche Säfte haben Sie? [vehlsh-e zehft-e haaben zee]

**full** voll [fol]; *(booked up)* ausgebucht [owsgebookht]; *(after eating)* satt [zat]
▶ I'm quite full, thank you ich bin ziemlich satt, danke [ish bin tseemlish zat dank-e]

**full up** *(after eating)* satt [zat]
▶ I'm full up ich bin satt [ish bin zat]

**fun** der Spaß [shpaas]
▶ to have fun Spaß haben [shpaas haaben]

**gallery** *(for art)* die Galerie [galeree]
▶ what time does the gallery open? wann öffnet die Galerie? [van eufnet dee galeree]

**game** das Spiel [shpeel]
▶ do you want to play a game of tennis tomorrow? wollen Sie morgen Tennis spielen? [vol-en zee morgen tehnis shpeelen]

**garage** *(for car repair)* die Werkstatt [vehrkshtat]
▶ is there a garage near here? ist hier in der Nähe eine Werkstatt? [ist heer in dehr nay-e ey-ne vehrkshtat]
▶ could you tow me to a garage? können Sie mich zu einer Werkstatt abschleppen? [keunen zee mish tsoo eyner vehrkshtat ap-shlehpen]

**garbage can** der Mülleimer [muuleymer]
▶ where is the garbage can? wo ist der Mülleimer? [voh ist dehr muuleymer]

**gas** *(for vehicle)* das Benzin [behntseen]; *(for domestic/medical use)* das Gas [gaas]
▶ where can I get gas? wo bekomme ich Benzin? [voh bekom-e ish behntseen]
▶ I've run out of gas ich habe kein Benzin mehr [ish haa-be keyn behntseen mehr]

**gas pump** die Zapfsäule [tsapf-zoyl-e]
▶ how do you use this gas pump? wie bedient man diese Zapfsäule? [vee bedeent man deez-e tsapf-zoyl-e]

**gas station** die Tankstelle [tankshtehl-e]
▶ where can I find a gas station? wo ist eine Tankstelle? [voh ist ey-ne tankshtehl-e]

**gas stove** der Gaskocher [gaaskokher]
▶ do you have a gas stove we could borrow? können Sie uns einen Gaskocher leihen? [keunen zee uns eynen gaaskokher leyen]

**gas tank** der Benzintank [behntseentank]
▶ the gas tank is leaking der Tank ist undicht [dehr behntseentank ist undisht]

**gate** *(of a garden, a town)* das Tor [tor]; *(at an airport)* der Flugsteig [flookshteyk], das Gate [gayt]

▸ where is Gate 2? wo ist Flugsteig 2? [voh ist flookshteyk tsvey]

**gear** *(of a car, a bike)* der Gang [gang]

▸ how many gears does the bike have? wie viele Gänge hat das Fahrrad? [vee feel-e gehng-e hat das faar-raat]

**get** *(obtain)* bekommen [bekom-en]; *(understand)* verstehen [fehrshtayen] ◆ *(make one's way)* kommen [kom-en]; *(tired, old)* werden [vehrden]

▸ where can we get something to eat this time of night? wo können wir um diese Zeit etwas zu essen bekommen? [voh keunen veer um deez-e tseyt ehtvas tsoo ehsen bekom-en]

▸ I can't get it into reverse ich bekomme den Rückwärtsgang nicht rein [ish bekom-e dayn ruukvehrtsgang nisht reyn]

▸ now I get it jetzt verstehe ich [yehtst fehrshtay-e ish]

▸ I got here a month ago ich bin vor einem Monat hierher gekommen [ish bin for eynem mohnaat heerhehr gekom-en]

▸ can you get there by car? kann man dort mit dem Auto hinkommen? [kan man dort mit daym owtoh hinkom-en]

▸ how can I get to … wie komme ich nach… [vee kom-e ish naakh]

▸ could you tell me the best way to get to Dresden? können Sie mir sagen, wie ich am besten nach Dresden komme? [keunen zee meer zaagen vee ish am behsten naakh drayzden kom-e]

▸ how do we get to Terminal 2? wie kommen wir zum Terminal 2? [vee kom-en veer tsum tehrminal tsvey]

**get back** *(money)* zurückbekommen [tsuruuk-bekom-en]

▸ I just want to get my money back ich möchte nur mein Geld zurückbekommen [ish meusht-e noor meyn gehlt tsuruuk-bekom-en]

**get back onto** *(road)* zurückkommen auf [tsuruuk-kom-en owf]

▸ how can I get back onto the freeway? wie komme ich zurück auf die Autobahn? [vee kom-e ish tsuruuk owf dee owtohbaan]

**get in** *(arrive)* ankommen [ankom-en]; *(into car, train)* einsteigen [eynshteygen] ◆ *(car)* einsteigen in [eynshteygen in]

▸ what time does the train get into Augsburg? wann kommt der Zug in Augsburg an? [van komt dehr tsook in owgzburg an]

▸ what time does the flight get in? wann kommt der Flug an? [van komt dehr flook an]

▸ do you have to pay to get in? muss man Eintritt zahlen? [mus man eyntrit tsaalen]

**get off** *(bus, train)* aussteigen aus [ows-shteygen ows]; *(bicycle)* absteigen von [ap-shteygen fon]; *(road)* abfahren von [apfaaren fon] ◆ *(out of bus, train)* aussteigen [ows-shteygen]; *(off bicycle)* absteigen [ap-shteygen]

▸ where do we get off the bus? wo steigen wir aus? [voh shteygen veer ows]

▸ where do I get off the freeway? wo fahre ich von der Autobahn ab? [voh faar-e ish fon dehr owtohbaan ap]

**get on** *(bus, train)* einsteigen in [eynshteygen in]; *(bicycle)* aufsteigen auf [owfshteygen owf]
> which bus should we get on to go downtown? in welchen Bus müssen wir einsteigen, um ins Zentrum zu kommen? [in vehlshen bus muusen veer eynshteygen um ins tsehntrum tsoo kom-en]

**get past** vorbeigehen [forbeygayen]
> sorry, can I get past, please? Entschuldigung, kann ich bitte vorbei? [ehntshuldigung kan ish bi-te forbey]

**get up** *(in morning)* aufstehen [owfshtayen]
> I got up very early ich bin sehr früh aufgestanden [ish bin zehr fruu owfgeshtanden]

**gift-wrap** als Geschenk verpacken [als geshehnk fehrpaken]
> could you gift-wrap it for me? können Sie mir das als Geschenk verpacken? [keunen zee meer das als geshehnk fehrpaken]

**girl** das Mädchen [maydshen]; *(daughter)* die Tochter [tokhter]
> who is that girl? wer ist das Mädchen? [vehr ist das maydshen]
> I've got two girls ich habe zwei Töchter [ish haa-be tsvey teushter]

**girlfriend** die Freundin [froyndin]
> is she your girlfriend? ist sie Ihre Freundin? [ist zee eer-e froyndin]

**give** geben [gayben]
> I can give you my e-mail address ich kann Ihnen meine E-Mail-Adresse geben [ish kan eenen meyn-e ee-mayl-adrehs-e gayben]
> can you give me a hand? können Sie mir helfen? [keunen zee meer hehlfen]

**glass** das Glas [glaas] ◆ **glasses** *(spectacles)* die Brille [bril-e]
> can I have a clean glass? kann ich ein sauberes Glas haben? [kan ish eyn zowberez glaas haaben]
> would you like a glass of champagne? möchten Sie ein Glas Sekt? [meushten zee eyn glaas zehkt]
> I've lost my glasses ich habe meine Brille verloren [ish haa-be meyn-e bril-e fehrloren]

**glove** der Handschuh [hantshoo]
> I've lost a brown glove ich habe einen braunen Handschuh verloren [ish haa-be eynen brownen hantshoo fehrloren]

**go** gehen [gayen]; *(vehicle, passenger)* fahren [faaren]; *(depart: vehicle)* abfahren [apfaaren]; *(path)* führen [fuuren]
> let's go to the beach lass uns an den Strand gehen [las uns an dayn shtrant gayen]
> where can we go for breakfast? wo können wir frühstücken gehen? [voh keunen veer fruushtuuken gayen]
> where does this path go? wohin führt dieser Weg? [voh-hin fuurt deezer vayk]
> the bus goes at 10 o'clock der Bus fährt um 10 Uhr ab [dehr bus fehrt um tseyn oor ap]
> I must be going ich muss gehen [ish mus gayen]
> we're going home tomorrow wir reisen morgen ab [veer reyzen morgen ap]

**go away** weggehen [vehk-gayen]

> go away and leave me alone! geh weg und lass mich in Ruhe! [gay vehk unt las mish in roo-e]

**go back** zurückgehen [tsuruukgayen]; *(vehicle, in vehicle)* zurückfahren [tsuruukfaaren]

> we're going back home tomorrow wir fahren morgen zurück nach Hause [veer faaren morgen zuruuk naakh howz-e]

**go down** hinuntergehen [hinuntergayen]

> go down that street and turn left at the bottom gehen Sie diese Straße hinunter und biegen am Ende links ab [gayen zee deez-e shtraas-e hinunter unt beegen am ehnd-e links ap]

**gold** *(metal)* das Gold [golt]

> is it made of gold? ist es aus Gold? [ist ehs ows golt]

**golf** das Golf [golf]

> I play golf ich spiele Golf [ish shpeel-e golf]

**golf club** *(instrument)* der Golfschläger [golfshlayger]; *(association)* der Golfklub [golfklub]

> where can I rent golf clubs? wo kann ich Golfschläger mieten? [voh kan ish golfshlayger meeten]

**golf course** der Golfplatz [golfplats]

> is there a golf course nearby? gibt es in der Nähe einen Golfplatz? [gipt ehs in dehr nay-e eynen golfplats]

**good** gut [goot]

> this isn't a very good restaurant dies ist kein besonders gutes Restaurant [deez ist keyn bezonderz gootez rehsteront]
> you're really good at surfing! du bist ein sehr guter Surfer! [doo bist eyn zehr gooter surfer]
> we had a good time wir hatten viel Spaß [veer hat-en feel shpaas]

**good afternoon** guten Tag! [gooten taak]

> good afternoon! isn't it a beautiful day? guten Tag! ist es heute nicht schön? [gooten taak ist ehs hoyt-e nisht sheun]

**goodbye** auf Wiedersehen! [owf veederzayen]

> I'd better say goodbye now ich sage jetzt besser auf Wiedersehen [ish zaag-e yehtst behser owf veederzayen]

**good evening** guten Abend! [gooten aabent]

> good evening! how are you tonight? guten Abend! wie geht es Ihnen? [gooten aabent vee gayt ehs eenen]

**good morning** guten Morgen! [gooten morgen]

> good morning! how are you today? guten Morgen! wie geht es Ihnen heute? [gooten morgen vee gayt ehs eenen hoyt-e]

**good night** *(when leaving)* auf Wiedersehen! [owf veederzayen]; *(when going to bed)* gute Nacht! [goot-e nakht]

**go out** *(leave house)* hinausgehen [hinowsgayen]; *(socially)* ausgehen [owsgayen]
  ▸ what's a good place to go out for a meal? wo kann man gut essen gehen? [voh kan man goot ehsen gayen]
  ▸ the tide's going out die Ebbe kommt [dee ehb-e komt]

**grapefruit** die Grapefruit [graypfroot]
  ▸ I'll just have the grapefruit ich nehme nur die Grapefruit [ish naym-e noor dee graypfroot]

**great** *(very good)* großartig [grohsartish], toll [tol]
  ▸ that's great! das ist großartig! [das ist grohsartish]
  ▸ it was really great! es war wirklich toll! [ehs var virklish tol]

**green** grün [gruun]
  ▸ the green one der Grüne [dehr gruun-e]

**grocery store** das Lebensmittelgeschäft [laybenzmitel-geshehft]
  ▸ is there a grocery store around here? gibt es hier in der Nähe ein Lebensmittelgeschäft? [gipt ehs heer in dehr nay-e eyn laybenzmitel-geshehft]

**ground cloth** die Bodenplane [bohdenplaan-e]
  ▸ I brought a ground cloth ich habe eine Bodenplane dabei [ish haa-be ey-ne bohdenplaan-e daabey]

**group** die Gruppe [grup-e]
  ▸ there's a group of 12 of us wir sind eine Zwölfergruppe [veer zint ey-ne tsveulfergrup-e]
  ▸ are there reductions for groups? gibt es Gruppenermäßigungen? [gipt ehs grupen-ehrmaysigungen]

**group rate** der Gruppentarif [grupentareef]
  ▸ are there special group rates? gibt es spezielle Gruppentarife? [gipt ehs shpehtsi-ehl-e grupentareef-e]

**guarantee** *(for purchased product)* die Garantie [garantee]
  ▸ it's still under guarantee es hat noch Garantie [ehs hat nokh garantee]

**guesthouse** die Pension [penziohn]
  ▸ we're looking for a guesthouse for the night wir suchen eine Pension für die Nacht [veer zookhen ey-ne penziohn fuur dee nakht]

**guide** *(person)* der Reiseleiter [reyzeleyter], die Reiseleiterin [reyzeleyterin]; *(book)* der Reiseführer [reyzefuurer]
  ▸ does the guide speak English? spricht der Reiseleiter/die Reiseleiterin Englisch? [shprisht dehr reyzeleyter/dee reyzeleyterin ehnglish]

**guidebook** der Reiseführer [reyzefuurer]
  ▸ do you have a guidebook in English? haben Sie einen englischen Reiseführer? [haaben zee eynen ehnglishen reyzefuurer]

**guided tour** die Führung [fuurung]
- what time does the guided tour begin? wann beginnt die Führung? [van begint dee fuurung]
- is there a guided tour in English? gibt es eine Führung auf Englisch? [gipt ehs eyn-e fuurung owf ehnglish]
- are there guided tours of the museum? gibt es Führungen durch das Museum? [gipt ehs fuurungen dursh das moozayum]

# h

**hair** das Haar [haar]
- she has short hair sie hat kurzes Haar [zee hat kurtsez haar]
- he has red hair er hat rotes Haar [ehr hat rohtez haar]

**hairbrush** die Haarbürste [haarbuurst-e]
- do you sell hairbrushes? verkaufen Sie Haarbürsten? [fehrkowfen zee haarbuursten]

**hairdryer** der Fön [feun]
- do the rooms have hairdryers? gibt es im Zimmer einen Fön? [gipt ehs im tsim-er eynen feun]

**hair salon** der Friseursalon [frizeursalon]
- does the hotel have a hair salon? gibt es im Hotel einen Friseursalon? [gipt ehs im hohtehl eynen frizeursalon]

**half** halb [halp] ♦ die Hälfte [hehlft-e]
- shall we meet in half an hour? wollen wir uns in einer halben Stunde treffen? [vol-en veer uns in eyner halben shtund-e trehfen]
- it's half past eight es ist halb neun [ehs ist halp noyn]

**half-bottle** die kleine Flasche [kleyn-e flash-e]
- a half-bottle of red wine, please eine kleine Flasche Rotwein, bitte [eyn-e kleyn-e flash-e rohtveyn bi-te]

**ham** der Schinken [shinken]
- I'd like five slices of ham ich hätte gern fünf Scheiben Schinken [ish heht-e gehm fuunf sheyben shinken]

**hand** die Hand [hant]
- where can I wash my hands? wo kann ich mir die Hände waschen? [voh kan ish meer dee hehnd-e vashen]

**handbag** die Handtasche [hant-tash-e]
- someone's stolen my handbag jemand hat mir die Handtasche gestohlen [yaymant hat meer dee hant-tash-e geshtohlen]

**hand baggage** das Handgepäck [hantgepehk]

▸ I have one suitcase and one piece of hand baggage ich habe einen Koffer und ein Handgepäck [ish haa-be eynen kof-er unt eyn hantgepehk]

**handkerchief** das Taschentuch [tashentookh]

▸ do you have a spare handkerchief? haben Sie ein Taschentuch für mich? [haaben zee eyn tashentookh fuur mish]

**handle** der Griff [grif]

▸ the handle's broken der Griff ist kaputt [dehr grif ist kaput]

**handmade** handgearbeitet [hant-ge-arbeytet]

▸ is this handmade? ist das Handarbeit? [ist das hantarbeyt]

**happen** *(occur)* passieren [paseeren]

▸ what happened? was ist passiert? [vas ist paseert]

▸ these things happen das kann vorkommen [das kan forkom-en]

**happy** *(not sad)* glücklich [gluuklish]; *(satisfied)* zufrieden [tsufreeden]

▸ I am very happy with the service at the hotel ich bin sehr zufrieden mit dem Service im Hotel [ish bin zehr tsufreeden mit daym sehrvis im hohtehl]

▸ I'd be happy to help ich helfe gerne [ish hehlf-e gehrn-e]

▸ Happy Birthday! Herzlichen Glückwunsch zum Geburtstag! [hehrtslishen gluuk-vunsh tsum geburtstaak]

▸ Happy New Year! Frohes Neues Jahr! [frohez noyez yaar]

**hat** der Hut [hoot]

▸ I think I left my hat here ich glaube, ich habe meinen Hut hier vergessen [ish glowb-e ish haa-be meynen hoot heer fehrgehsen]

**hate** hassen [has-en]

▸ I hate golf ich hasse Golf [ish has-e golf]

**have** haben [haaben]; *(meal)* essen [ehsen]; *(drink)* trinken [trinken] ◆ **have to** *(be obliged)* müssen [muusen]

▸ do you have any bread? haben Sie etwas Brot? [haaben zee ehtvas broht]

▸ do you have them in red? haben Sie sie in Rot? [haaben zee zee in roht]

▸ he has brown hair er hat braunes Haar [ehr hat brownez haar]

▸ where should we go to have a drink? wo wollen wir etwas trinken gehen? [voh vol-en veer ehtvas trinken gayen]

▸ I have to be at the airport by six (o'clock) ich muss um sechs (Uhr) am Flughafen sein [ish mus um zeks (oor) am flookhaafen zeyn]

▸ we have to go wir müssen gehen [veer muusen gayen]

**head** der Kopf [kopf]

▸ I hit my head when I fell ich habe mir beim Fallen den Kopf gestoßen [ish haa-be meer beym fal-en dayn kopf geshtohsen]

▸ the shower head is broken der Duschkopf ist kaputt [dehr dushkopf ist kaput]

**headache** die Kopfschmerzen [kopfshmehrtsen]
> I've got a headache ich habe Kopfschmerzen [ish haa-be kopfshmehrtsen]
> do you have anything for a headache? haben Sie etwas gegen Kopfschmerzen? [haaben zee ehtvas gaygen kopfshmehrtsen]

**headlight** der Scheinwerfer [sheynvehrfer]
> one of my headlights got smashed einer meiner Scheinwerfer wurde eingeschlagen [eyner meyner sheynvehrfer vurd-e eyngeshlaagen]

**headphones** die Kopfhörer [kopfheurer]
> did you find my headphones? haben Sie meine Kopfhörer gefunden? [haaben zee meyn-e kopfheurer gefunden]

**health** die Gesundheit [gezunt-heyt]
> in good/poor health bei guter/schlechter Gesundheit [bey gooter/shlehshter gezunt-heyt]

**hear** hören [heuren]
> I've heard a lot about you ich habe viel von Ihnen gehört [ish haa-be feel fon eenen geheurt]

**heart** das Herz [hehrts]
> he's got a weak heart er hat ein schwaches Herz [ehr hat eyn shvakhez hehrts]

**heart attack** der Herzinfarkt [hehrtsinfarkt]
> he had a heart attack er hatte einen Herzinfarkt [ehr hat-e eynen hehrtsinfarkt]
> I nearly had a heart attack! ich habe fast einen Herzinfarkt bekommen! [ish haa-be fast eynen hehrtsinfarkt bekom-en]

**heart condition** die Herzkrankheit [hehrtskrankheyt]
> to have a heart condition herzkrank sein [hehrtskrank zeyn]

**heat** *(warmth)* die Wärme [vehrm-e]; *(weather, for cooking)* die Hitze [hits-e]
> there's no heat from the radiator in my room der Heizkörper in meinem Zimmer wird nicht warm [dehr heytskeurper in meynem tsim-er virt nisht varm]

**heating** die Heizung [heytsung]
> how does the heating work? wie funktioniert die Heizung? [vee funktsiohneert dee heytsung]

**heavy** schwer [shvehr]
> my bags are very heavy meine Koffer sind sehr schwer [mey-ne kof-er zint zehr shvehr]

**heel** *(of foot)* die Ferse [fehr-ze]; *(of shoe)* der Absatz [apzats]
> can you put new heels on these shoes? können Sie auf diese Schuhe neue Absätze machen? [keunen zee owf dee-ze shoo-e noy-e apzehts-e makhen]

**hello** hallo [haloh]
  ▸ hello, is this ...? hallo, ist das ...? [haloh ist das]

**helmet** der Helm [hehlm]
  ▸ do you have a helmet you could lend me? haben Sie einen Helm, den Sie mir leihen können? [haaben zee eynen hehlm dayn zee meer leyen keunen]

**help** die Hilfe [hilf-e] ◆ helfen [hehlfen]
  ▸ help! Hilfe! [hilf-e]
  ▸ go and get help quickly! schnell, holen Sie Hilfe! [shnehl hohlen zee hilf-e]
  ▸ thank you for your help danke für Ihre Hilfe! [dank-e fuur ee-re hilf-e]
  ▸ could you help me? könnten Sie mir helfen? [keunten zee meer hehlfen]
  ▸ could you help us push the car? könnten Sie uns helfen, das Auto zu schieben? [keunten zee uns hehlfen das owtoh tsoo sheeben]
  ▸ let me help you with that lassen Sie mich Ihnen dabei helfen [las-en zee mish eenen daabey hehlfen]
  ▸ could you help me with my bags? könnten Sie mir mit meinem Gepäck helfen? [keunten zee meer mit meynem gepehk hehlfen]

**herbal tea** der Kräutertee [kroytertay]
  ▸ I'd like an herbal tea ich hätte gerne einen Kräutertee [ish heh-te gehrn-e eynen kroytertay]

**here** *(in this place)* hier [heer]; *(to this place)* hierher [heer-hehr]
  ▸ I've been here two days ich bin hier seit zwei Tagen [ish bin heer zeyt tsvey taagen]
  ▸ I came here three years ago ich bin vor drei Jahren hierher gekommen [ish bin for drey yaaren heer-hehr gekom-en]
  ▸ are you from around here? kommen Sie hier aus der Gegend? [kom-en zee heer ows dehr gaygent]
  ▸ I'm afraid I'm a stranger here myself es tut mir Leid, ich bin selbst fremd hier [ehs toot meer leyt ish bin zehlbst frehmt heer]
  ▸ it's five minutes from here es ist fünf Minuten von hier [ehs ist fuunf minooten fon heer]

## hitchhiking

Hitchhiking on the spur of the moment won't usually get you very far, although there might be exceptions in some particular regions or in the tourist season. Hitchhiking is also banned on highways. There is a very inexpensive alternative, however: car-shares arranged through the small ads that are put up in university dining halls or through *Mitfahrzentrale*, which can be found in every town.

▸ here is/are ... hier ist/sind ... [heer ist/zint]
▸ here are my passport and ticket hier sind mein Pass und mein Ticket [heer zint meyn pas unt meyn tikit]

**hi** hallo [haloh]
▸ hi, I'm Fiona hallo, ich bin Fiona [haloh ish bin fiohna]

**high beam** das Fernlicht [fehrnlisht]
▸ put your lights on high beam! stellen Sie das Fernlicht ein! [shtehlen zee das fehrnlisht eyn]

**high chair** der Hochstuhl [hohkh-shtool]
▸ could we have a high chair for the baby? könnten wir einen Hochstuhl für das Baby bekommen? [keunten veer eynen hohkh-shtool fuur das baybi bekom-en]

**high season** die Hochsaison [hohkh-sayzon]
▸ is it very expensive in the high season? ist es sehr teuer in der Hochsaison? [ist ehs zehr toyer in dehr hohkh-sayzon]

**high tide** die Flut [floot]
▸ what time is high tide? um wie viel Uhr setzt die Flut ein? [um vee feel oor zehtst dee floot eyn]

**hike** die Wanderung [vanderung]
▸ are there any good hikes around here? gibt es hier in der Gegend gute Wandermöglichkeiten? [gipt ehs heer in dehr gaygent goot-e vandermeuglishkeyten]

**hiking** das Wandern [vandern]
▸ to go hiking wandern gehen [vandern gayen]
▸ are there any hiking trails? gibt es Wanderwege? [gipt ehs vandervayg-e]

**hiking boot** der Wanderstiefel [vandershteefel]
▸ do you need to wear hiking boots? muss man Wanderstiefel tragen? [mus man vandershteefel traagen]

**hitchhike** per Anhalter fahren [per anhalter faaren]
▸ we hitchhiked here wir sind hierher per Anhalter gefahren [veer zint heer-hehr per anhalter gefaaren]

**holiday** der Feiertag [feyertaak]
▸ is tomorrow a holiday? ist morgen ein Feiertag? [ist morgen eyn feyertaak]

**home** *(house)* das Zuhause [tsoo-howz-e] ◆ zu Hause [tsoo howz-e]
- to stay at home zu Hause bleiben [tsoo howz-e bleyben]
- we're going home tomorrow wir fahren morgen nach Hause [veer faaren morgen naakh howz-e]

**homemade** selbst gemacht [zehlbst gemakht]
- is it homemade? ist es selbst gemacht? [ist ehs zehlbst gemakht]

**hood** *(vehicle)* die Motorhaube [mohtorhowb-e]
- I've dented the hood ich habe die Motorhaube eingedellt [ish haa-be dee mohtorhowb-e eyn-gedehlt]

**horrible** *(weather, day)* schrecklich [shrehklish]; *(person)* gemein [gemeyn]
- what horrible weather! was für schreckliches Wetter! [vas fuur shrehklishes vehter]

**horseback riding** das Reiten [reyten]
- can we go horseback riding? können wir reiten gehen? [keunen veer reyten gayen]

**hospital** das Krankenhaus [krankenhows]
- where is the nearest hospital? wo ist das nächste Krankenhaus? [voh ist das nehkst-e krankenhows]

**hot** *(in temperature)* heiß [heys]; *(spicy)* scharf [sharf]
- I'm too hot mir ist zu heiß [meer ist tsoo heys]
- this dish is really hot dieses Gericht ist wirklich scharf [deezes gerisht ist virklish sharf]
- there's no hot water es gibt kein heißes Wasser [ehs gipt keyn heysez vas-er]

**hotel** das Hotel [hohtehl]
- do you have a list of hotels in this area? haben Sie eine Liste der Hotels in dieser Gegend? [haaben zee ey-ne list-e dehr hohtehlz in deezer gaygent]
- are there any reasonably priced hotels near here? gibt es hier in der Nähe preiswerte Hotels? [gipt ehs heer in dehr nay-e preyzvehrt-e hohtehlz]

---

## at the hotel

- we'd like a double room/two single rooms wir hätten gerne ein Doppelzimmer/zwei Einzelzimmer [veer hehten gehrn-e eyn dop-el-tsimer/tsvey eyntsel-tsimer]
- I have a reservation in the name of Black ich habe eine Reservierung auf den Namen Black gemacht [ish haa-be ey-ne rehzerveerung owf dayn naamen blak gemakht]
- what time is breakfast served? um wie viel Uhr gibt es Frühstück? [um vee feel oor gipt ehs fruuhshtuuk]
- could I have a wake-up call at 7 a.m.? könnten Sie mich um sieben Uhr morgens wecken lassen? [keunten zee mish um zeeben oor morgenz vehken las-en]

▸ is the hotel downtown? ist das Hotel im Stadtzentrum? [ist das hohtehl im shtat-tsehntrum]

▸ could you recommend another hotel? könnten Sie ein anderes Hotel empfehlen? [keunten zee eyn anderez hohtehl ehmpfaylen]

**hour** die Stunde [shtund-e]

▸ I'll be back in an hour ich bin in einer Stunde wieder zurück [ish bin in eyner shtund-e tsuruuk]

▸ the flight takes three hours der Flug dauert drei Stunden [dehr flook dowert drey shtunden]

**house** das Haus [hows]

▸ is this your house? ist das Ihr Haus? [ist das eer hows]

**house wine** der Hauswein [howsveyn]

▸ a bottle of house wine, please eine Flasche des Hausweins, bitte [ey-ne flash-e dez howsveynz bi-te]

**how** wie [vee]

▸ how are you? wie geht es Ihnen? [vee gayt ehs eenen]

▸ how do you spell it? wie buchstabiert man das? [vee bookh-shtabeert man das]

▸ how about a drink? wie wäre es mit einem Drink? [vee vehr-e ehs mit eynem drink]

**humid** *(room)* feucht [foysht]; *(weather)* schwül [shvuul]

▸ it's very humid today es ist sehr schwül heute [ehs ist zehr shvuul hoy-te]

**hungry** hungrig [hungrish]

▸ to be hungry Hunger haben [hung-er haaben]

▸ I'm starting to get hungry ich werde langsam hungrig [ish vehrd-e langzaam hungrish]

**hurry**

▸ to be in a hurry in Eile sein [in ey-le zeyn]

**hurry up** sich beeilen [zish be-eylen]

▸ hurry up! beeil dich! [be-eyl dish]

**hurt** wehtun [vaytoon]

▸ you're hurting me! Sie tun mir weh! [zee toon meer vay]

▸ I hurt myself ich habe mich verletzt [ish haa-be mish fehrlehtst]

▸ I hurt my hand ich habe mich an der Hand verletzt [ish haa-be mish an dehr hant vehrlehtst]

▸ it hurts es tut weh [ehs toot vay]

# i

**ice** *(frozen water)* das Eis [eys]; *(cubes)* die Eiswürfel [eysvuurfel]
▸ a Diet Coke® without ice, please eine Cola light ohne Eis, bitte [ey-ne kohla leyt ohn-e eys bi-te]

**ice cream** das Eis [eys]
▸ I'd like some ice cream ich hätte gerne ein Eis [ish heht-e gehrn-e eyn eys]

**ice cube** der Eiswürfel [eysvuurfel]
▸ could I have a carafe of water with no ice cubes in it? könnte ich eine Karaffe Wasser ohne Eiswürfel bekommen? [keunt-e ish ey-ne karaf-e vas-er ohn-e eysvuurfel bekom-en]

**iced coffee** der Eiskaffee [eyskafay]
▸ I'd like an iced coffee ich hätte gerne einen Eiskaffee [ish heh-te gehrn-e eynen eyskafay]

**ice rink** die Eisbahn [eysbaan]
▸ is there an ice rink nearby? gibt es in der Nähe eine Eisbahn? [gipt ehs in dehr nay-e ei-ne eysbaan]

**ice skate** der Schlittschuh [shlit-shoo]
▸ I'd like to rent some ice skates ich möchte gerne Schlittschuhe mieten [ish meusht-e gehrn-e shlit-shoo-e meeten]

**ice-skate** Schlittschuh laufen [shlit-shoo lowfen]
▸ would you like to go ice-skating tomorrow? hast du Lust morgen Schlittschuh laufen zu gehen? [hast doo lust morgen shlit-shoo lowfen tsoo gayen]

**ID card** der Personalausweis [pehrzonaal-owsveys]
▸ I don't have an ID card: will a passport work? ich habe keinen Personalausweis, ist ein Reisepass in Ordnung? [ish haa-be keynen pehrzonaal-owsveys ist eyn reyzepas in ordnung]

**if** wenn [vehn]
▸ we can go if you want wir können gehen, wenn du willst [veer keunen gayen vehn doo vilst]

**ill** krank [krank]
▸ my son is ill mein Sohn ist krank [meyn zohn ist krank]

**immediately** sofort [zohfort]
▸ can you do it immediately? können Sie es sofort machen? [keunen zee ehs zohfort makhen]

**improve** verbessern [fehrbehsern]
▸ I'm hoping to improve my German while I'm here ich hoffe mein Deutsch zu

verbessern, während ich hier bin [ish hof-e meyn doytsh tsoo fehrbehsern vehrent ish heer bin]

**in** in [in]
- our bags are still in the room unsere Koffer sind noch im Zimmer [unzere kof-er zint nokh im tsim-er]
- do you live in Berlin? leben Sie in Berlin? [layben zee in behrleen]

**included** inbegriffen [inbegrif-en]
- is breakfast included? ist Frühstück inbegriffen? [ist fruushtuuk inbegrif-en]
- is sales tax included? ist Mehrwertsteuer inbegriffen? [ist mehrvehrt-shtoyer inbegrif-en]
- is the tip included? ist das Trinkgeld inbegriffen? [ist das trinkgehlt inbegrif-en]

**indoor** (pool, sport) Hallen- [hal-en]
- is there an indoor pool? gibt es ein Hallenbad? [gipt ehs eyn hal-en-baat]

**infection** die Infektion [infehktsiohn]
- I have an eye infection ich habe eine Augeninfektion [ish haa-be ey-ne owgen-infehktsiohn]

**information** (facts) die Informationen [informatsiohnen]; (service, department) die Information [informatsiohn]; (directory assistance) die Auskunft [owskunft]
- a piece of information eine Auskunft [ey-ne owskunft]
- may I ask you for some information? darf ich Sie um eine Auskunft bitten? [darf ish zee um ey-ne owskunft bit-en]
- where can I find information on...? wo kann ich Informationen über ... finden? [voh kan ish informatsiohnen uuber finden]

**injection** (medicine) die Spritze [shprits-e]
- am I going to need an injection? werde ich eine Spritze bekommen müssen? [vehrd-e ish ey-ne shprits-e bekom-en meus-en]

**injure** verletzen [fehrlehtsen]
- to injure oneself sich verletzen [zish fehrlehtsen]
- I injured myself ich habe mich verletzt [ish haa-be mish fehrlehtst]

**inside** (be) in [in]; (go) in ... hinein [in hineyn] ♦ innen [in-en]
- are you allowed inside the castle? darf man ins Schloss hinein? [darf man ins shlos hineyn]
- we'd prefer a table inside wir hätten lieber einen Tisch drinnen [veer hehten leeber eynen tish drin-en]

**insurance** die Versicherung [fehrzisherung]
- what does the insurance cover? was deckt die Versicherung ab? [vas dehkt dee fehrzisherung ap]

**insure** (house, car) versichern [fehrzishern]
- yes, I'm insured ja, ich bin versichert [yaa ish bin fehrzishert]

### Internet

Internet cafés are largely to be found in big towns. But if you use one, you'll need to keep your wits about you as German keyboards aren't the same as ours. And you'll need a telephone jack if you take your laptop with you.

---

**interesting** interessant [interehs-ant]
 ▸ it's not a very interesting place es ist kein besonders interessanter Ort [ehs ist keyn bezonders interehs-anter ort]

**international call** das Auslandsgespräch [owslandz-geshprehsh]
 ▸ I'd like to make an international call ich möchte ein Auslandsgespräch machen [ish meusht-e eyn owslandz-geshprehsh makhen]

**Internet** das Internet [interneht]
 ▸ where can I connect to the Internet? wo gibt es einen Internetanschluss? [voh gipt ehs eynen interneht-anshlus]

**introduce** *(present)* vorstellen [for-shtehlen]
 ▸ to introduce oneself sich vorstellen [zish for-shtehlen]
 ▸ allow me to introduce myself: I'm Mike darf ich mich vorstellen, ich bin Mike [darf ish mish for-shtehlen ish bin meyk]

**invite** einladen [eynlaaden]
 ▸ I'd like to invite you to dinner next weekend ich möchte Sie gerne nächstes Wochenende zum Abendessen einladen [ish meusht-e zee gehrn-e nehkstez wokhenehnd-e tsum aabent-ehsen eynlaaden]

**iron** *(for ironing)* das Bügeleisen [buugeleyzen] ◆ bügeln [buugeln]
 ▸ I need an iron ich brauche ein Bügeleisen [ish browkh-e eyn buugeleyzen]

**itch** der Juckreiz [yuk-reyts]
 ▸ I've got an itch on my left leg ich habe einen Juckreiz am linken Bein [ish haa-be eynen yuk-reyts am linken beyn]

**itinerary** die Reiseroute [reyz-e-root-e]
 ▸ is it possible to modify the planned itinerary? ist es möglich, die geplante Reiseroute abzuändern? [ist ehs meuglish dee geplaant-e reyz-e-root-e ap-tsoo-ehndern]

# j

**January** der Januar [yanuar]
- ▸ January 4th vierter Januar [feerter yanuar]

**Jet Ski®** der Jetski [dzheht-skee]
- ▸ I'd like to rent a Jet Ski® ich möchte gerne einen Jetski mieten [ish meusht-e gehrn-e eynen dzheht-skee meeten]

**job** *(employment)* die Stelle [shtehl-e]
- ▸ I'm looking for a summer job in the area ich suche einen Sommerjob in der Gegend [ish zookh-e eynen som-er-dzhob in dehr gaygent]

**joke** der Witz [vits] ♦ Witze machen [vits-e makhen]
- ▸ it's beyond a joke! das ist kein Witz mehr! [das ist keyn vits mehr]
- ▸ I was just joking ich habe nur Spaß gemacht [ish haa-be noor shpaas ge-makht]

**journey** die Reise [reyz-e]
- ▸ how long does the journey take? wie lange dauert die Reise? [vee lang-e dowert dee reyz-e]

**juice** der Saft [zaft]
- ▸ what types of juice do you have? was für Saft haben Sie? [vas fuur zaft haaben zee]

**July** der Juli [yooli]
- ▸ July 4th vierter Juli [feerter yooli]

**June** der Juni [yooni]
- ▸ June 2nd der zweite Juni [dehr tsveyt-e yooni]

**just** *(recently, at that moment)* gerade [geraad-e]; *(only, simply)* nur [noor]
- ▸ he just left er ist gerade gegangen [ehr ist geraad-e ge-gangen]
- ▸ I'll just have one ich nehme nur eins [ish naym-e noor eyns]

# k

**kayak** der Kajak [kayak]
- can we rent kayaks? können wir Kajaks mieten? [keunen veer kayaks meeten]

**keep** *(retain)* behalten [behalten]; *(promise)* halten [halten]; *(appointment)* einhalten [eynhalten]
- keep the change der Rest ist für Sie [dehr rehst ist fuur zee]

**key** *(for door, container)* der Schlüssel [shluusel]; *(on keyboard, phone)* die Taste [tast-e]
- where is the key to the front door? wo ist der Schlüssel für die Eingangstür? [voh ist dehr shluusel fuur dee eyngangstuur]

**kilometer** der Kilometer [keelohmayter]
- how much is it per kilometer? wie viel kostet es pro Kilometer? [vee feel kostet ehs proh keelohmayter]

**kind** *(nice)* nett [neht] ◆ *(sort, type)* die Art [art]
- that's very kind of you das ist sehr nett von Ihnen [das ist zehr neht fon eenen]
- what's your favorite kind of music? was für Musik hören Sie am liebsten? [vas fuur muzeek heuren zee am leebsten]

**kitchen** die Küche [kuukh-e]
- is the kitchen shared? ist es eine Gemeinschaftsküche? [ist ehs ey-ne gemeynshafts-kuukh-e]

**Kleenex**® das Papiertaschentuch [papeer-tashentookh]
- do you have any Kleenex®? haben Sie ein Papiertaschentuch? [haaben zee eyn papeer-tashentookh]

**knife** das Messer [mehser]
- could I have a knife? könnte ich ein Messer haben? [keun-te ish eyn mehser haaben]

**know** *(fact)* wissen [vis-en]; *(person, place)* kennen [ken-en]
- I don't know this town very well ich kenne diese Stadt nicht besonders gut [ish ken-e deez-e shtat nisht bezonderz goot]
- I know the basics but no more than that ich weiß über das Wesentliche Bescheid, aber nicht mehr [ish veys uuber das vayzentlish-e besheyd aaber nisht mehr]
- do you know each other? kennen Sie sich? [ken-en zee zish]

**knowledge** das Wissen [vis-en]
- she has a good knowledge of German sie hat gute Deutschkenntnisse [zee hat goot-e doytsh-kentnis-e]
- without my knowledge ohne mein Wissen [ohn-e meyn vis-en]

**ladies' room** die Damentoilette [daamen-toyleht-e]
- where's the ladies' room? wo ist die Damentoilette? [voh ist dee daamen-toyleht-e]

**lake** der See [zay]
- can you go swimming in the lake? kann man in dem See schwimmen? [kan man in daym zay shvim-en]

**lamp** die Lampe [lamp-e]
- the lamp doesn't work die Lampe geht nicht [dee lamp-e gayt nisht]

**land** *(plane)* landen [landen]
- what time is the plane scheduled to land? um wie viel Uhr soll das Flugzeug landen? [um vee feel oor zol das flooktsoyk landen]

**landmark** der Orientierungspunkt [oriehnteerungzpunkt]
- do you recognize any landmarks? erkennen Sie irgendwelche Orientierungspunkte? [ehrkehnen zee irgentvehlsh-e oriehnteerungzpunkt-e]

**lane** *(on a highway, for a bus)* die Spur [shpoor]
- a four-lane highway eine vierspurige Autobahn [ey-ne feershpoorig-e owtohbaan]

**laptop** der Laptop [lehptop]
- my laptop's been stolen mein Laptop ist gestohlen worden [meyn lehptop ist geshtohlen vorden]

**last** letzter [lehtster] ◆ *(go on, continue)* halten [halten]
- when does the last bus go? wann fährt der letzte Bus? [van fehrt dehr lehtst-e bus]
- when is the last subway train? wann fährt die letzte U-Bahn? [van fehrt dee lehtst-e oo-baan]

**last name** der Nachname [nakhnaam-e]
- could I have your last name? könnten Sie mir Ihren Nachnamen sagen? [keunten zee meer eeren nakhnaamen zaagen]

**late** spät [shpayt]
- the plane was two hours late das Flugzeug war zwei Stunden verspätet [das flooktsoyk var tsvey shtunden fehrshpaytet]
- could you tell me if the 1:17 to Ulm is running late? könnten Sie mir sagen, ob der Zug nach Ulm um ein Uhr siebzehn Verspätung hat? [keunten zee meer zaagen op dehr tsook naakh ulm um eyn oor zeebtsayn fehrshpaytung hat]

**later** später [shpayter]
- is there a later train? gibt es einen späteren Zug? [gipt ehs eynen shpayteren tsook]
- see you later! bis später! [bis shpayter]

**latest** *(most recent)* neuester [noyester]; *(very last)* spätester [shpaytester]
  ▸ what's the latest time we can check out? bis wann muss man spätestens auschecken? [bis van mus man shpaytestenz ows-tsehken]

**laugh** das Lachen [lakhen] ◆ lachen [lakhen]
  ▸ I just did it for a laugh ich habe es nur aus Spaß gemacht [ish haab-e ehs noor ows shpaas ge-makht]

**Laundromat®** der Waschsalon [vashzalon]
  ▸ is there a Laundromat® nearby? gibt es einen Waschsalon in der Nähe? [gipt ehs eynen vashzalon in dehr nay-e]

**laundry** *(clothes)* die Wäsche [vesh-e]; *(business)* die Wäscherei [vesherey]; *(room)* die Waschküche [vashkuukh-e]
  ▸ where can we do our laundry? wo können wir unsere Wäsche waschen? [voh keunen veer unzer-e vesh-e vashen]
  ▸ where's the nearest laundry? wo ist die nächste Wäscherei? [voh ist dee nehkst-e vesherey]

**lawyer** der Anwalt [anvalt], die Anwältin [anvehltin]
  ▸ I'm a lawyer ich bin Anwalt (Anwältin) [ish bin anvalt (anvehltin)]
  ▸ I need a lawyer ich brauche einen Anwalt [ish browkh-e eynen anvalt]

**leaflet** der Prospekt [prospehkt]
  ▸ do you have any leaflets in English? haben Sie Prospekte auf Englisch? [haaben zee prospehkt-e owf ehnglish]

**learn** lernen [lehrnen]
  ▸ I've just learned a few words from a book ich habe nur ein paar Wörter aus einem Buch gelernt [ish haa-be noorl eyn par weurter ows eynem bookh ge-lehrnt]

**least** geringster [geringster] ◆ das Mindeste [das mindest-e] ◆ am wenigsten [am vaynigsten]
  ▸ it's the least I can do das ist das Mindeste, was ich tun kann [das ist das mindest-e vas ish toon kan]
  ▸ not in the least nicht im Geringsten [nisht im geringsten]
  ▸ to say the least um es milde zu sagen [um ehs mild-e tsoo zaagen]
  ▸ at least mindestens [mindestenz]
  ▸ it's at least a three-hour drive es ist mindestens eine dreistündige Fahrt [ehs ist mindestenz ey-ne dreyshtuundig-e fart]

**leave** *(house, country)* verlassen [fehrlas-en]; *(open, alone, on table etc.)* lassen [las-en]; *(forget to take)* liegen lassen [leegen las-en] ◆ *(go away)* (weg)gehen [(vek)gayen]; *(in vehicle)* abfahren [ap-faaren]
  ▸ can I leave my backpack at the reception desk? kann ich meinen Rucksack an der Rezeption lassen? [kan ish meynen rukzak an dehr retsehptsiohn las-en]
  ▸ can I leave the car at the airport? kann ich das Auto am Flughafen lassen? [kan ish das owtoh am flookhaafen las-en]

- leave us alone! lassen Sie uns in Ruhe! [las-en zee uns in roo-e]
- I've left something on the plane ich habe etwas im Flugzeug liegen lassen [ish haa-be ehtvas im flooktsoyk leegen las-en]
- I'll be leaving at nine o'clock tomorrow morning ich werde morgen Früh um neun Uhr abfahren [ish vehrd-e morgen fruu um noyn oor ap-faaren]
- what platform does the train for Hamburg leave from? von welchem Bahnsteig fährt der Zug nach Hamburg ab? [fon vehlshem baanshteyk fehrt dehr tsook naakh hamburk ap]

**left** *(not right)* links [links] ♦ der Linke [link-e]; *(in politics, boxing)* die Linke [link-e]

- to be left *(remain)* übrig bleiben [uubrish bleyben]
- are there any tickets left for...? gibt es noch Tickets für ...? [gipt ehs nokh tikits fuur]
- to the left (of) links (von) [links fon]

**left-hand** linker [linker]

- on your left-hand side auf Ihrer linken Seite [owf eerer linken zeyt-e]

**leg** das Bein [beyn]

- I have a pain in my left leg mein linkes Bein tut weh [meyn linkez beyn toot vay]
- I can't move my leg ich kann mein Bein nicht bewegen [ish kan meyn beyn nisht bevaygen]

**lemon** die Zitrone [tsitrohn-e]

- can I have half a pound of lemons? kann ich ein halbes Pfund Zitronen bekommen? [kan ish eyn halbez pfunt tsitrohnen bekom-en]

**lend** leihen [leyen]

- could you lend us your car? könnten Sie uns Ihr Auto leihen? [keunten zee uns eer owtoh leyen]

**lens** *(of camera)* die Linse [linz-e]; *(contact lens)* die Kontaktlinse [kontaktlinz-e]

- there's something on the lens da ist etwas auf der Linse [daa ist ehtvas owf dehr linz-e]
- I have hard lenses ich habe harte Kontaktlinsen [ish haa-be hart-e kontaktlinzen]
- I have soft lenses ich habe weiche Kontaktlinsen [ish haa-be veysh-e kontaktlinzen]

**less** weniger [vayniger]

- less and less immer weniger [im-er vayniger]
- a little less ein bisschen weniger [eyn bis-shen vayniger]

**lesson** *(individual class)* die Stunde [shtund-e]

- how much do lessons cost? was kostet der Unterricht? [vas kostet dehr unterisht]
- can we take lessons? können wir Unterricht nehmen? [keunen veer unterisht naymen]

**let off** (allow to disembark) aussteigen lassen [ows-shteygen las-en]
- could you let me off here, please? könnten Sie mich hier bitte aussteigen lassen? [keunten zee mish heer bi-te ows-shteygen las-en]

**letter** der Brief [breef]
- I would like to send this letter to the States ich möchte gerne diesen Brief in die Vereinigten Staaten schicken [ish meush-te gehm-e deezen breef in dee fehreynigten shtaaten shik-en]
- I confirmed my reservation by letter ich habe meine Buchung brieflich bestätigt [ish haa-be meyn-e bookhung breeflish beshtaytisht]

**level** (amount) der Anteil [anteyl]; (of a building, a ship) das Stockwerk [shtokvehrk]
- do you know if cabin 27 is on this level? wissen Sie, ob Kabine siebenundzwanzig auf diesem Stockwerk ist? [vis-en zee op kabeen-e zeeben-unt-tsvantsish owf deezem shtokvehrk ist]

**license** (gen) die Berechtigung [berehshtigung]; (for driving) der Führerschein [fuurersheyn]
- do you need a license to hunt here? braucht man hier eine Jagdberechtigung? [browkht man heer ey-ne yaaktberehshtigung]
- I left my driver's license in my hotel room ich habe meinen Führerschein in meinem Hotelzimmer gelassen [ish haa-be meynen fuurersheyn in meynem hohtehl-tsim-er gelas-en]

**license number** das Kraftfahrzeugzeichen [kraftfaartsoyk-tseyshen]
- I got the license number ich habe das Kraftfahrzeugzeichen [ish haa-be das kraftfaartsoyk-tseyshen]

**lifebelt** der Rettungsgürtel [rehtungzguurtel]
- throw me a lifebelt! werfen Sie mir einen Rettungsgürtel zu! [vehrfen zee meer eynen rehtungzguurtel tsoo]

**lifeboat** das Rettungsboot [rehtungzboht]
- how many lifeboats are there? wie viele Rettungsboote gibt es? [vee feel-e rehtungzboht-e gipt ehs]

**lifejacket** die Schwimmweste [shvimvehst-e]
- are there any lifejackets? gibt es Schwimmwesten? [gipt ehs shvimvehsten]

**light** das Licht [lisht]; (regulating traffic) die Ampel [ampel]; (for a cigarette) das Feuer [foy-er]; (light bulb) die Glühbirne [gluubeern-e]
- the light doesn't work das Licht geht nicht [das lisht gayt nisht]
- could you check the lights? könnten Sie die Lichter nachsehen? [keunten zee dee lishter nakhzayen]
- stop at the next light halten Sie an der nächsten Ampel [halten zee an dehr nehksten ampel]
- do you have a light? haben Sie Feuer? [haaben zee foy-er]

## likes

▶ I really love that painting ich mag dieses Gemälde wirklich sehr [ish maak deezez gemehld-e virklish zehr]

▶ I like your brother ich mag Ihren Bruder [ish maak eeren brooder]

▶ I've got a soft spot for her ich habe eine Schwäche für sie [ish haa-be ey-ne shvehsh-e fuur zee]

▶ I think she's very nice ich finde sie sehr nett [ish fin-de zee zehr neht]

**lighter** das Feuerzeug [foy-er-tsoyk]

▶ can I borrow your lighter? kann ich Ihr Feuerzeug leihen? [kan ish eer foy-er-tsoyk leyen]

**like** (similar to) ähnlich [aynlish]; (such as) so wie [zoh vee] ♦ mögen [meugen]

▶ it's quite like English es ist ziemlich ähnlich wie Englisch [ehs ist tseemlish aynlish vee ehnglish]

▶ I like it ich mag es [ish maak ehs]

▶ I don't like it ich mag es nicht [ish maak ehs nisht]

▶ do you like it here? mögen Sie es hier? [meugen zee ehs heer]

▶ I like Chinese food very much ich mag chinesisches Essen sehr gerne [ish maak shinayzishes ehsen zehr gehrn-e]

▶ do you like the movies? gehen Sie gerne ins Kino? [gayen zee gehrn-e ins keenoh]

▶ would you like something to drink? - yes, please möchten Sie etwas zu trinken? - ja, bitte [meushten zee ehtvas tsoo trinken yaa bi-te]

▶ I'd like to speak to the manager ich möchte gerne mit dem Geschäftsführer sprechen [ish meusht-e gehrn-e mit daym geshehfts-fuurer shprehshen]

**limit** die Grenze [grehnts-e] ♦ begrenzen [begrehntsen]

▶ is that area off limits to the public? ist diese Gegend für die Öffentlichkeit gesperrt? [ist deez-e gaygent fuur dee eufentlishkeyt geshpehrt]

## dislikes

▶ I hate football ich hasse Fußball [ish has-e foosbal]

▶ I can't stand him ich kann ihn nicht ausstehen [ish kan een nisht ows-shtayen]

▶ I don't really like him/her ich mag ihn/sie nicht besonders [ish maak een/zee nisht bezonderz]

▶ I'm not really into walking Spazierengehen ist nicht so mein Fall [shpatseeren-gayen ist nisht zoh meyn fal]

**line** *(phone connection)* die Leitung [leytung]; *(of people waiting)* die Schlange [shlang-e]; *(on subway etc.)* die Linie [leeni-e]
- the line was busy die Leitung war besetzt [dee leytung var bezehtst]
- we had to stand in line for 15 minutes wir mussten fünfzehn Minuten anstehen [veer mussten fuunf-tsayn minooten an-shtayen]
- which line do I take to get to ...? welche Linie muss ich nach ... nehmen? [vehlsh-e leeni-e mus ish naakh naymen]

**lipstick** der Lippenstift [lip-en-shtift]
- I need to buy some lipstick ich muss einen Lippenstift kaufen [ish mus eynen lip-en-shtift kowfen]

**listen** zuhören [tsoo-heuren]
- listen, I really need to see a doctor hören Sie zu, ich muss wirklich mit einem Arzt sprechen [heuren zee tsoo ish mus virklish mit eynem artst shprehshen]
- listen to me carefully hören Sie mir genau zu [heuren zee meer genow tsoo]

**liter** der Liter [leeter]
- a two-liter bottle of mineral water eine Zweiliterflasche Mineralwasser [ey-ne tsveyleeterflash-e mineraal-vas-er]

**little** *(small)* klein [kleyn]; *(young)* jung [yung] ◆ wenig [vaynish]
- it's for a little girl es ist für ein kleines Mädchen [ehs ist fuur eyn kleynez maydshen]
- as little as possible so wenig wie möglich [zoh vaynish vee meuglish]
- I speak a little German ich spreche ein bisschen Deutsch [ish shprehsh-e eyn bis-shen doytsh]
- we've only got a little money left wir haben nur ein bisschen Geld übrig [veer haaben noor eyn bis-shen gehlt uubrish]
- a little bit ein kleines bisschen [eyn kleynez bis-shen]
- a little less ein bisschen weniger [eyn bis-shen vayniger]
- a little more ein bisschen mehr [eyn bish-shen mehr]

**live** *(life)* leben [layben]; *(reside)* wohnen [vohnen]
- do you live around here? wohnen Sie hier in der Gegend? [vohnen zee heer in dehr gaygent]
- I live in Leipzig ich wohne in Leipzig [ish vohn-e in leyptsish]

**live music** die Livemusik [leyvmuzeek]
- I'd like to go to a bar with live music ich möchte gerne in eine Bar mit Livemusik gehen [ish meusht-e gehrn-e in ey-ne bar mit leyvmuzeek gayen]

**living room** das Wohnzimmer [vohn-tsim-er]
- I can sleep in the living room ich kann im Wohnzimmer schlafen [ish kan im vohn-tsim-er shlaafen]

**loaf (of bread)** das Brot [broht]
- I'd like one of those large loaves ich hätte gerne eines dieser großen Brote [ish heh-te gehrn-e eynez deezer grohsen broht-e]

**local** *(newspaper, specialty)* lokal [lohkaal]; *(tradition, inhabitants)* örtlich [eurtlish]

▸ what's the local specialty? was ist die lokale Spezialität? [vas ist dee lohkaal-e shpehtsialitayt]

**lock** das Schloss [shlos] ◆ abschließen [ap-shleesen]
▸ the lock's broken das Schloss ist kaputt [das shlos ist kaput]
▸ I locked the door ich habe die Tür abgeschlossen [ish haa-be dee tuur ap-geshlos-en]

**lock out**
▸ to lock oneself out sich aussperren [zish ows-shpehren]
▸ I've locked myself out ich habe mich ausgesperrt [ish haa-be mish ows-ge-shpehrt]

**long** lang [lang] ◆ lange [lang-e]
▸ it's 10 feet long es ist zehn Fuß lang [ehs ist tsayn fus lang]
▸ I waited for a long time ich habe lange gewartet [ish haa-be lang-e ge-vartet]
▸ how long will it take? wie lange wird es dauern? [vee lang-e virt ehs dowern]
▸ we're not sure how long we're going to stay wir wissen noch nicht, wie lange wir bleiben [veer vis-en nokh nisht vee lang-e veer bleyben]

**look** (with eyes) der Blick [blik]; (appearance) das Aussehen [ows-zayen] ◆ (with eyes) schauen [showen]; (appear) aussehen [ows-zayen]
▸ could you have a look at my car? könnten Sie sich mein Auto ansehen? [keunten zee zish meyn owtoh anzayen]
▸ no, thanks, I'm just looking nein, danke, ich schaue mich nur um [neyn dank-e ish show-e mish noor um]
▸ what does she look like? wie sieht sie aus? [vee zeet zee ows]
▸ you look like your brother Sie sehen wie Ihr Bruder aus [zee zayen vee eer brooder ows]
▸ it looks like it's going to rain es sieht nach Regen aus [ehs zeet naakh raygen ows]

**look after** (ill person) sich kümmern um [zish kuumern um]; (child, luggage) aufpassen auf [owfpas-en owf]
▸ can someone look after the children for us? kann jemand für uns auf die Kinder aufpassen? [kan yaymant fuur uns owf dee kin-der owfpas-en]
▸ can you look after my things for a minute? können Sie für eine Minute auf meine Sachen aufpassen? [keunen zee fuur ey-ne minoot-e owf meyn-e zakhen owfpas-en]

**look for** suchen [zookhen]
▸ I'm looking for a good restaurant that serves regional cuisine ich suche ein gutes Restaurant, das regionale Gerichte serviert [ish zookh-e eyn gootez rehsteront das raygiohnaal-e gerisht-e zehrveert]

**lose** verlieren [fehrleeren]
▸ I've lost the key to my room ich habe meinen Zimmerschlüssel verloren [ish haa-be meynen tsim-er-shluusel fehrloren]
▸ I've lost my way ich habe mich verlaufen [ish haa-be mish fehrlowfen]

**lost** (key) verloren [fehrloren]
▸ who do you have to see about lost luggage? bei wem muss man verloren

gegangenem Gepäck melden? [bey vaym mus man fehrloren gegangenem gepehk mehlden]
- could you help me? I seem to be lost könnten Sie mir helfen? ich glaube, ich habe mich verirrt [keunten zee meer hehlfen ish glowb-e ish haab-e mish fehr-irt]
- to get lost sich verirren [zish fehr-ir-en]
- get lost! hau ab! [how ap]

**lost-and-found** das Fundbüro [funtbuuroh]
- where's the lost-and-found? wo ist das Fundbüro? [voh ist das funtbuuroh]

**(a) lot** viel [feel]
- a lot of viel [feel]
- are there a lot of things to see around here? gibt es hier in der Gegend viel zu sehen? [gipt ehs heer in dehr gaygent feel tsoo zayen]
- will there be a lot of other people there? werden dort viele Leute sein? [vehrden dort feel-e loyt-e zeyn]
- thanks a lot vielen Dank [feelen dank]

**loud** laut [lowt]
- the television is too loud der Fernseher ist zu laut [dehr fehrnzayer ist tsoo lowt]

**loudly** laut [lowt]
- can you speak a little more loudly? können Sie ein bisschen lauter sprechen? [keunen zee eyn bis-shen lowter shprehshen]

**love** lieben [leeben]
- I love you ich liebe dich [ish leeb-e dish]
- I love the movies ich gehe sehr gern ins Kino [ish gay-e zehr gehrn ins keenoh]
- I love cooking ich liebe es zu kochen [ish leeb-e ehs tsoo kokhen]

**lovely** wunderschön [vundersheun]; *(character)* nett [neht]
- what a lovely room! was für ein wunderschönes Zimmer! [vas fuur eyn vundersheunez tsim-er]
- it's lovely today es ist wunderschön heute [ehs ist vundersheun hoy-te]

**low** *(temperature, speed)* niedrig [needrish]
- temperatures are in the low twenties die Temperaturen liegen zwischen zwanzig und fünfundzwanzig Grad [dee tehmperatooren leegen tsvishen tsvantsish unt fuunf-unt-tsvantsish graat]

**low beam** das Abblendlicht [apblehndlisht]
- keep your lights on low beam fahren Sie mit Abblendlicht [faaren zee mit apblendlisht]

**lower** herunterlassen [hehrunterlas-en] ♦ *(in height)* niedriger [needriger]; *(part, level)* unterer [unterer]
- is it OK if I lower the blind a little? ist es in Ordnung, wenn ich das Rollo ein bisschen herunterlasse? [ist ehs in ordnung vehn ish das roloh eyn bis-shen hehrunterlas-e]

## lunch

Lunch (*Mittagessen*) used to be the main meal of the day but nowadays it's losing out to the modern practice of nibbling throughout the day! In Switzerland, it's called *Zmittag*.

▸ how do we get to the lower level? wie kommen wir in das untere Stockwerk? [vee kom-en veer in das unter-e shtokvehrk]

**low-fat** fettarm [fehtarm]
▸ do you have any low-fat yogurt? haben Sie fettarmen Jogurt? [haaben zee fehtarmen yogurt]

**low season** die Nebensaison [naybensayzon]
▸ what are prices like in the low season? wie sind die Preise in der Nebensaison? [vee zint dee preyz-e in dehr naybensayzon]

**low tide** die Ebbe [ehb-e]
▸ what time is low tide today? um wie viel Uhr setzt heute die Ebbe ein? [um vee feel oor zehtst hoy-te dee ehb-e eyn]

**luck** das Glück [gluuk]
▸ good luck! viel Glück! [feel gluuk]

**luggage** das Gepäck [gepehk]
▸ my luggage hasn't arrived mein Gepäck ist noch nicht angekommen [meyn gepehk ist nokh nisht an-gekom-en]
▸ I'd like to report the loss of my luggage ich möchte den Verlust meines Gepäcks melden [ish meusht-e dayn fehrlust meynez gepehks mehlden]

**luggage cart** der Gepäckwagen [gepehkvaagen]
▸ I'm looking for a luggage cart ich suche einen Gepäckwagen [ish zookh-e eynen gepehkvaagen]

**lunch** das Mittagessen [mitaak-ehsen]
▸ to have lunch zu Mittag essen [tsoo mitaak ehsen]
▸ what time is lunch served? um wie viel Uhr gibt es Mittagessen? [um vee feel oor gipt ehs mitaak-ehsen]

**machine-washable** waschmaschinenfest [vashmasheenenfehst]
▸ is it machine-washable? ist es waschmaschinenfest? [ist ehs vashmasheenenfehst]

**maid** das Zimmermädchen [tsim-er-maydshen]
▸ what time does the maid come? um wie viel Uhr kommt das Zimmermädchen? [um vee feel oor komt das tsim-er-maydshen]

**maid service** die Zimmerreinigung [tsim-er-reynigung]
▸ is there maid service? werden die Zimmer geputzt? [vehrden dee tsim-er ge-putst]

**mailbox** der Briefkasten [breefkasten]
▸ where's the nearest mailbox? wo ist der nächste Briefkasten? [voh ist dehr nehkste breefkasten]

**main course** der Hauptgang [howptgang]
▸ what are you having for your main course? was nehmen Sie als Hauptgang? [vas naymen zee als howptgang]

**mainline**
▸ where are the mainline trains? wo fahren die Schnellzüge ab? [voh faaren dee shnehl-tsuug-e ap]

**make** machen [makhen]
▸ how is this dish made? wie macht man dieses Gericht? [vee makht man deezez gerisht]
▸ I hope to make new friends here ich hoffe, dass ich hier neue Freunde finde [ish hof-e das ish heer noy-e froynd-e fin-de]

**make up** *(loss, difference)* ausgleichen [owsgleyshen]; *(invent)* sich ausdenken [zish owsdehnken]
▸ will we be able to make up the time we've lost? können wir die verlorene Zeit aufholen? [keunen veer dee fehrloren-e tseyt owfhohlen]

**man** der Mann [man]
▸ that man is bothering me dieser Mann belästigt mich [deezer man belehstisht mish]

**man-made** künstlich [kuunstlish]
▸ it's man-made es ist künstlich [ehs ist kuunstlish]

**many** viele [feel-e]
▸ there are many good restaurants here es gibt hier viele gute Restaurants [ehs gipt heer feel-e goot-e rehsteronts]
▸ how many? wie viele? [vee feel-e]
▸ how many days will you be staying? wie lange bleiben Sie? [vee lang-e bleyben zee]

**map** *(of country)* die Karte [kart-e]; *(of town, network)* der Plan [plan]
- where can I buy a map of the area? wo kann ich eine Karte dieser Gegend kaufen? [voh kan ish eyn-e kart-e deezer gaygent kowfen]
- can you show me where we are on the map? können Sie mir auf der Karte zeigen, wo wir sind? [keunen zee meer owf dehr kart-e tseygen voh veer zint]
- can I have a map of the subway? kann ich einen U-Bahn-Plan bekommen? [kan ish eynen oo-baan-plan bekom-en]

**March** der März [mehrts]
- March 1st der erste März [dehr ehrst-e mehrts]

**market** der Markt [markt]
- is there a market in the square every day? ist auf dem Platz jeden Tag Markt? [ist owf daym plats yayden taak markt]

**married** verheiratet [fehrheyraatet]
- are you married? sind Sie verheiratet? [zint zee fehrheyraatet]

**mass** *(religious)* die Messe [mehs-e]
- what time is mass? um wie viel Uhr ist Messe? [um vee feel oor ist mehs-e]

**match** *(for fire)* das Streichholz [shtreysh-holts]
- do you have any matches? haben Sie Streichhölzer? [haaben zee shtreysh-heultser]

**matter** wichtig sein [vishtish zeyn]
- it doesn't matter es macht nichts [ehs makht nishts]

**mattress** die Matratze [matrats-e]
- the mattresses are saggy die Matratzen sind durchgelegen [dee matratsen zint dursh-gelaygen]

**May** der Mai [mey]
- May 9th neunter Mai [noynter mey]

**maybe** vielleicht [feeleysht]
- maybe the weather will be better tomorrow vielleicht wird das Wetter morgen besser [feeleysht virt das veht-er morgen behs-er]

**meal** das Essen [ehsen]
- are meals included? ist das Essen inbegriffen? [ist das ehsen inbegrif-en]

**mean** *(signify)* bedeuten [bedoyten]; *(intend)* beabsichtigen [beapzishtigen]
- what does that word mean? was bedeutet das Wort? [vas bedoytet das vort]
- I mean it ich meine es ernst [ish meyn-e ehs ehrnst]
- I didn't mean it das war nicht meine Absicht [das var nisht meyn-e apzisht]

**meat** das Fleisch [fleysh]
- I don't eat meat ich esse kein Fleisch [ish ehs-e keyn fleysh]

**mechanic** der Mechaniker [mehkaaniker], die Mechanikerin [mehkaanikerin]
- what did the mechanic say was wrong with the car? was hat der Mechaniker gesagt, was mit dem Auto los ist? [vas hat dehr mehkaaniker gezaakt vas mit daym owtoh lohs ist]

## meeting up

In German-speaking countries punctuality reigns supreme. The Germans could be described as even more punctual than the Swiss! So, take care to arrive on time.

**medication** die Medikamente [mehdikamehnt-e]
> I'm not taking any other medication at the moment ich nehme im Moment keine anderen Medikamente [ish naym-e im mohmehnt keyn-e anderen mehdikamehnt-e]

**medicine** das Medikament [mehdikamehnt]
> how many times a day do I have to take the medicine? wie viel Mal am Tag muss ich das Medikament einnehmen? [vee feel mal am taak mus ish das mehdikamehnt eyn-naymen]

**medium** *(size)* mittlerer [mitlerer]; *(steak)* halbdurch [halpdursh] ♦ *(in size)* das Medium [maydium]
> I'd like my steak medium, please ich möchte mein Steak bitte halbdurch [ish meusht-e meyn stayk bi-te halpdursh]
> do you have this shirt in a medium? haben Sie dieses Hemd in Medium [haaben zee deezez hehmt in maydium]

**meet** *(by chance, arrangement)* treffen [trehfen]; *(make the acquaintance of)* kennen lernen [kehnenlehrnen] ♦ *(by chance, arrangement)* sich treffen [zish trehfen]; *(become acquainted)* sich kennen lernen [zish kehnen lehrnen]
> meet you at 9 o'clock in front of the town hall ich treffe Sie um neun Uhr vor dem Rathaus [ish trehf-e zee um noyn oor for daym raat-hows]
> I have to meet my friend at nine o'clock ich muss meinen Freund um neun Uhr treffen [ish mus meynen froynt um noyn oor trehfen]
> pleased to meet you freut mich, Sie kennen zu lernen [froyt mish zee kehnen tsoo lehrnen]
> goodbye! it was nice meeting you auf Wiedersehen! es war schön, Sie kennen zu lernen [owf veederzayen ehs var sheun zee kehnen tsoo lehrnen]
> Mr. Hendry, I'd like you to meet Mr. Merkle Herr Hendry, darf ich Ihnen Herrn Merkle vorstellen? [hehr hehndri darf ish eenen hehrn mehrkl-e for-shtehlen]
> where shall we meet? wo sollen wir uns treffen? [vo zol-en veer uns trehfen]
> what time are we meeting tomorrow? um wie viel Uhr treffen wir uns morgen? [um vee feel oor trehfen veer uns morgen]

**member** *(of club)* das Mitglied [mitgleet]
> do you have to be a member? muss man Mitglied sein? [mus man mitgleet zeyn]

**men's room** die Herrentoilette [hehrentoyleht-e]
> where's the men's room? wo ist die Herrentoilette? [voh ist dee hehrentoyleht-e]

**menu** die Speisekarte [shpeyzekart-e]

▸ can we see the menu? können Sie uns die Speisekarte bringen? [keunen zee uns dee shpeyzekart-e bringen]
▸ do you have a menu in English? haben Sie eine Speisekarte auf Englisch? [haaben zee ey-ne shpeyzekart-e owf ehnglish]
▸ do you have a children's menu? haben Sie eine Kinderkarte? [haaben zee ey-ne kin-der-kart-e]

**message** die Nachricht [naakh-risht]
▸ can you take a message? können Sie etwas ausrichten? [keunen zee ehtvas owsrishten]
▸ can I leave a message? kann ich eine Nachricht hinterlassen? [kan ish ey-ne naakh-risht hinterlas-en]
▸ did you get my message? haben Sie meine Nachricht bekommen? [haaben zee mey-ne naakh-risht bekom-en]

**meter** *(measurement)* der Meter [mayter]; *(device)* der Zähler [tsayler]
▸ it's about five meters long es ist ungefähr fünf Meter lang [ehs ist un-gefehr fuunf mayter lang]

**midday** der Mittag [mitaak]
▸ we have to be there by midday wir müssen um die Mittagszeit dort sein [veer meusen um dee mitaakz-tseyt dort zeyn]

**midnight** die Mitternacht [mit-er-nakht]
▸ it's midnight es ist Mitternacht [ehs ist mit-er-nakht]

**mileage** *(distance)* die Meilenzahl [meylen-tsaal]
▸ is there unlimited mileage? ist die Meilenzahl unbegrenzt? [ist dee meylen-tsaal un-be-grehntst]

**milk** die Milch [milsh]
▸ a gallon of milk eine Gallone Milch [ey-ne galohn-e milsh]
▸ tea with milk Tee mit Milch [tay mit milsh]

**milk chocolate** die Milchschokolade [milsh-shokohlaad-e]
▸ I prefer milk chocolate ich mag Milchschokolade lieber [ish maak milsh-shokohlaad-e leeber]

**mind** *(object)* etwas dagegen haben [ehtvas daagaygen haaben]
▸ I don't mind ich habe nichts dagegen [ish haa-be nishts daagaygen]
▸ do you mind if I smoke? haben Sie etwas dagegen, wenn ich rauche? [haaben zee ehtvas daagaygen vehn ish rowkh-e]
▸ do you mind if I open the window? haben Sie etwas dagegen, wenn ich das Fenster öffne? [haaben zee ehtvas daagaygen vehn ish das fehnster euf-ne]
▸ never mind macht nichts [makht nishts]

**mineral water** das Mineralwasser [mineraal-vas-er]
▸ could I have a bottle of mineral water, please? könnte ich bitte eine Flasche Mineralwasser haben? [keun-te ish bi-te ey-ne flash-e mineraal-vas-er haaben]

**minus** minus [meenus]

▸ it's minus two degrees outside! es sind draußen minus zwei Grad! [ehs zint drowsen meenus tsvey graat]

**minute** die Minute [minoot-e]

▸ we'll go in a minute wir gehen in einer Minute [veer gayen in eyner minoot-e]

**mirror** der Spiegel [shpeegel]

▸ the mirror's cracked der Spiegel hat einen Sprung [dehr shpeegel hat eynen shprung]

**miss** *(be too late for)* verpassen [fehrpas-en]; *(regret the absence of)* vermissen [fehrmis-en]

▸ I've missed my connection ich habe meinen Anschluss verpasst [ish haa-be meynen anshlus fehrpast]

▸ we're going to miss the train wir werden den Zug verpassen [veer vehrden dayn tsook fehrpas-en]

▸ I miss you ich vermisse dich [ish fehrmis-e dish]

**missing** *(person, aircraft)* vermisst [fehrmist]; *(object)* verschwunden [fehrsh-vunden]

▸ one of my suitcases is missing einer meiner Koffer fehlt [eyner meyner kof-er faylt]

**mistake** der Fehler [fayler]

▸ I think there's a mistake with the bill ich glaube, mit der Rechnung stimmt etwas nicht [ish glowb-e mit dehr rehshnung shtimt ehtvas nisht]

▸ you've made a mistake with my change Sie haben sich beim Rausgeben geirrt [zee haaben zish beym rowsgayben ge-irt]

**moment** der Augenblick [owgenblik]

▸ for the moment, we prefer staying in Berlin im Augenblick bleiben wir lieber in Berlin [im owgenblik bleyben veer leeber in behrleen]

**Monday** der Montag [mohntaak]

▸ we're arriving/leaving on Monday wir kommen am Montag an/wir reisen am Montag ab [veer kom-en am mohntaak an/veer reyzen am mohntaak ap]

**money** das Geld [gehlt]

▸ I don't have much money ich habe nicht viel Geld [ish haa-be nisht feel gehlt]

▸ where can I change money? wo kann ich Geld umtauschen? [voh kan ish gehlt umtowshen]

▸ I want my money back ich möchte mein Geld zurück [ish meusht-e meyn gehlt tsuruuk]

**money order** die Geldanweisung [gehlt-anveyzung]

▸ I'm waiting for a money order ich warte auf eine Geldanweisung [ish vart-e owf ey-ne gehlt-anveyzung]

**month** der Monat [mohnaat]

▸ I'm leaving in a month ich reise in einem Monat ab [ish reyz-e in eynem mohnaat ap]

**monument** das Denkmal [dehnkmal]
- what does this monument commemorate? woran erinnert dieses Denkmal? [vohran ehrinert deezez dehnkmal]

**more** mehr [mehr]
- this church is more beautiful diese Kirche ist schöner [deez-e kirsh-e ist sheuner]
- can we have some more bread? können wir etwas mehr Brot haben? [keunen vee ehtvas mehr broht haaben]
- a little more ein bisschen mehr [eyn bish-shen mehr]
- could I have a little more wine? könnte ich ein bisschen mehr Wein bekommen? [keun-te ish eyn bish-shen mehr veyn bekom-en]
- I don't want any more, thank you ich möchte nicht mehr, danke [ish meusht-e nisht mehr dank-e]
- I don't want to spend any more ich möchte nicht mehr ausgeben [ish meusht-e nisht mehr owsgayben]

**morning** der Morgen [morgen]
- the museum is open in the morning das Museum ist morgens geöffnet [das moozayum ist morgenz ge-eufnet]

**morning-after pill** die Pille danach [pil-e daanakh]
- I need the morning-after pill ich brauche die Pille danach [ish browkh-e dee pil-e daanakh]

**mosque** die Moschee [moshay]
- where's the nearest mosque? wo ist die nächste Moschee? [voh ist dee nehkst-e moshay]

**most** meiste [meyst-e] ♦ das meiste [meyst-e] ♦ *(to the greatest extent)* am meisten [am meysten]; *(very)* äußerst [oyserst]
- are you here most days? sind Sie meistens hier? [zint zee meystenz heer]
- that's the most I can offer mehr kann ich nicht bieten [mehr kan ish nisht beeten]

**mother** die Mutter [mut-er]
- this is my mother das ist meine Mutter [das ist meyn-e mut-er]

**motorboat** das Motorboot [mohtorboht]
- can we rent a motorboat? können wir ein Motorboot mieten? [keunen veer eyn mohtorboht meeten]

**motorcycle** das Motorrad [mohtor-raat]
- I'd like to rent a motorcycle ich möchte gerne ein Motorrad mieten [ish meusht-e gehrn-e eyn mohtor-raat meeten]

**mountain** der Berg [behrk]
- in the mountains in den Bergen [in dayn behrgen]

**mountain hut** die Berghütte [behrkhuut-e]
- we slept in a mountain hut wir haben in einer Berghütte geschlafen [veer haaben in eyner behrkhuut-e geshlaafen]

**move** *(movement)* die Bewegung [bevaygung]; *(step, measure)* der Schritt [shrit]
+ bewegen [bevaygen] + sich bewegen [zish bevaygen]
▶ I can't move my leg ich kann mein Bein nicht bewegen [ish kan meyn beyn nisht bevaygen]
▶ don't move him bewegen Sie ihn nicht [bevaygen zee een nisht]

**movie** der Film [film]
▶ have you seen his latest movie? haben Sie seinen neuesten Film gesehen? [haaben zee zeynen noyesten film gezayen]
▶ it's a subtitled movie es ist ein Film mit Untertiteln [ehs ist eyn film mit unterteeteln]

**movie theater** das Kino [keenoh]
▶ where is there a movie theater? wo ist hier ein Kino? [voh ist heer eyn keenoh]
▶ what's on at the movie theater? was läuft im Kino? [vas loyft im keenoh]

**much** viel [feel]
▶ I don't have much money ich habe nicht viel Geld [ish haa-be nisht feel gehlt]
▶ how much is it? wie viel kostet es? [vee feel kostet ehs]
▶ how much is it for one night? wie viel kostet eine Übernachtung? [vee feel kostet ey-ne uubernakhtung]
▶ how much is it per day and per person? wie viel kostet es pro Tag und pro Person? [vee feel kostet ehs proh taak unt proh pehrzohn]
▶ how much does it cost per hour? wie viel kostet es pro Stunde? [vee feel kostet ehs proh shtund-e]
▶ how much is a ticket to Bremen? wie viel kostet eine Fahrkarte nach Bremen? [vee feel kostet ey-ne faarkart-e naakh braymen ]

**museum** das Museum [moozayum]
▶ what time does the museum open? um wie viel Uhr macht das Museum auf? [um vee feel oor makht das moozayum owf]

**music** die Musik [muzeek]
▶ what kind of music do they play in that club? was für Musik spielen sie in dem Klub? [vas fuur muzeek shpeelen zee in daym klub]

**must** müssen [meus-en]
▶ that must cost a lot dass muss sehr teuer sein [das mus zehr toyer zeyn]

**mustard** der Senf [zehnf]
▶ is it strong mustard? ist der Senf würzig? [ist dehr zehnf vuurtsish]

# n

**nail** der Nagel [naagel]
- ▶ I need to cut my nails ich muss meine Nägel schneiden [ish mus meyn-e naygel shneyden]

**nail polish** der Nagellack [naagel-lak]
- ▶ I'd like to find nail polish in a dark shade of red ich suche einen Nagellack in einem dunklen Rot-Ton [ish zookh-e eynen naagel-lak in eynem dunklen roht-tohn]

**name** der Name [naam-e]
- ▶ what is your name? wie heißen Sie? [vee heysen zee]
- ▶ my name is Patrick ich heiße Patrick [ish heys-e patrik]
- ▶ I have a reservation in the name of Koch ich habe eine Reservierung auf den Namen Koch [ish haa-be ey-ne rehzerveerung owf dayn naamen kokh]

**napkin** die Serviette [sehrvi-et-e]
- ▶ could I have a clean napkin, please? könnte ich bitte eine saubere Serviette bekommen? [keun-te ish bi-te ey-ne zowber-e sehrvi-et-e bekom-en]

**national holiday** der gesetzliche Feiertag [gezehts-lish-e feyertaak]
- ▶ tomorrow is a national holiday morgen ist ein gesetzlicher Feiertag [morgen ist eyn gezehts-lisher feyertaak]

**nationality** die Staatsangehörigkeit [shtaats-angeheurishkeyt]
- ▶ what nationality are you? welche Staatsangehörigkeit haben Sie? [vehlsh-e shtaats-angeheurishkeyt haaben zee]

**nature** *(plants and animals)* die Natur [natoor]; *(essential qualities)* die Beschaffenheit [beshaf-en-heyt]; *(character)* das Wesen [vayzen]
- ▶ I like to take long walks and enjoy nature ich mache gerne lange Spaziergänge und genieße die Natur [ish makh-e gehrn-e lang-e shpatseer-gehng-e unt genees-e dee natoor]

**nausea** die Übelkeit [uubelkeyt]
- ▶ I've had nausea all day mir ist schon den ganzen Tag übel [meer ist shohn dayn gantsen taak uubel]

**near** nahe [naa-e] ◆ in der Nähe von [in dehr nay-e fon]
- ▶ where's the nearest subway station? wo ist die nächste U-Bahn-Station? [voh ist dee nehkst-e oo-baan-shtatsiohn]
- ▶ it's near the station es ist in der Nähe des Bahnhofs [ehs ist in dehr nay-e dez baanhohfs]
- ▶ very near ... ganz in der Nähe von ... [gants in dehr nay-e fon]

**nearby** in der Nähe [in dehr nay-e]
- is there a supermarket nearby? gibt es einen Supermarkt in der Nähe? [gipt ehs eynen zoopermarkt in dehr nay-e]

**neck** der Hals [hals]
- I have a sore neck mir tut der Hals weh [meer toot dehr hals vay]

**need** das Bedürfnis [beduurfnis] ♦ brauchen [browkhen] ♦ müssen [muus-en]
- I need something for a cough ich brauche etwas gegen Husten [ish browkh-e ehtvas gaygen husten]
- I need to be at the airport by six o'clock ich muss um sechs Uhr am Flughafen sein [ish mus um zeks oor am flookhaafen zeyn]
- we need to go wir müssen gehen [veer muus-en gayen]

**neither** keiner [keyner] ♦ weder [vayder]; auch nicht [owkh nisht]
- neither of us keiner von uns [keyner fon uns]
- me neither ich auch nicht [ish owkh nisht]

**neutral** neutral [noytraal]
- make sure the car's in neutral vergessen Sie nicht den Gang herauszunehmen [fehrgehs-en zee nisht dayn gang hehrows-tsunaymen]

**never** nie [nee]
- I've never been to Germany before ich bin noch nie in Deutschland gewesen [ish bin nokh nee in doytshlant gevayzen]

**new** neu [noy]
- could we have a new tablecloth, please? könnten wir bitte eine neue Tischdecke bekommen? [keunten veer bi-te ey-ne noy-e tishdek-e bekom-en]

**news** (information) die Nachricht [nakh-risht]; (on TV, radio) die Nachrichten [nakh-rishten]; (recent development) die Neuigkeit [noyishkeyt]
- a piece of news eine Neuigkeit [ey-ne noyishkeyt]
- that's great news! das sind wunderbare Nachrichten! [das zint vunderbar-e nakh-rishten]
- I heard it on the news ich habe es in den Nachrichten gehört [ish haa-be ehs in dayn nakh-rishten geheurt]

**newspaper** der Zeitung [tseytung]
- do you have any English-language newspapers? haben Sie englische Zeitungen? [haaben zee ehnglish-e tseytungen]

**New Year** das Neujahr [noy-yaar]
- Happy New Year! gutes neues Jahr! [gootez noyez yaar]

**New Year's Day** das Neujahr [noy-yaar]
- are stores open on New Year's Day? sind die Geschäfte an Neujahr geöffnet? [zint dee geshehft-e an noy-yaar ge-eufnet]

**next** nächster [nehkster] ◆ **next to** neben [nayben]

▸ when is the next guided tour? wann findet die nächste Führung statt? [van findet dee nehkst-e fuurung shtat]

▸ when is the next train to Hamburg? wann fährt der nächste Zug nach Hamburg? [van fehrt dehr nehkst-e tsook naakh hamburk]

▸ what time is the next flight to Berlin? wann geht der nächste Flug nach Berlin? [van gayt dehr nehkst-e flook naakh behrleen]

▸ can we park next to the tent? können wir neben dem Zelt parken? [keunen veer nayben daym tsehlt parken]

**nice** *(vacation)* schön [sheun]; *(food)* gut [goot]; *(kind, likable)* nett [neht]

▸ have a nice vacation! schöne Ferien! [sheun-e fehrien]

▸ we found a really nice little hotel wir haben ein richtig nettes kleines Hotel gefunden [veer haaben eyn rishtish nehtez kleynez hohtehl gefunden]

▸ it was nice meeting you ich habe mich gefreut Sie kennen zu lernen [ish haa-be mish gefroyt zee kehnen tsoo lehrnen]

**night** die Nacht [nakht]

▸ how much is it per night? wie viel kostet es pro Nacht? [vee feel kostet ehs proh nakht]

▸ I'd like to stay an extra night ich möchte gerne eine weitere Nacht bleiben [ish meusht-e gehrn-e ey-ne veyter-e nakht bleyben]

**nightclub** der Nachtklub [nakhtklub]

▸ are there any good nightclubs in this town? gibt es gute Nachtklubs hier in der Stadt? [gipt ehs goot-e nakhtklubs heer in dehr shtat]

**nine** neun [noyn]

▸ there are nine of us wir sind zu neunt [veer zint tsoo noynt]

▸ we have a reservation for nine o'clock wir haben eine Reservierung für neun Uhr [veer haaben ey-ne rehzerveerung fuur noyn oor]

**no** nein [neyn] ◆ **kein** [keyn]

▸ no thanks! nein danke! [neyn dank-e]

▸ a cup of tea with no milk or sugar, please eine Tasse Tee ohne Milch und Zucker, bitte [ey-ne tas-e tay ohn-e milsh unt tsuk-er bi-te]

**nobody** niemand [neemant]

▸ there's nobody at the reception desk es ist niemand an der Rezeption [ehs ist neemant an dehr reh-tsehp-tsiohn]

**noise** *(sound)* das Geräusch [geroysh]; *(loud, irritating)* der Lärm [lehrm]

▸ to make a noise ein Geräusch machen [eyn geroysh makhen]

▸ I heard a funny noise ich habe ein komisches Geräusch gehört [ish haa-be eyn kohmishez geroysh geheurt]

**noisy** laut [lowt]

▸ I'd like another room: mine is too noisy ich hätte gerne ein anderes Zimmer, meines ist zu laut [ish heh-te gehrn-e eyn anderez tsim-er meynez ist tsoo lowt]

**nonsmoker** der Nichtraucher [nishtrowkher], die Nichtraucherin [nisthrowkherin]
▸ we're nonsmokers wir sind Nichtraucher [veer zint nishtrowkher]

**nonsmoking** Nichtraucher- [nishtrowkher]
▸ is this restaurant nonsmoking? ist dies ein Nichtraucherrestaurant? [ist deez eyn nishtrowkher-rehsteront]

**nonsmoking compartment** das Nichtraucherabteil [nishtrowkher-apteyl]
▸ I'd like a seat in a nonsmoking compartment ich hätte gerne einen Platz in einem Nichtraucherabteil [ish heh-te gehrn-e eynen plats in eynem nishtrowkher-apteyl]

**nonsmoking section** der Nichtraucherbereich [nishtrowkher-bereysh]
▸ do you have a nonsmoking section? haben Sie einen Nichtraucherbereich? [haaben zee eynen nishtrowkher-bereysh]

**nonstop** *(flight)* Nonstop- [nonstop]; *(train)* durchgehend [durshgayent] ◆ *(fly)* nonstop [nonstop]; *(talk)* ununterbrochen [ununterbrokhen]
▸ I'd like a nonstop flight from Berlin to Chicago ich möchte einen Nonstopflug von Berlin nach Chicago [ish meusht-e eynen nonstopflook fon berhleen naakh shikaagoh]

**noon** der Mittag [mitaak]
▸ we leave at noon wir fahren um zwölf Uhr mittags [veer faaren um tsveulf oor mitaakz]

**no one** niemand [neemant]
▸ there's no one there es ist niemand da [ehs ist neemant daa]

**normal** normal [normaal]
▸ is it normal for it to rain as much as this? ist es normal, dass es so viel wie jetzt regnet? [ist ehs normaal das ehs zoh feel vee yehtst raygnet]

**not** nicht [nisht]
▸ I don't like spinach ich mag keinen Spinat [ish maak keynem shpinaat]
▸ I don't think so ich glaube nicht [ish glowb-e nisht]
▸ not at all ganz und gar nicht [gants unt gar nisht]

**note** die Notiz [nohtits]
▸ could I leave a note for him? könnte ich ihm eine Notiz hinterlassen? [keun-te ish eem ey-ne nohtits hinterlas-en]

**nothing** nichts [nishts]
▸ there's nothing to do here in the evening hier ist abends nichts los [heer ist aabents nishts lohs]
▸ there's nothing I can do about it da kann ich nichts machen [daa kan ish nishts makhen]

**November** der November [nohvehmber]
▸ November 7th siebter November [zeebter nohvehmber]

**now** jetzt [yehtst]
  ▸ what should we do now? was sollen wir jetzt machen? [vas zol-en veer yehtst makhen]

**number** *(of phone, room etc.)* die Nummer [num-er]; *(numeral)* die Zahl [tsaal]; *(quantity)* die Anzahl [antsaal]
  ▸ my name is... and my number is... mein Name ist ... und meine Nummer ist ... [meyn naam-e ist unt meyn-e num-er ist]

**occupied** *(bathroom)* besetzt [bezehtst]
  ▸ the restroom's occupied die Toilette ist besetzt [dee toyleht-e ist bezehtst]

**ocean** das Meer [mehr]
  ▸ we'd like to see the ocean while we're here wir würden gerne ans Meer fahren, während wir hier sind [veer vuurden gehrn-e ans mehr faaren vehrent veer heer sint]

**o'clock**
  ▸ it's eight o'clock es ist acht Uhr [ehs ist akht oor]

**October** der Oktober [oktohber]
  ▸ October 12th zwölfter Oktober [tsveulfter oktohber]

**of** von [fon]
  ▸ one of us einer von uns [eyner fon uns]

**off** *(indicating movement)* weg [vehk] ◆ *(at a distance from)* entfernt [ehntfehrnt]; *(deducted from)* billiger [biliger]
  ▸ an island off the coast of Germany eine Insel vor der Küste Deutschlands [ey-ne inzel for dehr kuust-e doytshlants]
  ▸ this sweater is 50 percent off! dieser Pullover ist fünfzig Prozent billiger! [deezer pulohver ist fuunf-tsish proh-tsehnt biliger]

**offer** anbieten [anbeeten]
  ▸ can I offer you a cigarette? kann ich Ihnen eine Zigarette anbieten? [kan ish eenen ey-ne tsigareht-e anbeeten]

**office** das Büro [buuroh]
  ▸ where is the hotel office? wo ist das Hotelbüro? [voh ist das hohtehl-buuroh]

**often** oft [oft]
  ▸ how often does the ferry sail? wie oft fährt die Fähre? [vee oft fehrt dee fehr-e]

**oil** das Öl [eul]
  ▸ could you check the oil, please? könnten Sie bitte das Öl nachsehen? [keunten zee bi-te das eul nakhzayen]

**OK** okay [ohkay]
- ▶ that's OK das ist okay [das ist ohkay]
- ▶ I'd like to have breakfast at 6 if that's OK ich möchte um sechs frühstücken. wenn das geht [ish meusht-e um zehks fruushtuuken vehn das gayt]

**old** alt [alt]
- ▶ how old are you? wie alt sind Sie? [vee alt zint zee]
- ▶ I'm 18 years old ich bin achtzehn Jahre alt [ish bin akht-tsayn yaar-e alt]
- ▶ have you visited the old town? haben Sie die Altstadt besucht? [haaben zee dee altshtat bezookht]

**on** *(working)* an [an] ◆ *(on top of)* auf [owf]
- ▶ the tickets are on the table die Fahrkarten liegen auf dem Tisch [dee faarkarten leegen owf daym tish]
- ▶ how long is the film on for at the cinema? wie lange wird der Film im Kino gezeigt? [vee lang-e virt dehr film im Kino getseykt]

**once** einmal [eynmal] ◆ **at once** sofort [zohfort]
- ▶ I've been here once before ich war schon einmal hier [ish var shohn eynmal heer]
- ▶ please do it at once machen Sie es bitte sofort [makhen zee ehs bi-te zohfort]

**one** eins [eyns]
- ▶ a table for one, please ein Tisch für eine Person, bitte [eyn tish fuur ey-ne pehrzohn bi-te]

**one-way (ticket)** die einfache Fahrkarte [eynfakh-e faarkart-e]
- ▶ how much is a one-way ticket downtown? wie viel kostet eine einfache Fahrkarte ins Stadtzentrum? [vee feel kostet ey-ne eynfakh-e faarkart-e ins shtat-tsehntrum]
- ▶ a second-class one-way ticket to Ulm eine einfache Fahrkarte zweiter Klasse nach Ulm [ey-ne eynfakh-e faarkart-e tsveyter klas-e naakh ulm]

**only** nur [noor]
- ▶ that's the only one left das ist das Einzige, das es noch gibt [das ist das eyntsig-e das ehs nokh gipt]

---

### opinions

- ▶ personally, I don't think it's fair ich persönlich finde es nicht fair [ish pehrzeunlish fin-de ehs nisht fehr]
- ▶ I think he's right ich finde er hat Recht [ish fin-de ehr hat rehsht]
- ▶ I don't want to say ich will es nicht sagen [ish vil ehs nisht zaagen]
- ▶ I'm not sure ich bin mir nicht sicher [ish bin meer nisht zisher]
- ▶ no idea! keine Ahnung! [keyn-e aanung]
- ▶ it depends es kommt darauf an [ehs komt daarowf an]

A waiter will come and take your order and not expect you to pay until later. In a bar he often marks what you're having on a cardboard coaster and tallies it up at the end.

**open** *(door, window)* offen [offen]; *(store)* geöffnet [ge-eufnet] ♦ *(door, window)* aufmachen [owfmakhen]; *(store)* öffnen [eufnen] ♦ *(of door, window)* aufgehen [owfgayen]

> ‣ is the bank open at lunchtime? hat die Bank mittags geöffnet? [hat dee bank mitaakz ge-eufnet]
> ‣ is the museum open all day? hat das Museum den ganzen Tag geöffnet? [hat das moozayum dayn gantsen taak ge-eufnet]
> ‣ at what time is ... open? um wie viel Uhr öffnet ...? [um vee feel oor eufnet]
> ‣ can I open the window? kann ich das Fenster aufmachen? [kan ish das fehnster owfmakhen]
> ‣ what time do you open? um wie viel Uhr öffnen Sie? [um vee feel oor eufnen zee]

**open-air** im Freien [im freyen]

> ‣ is there an open-air swimming pool? gibt es dort ein Freibad? [gipt ehs dort eyn freybaat]

**operating room** der Operationssaal [operatsiohnz-zaal]

> ‣ is she still in the operating room? ist sie noch im Operationssaal? [ist zee nokh im operatsiohnz-zaal]

**opinion** die Meinung [meynung]

> ‣ in my opinion, ... meiner Meinung nach ... [meyner meynung naakh] ♦ see box on p. 97

**orange** *(flavor)* Orangen- [orondzhen]; *(in color)* orangefarben [orondzh-e-farben] ♦ *(fruit)* die Orange [orondzh-e]; *(color)* das Orange [orondzh-e]

> ‣ I'd like a pound of oranges ich hätte gerne ein Pfund Orangen [ish heh-te gehrn-e eyn pfunt orondzhen]

**orange juice** der Orangensaft [orondzhenzaft]

> ‣ I'll have a glass of orange juice ich nehme ein Glas Orangensaft [ish naym-e eyn glaas orondzhenzaft]
> ‣ I'd like a freshly squeezed orange juice ich hätte gerne einen frisch gepressten Orangensaft [ish heh-te gehrn-e eynen frish ge-prehsten orondzhenzaft]

**order** *(for food, goods)* die Bestellung [beshtehlung] ♦ *(food, goods, in café)* bestellen [beshtehlen]

> ‣ this isn't what I ordered: I asked for... das ist nicht, was ich bestellt habe; ich habe ... bestellt [das ist nisht vas ish beshtehlt haa-be ish haa-be beshtehlt]
> ‣ I ordered a coffee ich habe einen Kaffee bestellt [ish haa-be eynen kafay beshtehlt]
> ‣ we'd like to order now wir möchten jetzt gerne bestellen [veer meushten yehtst gehrn-e beshtehlen]

**organize** organisieren [organizeeren]
- can you organize the whole trip for us? können Sie die ganze Reise für uns organisieren? [keunen zee dee gants-e reyz-e fuur uns organizeeren]

**other** anderer [anderer] ◆ andere [ander-e]
- I'll have the other one ich nehme das andere [ish naym-e das ander-e]
- on the other side of the street auf der anderen Straßenseite [owf dehr anderen shtraasen-zeyt-e]
- I'm going to wait for the others ich warte noch auf die anderen [ish vaart-e nokh owf dee anderen]

**out-of-date** *(passport)* abgelaufen [apgelowfen]; *(old-fashioned)* veraltet [fehraltet]
- I think my passport is out-of-date ich glaube, mein Reisepass ist abgelaufen [ish glowb-e meyn reyzepas ist apgelowfen]

**outside call** der externe Anruf [ehkstern-e anroof]
- I'd like to make an outside call ich möchte gerne einen externen Anruf machen [ish meusht-e gehrn-e eynen ehksternen anroof makhen]

**outside line** die externe Leitung [ehkstern-e leytung]
- how do I get an outside line? wie bekomme ich eine externe Leitung? [vee bekom-e ish eyn-e ehkstern-e leytung]

**overheat** heiß laufen [heys lowfen]
- the engine is overheating der Motor läuft heiß [dehr mohtor loyft heys]

**owner** der Besitzer [bezitser], die Besitzerin [bezitserin]
- do you know who the owner is? kennen Sie den Besitzer? [kehnen zee dayn bezitser]

# p

**pack** *(of cigarettes, chewing gum)* die Packung [pakung] ◆ packen [pak-en]
- how much is a pack of cigarettes? was kostet eine Packung Zigaretten? [vas kostet ey-ne pakung tsigarehten]
- I need to pack ich muss packen [ish mus pak-en]

**package** das Paket [pakayt]
- I'd like to send this package to Hamburg by airmail ich möchte dieses Paket per Luftpost nach Hamburg schicken [ish meusht-e deezez pakayt per luftpost naakh hamburg shiken]

**package tour** die Pauschalreise [powshaalreyz-e]
- it's my first time on a package tour ich mache zum ersten Mal eine Pauschalreise [ich makh-e tsum ehrsten mal ey-ne powshaalreyz-e]

**padlock** das Vorhängeschloss [for-hehng-e-shlos]
▸ I'd like to buy a padlock for my bike **ich möchte ein Fahrradschloss kaufen** [ish meusht-e eyn faar-raat-shlos kowfen]

**pain** *(physical)* der Schmerz [shmehrts]
▸ I'd like something for pain **ich hätte gerne etwas gegen Schmerzen** [ish heht-e gehrn-e ehtvas gaygen shmehrtsen]
▸ I have a pain here **ich habe hier Schmerzen** [ish haab-e heer shmehrtsen]

**painkiller** das Schmerzmittel [shmehrtsmitel]
▸ I have a really bad toothache: can you give me a painkiller, please? **ich habe starke Zahnschmerzen, können Sie mir bitte ein Schmerzmittel geben?** [ish haab-e shtark-e tsaanshmehrtsen keunen zee meer bi-te eyn shmehrtsmitel gayben]

**pair** *(of gloves, socks)* das Paar [par]
▸ a pair of shoes **ein Paar Schuhe** [eyn par shoo-e]
▸ a pair of pants **eine Hose** [ey-ne hohz-e]
▸ do you have a pair of scissors? **haben Sie eine Schere?** [haaben zee ey-ne shehr-e]

**pants** die Hose [hohz-e]
▸ a pair of pants **eine Hose** [ey-ne hohz-e]
▸ there is a hole in these pants **die Hose hat ein Loch** [dee hohz-e hat eyn lokh]

**pantyhose** die Strumpfhose [shtrumpfhohz-e]
▸ I got a run in my pantyhose **ich habe eine Laufmasche in meiner Strumpfhose** [ish haab-e ey-ne lowfmash-e in meyner shtrumpfhohz-e]

**paper** *(for writing on)* das Papier [papeer]; *(newspaper)* die Zeitung [tseytung]
**• papers** *(official documents)* die Papiere [papeer-e]
▸ a piece of paper **ein Blatt Papier** [eyn blat papeer]
▸ here are my papers **hier sind meine Papiere** [heer zint meyn-e papeer-e]

**parasol** der Sonnenschirm [zon-en-shirm]
▸ can you rent parasols? **kann man Sonnenschirme mieten?** [kan man zon-en-shirm-e meeten]

**pardon** *(forgive)* verzeihen [fehrtseyen]
▸ I beg your pardon! *(to apologize)* **Verzeihung!** [fehrtseyung]; *(showing disagreement)* **erlauben Sie mal!** [ehrlowben zee mal]
▸ I beg your pardon? *(asking for repetition)* **wie bitte?** [vee bi-te]
▸ pardon me? *(asking for repetition)* **wie bitte?** [vee bi-te]
▸ pardon me! *(to get past, to apologize)* **Verzeihung!** [fehrtseyung]; *(showing disagreement)* **erlauben Sie mal!** [ehrlowben zee mal]

**park** parken [parken]
▸ can we park our trailer here? **können wir unseren Wohnwagen hier parken?** [keunen veer unzeren vohnvaagen heer parken]
▸ am I allowed to park here? **darf ich hier parken?** [darf ish heer parken]

**parking** die Parkmöglichkeit [parkmeuglishkeyt]

▸ is there any parking near the hostel? **gibt es eine Parkmöglichkeit in der Nähe der Jugendherberge?** [gipt ehs ey-ne parkmeuglishkeyt in dehr nay-e dehr yoogent-hehrbehrg-e]

**parking lot** der Parkplatz [parkplats]

▸ is there a parking lot nearby? **gibt es in der Nähe einen Parkplatz?** [gipt ehs in dehr nay-e eynen parkplats]

**parking space** der Parkplatz [parkplats]

▸ is it easy to find a parking space in town? **findet man leicht einen Parkplatz in der Stadt?** [fin-det man leysht eynen parkplats in dehr shtat]

**part** der Teil [teyl]

▸ what part of Germany are you from? **aus welchem Teil Deutschlands kommen Sie?** [aus vehlshem teyl doytshlants kom-en zee ]

▸ I've never been to this part of Germany before **in diesem Teil Deutschlands bin ich noch nie gewesen** [in deezem teyl doytshlants bin ish nokh nee gevayzen]

**party** *(celebration)* die Party [parti] ◆ feiern [feyern]

▸ I'm planning a little party tomorrow **ich will morgen eine kleine Party machen** [ish vil morgen ey-ne kleyn-e parti makhen]

**pass** *(hand)* reichen [reyshen]; *(in a car)* überholen [uuberhohlen]

▸ can you pass me the salt? **können Sie mir das Salz reichen?** [keunen zee meer das zalts reyshen]

▸ can you pass on this road? **darf man auf dieser Straße überholen?** [darf man owf deezer shtraas-e uuberhohlen]

**passage** *(corridor)* der Gang [gang]

▸ I heard someone outside in the passage **ich habe draußen auf dem Gang jemanden gehört** [ish haab-e drowsen owf daym gang yaymanden geheurt]

**passenger** der Passagier [pasa-zheer], die Passagierin [pasa-zheerin]

▸ is this where the passengers from the Cologne flight arrive? **kommen hier die Passagiere aus Köln an?** [kom-en heer dee pasa-zheer-e ows keuln an]

**passport** der Pass [pas]

▸ I've lost my passport **ich habe meinen Pass verloren** [ish haab-e meynen pas fehrlohren]

▸ I forgot my passport **ich habe meinen Pass vergessen** [ish haab-e meynen pas fehrgehsen]

▸ my passport has been stolen **mein Pass wurde gestohlen** [meyn pas vurd-e geshtohlen]

**past** *(in place)* an ... vorbei [an forbey]; *(in time)* nach [naakh]

▸ we've just gone past the castle **wir sind gerade am Schloss vorbeigefahren** [veer zint geraad-e am shlos forbeygefaaren]

▸ twenty past twelve **zwanzig nach zwölf** [tsvantsish naakh tsveulf]

**path** *(track)* der Weg [vayk]
> is the path well-marked? ist der Weg gut ausgeschildert? [ist dehr vayk goot owsgeshildert]

**pay** zahlen [tsaalen] ◆ *(person, bill, fine)* bezahlen [betsaalen]
> do you have to pay to get in? muss man Eintritt zahlen? [mus man eyntrit tsaalen]
> can you pay by credit card? kann man mit Kreditkarte zahlen? [kan man mit krehdeetkart-e tsaalen]
> do I have to pay a deposit? muss ich eine Anzahlung machen? [mus ish ey-ne antsaalung makhen]
> we're going to pay separately wir zahlen getrennt [veer tsaalen getrehnt]

**paying guest** der zahlende Gast [tsaalend-e gast]
> how many paying guests do you have? wie viele zahlende Gäste haben Sie? [vee feel-e tsaalend-e gehst-e haaben zee]

**pay-per-view TV** das Pay-per-View-Fernsehen [pay-per-vyoo-fehrnzayen]
> is there pay-per-view TV in the room? gibt es Pay-per-View-Fernsehen im Zimmer? [gipt ehs pay-per-vyoo-fehrnzayen im tsim-er]

**pedestrian** der Fußgänger [foosgehnger], die Fußgängerin [foosgehngerin] ◆ Fußgänger- [foosgehnger]
> is this just a pedestrian street? ist die Straße nur für Fußgänger? [ist dee shtraas-e noor fuur foosgehnger]

**pedestrian mall** die Fußgängerzone [foosgehnger-tsohn-e]
> can you direct me to the pedestrian mall? können Sie mir sagen, wie ich zur Fußgängerzone komme? [keunen zee meer zaagen vee ish tsoor foosgehnger-tsohn-e kom-e]

**pen** der Stift [shtift]
> can you lend me a pen? können Sie mir einen Stift leihen? [keunen zee meer eynen shtift leyen]

**pencil** der Bleistift [bleyshtift]
> can you lend me a pencil? können Sie mir einen Bleistift leihen? [keunen zee meer eynen bleyshtift leyen]

**penicillin** das Penicillin [pehnitsileen]

> I'm allergic to penicillin ich bin allergisch gegen Penicillin [ish bin alehrgish gaygen pehnitsileen]

**pepper** der Pfeffer [pfehfer]

> pass the pepper, please können Sie mir bitte den Pfeffer reichen? [keunen zee meer bi-te dayn pfehfer reyshen]

**percent** das Prozent [prohtsehnt]

> could you knock 10 percent off the price? können Sie mir zehn Prozent Preisnachlass geben? [keunen zee meer tsayn prohtsehnt preysnakhlas gayben]

**performance** *(show)* die Vorführung [forfuurung]; *(in a movie theater)* die Vorstellung [forshtehlung]

> what time does the performance begin? wann beginnt die Vorführung? [van begint dee forfuurung]

**perfume** das Parfüm [parfuum]

> how much is this perfume? was kostet das Parfüm? [vas kostet das parfuum]

**perhaps** vielleicht [feeleysht]

> perhaps you can help me? können Sie mir vielleicht helfen? [keunen zee meer feeleysht hehlfen]

**person** die Person [pehrzohn]

> how much is it per hour and per person? was kostet es pro Stunde und pro Person? [vas kostet ehs proh shtund-e unt proh pehrzohn]

**pet** das Haustier [howsteer]

> are pets allowed? sind Haustiere erlaubt? [zint howsteer-e ehrlowbt]

**phone** das Telefon [tehlefohn] ♦ anrufen [anroofen] ♦ telefonieren [tehlefohneeren]

> can I use the phone? kann ich das Telefon benutzen? [kan ish das tehlefohn benutsen]

---

## on the phone

> hello? hallo? [haloh]
> Joe Stewart speaking hier spricht Joe Stewart [heer shprisht dzhoh stooart]
> I'd like to speak to Jack Adams ich möchte gerne mit Jack Adams sprechen [ish meusht-e gehrn-e mit dzhak adamz shprehshen]
> please hold the line bitte warten Sie [bi-te varten zee]
> can you call back in ten minutes? können Sie in zehn Minuten zurückrufen? [keunen zee in tsayn minooten tsuruukroofen]
> would you like to leave a message? möchten Sie eine Nachricht hinterlassen? [meushten zee ey-ne nakh-risht hinterlas-en]
> you have the wrong number Sie haben sich verwählt [zee haaben zish fehrvaylt]

**phone booth** die Telefonzelle [tehlefohn-tsehl-e]
- is there a phone booth near here? **gibt es in der Nähe eine Telefonzelle?** [gipt ehs in dehr nay-e ey-ne tehlefohn-tsehl-e]

**phone call** der Anruf [anroof]
- there's a call for you! **ein Anruf für Sie!** [eyn anroof fuur zee]
- I'd like to make a phone call **ich würde gerne telefonieren** [ish vuurd-e gehrn-e tehlefohneeren]

**phonecard** die Telefonkarte [tehlefohnkart-e]
- where can I buy a phonecard? **wo kann ich eine Telefonkarte kaufen?** [voh kan ish ey-ne tehlefohnkart-e kowfen]

**photo** das Foto [fohtoh]
- could you take a photo of us? **können Sie ein Foto von uns machen?** [keunen zee eyn fohtoh fon uns makhen]
- I'd like copies of some photos **ich möchte ein paar Fotos nachmachen lassen** [ish meusht-e eyn par fohtohz nakhmakhen las-en]
- can I take photos in here? **darf ich hier fotografieren?** [darf ish heer fohtohgrafeeren]

**photography**
- is photography allowed in the museum? **darf man im Museum fotografieren?** [darf man im moozayum fohtohgrafeeren]

**picnic** das Picknick [piknik]
- shall we go for a picnic by the river? **wollen wir ein Picknick am Fluss machen?** [vol-en veer eyn piknik am floos makhen]

**piece** das Stück [shtuuk]
- a piece of cake, please **ein Stück Kuchen, bitte** [eyn shtuuk kookhen bi-te]
- a piece of advice **ein Ratschlag** [eyn raatshlaak]
- a piece of news **eine Neuigkeit** [ey-ne noyishkeyt]

**pill** die Tablette [tableht-e]
- a bottle of pills **ein Tablettenfläschchen** [eyn tablehten-flehsh-shen]
- the Pill *(contraceptive)* **die Pille** [dee pil-e]

**pillow** das Kissen [kis-en]
- could I have another pillow? **kann ich noch ein Kissen haben?** [kan ish nokh eyn kis-en haaben]

**pizza** die Pizza [pitsa]
- I'd like a large mushroom pizza **ich hätte gerne eine große Pizza mit Pilzen** [ish heht-e gehrn-e ey-ne grohs-e pitsa mit piltsen]

**place** *(area, town)* der Ort [ort]; *(house)* die Wohnung [vohnung]; *(seat)* der Platz [plats]; *(place setting)* das Gedeck [gedehk]
- do you want to change places with me? **wollen wir Plätze tauschen?** [vol-en veer plehts-e towshen]

▸ can you recommend a nice place to eat? **können Sie mir ein gutes Restaurant empfehlen?** [keunen zee meer eyn gootez rehsteront ehmpfaylen]

**plain** *(simple)* einfach [eynfakh]; *(clear)* klar [klar]; *(yoghurt)* Natur- [natoor]

▸ do you have any plain yogurt? **haben Sie Naturjoghurt?** [haaben zee natoor-yogoort]

**plan** der Plan [plan] ◆ *(organize)* planen [planen]; *(intend)* vorhaben [forhaaben]

▸ do you have plans for tonight? **haben Sie heute Abend etwas vor?** [haaben zee hoyt-e aabent ehtvas for]

▸ I'm planning to stay for just one night **ich will nur eine Nacht bleiben** [ish vil noor ey-ne nakht bleyben]

**plane** das Flugzeug [flooktsoyk]

▸ when's the next plane to Stuttgart? **wann geht der nächste Flug nach Stuttgart?** [van gayt dehr nehkst-e flook nakh shtutgart]

▸ which gate does the plane depart from? **von welchem Gate startet der Flug?** [fon vehlshem gayt shtartet dehr flook]

**plate** der Teller [tehler]

▸ this plate's got a crack in it **der Teller hat einen Sprung** [dehr tehler hat eynen shprung]

**platform** *(at a station)* der Bahnsteig [baanshteyk]

▸ which platform does the train leave from? **von welchem Bahnsteig fährt der Zug?** [fon vehlshem baanshteyk fehrt dehr tsook]

**play** *(at a theater)* das Stück [shtuuk] ◆ spielen [shpeelen]

▸ do you play tennis? **spielen Sie Tennis?** [shpeelen zee tehnis]

▸ I play the cello **ich spiele Cello** [ish shpeel-e tshehloh]

**playroom** das Spielzimmer [shpeeltsim-er]

▸ is there a children's playroom? **haben Sie ein Kinderspielzimmer?** [haaben zee eyn kin-der-shpeeltsim-er]

**please** bitte [bi-te]

▸ please sit down **bitte setzen Sie sich** [bi-te zehtsen zee zish]

▸ can I come in? – please do **kann ich hereinkommen? – ja, bitte** [kan ish hehreynkom-en yaa bi-te]

**pleased** erfreut [ehrfroyt]

▸ pleased to meet you **es freut mich, Sie kennenzulernen** [ehs froyt mish zee kehnen-tsu-lehrnen]

**pleasure** das Vergnügen [fehrgnuugen]

▸ with pleasure! **mit Vergnügen!** [mit fehrgnuugen]

▸ it's a pleasure **es ist mir ein Vergnügen** [ehs ist meer eyn fehrgnuugen]

## police

German police officers are usually very pleasant with tourists (some of them do speak English). You'll spot their cars with their green paint jobs and the word *Polizei* written on them. However, if one of them asks you to *bitte folgen*, it's best to do as he says and follow him.

**plug** *(on electrical equipment)* der Stecker [shtehker]
▸ where can I find an adaptor for the plug on my hairdryer? wo bekomme ich einen Steckeradapter für meinen Fön? [voh bekom-e ish eynen shtehkeradapter fuur meynen feun]

**plug in** einstöpseln [eynshteupseln]
▸ can I plug my cellphone in here to recharge it? kann ich mein Handy hier zum Aufladen einstöpseln? [kan ish meyn hehndi heer tsum owfladen eynshteupseln]

**point** *(moment)* der Moment [mohmehnt]; *(spot, location)* die Stelle [shtehl-e]
◆ *(direct)* zeigen [tseygen]
▸ points of the compass Himmelsrichtungen [himelzrishtungen]
▸ can you point me in the direction of the freeway? in welcher Richtung ist die Autobahn? [in vehlsher rishtung ist dee owtohbaan]

**police** die Polizei [politsey]
▸ call the police! rufen Sie die Polizei! [roofen zee dee politsey]
▸ what's the number for the police? welche Nummer hat die Polizei? [vehlsh-e numer hat dee politsey]

**police station** die Polizeiwache [politsey-vakh-e]
▸ where is the nearest police station? wo ist die nächste Polizeiwache? [voh ist dee nehkst-e politsey-vakh-e]

**pool** *(for swimming)* das Schwimmbecken [shvimbehken]
▸ the main pool das Hauptbecken [howptbehken]
▸ the children's pool das Kinderbecken [kin-der-behken]
▸ is the pool heated? ist das Becken beheizt? [ist das behken beheytst]
▸ is there an indoor pool? gibt es ein Innenbecken? [gipt ehs eyn inenbehken]

**pork** das Schweinefleisch [shveyn-e-fleysh]
▸ I don't eat pork ich esse kein Schweinefleisch [ish ehs-e keyn shveyn-e-fleysh]

**portable** tragbar [traakbar]
▸ do you have a portable heater we could borrow? können Sie uns ein tragbares Heizgerät leihen? [keunen zee uns eyn traakbarez heytsgerayt leyen]

**portion** die Portion [portsiohn]
▸ the portions at that restaurant are just right in dem Restaurant sind die Portionen gerade richtig [in daym rehstoront zint dee portsiohnen geraad-e rishtish]

**possible** möglich [meuglish]
- without sauce, if possible wenn möglich ohne Soße [vehn meuglish ohn-e zohs-e]

**postcard** die Postkarte [postkart-e]
- where can I buy postcards? wo kann ich Postkarten kaufen? [voh kan ish postkarten kowfen]
- how much are stamps for postcards to the States? was kostet eine Postkarte in die Vereinigten Staaten? [vas kostet ey-ne postkart-e in dee fehreynishten shtaaten]

**post office** die Post [post]
- where is the nearest post office? wo ist die nächste Post? [voh ist dee nehkst-e post]

**power** *(electricity)* der Strom [shtrohm]
- there's no power es gibt keinen Strom [ehs gipt keynen shtrohm]

**power failure** der Stromausfall [shtrohm-owsfal]
- there's a power failure der Strom ist ausgefallen [dehr shtrohm ist owsgefal-en]
- how long is the power failure expected to last? wie lange soll der Stromausfall dauern? [vee lang-e zol dehr shtrohm-owsfal dowern]

**prawn** die Garnele [garnehl-e]
- I'd like to try a dish with shrimp or prawns ich würde gerne etwas mit Shrimps oder Garnelen probieren [ish vuurd-e gehrn-e ehtvas mit shrimps ohder garnehlen prohbeeren]

**prefer** vorziehen [fortsee-en]; lieber mögen [leeber meugen]
- I prefer this one ich ziehe diesen vor [ish tsee-e deezen for]
- I prefer black tea ich mag lieber schwarzen Tee [ish maak leeber shvartsen tay]
- I'd prefer you not smoke es wäre mir lieber, wenn Sie nicht rauchen [ehs vehr-e meer leeber vehn zee nisht rowshen]

**prescription** *(medicine)* das Rezept [rehtsehpt]
- is it only available by prescription? benötige ich dafür ein Rezept? [beneutig-e ish dafuur eyn rehtsehpt]

---

### expressing a preference

- I prefer red wine to white wine ich trinke lieber Rotwein als Weißwein [ish trink-e leeber rohtveyn als veysveyn]
- I'd rather fly than go by train ich fliege lieber, als dass ich mit dem Zug fahre [ish fleeg-e leeber als das ish mit daym tsook faar-e]
- Saturday would suit me better Samstag würde mir besser passen [zamztaak vuurd-e meer besher pas-en]

**present** *(gift)* das Geschenk [geshehnk]
- where can I buy presents around here? wo kann ich hier in der Nähe Geschenke kaufen? [voh kan ish heer in dehr nay-e geshehnk-e kowfen]

**pretty** hübsch [huubsh]
- she's a very pretty girl sie ist sehr hübsch [zee ist zehr huubsh]

**price** der Preis [preys]
- if the price is right wenn der Preis stimmt [vehn dehr preys shtimt]
- what's the price of gas today? was kostet Benzin heute? [vas kostet behntseen hoyt-e]

**price list** die Preisliste [preyslist-e]
- do you have a price list? haben Sie eine Preisliste? [haaben zee ey-ne preyslist-e]

**print** *(photograph)* der Abzug [aptsook]
- could I have another set of prints? könnte ich die Abzüge nachmachen lassen? [keunt-e ish dee aptsuug-e nakhmakhen las-en]

**private** *(not public)* privat [privaat]; *(personal)* persönlich [pehrzeunlish]
- is it a private beach? ist das ein Privatstrand? [ist das eyn privaat-shtrant]

**problem** das Problem [problaym]
- there's a problem with the central heating wir haben ein Problem mit der Zentralheizung [veer haaben eyn problaym mit dehr tsehntraal-heytsung]
- no problem kein Problem [keyn problaym]

**program** *(for a play, concert)* das Programm [prohgram]
- could I see a program? haben Sie ein Programm für mich? [haaben zee eyn prohgram fuur mish]

**pronounce** *(word)* aussprechen [ows-shprehshen]
- how is that pronounced? wie wird das ausgesprochen? [vee virt das owsgeshprokhen]

**public** öffentlich [eufentlish] ♦ die Öffentlichkeit [eufentlishkeyt]
- is there a public swimming pool? gibt es ein öffentliches Schwimmbad? [gipt ehs eyn eufentlishez shvimbaat]
- let's go somewhere less public gehen wir irgendwo hin, wo weniger Menschen sind [gayen veer irgehntvoh hin voh vayniger mehnshen zint]
- is the castle open to the public? kann man das Schloss besichtigen? [kan man das shlos bezishtigen]

**public holiday** der Feiertag [feyertaak]
- is tomorrow a public holiday? ist morgen ein Feiertag? [ist morgen eyn feyertaak]

**public transportation** die öffentlichen Verkehrsmittel [eufentlishen fehrkehrzmitel]
- can you get there by public transportation? kommt man dort mit öffentlichen Verkehrsmitteln hin? [komt man dort mit eufentlishen fehrkehrzmiteln hin]

### public transportation

There's a subway system (*U-Bahn*) in most of the big towns (Berlin, Munich, Hamburg, etc.). This is often supported by networks of trams or commuter trains (*S-Bahn*). Tickets and cards can be used on all of these and also on the bus network.

**pull** ziehen [tsee-en]; *(muscle)* zerren [tsehren]
▸ I've pulled a muscle ich habe eine Muskelzerrung [ish haab-e ey-ne muskel-tsehrung]

**puncture** *(flat tire)* die Panne [pan-e]
▸ we had a puncture wir hatten eine Panne [veer hat-en ey-ne pan-e]

**purpose** *(reason)* der Zweck [tsvehk]; *(aim)* das Ziel [tseel] ✦ **on purpose** absichtlich [apzishtlish]
▸ sorry, I didn't do it on purpose tut mir Leid, das habe ich nicht absichtlich getan [toot meer leyt das haab-e ish nisht apzishtlish getaan]

**purse** *(handbag)* die Handtasche [hant-tash-e]; *(change purse)* das Portmonee [portmonay]
▸ my purse was stolen meine Handtasche wurde gestohlen [meyn-e hant-tash-e vurd-e geshtohlen]

**push** *(button)* drücken [druuken]; *(car)* anschieben [ansheeben]
▸ can you help us push the car? können Sie uns helfen, den Wagen anzuschieben? [keunen zee uns hehlfen dayn vaagen antsusheeben]

**put** *(into place, position)* stellen [shtehlen]; *(lay horizontally)* legen [laygen]; *(into bag, pocket)* stecken [shtehken]
▸ is there somewhere I can put my bags? wo kann ich meine Taschen hinstellen? [voh kan ish meyn-e tashen hin-shtehlen]

**put down** *(set down)* hinstellen [hin-shtehlen]; *(lay down)* hinlegen [hinlaygen]
▸ can we put our things down in the corner? können wir unsere Sachen in die Ecke hinstellen? [keunen veer unzer-e zakhen in dee ehk-e hin-shtehlen]

**put on** *(clothes)* anziehen [antsee-en]; *(TV, radio, heating)* einschalten [eynshalten]
▸ can you put the heat on? können Sie die Heizung einschalten? [keunen zee dee heytsung eynshalten]
▸ can you put Mrs. Martin on, please? können Sie mir bitte Frau Martin geben? [keunen zee meer bi-te frow martin gayben]

**put out** *(cigarette, fire)* ausmachen [owsmakhen]
▸ can you please put your cigarette out? können Sie bitte Ihre Zigarette ausmachen? [keunen zee bi-te eer-e tsigareht-e owsmakhen]

**put up** *(erect)* aufbauen [owfbowen]
▸ can we put up our tent here? können wir unser Zelt hier aufbauen? [keunen veer unzer tsehlt heer owfbowen]

# q

**quarter** *(fourth)* das Viertel [feertel]
- a quarter past/after one Viertel nach eins [feertel naakh eyns]
- a quarter to/of one Viertel vor eins [feertel for eyns]
- I'll be back in a quarter of an hour ich bin in einer Viertelstunde zurück [ish bin in eyner feertelshtund-e tsuruuk]

**quay** der Kai [key]
- is the boat at the quay? liegt das Boot am Kai? [leekt das boht am key]

**question** die Frage [fraag-e]
- can I ask you a question? darf ich Sie etwas fragen? [darf ish zee ehtvas fraagen]

**quickly** schnell [shnehl]
- everyone speaks so quickly sie sprechen alle so schnell [zee shprehshen al-e zoh shnehl]

**quiet** ruhig [rooish]
- is it a quiet beach? ist der Strand ruhig? [ist dehr shtrant rooish]
- do you have anything quieter? haben Sie ein ruhigeres Zimmer? [haaben zee eyn rooigerez tsim-er]

**quite** *(rather)* ziemlich [tseemlish]
- it's quite expensive around here hier ist es ziemlich teuer [heer ist ehs tseemlish toyer]

# r

**racket** *(for tennis)* der Schläger [shlayger]
- can you rent rackets? kann man Tennisschläger leihen? [kan man tehnis-shlayger leyen]

**radiator** der Heizkörper [heytskeurper]
- the radiator's leaking der Heizkörper leckt [dehr heytskeurper lehkt]

**radio** das Radio [raadioh]
- the radio doesn't work das Radio funktioniert nicht [das raadioh funktsiohneert nisht]

**radio station** der Radiosender [raadioh-zehnder]
- can you get any English-language radio stations here? gibt es hier englischsprachige Radiosender? [gipt ehs heer ehnglish-shpraakhig-e raadioh-zehnder]

**rain** regnen [raygnen]
- it's raining es regnet [ehs raygnet]

**random**
- at random aufs Geratewohl [owfs geraat-e-vohl]

**rare** *(meat)* blutig [blootish]
- rare, please blutig, bitte [blootish bi-te]

**rate** *(price)* der Satz [zats]
- what's your daily rate? wie hoch ist Ihr Tagessatz? [vee hohkh ist eer taagez-zats]

**rate of exchange** der Wechselkurs [vehkselkoors]
- they offer a good rate of exchange man bekommt dort einen guten Wechselkurs [man bekomt dort eynen gooten vehkselkoors]

**razor** *(for wet shaving)* der Rasierer [razeerer]; *(electric)* der Rasierapparat [razeer-aparaat]
- where can I buy a new razor? wo kann ich einen neuen Rasierapparat kaufen? [voh kan ish eynen noyen razeer-aparaat kowfen]

**razor blade** die Rasierklinge [razeer-kling-e]
- I need to buy some razor blades ich muss Rasierklingen kaufen [ish mus razeer-klingen kowfen]

**ready** *(prepared)* fertig [fehrtish]; *(willing)* bereit [bereyt]
- when will it be ready? wann ist es fertig? [van ist ehs fehrtish]

**really** *(actually, very)* wirklich [virklish]
- really? wirklich? [virklish]
- not really eigentlich nicht [eygentlish nisht]

**rear** *(of a train, building)* der hintere Teil [hinter-e teyl]
- your seats are in the rear of the train Ihre Plätze befinden sich im hinteren Teil des Zuges [eer-e plehts-e befinden zish im hinteren teyl dehz tsoogez]

**receipt** *(for a purchase)* der Kassenbon [kas-en-bohn]; *(for a bill, a meal, rent)* die Rechnung [rehshnung]; *(for a taxi)* die Quittung [kvitung]
- can I have a receipt, please? kann ich bitte eine Quittung haben? [kan ish bi-te ey-ne kvitung haaben]

**receive** *(package, letter)* bekommen [bekom-en]
- I should have received the package this morning ich hätte das Päckchen heute Vormittag bekommen müssen [ish heht-e das pehkshen hoyt-e formitaak bekom-en meusen]

**reception** *(celebration)* der Empfang [ehmpfang]; *(desk in hotel)* die Rezeption [rehtsehptsiohn]
- I'm looking for the Mackenzie wedding reception ich suche den Hochzeitsempfang der Mackenzies [ish zookh-e dayn hohkhtseyts-ehmpfang dehr makehnzeez]

**reception desk** *(at hotel)* die Rezeption [rehtsehptsiohn]
- can I leave my backpack at the reception desk? kann ich meinen Rucksack an der Rezeption lassen? [kan ish meynen rukzak an dehr rehtsehptsiohn las-en]

**recline** nach hinten stellen [naakh hinten shtehlen]
- do you mind if I recline my seat? macht es Ihnen etwas aus, wenn ich meinen Sitz nach hinten stelle? [makht ehs eenen ehtvas ows vehn ish meynen zits naakh hinten shtehl-e]

**recommend** empfehlen [ehmpfaylen]
- could you recommend another hotel? können Sie mir ein anderes Hotel empfehlen? [keunen zee meer eyn anderez hohtehl ehmpfaylen]
- could you recommend a restaurant? können Sie mir ein Restaurant empfehlen? [keunen zee meer eyn rehstoront ehmpfaylen]
- what do you recommend? was würden Sie empfehlen? [vas vuurden zee ehmpfaylen]

**record store** der Plattenladen [plat-en-laaden]
- I'm looking for a record store ich suche einen Plattenladen [ish zookh-e eynen plat-en-laaden]

**rec center, recreation center** das Freizeitzentrum [frey-tseyt-tsehntrum]
- what kinds of activities does the recreation center offer? welche Aktivitäten werden im Freizeitzentrum angeboten? [vehlsh-e aktivitayten vehrden im frey-tseyt-tsehntrum angebohten]

**red** rot [roht] ♦ *(color)* das Rot [roht]; *(wine)* der Rote [roht-e]
- dressed in red rot gekleidet [roht gekleydet]
- what kinds of red wine do you have? was für Rotweine haben Sie? [vas fuur rohtveyn-e haaben zee]

**redhead** der, die Rothaarige [roht-haarig-e]
- a tall redhead wearing glasses ein großer Rothaariger mit Brille [eyn grohser roht-haariger mit bril-e]

**red light** *(on traffic lights)* die rote Ampel [roht-e ampel]
- you failed to stop at a red light Sie haben die rote Ampel überfahren [zee haaben dee roht-e ampel uuberfaaren]

**reduced** *(rate)* ermäßigt [ehrmaysisht]
- is there a reduced rate for students? gibt es einen ermäßigten Preis für Studenten? [gipt ehs eynen ehrmaysishten preys fuur shtoodehnten]

**reduced-price** *(ticket)* ermäßigt [ehrmaysisht]
- two reduced-price tickets and one full-price zweimal ermäßigt und einmal normal [tsveymal ehrmaysisht unt eynmal normaal]

**reduction** die Ermäßigung [ehrmaysigung]
- do you have reductions for groups? haben Sie Gruppenermäßigungen? [haaben zee grup-en-ehrmaysigungen]

**red wine** der Rotwein [rohtveyn]
- a bottle of red wine eine Flasche Rotwein [ey-ne flash-e rohtveyn]

**refresher course** der Auffrischungskurs [owf-frishungz-kurs]
- I need a refresher course ich muss einen Auffrischungskurs machen [ish mus eynen owf-frishungz-kurs makhen]

**refuge** *(for animals)* das Naturschutzgebiet [natoor-shutsgebeet]
- we'd like to visit the wildlife refuge wir würden gerne das Wildschutzgebiet besuchen [veer vuurden gehrn-e das vilt-shutsgebeet bezookhen]

**refundable**
- are the tickets refundable? kann ich die Karten zurückgeben? [kan ish dee karten zuruukgayben]

**regard(s)**
- give my regards to your parents! grüßen Sie bitte Ihre Eltern von mir! [gruusen zee bi-te eer-e ehltern fon meer]
- I'm calling you with regard to ... ich rufe wegen ... an [ish roof-e vaygen an]

**region** die Region [rehgiohn]
- the Munich region die Region um München [dee rehgiohn um muunshen]

**registered mail**
- I would like to send a letter by registered mail ich möchte gerne einen Brief per Einschreiben versenden [ish meusht-e gehrn-e eynen breef per eynshreyben fehrzehnden]

**registration** *(of vehicle)* das Kraftfahrzeugzeichen [kraft-faartsoyk-tseyshen]
- here's the car's registration hier ist das Kraftfahrzeugzeichen [heer ist das kraft-faartsoyk-tseyshen]

**relative** der, die Verwandte [fehrvant-e]
- I have relatives in Berlin ich habe Verwandte in Berlin [ish haab-e fehrvant-e in behrleen]

**remember** sich erinnern an [zish ehrinern an]
- do you remember me? erinnern Sie sich an mich? [ehrinern zee zish an mish]
- I can't remember his name ich kann mich nicht an seinen Namen erinnern [ish kan mish nisht an seynen naamen ehrinern]

**remote (control)** die Fernbedienung [fehrnbedeenung]
- I can't find the remote for the TV ich kann die Fernbedienung für den Fernseher nicht finden [ish kan dee fehrnbedeenung fuur dayn fehrnzayer nisht fin-den]

**rent** die Miete [meet-e] ♦ mieten [meeten]
- how much is the rent per week? was kostet die Miete für eine Woche? [vas kostet dee meet-e fuur ey-ne vokh-e]
- I'd like to rent a car for a week ich möchte gerne für eine Woche einen Wagen mieten [ish meusht-e gehrn-e fuur ey-ne vokh-e eynen vaagen meeten]
- I'd like to rent a boat ich möchte gerne ein Boot mieten [ish meusht-e gehrn-e eyn boht meeten]

## reservations

As far as overnight accommodations are concerned, you should book as early as you can. On the trains, you must have a reservation to travel on trains marked with an *R* in a circle, and it's advisable to reserve a seat on intercity trains and when you're traveling during the tourist season. You can book your ticket in the *Reisezentrum* at any station.

▸ does it work out cheaper to rent the equipment by the week? wird es billiger, wenn ich die Ausrüstung für eine Woche miete? [virt ehs biliger vehn ish dee owsruustung fuur ey-ne vokh-e meet-e]

**rental** *(renting)* die Vermietung [fehrmeetung]; *(on apartment, house, car)* die Miete [meet-e]

▸ we have the rental for two weeks wir haben die Miete für zwei Wochen [veer haaben dee meet-e fuur tsvey vokhen]

**repair** die Reparatur [rehparatoor] ◆ reparieren [rehpareeren]

▸ will you be able to make the repairs today? werden Sie die Reparatur heute machen können? [vehrden zee dee rehparatoor hoyt-e makhen keunen]

▸ how long will it take to repair? wie lange wird die Reparatur dauern? [vee lang-e virt dee rehparatoor dowern]

**repeat** wiederholen [veederhohlen]

▸ can you repeat that, please? können Sie das bitte noch einmal wiederholen? [keunen zee das bi-te nokh eynmal veederhohlen]

**report** *(theft)* melden [mehlden]

▸ I'd like to report something stolen ich möchte einen Diebstahl melden [ish meusht-e eynen deebshtaal mehlden]

▸ I'd like to report the loss of my credit cards ich möchte den Verlust meiner Kreditkarten melden [ish meusht-e dayn fehrlust meyner krehdeetkarten mehlden]

**reservation** die Reservierung [rehzerveerung]

▸ do you have to make a reservation? muss man reservieren? [mus man rehzerveeren]

▸ I have a reservation in the name of Jones ich habe eine Reservierung auf den Namen Jones [ish haab-e ey-ne rehzerveerung owf dayn naamen dzhohnz]

**reserve** *(ticket, room)* reservieren [rehzerveeren]

▸ hello, I'd like to reserve a table for tomorrow night at 8 guten Tag, ich möchte für morgen Abend um acht Uhr einen Tisch für zwei Personen reservieren [gooten taak ish meusht-e fuur morgen aabent um akht oor eynen tish fuur tsvey pehrzohnen rehzerveeren]

**reserved** *(booked)* reserviert [rehzerveert]

▸ is this table reserved? ist der Tisch reserviert? [ist dehr tish rehzerveert]

**rest** *(while walking)* die Pause [powz-e] ♦ *(relax)* sich ausruhen [zish owsrooen]
- I've come here to get some rest ich bin hergekommen, um mich auszuruhen [ish bin hehrgekom-en um mish ows-tsu-rooen]
- to have a rest *(while walking)* eine Pause machen [eyn-e powz-e makhen]; *(relax)* sich ausruhen [zish owsrooen]

**restaurant** das Restaurant [rehstoront]
- are there any good restaurants around here? gibt es hier in der Nähe gute Restaurants? [gipt ehs heer in dehr nay-e goot-e rehsteronts]

**restriction** die Begrenzung [begrehntsung]
- are there restrictions on how much luggage you can take? gibt es eine Gepäckbegrenzung? [gipt ehs ey-ne gepehk-begrehntsung]

**restroom** die Toilette [toyleht-e]
- is there a restroom on the bus? gibt es im Bus eine Toilette? [gipt ehs im bus ey-ne toyleht-e]

**retired** im Ruhestand [im roo-e-shtant]
- I'm retired now ich bin jetzt im Ruhestand [ish bin yehtst im roo-e-shtant]

**return** *(arrival back)* die Rückkehr [ruuk-kehr] ♦ *(rental car)* zurückbringen [tsuruukbringen]; *(smile)* erwidern [ehrvidern]
- when do we have to return the car? wann müssen wir den Wagen zurückbringen? [van muusen veer dayn vaagen tsuruukbringen]

**return trip** die Rückfahrt [ruukfart]
- the return trip is scheduled for 6 o'clock die Rückfahrt ist für sechs Uhr geplant [dee ruukfart ist fuur zehks oor geplant]

**rice** der Reis [reys]
- I'd like some rice, please ich hätte gerne etwas Reis, bitte [ish heht-e gehrn-e ehtvas reys bi-te]

---

## at a restaurant

- I'd like to reserve a table for tonight ich möchte gerne für heute Abend einen Tisch reservieren [ish meusht-e gehrn-e fuur hoyt-e aabent eynen tish rehzerveeren]
- can we see the menu? können wir bitte die Speisekarte haben? [keunen veer bi-te dee shpeyzekart-e haaben]
- do you have a set menu? gibt es ein Menü? [gipt ehs eyn mehnyuu]
- rare/medium/well done, please blutig/medium/durchgebraten, bitte [blootish/maydium/durshgebraaten bi-te]
- can I have the check, please? kann ich bitte die Rechnung haben? [kan ish bi-te dee rehshnung haaben]

**ride**

▸ do you want a ride? wollen Sie mitfahren? [vol-en zee mitfaaren]

▸ where can we go for a ride around here? wo können wir hier in der Nähe ein bisschen herumfahren? [voh keunen veer heer in dehr nay-e eyn bis-shen hehrumfaaren]

**riding** *(on horseback)* das Reiten [reyten]

▸ to go riding reiten gehen [reyten gayen]

**right** *(correct)* richtig [rishtish]; *(not left)* rechts [rehshts] ♦ *(right side)* die rechte Seite [rehsht-e zeyt-e] ♦ *(correctly)* richtig [rishtish]

▸ to the right (of) rechts (von) [rehshts (fon)]

▸ that's right das ist richtig [das ist rishtish]

▸ is this the right train for Vienna? ist dies der richtige Zug nach Wien? [ist deez dehr rishtig-e tsook naakh veen]

▸ is this the right number? ist das die richtige Nummer? [ist das dee rishtig-e num-er]

▸ take the next right fahren Sie die Nächste rechts [faaren zee dee nehkst-e rehshts]

▸ you have to turn right Sie müssen rechts abbiegen [zee muusen rehshts apbeegen]

**right-hand** rechter [rehshter]

▸ on the right-hand side auf der rechten Seite [owf dehr rehshten zeyt-e]

**right of way** die Vorfahrt [forfaart]

▸ who has the right of way here? wer hat hier Vorfahrt? [vehr hat heer forfaart]

**road** die Straße [shtraas-e ]

▸ which road do I take for Dortmund? welche Straße geht nach Dortmund? [vehlsh-e shtraas-e gayt naakh dortmunt]

▸ what is the speed limit on this road? wie schnell darf ich auf dieser Straße fahren? [vee shnehl darf ish owf deezer shtraas-e faaren]

**rob** *(person)* bestehlen [beshtaylen]

▸ I've been robbed ich wurde bestohlen [ish vurd-e beshtohlen]

**rock climbing** das Klettern [klehtern]

▸ can you go rock climbing here? kann man hier klettern gehen? [kan man heer klehtern gayen]

**roller skate** der Rollschuh [rolshoo]

▸ where can we rent roller skates? wo kann man Rollschuhe leihen? [voh kan man rolshoo-e leyen]

**room** *(in a house, hotel)* das Zimmer [tsim-er]; *(space)* der Platz [plats]

▸ do you have any rooms available? haben Sie freie Zimmer? [haaben zee frey-e tsim-er]

▸ how much is a room with a bathroom? was kostet ein Zimmer mit Bad? [vas kostet eyn tsim-er mit baat]

▸ I've reserved a room for tonight under the name Pearson ich habe für heute Abend ein Zimmer auf den Namen Pearson reserviert [ish haab-e fuur hoyt-e aabent eyn tsim-er owf dayn naamen peerson rehzervee rt]

▸ can I see the room? kann ich das Zimmer sehen? [kan ish das tsim-er zayen]

**rosé** der Rosé [rohzay]
- could you recommend a good rosé? können Sie mir einen guten Rosé empfehlen? [keunen zee meer eynen gooten rohzay ehmpfaylen]

**round trip** die Rundreise [runtreyz-e]
- how long will the round trip take? wie lange dauert die Rundreise? [vee lang-e dowert dee runtreyz-e]

**round-trip ticket** die Rückfahrkarte [ruukfaarkart-e]
- two second-class round-trip tickets to Hamburg, please zwei Rückfahrkarten zweiter Klasse nach Hamburg, bitte [tsvey ruukfaarkarten tsveyter klas-e naakh hamburk bi-te]
- I'd like a round-trip ticket to Kiel, leaving on the 3rd and coming back on the 9th ich hätte gerne eine Rückfahrkarte nach Kiel, am Dritten hin und am Neunten zurück [ish heht-e gehrn-e ey-ne ruukfaarkart-e naakh keel am driten hin unt am noynten tsuruuk]
- a round-trip ticket for one car, two adults and two children, please eine Rückfahrkarte für ein Auto, zwei Erwachsene und zwei Kinder, bitte [ey-ne ruukfaarkart-e fuur eyn owtoh tsvey ehrvaksene unt tsvey kin-der bi-te]

**route** *(itinerary)* die Strecke [shtrehk-e], die Route [root-e]; *(of bus, train, plane)* die Linie [leeni-e]
- is there an alternative route we could take? gibt es eine Alternativstrecke? [gipt ehs ey-ne altehrnateev-shtrehk-e]

**row** *(of seats)* die Reihe [rey-e]
- can we have seats in the front row? können wir Sitzplätze in der ersten Reihe haben? [keunen veer zitsplehts-e in der ehrsten rey-e haaben]

**rowboat** das Ruderboot [rooderboht]
- can we rent a rowboat? können wir ein Ruderboot mieten? [keunen veer eyn rooderboht meeten]

**rubber ring** der Gummiring [gumiring]
- where can I buy a rubber ring? wo kann ich einen Gummiring kaufen? [voh kan ish eynen gumiring kowfen]

**run** *(on foot)* der Lauf [lowf]; *(in a car)* die Fahrt [fart]; *(for skiing)* die Piste [pist-e] ◆ *(on foot)* laufen [lowfen], rennen [rehnen]; *(bus, train)* fahren [faaren]; *(engine)* laufen [lowfen] ◆ *(traffic light)* überfahren [uuberfaaren]
- I'm going for a run ich gehe laufen [ish gay-e lowfen]
- the bus runs every half hour der Bus fährt jede halbe Stunde [dehr bus fehrt yayd-e halb-e shtund-e]

**running** das Laufen [lowfen]
- where can you go running here? wo kann man hier laufen gehen? [voh kan man heer lowfen gayen]

**run out of**
- I've run out of gas mir ist das Benzin ausgegangen [meer ist das behntseen owsgegangen]

▸ I've run out of money ich habe kein Geld mehr [ish haab-e keyn gehlt mehr]
▸ we're running out of time die Zeit wird knapp [dee tseyt virt knap]

# S

**safe** sicher [zisher] ♦ *(for valuables)* der Safe [sayf]
▸ is it safe to swim here? ist es sicher, hier zu schwimmen? [ist ehs zisher heer tsoo shvimen]
▸ is it safe to camp here? ist es sicher, hier zu zelten? [ist ehs zisher heer tsoo tsehlten]
▸ is there a safe in the room? gibt es einen Safe im Zimmer? [gipt ehs eynen sayf im tsim-er]

**sail** *(of a boat)* das Segel [zaygel]
▸ we need to adjust that sail wir müssen das Segel richten [veer muusen das zaygel rishten]

**sailboat** das Segelboot [zaygelboht]
▸ can we rent a sailboat? können wir ein Segelboot mieten? [keunen veer eyn zaygelboht meeten]

**sailing** das Segeln [zaygeln]
▸ to go sailing segeln gehen [zaygeln gayen]
▸ I'd like to take beginners' sailing classes ich würde gerne einen Segelkurs für Anfänger machen [ish vuurd-e gehrn-e eynen zaygelkurs fuur anfehnger makhen]

**salad** der Salat [zalaat]
▸ can I just have a salad? kann ich bitte nur einen Salat haben? [kan ish bi-te noor eynen zalaat haaben]

**sale** *(selling)* der Verkauf [fehrkowf]; *(at reduced prices)* der Ausverkauf [owsfehrkowf]
▸ is it for sale? kann man das kaufen? [kan man das kowfen]
▸ can you get your money back on sale items? bekommt man das Geld für reduzierte Waren zurück? [bekomt man das gehlt fuur rehdootseert-e vaaren tsuruuk]

**sales tax** die Mehrwertsteuer [mehrvehrt-shtoyer]
▸ is sales tax included? ist das einschließlich Mehrwertsteuer? [ist das eynshleeslish mehrvehrt-shtoyer]
▸ can you deduct the sales tax? können Sie die Mehrwertsteuer absetzen? [keunen zee dee mehrvehrt-shtoyer apzehtsen]

**salt** das Salz [zalts] ♦ salzen [zaltsen]
▸ can you pass me the salt? können Sie mir das Salz reichen? [keunen zee meer das zalts reyshen]

▸ it doesn't have enough salt es ist nicht genug gesalzen [ehs ist nisht genookh gezaltsen]

▸ are they going to salt the roads tonight? werden heute Abend die Straßen mit Salz gestreut? [vehrden hoyt-e aabent dee shtraasen mit zalts geshtroyt]

**salty** *(food)* salzig [zaltsish]; *(water)* Salz- [zalts]

▸ it's too salty es ist zu salzig [ehs ist tsoo zaltsish]

**same** gleicher [gleysher]

▸ I'll have the same ich nehme das Gleiche [ish naym-e das gleysh-e]

▸ he's wearing the same coat as I am er trägt den gleichen Mantel wie ich [ehr traykt dayn gleyshen mantel vee ish]

▸ the same (as) dasselbe (wie) [das-zehlb-e (vee)]

▸ it's the same as yours ich habe das Gleiche wie Sie [ish haab-e das gleysh-e vee zee]

**sandwich** das Sandwich [sehntvitsh]

▸ a chicken sandwich, please ein Sandwich mit Hühnerfleisch, bitte [eyn sehntvitsh mit huunerfleysh bi-te]

**Saturday** der Samstag [zamztaak]

▸ Saturday, September 13th Samstag, den dreizehnten September [zamztaak dayn dreytsaynten zehptehmber]

▸ it's closed on Saturdays es hat samstags geschlossen [ehs hat zamztaakz geshlossen]

**sauce** die Soße [zohs-e]

▸ do you have a sauce that isn't too strong? haben Sie eine Soße, die nicht so kräftig ist? [haaben zee ey-ne zohs-e dee nisht zoh krehftish ist]

**sauna** die Sauna [zowna]

▸ is there a sauna? gibt es eine Sauna? [gipt ehs ey-ne zowna]

**sausage** die Wurst [vurst]

▸ I'd like to try some local sausages ich möchte gerne ein paar Würste aus dieser Gegend probieren [ish meusht-e gehrn-e eyn par vuurst-e ows deezer gaygent prohbeeren]

**say** sagen [zaagen]

▸ how do you say "good luck" in German? wie sagt man "good luck" auf Deutsch? [vee zaakt man good luck owf doytsh]

**scared**

▸ to be scared Angst haben [angst haaben]

▸ I'm scared of spiders ich habe Angst vor Spinnen [ish haab-e angst for shpin-en]

**scheduled flight** der Linienflug [leeni-en-flook]

▸ when is the next scheduled flight to Berlin? wann geht der nächste Linienflug nach Berlin? [van gayt dehr nehkst-e leeni-en-flook naakh behrleen]

**school** *(for children)* die Schule [shool-e]; *(college, university)* die Universität [ooniversitayt]

▶ are you still in school? gehst du noch zur Schule? [gayst doo nokh tsur shool-e]

**scoop** *(of ice cream)* die Kugel [koogel]

▶ I'd like a cone with two scoops ich hätte gern eine Waffel mit zwei Kugeln [ish heht-e gehrn ey-ne vafel mit tsvey koogeln]

**scooter** der Motorroller [mohtor-rol-er]

▶ I'd like to rent a scooter ich möchte gerne einen Motorroller mieten [ish meusht-e gehrn-e eynen mohtor-rol-er meeten]

**Scotch** *(whiskey)* der Scotch [skotsh]

▶ a Scotch on the rocks, please einen Scotch mit Eis, bitte [eynen skotsh mit eys bi-te]

**Scotch tape**® der Tesafilm® [tayzafilm]

▶ do you have any Scotch tape®? haben Sie Tesafilm®? [haaben zee tayzafilm]

**scrambled eggs** das Rührei [ruurey]

▶ I'd like scrambled eggs for breakfast ich hätte gerne Rührei zum Frühstück [ish heht-e gehrn-e ruurey tsum fruushtuuk]

**screen** *(room in a movie theater)* der Kinosaal [keenohzaal]

▶ how many screens does the movie theater have? wie viele Kinosäle gibt es? [vee feel-e keenohzayl-e gipt ehs]

**scuba diving** das Sporttauchen [shport-towkhen]

▶ can we go scuba diving? können wir Sporttauchen gehen? [keunen veer shport-towkhen gayen]

**sea** das Meer [mehr], die See [zay]

▶ the sea is rough die See ist rau [dee zay ist row]

▶ how long does it take to walk to the sea? wie lange läuft man zum Meer? [vee lang-e loyft man tsum mehr]

**seasick** seekrank [zaykrank]

▶ I feel seasick ich bin seekrank [ish bin zaykrank]

**seasickness** die Seekrankheit [zaykrankheyt]

▶ can you give me something for seasickness, please? können Sie mir etwas gegen Seekrankheit geben, bitte? [keunen zee meer ehtvas gaygen zaykrankheyt gayben bi-te]

**seaside resort** das Seebad [zaybaat]

▶ what's the nearest seaside resort? wo ist das nächste Seebad? [voh ist das nehkst-e zaybaat]

**season** *(of the year)* die Jahreszeit [yaarez-tseyt]

▶ what is the best season to come here? in welcher Jahreszeit kommt man am besten hierher? [in vehlsher yaarez-tseyt komt man am behsten heerhehr]

**season ticket** *(for train)* die Dauerkarte [dowerkart-e]
- how much is a season ticket? was kostet eine Dauerkarte? [vas kostet ey-ne dowerkart-e]

**seat** *(chair)* der Stuhl [shtool]; *(in a bus, a train)* der Sitzplatz [zitsplats]; *(in a car)* der Sitz [zits]; *(in a theater, a movie theater)* der Platz [plats]
- is this seat taken? ist der Platz noch frei? [ist dehr plats nokh frey]
- excuse me, I think you're (sitting) in my seat Entschuldigung, ich glaube, Sie sitzen auf meinem Platz [ehntshuldigung ish glowb-e zee zitsen owf meynem plats]

**second** *(unit of time)* die Sekunde [zehkund-e]; *(gear)* der Zweite [tsveyt-e]
+ zweite [tsveyt-e]
- wait a second! eine Sekunde! [ey-ne zehkund-e]
- is it in second? ist der Zweite eingelegt? [ist dehr tsveyt-e eyngelaykt]
- it's the second street on your right es ist die zweite Straße rechts [ehs ist dee tsveyt-e shtraas-e rehshts]

**second class** die zweite Klasse [tsveyt-e klas-e] + zweiter Klasse [tsveyter klas-e]
- your seat's in second class Ihr Sitzplatz ist in der zweiten Klasse [eer zitsplats ist in dehr tsveyten klas-e]
- to travel second class zweiter Klasse reisen [tsveyter klas-e reyzen]

**see** sehen [zayen]
- can I see the room? kann ich das Zimmer sehen? [kan ish das tsim-er zayen]
- I'd like to see the dress in the window ich würde gerne das Kleid aus dem Schaufenster sehen [ish vuurd-e gehrn-e das kleyt ows daym showfehnster zayen]
- see you soon! bis bald! [bis balt]
- see you later bis später [bis shpayter]
- see you (on) Thursday! bis Donnerstag [bis don-erz-taak]
- I'm here to see Dr. Brown ich möchte zu Dr. Brown [ish meusht-e tsoo doktor brown]

**self-service** *(restaurant, gas station)* Selbstbedienungs- [zehlbstbedeenungz]
+ *(restaurant, gas station)* die Selbstbedienung [zehlbstbedeenung]
- is it self-service? ist hier Selbstbedienung? [ist heer zehlbstbedeenung]

**sell** verkaufen [fehrkowfen]
- do you sell stamps? verkaufen Sie Briefmarken? [fehrkowfen zee breefmarken]
- the radio I was sold is defective das Radio, das man mir verkauft hat, ist kaputt [das raadioh das man meer fehrkowft hat ist kaput]

**send** schicken [shiken]
- I'd like to send this package to Hamburg by airmail ich möchte dieses Paket per Luftpost nach Hamburg schicken [ish meusht-e deezez pakayt per luftpost nakh hamburk shiken]
- could you send a tow truck? können Sie einen Abschleppwagen schicken? [keunen zee eynen apshlehpvaagen shiken]

**separately** *(individually)* getrennt [getrehnt]
▸ is it sold separately? wird es getrennt verkauft? [virt ehs getrennt fehrkowft]

**September** der September [zehptehmber]
▸ September 9th neunter September [noynter zehptehmber]

**serve** *(meal, drink)* servieren [zehrveeren]; *(customer)* bedienen [bedeenen]
▸ when is breakfast served? wann wird das Frühstück serviert? [van virt das fruushtuuk zehrveert]
▸ are you still serving lunch? gibt es noch Mittagessen? [gipt ehs nokh mitaakehsen]

**service** *(in a restaurant)* die Bedienung [bedeenung]
▸ the service was terrible die Bedienung war unmöglich [dee bedeenung var unmeuglish]
▸ we have to have the car serviced der Wagen muss zur Inspektion [dehr vaagen mus tsur inspehktsiohn]

**service charge** der Bedienungszuschlag [bedeenungz-tsuushlaak]
▸ is the service charge included? ist die Bedienung inbegriffen? [ist dee bedeenung inbegrif-en]

**set** *(collection)* der Satz [zats] ◆ *(sun)* untergehen [untergayen]
▸ do you have a spare set of keys? haben Sie Ersatzschlüssel? [haaben zee ehrzatsshluusel]
▸ what time does the sun set? wann geht die Sonne unter? [van gayt dee zon-e unter]

**seven** sieben [zeeben]
▸ there are seven of us wir sind zu siebt [veer zint tsoo zeebt]

**several** mehrere [mehrer-e], einige [eynig-e]
▸ I've been here before, several years ago ich war hier vor mehreren Jahren schon einmal [ish var heer for mehreren yaaren shohn eynmal]

**shade** *(shadow)* der Schatten [shat-en]
▸ can we have a table in the shade? können wir einen Tisch im Schatten haben? [keunen veer eynen tish im shat-en haaben]

**shake** *(bottle)* schütteln [shuuteln]
▸ to shake hands sich die Hand geben [zish dee hant gayben]
▸ let's shake *(in agreement)* schlagen Sie ein [shlaagen zee eyn]

### shame

▸ (what a) shame! wie schade! [vee shaad-e]

▸ it's a shame that ... wie schade, dass ... [vee shaad-e das]

**shampoo** das Shampoo [shampoo]

▸ do you have any shampoo? haben Sie Shampoo? [haaben zee shampoo]

**share** teilen [teylen]

▸ we're going to share it: can you bring us two plates? wir wollen teilen, können Sie uns bitte zwei Teller bringen? [veer vol-en teylen keunen zee uns bi-te tsvey tehler bringen]

**shared** *(bathroom, kitchen)* Gemeinschafts- [gemeynshafts]

▸ is the bathroom shared? ist es ein Gemeinschaftsbad? [ist ehs eyn gemeyn-shaftsbaat]

**shaver** der Rasierapparat [razeer-aparaat]

▸ where can I buy a new shaver? wo kann ich einen neuen Rasierapparat kaufen? [voh kan ish eynen noyen razeer-aparaat kowfen]

**sheet** *(for a bed)* das Laken [laaken]; *(of paper)* das Blatt [blat]

▸ could you change the sheets? könnten Sie die Laken wechseln? [keunten zee dee laaken vehkseln]

**ship** das Schiff [shif]

▸ when does the ship dock? wann legt das Schiff an? [van laykt das shif an]

**shoe** der Schuh [shoo]

▸ what sort of shoes should you wear? welche Art Schuhe soll man tragen? [vehlsh-e art shoo-e zol man traagen]

**shoe size** die Schuhgröße [shoogreus-e]

▸ what's your shoe size? welche Schuhgröße haben Sie? [vehlsh-e shoogreus-e haaben zee]

**shop** das Geschäft [geshehft], der Laden [laaden]

▸ what time do the shops downtown close? wann schließen die Geschäfte in der Innenstadt? [van shleesen dee geshehft-e in dehr inen-shtat]

**shopping** das Einkaufen [eynkowfen]

▸ where can you go shopping around here? wo kann man hier in der Nähe einkaufen gehen? [voh kan man heer in dehr nay-e eynkowfen gayen]

**shopping bag** die Tragetasche [traag-e-tash-e]
▸ can I have a plastic shopping bag, please? kann ich bitte eine Plastiktragetasche haben? [kan ish bi-te ey-ne plasteek-traag-e-tash-e haaben] ▸ see box on p. 123

**shopping center** das Einkaufszentrum [eynkowfs-tsehntrum]
▸ I'm looking for a shopping center ich suche ein Einkaufszentrum [ish zookh-e ey-n eynkowfs-tsehntrum]

**shop window** das Schaufenster [showfehnster]
▸ we've just been peeking in the shop windows wir haben nur einen Schaufensterbummel gemacht [veer haaben noor eynen showfehnsterbumel ge-makht]

**short** *(in time, in length)* kurz [kurts]; *(in height)* klein [kleyn]
▸ we're only here for a short time wir sind nur für kurze Zeit hier [veer zint noor fuur kurts-e tseyt heer]
▸ we'd like to do a shorter trip wir würden gerne einen kürzeren Ausflug machen [veer vuurden gehrn-e eynen kuurtseren owsflook makhen]
▸ I'm two euros short mir fehlen zwei Euro [meer faylen tsvey oyroh]

**shortcut** die Abkürzung [apkuurtsung]
▸ is there a shortcut? gibt es eine Abkürzung? [gipt ehs ey-ne apkuurtsung]

**short wave** die Kurzwelle [kurts-vehl-e]
▸ can you get any English stations on short wave? kann man englische Sender über Kurzwelle empfangen? [kan man ehnglish-e zehnder uuber kurts-vehl-e ehmpfangen]

**should** sollen [zol-en]
▸ what should I do? was soll ich tun? [vas zol ish toon]

**show** *(at the theater, movies)* die Vorstellung [forshtehlung] ◆ zeigen [tseygen]
▸ what time does the show begin? wann beginnt die Vorstellung? [van begint dee vorshtehlung]
▸ could you show me where that is on the map? können Sie mir das auf der Karte zeigen? [keunen zee meer das owf der kart-e tseygen]
▸ could you show me the room? können Sie mir das Zimmer zeigen? [keunen zee meer das tsim-er tseygen]

**shower** *(device)* die Dusche [dush-e]; *(of rain)* der Schauer [shower]
▸ I'd like a room with a shower, please ein Zimmer mit Dusche, bitte [eyn tsim-er mit dush-e bi-te]
▸ how does the shower work? wie funktioniert die Dusche? [vee funktsiohneert dee dush-e]
▸ the shower is leaking die Dusche tropft [dee dush-e tropft]

**shower head** der Duschkopf [dushkopf]
▸ the shower head is broken der Duschkopf ist kaputt [dehr dushkopf ist kaput]

**shrimp** der Shrimp [shrimp]
- I'm allergic to shrimp ich bin allergisch gegen Shrimps [ish bin alehrgish gaygen shrimps]

**shut** (door, window) schließen [shleesen]
- the window won't shut das Fenster schließt nicht [das fehnster shleest nisht]

**shutter** (on a window) der Fensterladen [fehnsterlaaden]; (on a camera) die Blende [blehnd-e]
- are there shutters on the windows? haben die Fenster Fensterläden? [haaben dee fehnster fehnsterlayden]

**shuttle** (vehicle) der Zubringer [tsoobringer], der Shuttle [shut-el]
- is there a shuttle to the airport? gibt es einen Zubringer zum Flughafen? [gipt ehs eynen tsoobringer tsum flookhaafen]

**sick** (unwell) krank [krank]
- I feel sick ich fühle mich schlecht [ish fuul-e mish shlehsht]
- to be sick (be unwell) krank sein [krank zeyn]; (vomit) sich übergeben [zish uubergayben]

**side** die Seite [zeyt-e]; (edge) der Rand [rant]
- I have a pain in my right side ich habe Schmerzen auf der rechten Seite [ish haab-e shmehrtsen owf dehr rehshten zeyt-e]
- could we have a table on the other side of the room? könnten wir einen Tisch auf der anderen Seite des Raums haben? [keunten veer eynen tish owf dehr anderen zeyt-e dez rowmz haaben]
- which side of the road do they drive on here? auf welcher Straßenseite fährt man hier? [owf vehlsher shtraasenzeyt-e fehrt man heer]

**sidewalk** der Bürgersteig [buurgershteyk]
- the sidewalks are very clean here die Bürgersteige sind hier sehr sauber [dee buurgershteyg-e zint heer zehr zowber]

**sight** (seeing) die Sicht [zisht] ♦ **sights** (of a place) die Sehenswürdigkeiten [zayenzvuurdishkeyten]
- I'm having problems with my sight ich kann schlecht sehen [ish kan shlehsht zayen]
- what are the sights that are most worth seeing? welche Sehenswürdigkeiten lohnen sich am meisten? [vehlsh-e zayenzvuurdishkeyten lohnen zish am meysten]

**sign** unterschreiben [untershreyben]
- do I sign here? muss ich hier unterschreiben? [mus ish heer untershreyben]

**signpost** der Wegweiser [vaykveyzer]
- does the route have good signposts? ist die Strecke gut beschildert? [ist dee shtrehk-e goot beshildert]

**silver** (metal) das Silber [zilber]
- is it made of silver? ist es aus Silber? [ist ehs ows zilber]

**since** seit [zeyt] ◆ *(in time)* seitdem [zeytdaym]; *(because)* da [daa]

> ▸ I've been here since Tuesday ich bin seit Dienstag hier [ish bin zeyt deenstaak heer]
> ▸ it hasn't rained once since we've been here seitdem wir hier sind, hat es nicht einmal geregnet [zeytdaym veer heer zint hat ehs nisht eynmal gerraygnet]

**single** *(only one)* einzige [eyntsig-e]; *(unmarried)* ledig [laydish] ◆ *(CD)* die Single [singel]

> ▸ not a single one nicht ein Einziger [nisht eyn eyntsiger]
> ▸ I'm single ich bin ledig [ish bin laydish]
> ▸ she's a single woman in her thirties sie ist unverheiratet und um die dreißig [zee ist laydish unt um dee dreysish]

**single bed** das Einzelbett [eyntselbeht]

> ▸ we'd prefer two single beds wir hätten lieber zwei Einzelbetten [veer hehten leeber tsvey eyntselbehten]

**single room** das Einzelzimmer [eyntsel-tsim-er]

> ▸ I'd like to book a single room for 5 nights, please ich möchte bitte ein Einzelzimmer für fünf Nächte buchen [ish meusht-e bi-te eyn eyntsel-tsim-er fuur fuunf nehsht-e bookhen]

**sister** die Schwester [shvehster]

> ▸ I have two sisters ich habe zwei Schwestern [ish haab-e tsvey shvehstern]

**sit** *(be sitting)* sitzen [zitsen]; *(sit down)* sich setzen [zish zehtsen]

> ▸ may I sit at your table? darf ich mich mit an Ihren Tisch setzen? [darf ish mish mit an eeren tish zehtsen]
> ▸ is anyone sitting here? sitzt hier schon jemand? [zitst heer shohn yaymant]

**site** *(of a town, a building)* die Lage [laag-e]; *(archaeological)* die Fundstätte [fundshteht-e]

> ▸ can we visit the site? kann man die Fundstätte besichtigen? [kan man dee fundshteht-e bezishtigen]

**sitting** *(for a meal)* die Essenszeit [ehsenz-tseyt]

> ▸ is there more than one sitting for lunch? gibt es mittags mehr als eine Essenszeit? [gipt ehs mitaaks mehr als ey-ne ehsenz-tseyt]

**six** sechs [zehks]

> ▸ there are six of us wir sind zu sechst [veer zint tsoo zehkst]

**sixth** sechste [zehkst-e] ◆ der Sechste [zehkst-e]

> ▸ our room is on the sixth floor unser Zimmer ist im fünften Stock [unzer tsim-er ist im fuunften shtok]

**size** *(of a person, clothes)* die Größe [greus-e]

> ▸ do you have another size? haben Sie eine andere Größe? [haaben zee ey-ne ander-e greus-e]
> ▸ do you have it in a smaller size? haben sie eine kleinere Größe? [haaben zee ey-ne kleyner-e greus-e]

‣ I take/I'm a size 38 *(shoes, clothes)* ich habe Größe achtunddreißig [ish haab-e greus-e akht-unt-dreysish]

**skate** *(for ice skating)* der Schlittschuh [shlit-shoo] ♦ Schlittschuh laufen [shlit-shoo lowfen]

‣ can you skate? können Sie Schlittschuh laufen? [keunen zee shlit-shoo lowfen]

‣ how much is it to rent skates? was kostet es, Schlittschuhe zu leihen? [vas kostet ehs shlit-shoo-e tsoo leyen]

**skating** das Schlittschuhlaufen [shlit-shoo-lowfen]

‣ where can we go skating? wo können wir Schlittschuhlaufen gehen? [voh keunen veer shlit-shoo-lowfen gayen]

**ski** der Ski [shee]

‣ I'd like to rent a pair of skis for the week, please ich möchte bitte für eine Woche ein Paar Skier leihen [ish meusht-e bi-te fuur ey-ne vokh-e eyn par shee-er leyen]

**ski boots** die Skistiefel [shee-shteefel]

‣ I'd like to rent ski boots ich möchte gerne Skistiefel mieten [ish meusht-e gehrn-e shee-shteefel meeten]

**skiing** das Skifahren [sheefaaren]

‣ where can we go skiing near here? wo kann man hier in der Nähe Skifahren gehen? [voh kan man heer in dehr nay-e sheefaaren gayen]

**sleep** schlafen [shlaafen]

‣ I slept well ich habe gut geschlafen [ish haab-e goot geshlaafen]

‣ I can't sleep ich kann nicht schlafen [ish kan nisht shlaafen]

**sleeping bag** der Schlafsack [shlaafzak]

‣ where can I buy a new sleeping bag? wo kann ich einen neuen Schlafsack kaufen? [voh kan ish eynen noyen shlaafzak kowfen]

**sleeping pill** die Schlaftablette [shlaaftableht-e]

‣ I'd like some sleeping pills ich hätte gerne Schlaftabletten [ish heht-e gehrn-e shlaaftabletten]

**slice** *(of bread, ham)* die Scheibe [sheyb-e] ♦ in Scheiben schneiden [in sheyben shneyden]

‣ a thin slice of ham eine dünne Scheibe Schinken [ey-ne duun-e sheyb-e shinken]

**slim** *(person)* schlank [shlank]

‣ she's slim sie ist schlank [zee ist shlank]

**slow** langsam [langzaam]

‣ the fog was slow to clear der Nebel löste sich nur langsam auf [dehr naybel leuzt-e zish noor langzaam owf]

‣ is that clock slow? geht die Uhr nach? [gayt dee oor naakh]

**slowly** langsam [langzaam]

‣ could you speak more slowly, please? können Sie bitte etwas langsamer sprechen? [keunen zee bi-te ehtvas langzaamer shprehshen]

**small** klein [kleyn]
- do you have anything smaller? haben Sie etwas Kleineres? [haaben zee ehtvas kleynerez]

**smell** riechen [reeshen] ◆ *(have a bad smell)* stinken [shtinken]
- can you smell something burning? riecht es nicht verbrannt? [reesht ehs nisht fehrbrant]
- it smells in here hier stinkt es [heer shtinkt ehs]

**smoke** der Rauch [rowkh] ◆ *(person)* rauchen [rowkhen]
- is the smoke bothering you? stört Sie der Rauch? [shteurt zee dehr rowkh]
- do you mind if I smoke? stört es Sie, wenn ich rauche? [shteurt ehs zee vehn ish rowkh-e]
- no thanks, I don't smoke nein danke, ich rauche nicht [neyn dank-e ish rowkh-e nisht]

**smoker** der Raucher [rowkher], die Raucherin [rowkherin]
- are you smokers or nonsmokers? Raucher oder Nichtraucher? [rowkher ohder nishtrowkher]

**smoking** das Rauchen [rowkhen]
- is smoking allowed here? ist Rauchen hier erlaubt? [ist rowkhen heer ehrlowbt]
- I can't stand smoking ich hasse Rauchen [ish has-e rowkhen]

**smoking compartment** das Raucherabteil [rowkher-apteyl]
- I'd like a seat in a smoking compartment ich hätte gerne einen Sitzplatz in einem Raucherabteil [ish heht-e gehrn-e eynen zitsplats in eynem rowkher-apteyl]
- is there a smoking compartment? gibt es ein Raucherabteil? [gipt ehs eyn rowkher-apteyl]

**smoking section** die Raucherzone [rowkher-tsohn-e]
- I'd like a table in the smoking section ich hätte gerne einen Tisch in der Raucherzone [ish heht-e gehrn-e eynen tish in dehr rowkher-tsohn-e]

**sneaker** der Turnschuh [turnshoo]
- your sneakers are really trendy! Ihre Turnschuhe sind total schick! [eer-e turnshoo-e zint tohtaal shik]

**snorkel** der Schnorchel [shnorshel]
- I'd like to rent a snorkel and mask, please ich möchte bitte einen Schnorchel und eine Taucherbrille leihen [ish meusht-e bi-te eynen shnorshel unt ey-ne towkherbril-e leyen]

**snow** schneien [shneyen]
- it's snowing es schneit [ehs shneyt]

**snowboard** das Snowboard [snohbord]
- I'd like to rent a snowboard ich möchte gerne ein Snowboard mieten [ish meusht-e gehrn-e eyn snohbord meeten]

**snowboarding** das Snowboarden [snohborden]
 ▸ where can we go snowboarding near here? wo können wir hier in der Nähe Snowboarden gehen? [voh keunen veer heer in dehr nay-e snohborden gayen]

**snow tire** der Winterreifen [vinter-reyfen]
 ▸ do I need snow tires? brauche ich Winterreifen? [browkh-e ish vinter-reyfen]

**so** (to such a degree) so [zoh]; (consequently) also [alzoh]
 ▸ it's so big! es ist so groß! [ehs ist zoh grohs]
 ▸ there's so many choices I don't know what to have es gibt so viel Auswahl, ich weiß gar nicht, was ich nehmen soll [ehs gipt zoh feel owsvaal ish veys gar nisht vas ish naymen zol]
 ▸ I'm hungry – so am I! ich habe Hunger – ich auch! [ish haab-e hunger ish owkh]

**soap** die Seife [zeyf-e]
 ▸ there's no soap wir haben keine Seife [veer haaben keyn-e zeyf-e]

**socket** (in a wall) die Steckdose [shtehkdohz-e]
 ▸ is there a socket I can use to recharge my cell? gibt es eine Steckdose, wo ich mein Handy aufladen kann? [gipt ehs ey-ne shtehkdohz-e voh ish meyn hehndi owflaaden kan]

**solution** die Lösung [leuzung]
 ▸ that seems to be the best solution das scheint die beste Lösung zu sein [das sheynt dee behst-e leuzung tsoo zeyn]
 ▸ I'd like some rinsing solution for soft lenses ich hätte gerne eine Reinigungslösung für weiche Kontaktlinsen [ish heht-e gehrn-e ey-ne reynigung-zleuzung fuur veysh-e kontaktlinzen]

**some** (an amount of) etwas [ehtvas]; (a number of) einige [eynig-e] ◆ (an amount) etwas [ehtvas]; (a number) einige [eynig-e]
 ▸ I'd like some coffee ich hätte gerne etwas Kaffee [ish heht-e gehrn-e ehtvas kafay]
 ▸ some friends recommended you ein paar Freunde haben Sie empfohlen [eyn par froynd-e haaben zee ehmpfohlen]
 ▸ can I have some? geben Sie mir etwas ab? [gayben zee meer ehtvas ap]

**somebody, someone** jemand [yaymant]
 ▸ somebody left this for you jemand hat das für Sie abgegeben [yaymant hat das fuur zee apgegayben]

**something** etwas [ehtvas]
 ▸ is something wrong? stimmt etwas nicht? [shtimt ehtvas nisht]

**somewhere** irgendwo [irgentvoh]
 ▸ somewhere near here irgendwo in der Nähe [irgentvoh in dehr nay-e]
 ▸ somewhere else irgendwo anders [irgentvoh anderz]
 ▸ I'm looking for somewhere to stay ich suche eine Unterkunft [ish zookh-e ey-ne unterkunft]

**son** der Sohn [zohn]
 ▸ this is my son das ist mein Sohn [das ist meyn zohn]

**saying sorry**

People usually say *Entschuldigung* when they apologize. But if you want to be very formal, you should say *Entschuldigen Sie, bitte*.

**soon** bald [balt]
▶ see you soon! bis bald! [bis balt]
▶ as soon as possible so bald wie möglich [zoh balt vee meuglish]

**sore throat** die Halsschmerzen [hals-shmehrtsen]
▶ I have a sore throat ich habe Halsschmerzen [ish haab-e hals-shmehrtsen]

**sorry**
▶ I'm sorry! Entschuldigung! [ehntshuldigung]
▶ sorry I'm late Entschuldigung, dass ich zu spät komme [ehntshuldigung das ish tsoo shpayt kom-e]
▶ I'm sorry, but this seat is taken es tut mir Leid, aber dieser Platz ist schon besetzt [ehs toot meer leyt aaber deezer plats ist shohn bezehtst]
▶ sorry to bother you entschuldigen Sie die Störung [ehntshuldigen zee dee shteurung]
▶ sorry? *(asking for repetition)* wie bitte? [vee bi-te]
▶ no, sorry nein, tut mir Leid [neyn toot meer leyt]

**sound** *(of footsteps, conversation)* das Geräusch [geroysh]; *(of a voice)* der Klang [klang]; *(of a TV, radio)* der Ton [tohn]
▶ can you turn the sound down? können Sie den Ton leiser stellen? [keunen zee dayn tohn leyzer shtehlen]

**souvenir** das Andenken [andehnken], das Souvenir [zooveneer]
▶ where can I buy souvenirs? wo kann ich Souvenirs kaufen? [voh kan ish zooveneerz kowfen]

**souvenir shop** der Souvenirladen [zooveneerlaaden]
▶ I'm looking for a souvenir shop ich suche einen Souvenirladen [ish zookh-e eynen zooveneerlaaden]

**spa** *(town)* der Kurort [koorort]; *(health club)* das Heilbad [heylbaat]; *(bathtub)* der Whirlpool [werlpool]
▶ the spa's not working der Whirlpool ist kaputt [dehr werlpool ist kaput]

**space** *(room)* der Platz [plats]; *(for parking)* der Parkplatz [parkplats]; *(for a tent, a trailer)* der Stellplatz [shtehlplats]
▶ is there space for another bed in the room? ist im Zimmer noch Platz für ein weiteres Bett? [ist im tsim-er nokh plats fuur eyn veyterez beht]
▶ I'd like a space for one tent for two days ich hätte gerne einen Stellplatz für ein Zelt für zwei Tage [ish heht-e gehrn-e eynen shtehlplats fuur eyn tsehlt fuur tsvey taag-e]

▸ do you have any spaces farther from the road? haben Sie noch Stellplätze, die weiter von der Straße entfernt sind? [haaben zee nokh stehlplehts-e dee veyter fon dehr shtraas-e ehntfehrnt zint]

**spade** *(tool)* der Spaten [shpaaten]; *(child's toy)* die Schaufel [showfel]

▸ my son's left his spade at the beach mein Sohn hat seine Schaufel am Strand liegen lassen [meyn zohn hat zeyn-e showfel am shtrant leegen las-en]

**spare** *(clothes)* zum Wechseln [tsum vehkseln]; *(battery)* Ersatz- [ehrzats] ◆ *(tire)* der Ersatzreifen [ehrzatsreyfen]; *(part)* das Ersatzteil [ehrzatsteyl]

▸ should I take some spare clothes? sollte ich Kleidung zum Wechseln mitnehmen? [zol-te ish kleydung tsum vehkseln mitnaymen]

▸ I don't have any spare cash ich habe kein Bargeld mehr übrig [ish haab-e keyn bargehlt mehr uubrish]

▸ I've got a spare ticket for the game ich habe noch eine Karte für das Spiel übrig [ish haab-e nokh ey-ne kart-e fuur das shpeel uubrish]

**spare part** das Ersatzteil [ehrzatsteyl]

▸ where can I get spare parts? wo bekomme ich Ersatzteile? [voh bekom-e ish ehrzatsteyl-e]

**spare tire** der Ersatzreifen [ehrzatsreyfen]

▸ the spare tire's flat too der Ersatzreifen ist auch platt [dehr ehrzatsreyfen ist owkh plat]

**spare wheel** das Ersatzrad [ehrzatsraat]

▸ there's no spare wheel es gibt kein Ersatzrad [ehs gipt keyn ehrzatsraat]

**sparkling** *(water)* mit Kohlensäure [mit kohlenzoyr-e]

▸ could I have a bottle of sparkling water, please? könnte ich bitte eine Flasche Mineralwasser mit Kohlensäure bekommen? [keunt-e ish bi-te ey-ne flash-e mineraalvas-er mit kohlenzoyr-e bekom-en]

▸ can I have a glass of sparkling wine? kann ich ein Glas Sekt bekommen? [kan ish eyn glaas zehkt bekom-en]

**speak** *(utter)* sagen [zaagen]; *(language)* sprechen [shprehshen] ◆ sprechen [shprehshen]

▸ I speak hardly any German ich spreche fast kein Deutsch [ish shprehsh-e fast keyn doytsh]

▸ is there anyone here who speaks English? spricht hier jemand Englisch? [shprisht heer yaymant ehnglish]

▸ could you speak more slowly? könnten Sie langsamer sprechen? [keunten zee langzaamer shprehshen]

▸ hello, I'd like to speak to Mr...; this is... hallo, ich möchte mit Herrn ... sprechen; hier ist ... [haloh ish meusht-e mit hehrn shprehshen heer ist]

▸ who's speaking please? wer spricht bitte? [vehr shprisht bi-te]

▸ hello, Gary speaking hallo, hier ist Gary [haloh heer ist gari]

**special** *(in restaurant)* das Tagesgericht [taagezgerisht]; *(TV programme)* die Sondersendung [zonderzehndung]
- what's today's special? was gibt es heute als Tagesgericht? [vas gipt ehs hoyt-e als taagezgerisht]

**specialist** der Spezialist [shpehtsialist], die Spezialistin [shpehtsialistin]
- could you refer me to a specialist? könnten Sie mich zu einem Spezialisten/ einer Spezialistin überweisen? [keunten zee mish tsoo eynem shpehtsialisten/eyner shpehtsialistin uuberveyzen]

**specialty** die Spezialität [shpehtsialitayt]
- what are the local specialties? was sind die lokalen Spezialitäten? [vas zint dee lohkaalen shpehtsialitayten]

**speed limit** die Geschwindigkeitsbegrenzung [geshvindishkeyts-begrehntsung]
- what's the speed limit on this road? was ist die Geschwindigkeitsbegrenzung auf dieser Straße? [vas ist dee geshvindishkeyts-begrehntsung owf deezer shtraas-e]

**speedometer** der Tachometer [takhohmayter]
- the speedometer's broken der Tachometer ist kaputt [dehr takhohmayter ist kaput]

**speed trap** die Radarfalle [radaarfal-e]
- are there lots of speed traps in the area? gibt es viele Radarfallen in der Gegend? [gipt ehs feel-e radaarfal-en in dehr gaygent]

**spell** *(write)* schreiben [shreyben]; *(aloud)* buchstabieren [bookh-shtabeeren]
- how do you spell your name? wie schreibt sich Ihr Name? [vee shreybt zish eer naam-e]

**spend** *(money)* ausgeben [owsgayben]; *(time, vacation)* verbringen [fehrbringen]
- we are prepared to spend up to 200 euros wir sind bereit, bis zu zweihundert Euro auszugeben [veer zint bereyt bis tsoo tsveyhundert oyroh ows-tsugayben]
- I spent a month in Germany a few years ago ich war vor ein paar Jahren für einen Monat in Deutschland [ish var for eyn par yaaren fuur eynen mohnaat in doytshlant]

**spicy** stark gewürzt [shtark gevuurst]
- is this dish spicy? ist dieses Gericht stark gewürzt? [ist deezes gerisht shtark gevuurst]

**spoon** der Löffel [leufel]
- could I have a spoon? könnte ich einen Löffel bekommen? [keunt-e ish eynen leufel bekom-en]

**sport** der Sport [shport]
- do you play any sports? treiben Sie Sport? [treyben zee shport]
- I play a lot of sports ich treibe viel Sport [ish treyb-e feel shport]

**sporty** *(person)* sportlich [shportlish]
- I'm not very sporty ich bin nicht sehr sportlich [ish bin nisht zehr shportlish]

You can buy stamps in the *Deutsche Post* offices, from stamp machines and in stores that sell postcards.

**sprain** verstauchen [fehrshtowkhen]
- ▸ I think I've sprained my ankle ich glaube, ich habe mir den Knöchel verstaucht [ish glowb-e ish haab-e meer dayn kneushel fehrshtowkht]
- ▸ my wrist is sprained mein Handgelenk ist verstaucht [meyn hantgelehnk ist fehrshtowkht]

**square** *(in a town)* der Platz [plats]
- ▸ where is the market square? wo ist der Marktplatz? [voh ist dehr marktplats]

**stain** der Fleck [flehk]
- ▸ can you remove this stain? können Sie diesen Fleck entfernen? [keunen zee deezen flehk ehntfehrnen]

**stairs** die Treppe [trep-e]
- ▸ where are the stairs? wo ist die Treppe? [voh ist dee trep-e]

**stall** *(car, engine)* absterben [apshtehrben]
- ▸ the engine keeps stalling der Motor stirbt ständig ab [dehr mohtor shtirbt shtehndish ap]

**stamp** *(for letter, postcard)* die Briefmarke [breefmark-e]
- ▸ do you sell stamps? verkaufen Sie Briefmarken? [fehrkowfen zee breefmarken]

**stand** *(stall, booth)* der Stand [shtant]; *(in a stadium)* die Tribüne [tribuun-e]
- ♦ *(tolerate)* ausstehen [ows-shtayen] ♦ *(be upright)* stehen [shtayen]; *(get up)* aufstehen [owfshtayen]

**start** *(begin)* anfangen [anfangen]; *(engine)* starten [shtarten]
- ▸ when does the concert start? wann fängt das Konzert an? [van fehnkt das kontsehrt an]
- ▸ the car won't start das Auto startet nicht [das owtoh shtartet nisht]

**starving** sehr hungrig [zehr hungrish]
- ▸ I'm absolutely starving ich bin am Verhungern [ish bin am fehrhungern]

**States**
- ▸ the States die (Vereinigten) Staaten [dee (fehreynishten) shtaaten]
- ▸ I'm from the States ich komme aus den (Vereinigten) Staaten [ish kom-e ows dayn (fehreynishten) shtaaten]
- ▸ I live in the States ich lebe in den (Vereinigten) Staaten [ish layb-e in dayn (fehreynishten) shtaaten]
- ▸ have you ever been to the States? waren Sie schon einmal in den (Vereinigten) Staaten? [vaaren zee shohn eynmal in dayn (fehreynishten) shtaaten]

**station** *(railroad)* der Bahnhof [baanhohf]; *(bus)* der Busbahnhof [busbaanhohf]; *(subway)* die U-Bahn-Station [oo-baan-shtatsiohn]; *(TV, radio)* der Sender [zehnder]; *(police)* die Wache [vakh-e]
- to the train station, please! zum Bahnhof, bitte! [tsum baanhohf bi-te]
- where is the nearest subway station? wo ist die nächste U-Bahn-Station? [voh ist dee nehkst-e oo-baan-shtatsiohn]

**stay** bleiben [bleyben] ◆ *(visit)* der Aufenthalt [owfehnt-halt]
- we're planning to stay for two nights wir planen zwei Nächte zu bleiben [veer plaanen tsvey nehsht-e tsoo bleyben]
- a two-week stay ein zweiwöchiger Aufenthalt [eyn tsvey-veushiger owfehnt-halt]

**steak** das Steak [stayk]
- I'd like a steak and fries ich hätte gerne ein Steak mit Pommes frites [ish heht-e gehrn-e eyn stayk mit pom-ez frit-ez]

**steal** stehlen [shtaylen]
- my passport was stolen mein Pass ist gestohlen worden [meyn pas ist geshtohlen vorden]
- our car has been stolen unser Auto ist gestohlen worden [unzer owtoh ist geshtohlen vorden]

**steering** die Lenkung [lehnkung]
- there's a problem with the steering es stimmt etwas nicht mit der Lenkung [ehs shtimt ehtvas nisht mit dehr lehnkung]

**steering wheel** das Lenkrad [lehnkraat]
- the steering wheel is very stiff das Lenkrad ist sehr steif [das lehnkraat ist zehr shteyf]

**stick shift** *(lever)* der Schalthebel [shalt-haybel]; *(car)* der Schaltwagen [shaltvaagen]
- is it a stick shift or an automatic? ist es ein Schaltwagen oder ein Automatikwagen? [ist ehs eyn shaltvaagen ohder eyn owtohmaateek-vaagen]

**still** noch [nokh]; *(for emphasis)* immer noch [im-er nokh]
- how many miles are there still to go? wie viele Meilen sind es noch? [vee feel-e meylen zint ehs nokh]
- we're still waiting to be served wir warten noch immer auf die Bedienung [veer varten nokh im-er owf dee bedeenung]

**sting** *(wasp)* stechen [shtekhen]; *(nettle)* verbrennen [fehrbrehnen]
- I've been stung by a wasp ich bin von einer Wespe gestochen worden [ish bin fon eyner vehsp-e geshtokhen vorden]

**stomach** der Magen [maagen]
- my stomach hurts mein Magen tut weh [meyn maagen toot vay]

**stomachache** die Magenschmerzen [maagenshmehrtsen]
- I have a really bad stomachache ich habe ganz starke Magenschmerzen [ish haab-e gants shtark-e maagenshmehrtsen]

**stop** *(for buses, trains)* die Haltestelle [halt-e-shtel-e]; *(on a journey)* der Halt [halt]; *(on a flight)* die Zwischenlandung [tsvishenlandung] ◆ anhalten [anhalten] ◆ (an)halten [(an)halten]

> is this the right stop for ...? ist dies die richtige Haltestelle für ...? [ist deez dee rishtish-e halt-e-shtel-e fuur]

> stop it! Schluss damit! [shlus daamit]

> where in town does the shuttle stop? wo in der Stadt hält der Shuttle? [voh in dehr shtat hehlt dehr shutel]

> please stop here bitte halten Sie hier [bi-te halten zee heer]

> which stations does this train stop at? wo überall hält dieser Zug? [voh uuberal hehlt deezer tsook]

> do we stop at Weimar? halten wir in Weimar? [halten veer in veymar]

**store** *(place selling goods)* der Laden [laaden]

> are there any bigger stores in the area? gibt es in der Gegend größere Läden? [gipt ehs in dehr gaygent greuser-e layden]

**store window** das Schaufenster [showfehnster]

> the store windows are beautifully decorated at Christmas die Schaufenster sind an Weihnachten wunderschön dekoriert [dee showfehnster zint an veynahkten vundersheun dehkoreert]

**storm** *(strong wind)* der Sturm [shturm]; *(with thunder and lightning)* das Gewitter [gevit-er]

> is there going to be a storm? wird es ein Gewitter geben? [virt ehs eyn gevit-er gayben]

**straight** *(line, road)* gerade [geraad-e]; *(hair)* glatt [glat] ◆ *(in a straight line)* geradeaus [geraad-e-ows]

> you have to keep going straight Sie müssen immer geradeaus fahren [zee meusen im-er geraad-e-ows faaren]

---

### in a store

> no, thanks, I'm just looking nein, danke, ich sehe mich nur um [neyn dank-e ish zay-e mish noor um]

> how much is this? wie viel kostet das? [vee feel kostet das]

> I take a size 38/I'm a size 38 ich brauche Größe achtunddreißig/ich habe Größe achtunddreißig [ish browkh-e greus-e akht-unt-dreysish/ish haab-e greus-e akht-unt-dreysish]

> can I try this coat on? kann ich diesen Mantel anprobieren? [kan ish deezen mantel anprohbeeren]

> can it be exchanged? kann man es umtauschen? [kan man ehs umtowshen]

**street** die Straße [shtraas-e]
- will this street take me to the station? komme ich auf dieser Straße zum Bahnhof? [kom-e ish owf deezer shtraas-e tsum baanhof]

**streetcar** die Straßenbahn [shtraasenbaan]
- can you buy tickets on the streetcar? kann man Fahrkarten in der Straßenbahn kaufen? [kan man faarkarten in dehr shtraasenbaan kowfen]
- which streetcar line do we have to take? welche Straßenbahn müssen wir nehmen? [vehlshe shtraasenbaan meusen veer naymen]
- where is the nearest streetcar stop? wo ist die nächste Straßenbahnhaltestelle? [voh ist dee nehkst-e shtraasenbaan-halt-e-shtehl-e]

**street map** der Stadtplan [shtatplan]
- where can I buy a street map? wo kann ich einen Stadtplan kaufen? [voh kan ish eynen shtatplan kowfen]

**strong** (wind, current) stark [shtark]; (smell, taste) intensiv [intehnzeev]
- is the current very strong here? ist die Strömung stark hier? [ist dee shtreumung shtark heer]

**stuck**
- to be stuck (jammed, trapped) festsitzen [fehst-zitsen]
- someone is stuck in the elevator jemand sitzt im Aufzug fest [yaymant zitst im owftsook fehst]

**student** der Student [shtudehnt], die Studentin [shtudehntin]
- I'm a student ich bin Student/Studentin [ish bin shtudehnt/shtudehntin]

**student discount** die Studentenermäßigung [shtudehnten-ehrmaysigung]
- do you have student discounts? gibt es bei Ihnen Studentenermäßigung? [gipt ehs bey eenen shtudehnten-ehrmaysigung]

**studio (apartment)** die Studiowohnung [shtoodioh-vohnung]
- I'm renting a studio apartment ich miete eine Studiowohnung [ish meet-e ey-ne shtoodioh-vohnung]

**style** der Stil [shteel]
- she has a lot of style sie hat viel Stil [zee hat feel shteel]

**subway** die U-Bahn [oo-baan]
- can I have a map of the subway? kann ich einen U-Bahn-Plan bekommen? [kan ish eynen oo-baan-plan bekom-en]

**subway train** der U-Bahn-Zug [oo-baan-tsook]
- when's the last subway train from this station? wann fährt der letzte U-Bahn-Zug von dieser Haltestelle? [van fehrt dehr lehtst-e oo-baan-tsook fon deezer halt-e-shtehl-e]

**sudden** plötzlich [pleutslish]
- all of a sudden ganz plötzlich [gants pleutslish]

**sugar** der Zucker [tsuker]

▸ can you pass me the sugar? können Sie mir den Zucker reichen? [keunen zee meer dayn tsuker reyshen]

**suggest** *(propose)* vorschlagen [forshlaagen]

▸ do you have anything else you can suggest? können Sie etwas anderes vorschlagen? [keunen zee ehtvas anderez forshlaagen]

**suit** *(be convenient for)* passen [pas-en]

▸ that suits me perfectly das passt wunderbar [das past vunderbar]

▸ it doesn't suit me das geht bei mir nicht [das gayt bey meer nisht]

**suitcase** der Koffer [kof-er]

▸ one of my suitcases is missing einer meiner Koffer fehlt [eyner meyner kof-er faylt]

▸ my suitcase was damaged in transit mein Koffer ist auf dem Transport beschädigt worden [meyn kof-er ist owf daym transport beshaydisht vorden]

**summer** der Sommer [zom-er]

▸ in (the) summer im Sommer [im zom-er]

**summer vacation** die Sommerferien [zom-er-fayri-en]

▸ we've come here for our summer vacation wir sind für unsere Sommerferien hierher gekommen [veer zint fuur unzer-e zom-er-fayri-en heerhehr gekom-en]

**sun** die Sonne [zon-e]

▸ the sun's very strong at this time of day die Sonne ist zu dieser Tageszeit sehr stark [dee zon-e ist tsoo deezer taagez-tseyt zehr shtark]

**sunburn** der Sonnenbrand [zon-en-brant]

▸ I've got a bad sunburn ich habe einen schlimmen Sonnenbrand [ish haab-e eynen shlim-en zon-en-brant]

▸ do you have cream for a sunburn? haben Sie eine Creme für Sonnenbrand? [haaben zee ey-ne kraym-e fuur zon-en-brant]

**Sunday** der Sonntag [zontaak]

▸ where can I find a doctor on a Sunday? wo kann ich am Sonntag einen Arzt finden? [voh kan ish am zontaak eynen artst fin-den]

▸ are the stores open on Sunday? sind die Läden am Sonntag geöffnet? [zint dee layden am zontaak ge-eufnet]

**sun deck** das Sonnendeck [zon-en-dehk]

▸ how do I get onto the sun deck? wie komme ich aufs Sonnendeck? [vee kom-e ish owfs zon-en-dehk]

**sunglasses** die Sonnenbrille [zon-en-bril-e]

▸ I've lost my sunglasses ich habe meine Sonnenbrille verloren [ish haab-e meyn-e zon-en-bril-e fehrloren]

**sunny** *(day, weather)* sonnig [zon-ish]

▸ it's sunny die Sonne scheint [dee zon-e sheynt]

**sunrise** der Sonnenaufgang [zon-en-owfgang]

▸ what time is sunrise? um wie viel Uhr ist Sonnenaufgang? [um vee feel oor ist zon-en-owfgang]

**sunset** der Sonnenuntergang [zon-en-untergang]
▸ isn't the sunset beautiful? ist der Sonnenuntergang nicht wunderschön? [ist dehr zon-en-untergang nisht vundersheun]

**suntan lotion** das Sonnenöl [zon-en-eul]
▸ I'd like SPF 30 suntan lotion ich hätte gerne Sonnenöl mit Sonnenschutzfaktor dreißig [ish heht-e gehrn-e zon-en-eul mit zon-en-shutsfaktor dreysish]

**supermarket** der Supermarkt [zoopermarkt]
▸ is there a supermarket nearby? gibt es einen Supermarkt in der Nähe? [gipt ehs eynen zoopermarkt in dehr nay-e]

**surcharge** *(excess charge)* der Zuschlag [tsooshlaak]; *(for postage)* das Nachporto [nakhportoh]
▸ do I have to pay a surcharge? muss ich einen Zuschlag bezahlen? [mus ish eynen tsooshlaak betsaalen]

**sure** sicher [zisher]
▸ are you sure that's how you say it? sind Sie sich sicher, dass man es so sagt? [zint zee zisher das man ehs zoh zaakt]

**surfboard** das Surfbrett [serfbreht]
▸ is there somewhere we can rent surfboards? kann man irgendwo Surfbretter mieten? [kan man irgehntvoh serfbrehter meeten]

**surfing** das Surfen [serfen]
▸ can we go surfing around here? können wir hier in der Gegend surfen gehen? [keunen veer heer in dehr gaygent serfen gayen]

**surprise** die Überraschung [uuber-rashung]
▸ what a nice surprise! was für eine schöne Überraschung! [vas fuur ey-ne sheun-e uuber-rashung]

**surrounding area** die Umgebung [umgaybung]
▸ Lindau and the surrounding area Lindau und die Umgebung [lindow unt dee umgaybung]

**swallow** schlucken [shluk-en]
▸ the ATM outside has swallowed my credit card der Geldautomat draußen hat meine Kreditkarte geschluckt [dehr gehltowtohmaat drowsen hat meyn-e krehdeetkart-e geshlukt]
▸ it hurts when I swallow es tut weh, wenn ich schlucke [ehs toot vay vehn ish shluk-e]

**swim** schwimmen [shvim-en] ✦ das Schwimmen [shvim-en]
▸ is it safe to swim here? ist es hier sicher zu schwimmen? [ist ehs heer zisher tsoo shvim-en]
▸ to go for a swim schwimmen gehen [shvim-en gayen]

**swimming pool** das Schwimmbad [shvimbaat]
 ▸ is there an open-air swimming pool? gibt es ein Freibad? [gipt ehs eyn freybaat]

**switch** der Schalter [shalter]
 ▸ the switch doesn't work der Schalter funktioniert nicht [dehr shalter funktsiohneert nisht]

**switch off** *(light, appliance, radio)* ausschalten [ows-shalten]; *(electricity)* abstellen [apshtehlen]
 ▸ where do you switch the light off? wo schaltet man das Licht aus? [voh shaltet man das lisht ows]
 ▸ my cell was switched off mein Handy war ausgeschaltet [meyn hehndi var owsgeshaltet]

**switch on** *(light, heating, TV)* einschalten [eynshalten]; *(engine)* anlassen [anlasen]
 ▸ where do I switch this light on? wo kann ich diese Lampe einschalten? [voh kan ish deez-e lampe-e eynshalten]
 ▸ how do you switch the engine on? wie lasse ich den Motor an? [vee las-e ish dayn mohtor an]

**synagogue** die Synagoge [zuunagohg-e]
 ▸ where's the nearest synagogue? wo ist die nächste Synagoge? [voh ist dee nehkst-e zuunagohg-e]

**table** der Tisch [tish]
 ▸ I've reserved a table in the name of... ich habe einen Tisch auf den Namen ... reserviert [ish haab-e eynen tish owf dayn naamen rehzerveert]
 ▸ a table for four, please! einen Tisch für vier, bitte! [eynen tish fuur feer bi-te]

**table tennis** das Tischtennis [tishtehnis]
 ▸ are there tables for table tennis? gibt es Tische zum Tischtennisspielen? [gipt ehs tish-e tsum tishtehnis-shpeelen]

**table wine** der Tafelwein [taafelveyn]
 ▸ a bottle of red table wine eine Flasche roten Tafelwein [ey-ne flash-e rohten taafelveyn]

**take** *(get hold of, transport)* nehmen [naymen]; *(steal)* stehlen [shtaylen]; *(carry, lead, accompany)* bringen [bringen]; *(in time)* dauern [dowern]; *(size)* tragen [traagen]
 ▸ someone's taken my bag jemand hat meine Tasche gestohlen [yaymant hat meyn-e tash-e geshtohlen]
 ▸ can you take me to this address? können Sie mich zu dieser Adresse bringen?

[keunen zee mish tsoo deezer adrehs-e bringen]

- are you taking the plane or the train to Berlin? **fliegen Sie oder fahren Sie mit dem Zug nach Berlin?** [fleegen zee ohder faaren zee mit daym tsook naakh behrleen]
- which road should I take? **welche Straße soll ich nehmen?** [vehlsh-e shtraas-e zol ish naymen]
- I take a size 40 **ich trage Größe vierzig** [ish traag-e greus-e feertsish]
- how long does the trip take? **wie lange dauert die Reise?** [vee lang-e dowert dee reyz-e]
- how long does it take to get to Hamburg? **wie lange fährt man bis Hamburg?** [vee lang-e fehrt man bis hamburk]
- could you take a photo of us? **könnten Sie ein Photo von uns machen?** [keunten zee eyn fohtoh fon uns makhen]

**take back** *(to a store)* zurückbringen [tsuruukbringen]; *(to one's home)* mitbringen [mitbringen]

- I'm looking for a present to take back to my son **ich suche ein Geschenk, dass ich meinem Sohn mitbringen kann** [ish zookh-e eyn geshehnk das ish meynem zohn mitbringen kan]

**take down** *(from shelf)* herunterheben [hehrunterhayben]; *(downstairs)* heruntertragen [hehruntertraagen]

- could you take these bags down, please? **könnten Sie bitte diese Koffer heruntertragen?** [keunten zee bi-te deez-e kof-er hehruntertraagen]

**take in** *(bags, luggage)* hereinbringen [hehreynbringen]

- can you have someone take in my bags, please? **können Sie bitte jemanden meine Koffer hereinbringen lassen?** [keunen zee bi-te yaymanden meyn-e kof-er hehreynbringen las-en]

**taken** *(seat)* besetzt [bezehtst]

- sorry, this seat is taken **tut mir Leid, dieser Platz ist besetzt** [toot meer leyt deezer plats ist bezehtst]

**take up** *(bags, luggage)* hochbringen [hohkhbringen]

- can someone take our bags up to our room? **kann jemand unsere Koffer in unser Zimmer hochbringen?** [kan yaymant unzer-e kof-er in unzer tsim-er hohkhbringen]

**talk** sprechen [shprehshen]

- could I talk with you for a moment? **kann ich Sie kurz sprechen?** [kan ish zee kurts shprehshen]
- you have no right to talk to me like that **Sie haben kein Recht so mit mir zu sprechen** [zee haaben keyn rehsht zoh mit meer tsoo shprehshen]

**tall** groß [grohs]

- what's that tall building over there? **was ist das große Gebäude da drüben?** [vas ist das grohs-e geboyd-e daa druuben]

## taxis

Taxis aren't particularly economical unless there are a few of you. If you are a woman on your own you can take advantage of the *Frauentaxis* in most big towns which will take you where you need to go for the price of a bus journey after 9 p.m.

**tank** *(for gas)* der Tank [tank]
 ▸ is the tank full? ist der Tank voll? [ist dehr tank fol]

**tap water** das Leitungswasser [leytungz-vas-er]
 ▸ just some tap water, please nur etwas Leitungswasser, bitte [noor ehtvas leytungz-vas-er bi-te]

**taste** der Geschmack [geshmak] ◆ schmecken [shmehken]; *(try)* probieren [prohbeeren]
 ▸ I can't taste anything ich schmecke gar nichts [ish shmehk-e gar nishts]
 ▸ would you like to taste the wine? möchten Sie den Wein probieren? [meushten zee dayn veyn prohbeeren]
 ▸ it tastes funny es schmeckt komisch [ehs shmehkt kohmish]

**tax** die Steuer [shtoyer]
 ▸ does this price include tax? ist in diesem Preis die Steuer enthalten? [ist in deezem preys dee shtoyer ehnt-halten]

**taxi** das Taxi [taksi]
 ▸ how much does a taxi cost from here to the station? wie viel kostet ein Taxi von hier zum Bahnhof? [vee feel kostet eyn taksi fon heer tsum baanhohf]
 ▸ I'd like to reserve a taxi to take me to the airport, please ich möchte bitte ein Taxi zum Flughafen reservieren [ish meusht-e bi-te eyn taksi tsum flookhaafen rehzehrveeren]

## taking a taxi

 ▸ could you call me a taxi, please? könnten Sie mir bitte ein Taxi rufen? [keunten zee meer bi-te eyn taksi roofen]
 ▸ to the station/airport, please zum Bahnhof/Flughafen, bitte [tsum baanhohf/flookhaafen bi-te]
 ▸ stop here/at the lights/at the corner, please halten Sie bitte hier/an der Ampel/an der Ecke [halten zee bi-te heer/an dehr ampel/an dehr ehk-e]
 ▸ can you wait for me? können Sie auf mich warten? [keunen zee owf mish varten]
 ▸ how much is it? wie viel macht es? [vee feel makht ehs]
 ▸ keep the change behalten Sie den Rest [behalten zee dayn rehst]

## using the telephone

Calling someone is very simple: you say *Hallo, hier ist* and then your name, and when you answer a call you just say your name. On the other hand, when you hang up, don't say *auf Wiedersehen* (which is from *sehen*, to see) but *auf Wiederhören* (from *hören*, to hear).

**taxi driver** der Taxifahrer [taksifaarer], die Taxifahrerin [taksifaarerin]
▸ can you ask the taxi driver to wait? können Sie den Taxifahrer/die Taxifahrerin bitten zu warten? [keunen zee dayn taksifaarer/dee taksifaarerin bit-en tsoo varten]

**taxi stand** der Taxistand [taksi-shtant]
▸ where can I find a taxi stand? wo finde ich einen Taxistand? [voh fin-de ish eynen taksi-shtant]

**tea** *(drink)* der Tee [tay]
▸ tea with milk Tee mit Milch [tay mit milsh]
▸ tea without milk Tee ohne Milch [tay ohn-e milsh]

**teach** *(in school)* unterrichten [unter-rishten]
▸ so, you teach German? maybe you could help me! Sie unterrichten also Deutsch? vielleicht könnten Sie mir helfen! [zee unter-rishten alzoh doytsh feeleysht keunten zee meer hehlfen]

**teacher** der Lehrer [lehrer], die Lehrerin [lehrerin]
▸ I'm a teacher ich bin Lehrer/Lehrerin [ish bin lehrer/lehrerin]

**telephone** das Telefon [tehlefohn] ✦ anrufen [anroofen] ✦ telefonieren [tehlefohneeren]
▸ can I use the telephone? kann ich das Telefon benutzen? [kan ish das tehlefohn benutsen]

**telephone booth** die Telefonzelle [tehlefohn-tsehl-e]
▸ is there a telephone booth near here? ist hier in der Nähe eine Telefonzelle? [ist heer in dehr nay-e ey-ne tehlefohn-tsehl-e]

**telephone call** der Telefonanruf [tehlefohn-anroof]
▸ I'd like to make a telephone call ich möchte einen Telefonanruf machen [ish meusht-e eynen tehlefohn-anroof makhen]

**television** *(system, broadcasts)* das Fernsehen [fehmzayen]; *(set)* der Fernseher [fehmzayer]
▸ what's on television tonight? was gibt es heute Abend im Fernsehen? [vas gipt ehs hoyt-e aabent im fehmzayen]

**tell** *(say)* sagen [zaagen]; *(relate)* erzählen [ehrtsaylen]
▸ can you tell me the way to the museum? können Sie mir sagen, wie ich zum Museum komme? [keunen zee meer zaagen vee ish tsum moozayum kom-e]
▸ can you tell me what time it is? können Sie mir sagen, wie spät es ist? [keunen zee meer zaagen vee shpayt ehs ist]

---

## saying thank you (i)

'Thank you' is *Vielen Dank!*, *Danke schön!* or just *Danke!* In German-speaking Switzerland you might hear *Merci* or *Merci vielmals* as well. To this you'd reply *Bitte schön*, *Bitte sehr* or *Gern geschehen*. In Austria you'd say *Gerne*.

---

**temperature** *(outside, of water)* die Temperatur [tehmperatoor]; *(fever)* das Fieber [feeber]

  ▸ what's the temperature? was ist die Temperatur? [vas ist dee tehmperatoor]
  ▸ I've got a temperature ich habe Fieber [ish haab-e feeber]

**ten** zehn [tsayn]

  ▸ there are ten of us wir sind zu zehnt [veer zint tsoo tsaynt]

**tennis** das Tennis [tehnis]

  ▸ where can we play tennis? wo können wir Tennis spielen? [voh keunen veer tehnis shpeelen]

**tennis racket** der Tennisschläger [tehnis-shlayger]

  ▸ can you rent tennis rackets? kann man Tennisschläger mieten? [kan man tehnis-shlayger meeten]

**tent** das Zelt [tsehlt]

  ▸ I'd like to book space for a tent, please ich möchte bitte einen Stellplatz für ein Zelt buchen [ish meusht-e bi-te eynen stehlplats fuur eyn tsehlt bookhen]
  ▸ can you put up your tent anywhere? kann man sein Zelt irgendwo aufschlagen? [kan man zeyn tsehlt irgehntvoh owfshlaagen]

**tent peg** der Zeltpflock [tsehltpflok]

  ▸ we're short of tent pegs wir sind knapp an Zeltpflöcken [veer zint knap an tsehltpfleuken]

**terminal** *(in airport)* der Terminal [tehrminal]

  ▸ where is terminal 1? wo ist Terminal eins? [voh ist tehrminal eyns]
  ▸ is there a shuttle between terminals? gibt es einen Shuttle zwischen den Terminals? [gipt ehs eynen shutel tsvishen dayn tehrminalz]

**tetanus** der Tetanus [taytanus]

  ▸ I've been vaccinated for tetanus ich bin gegen Tetanus geimpft worden [ish bin gaygen taytanus ge-impft vorden]

**thank** danken [danken] ♦ **thanks** danke [dank-e]

  ▸ I can't thank you enough ich kann Ihnen nicht genug danken [ish kan eenen nisht genookh danken]
  ▸ thanks for everything danke für alles [dank-e fuur al-es]

**thank you!** danke! [dank-e]

  ▸ thank you very much! vielen Dank! [feelen dank]
  ▸ thank you for your help danke für Ihre Hilfe [dank-e fuur eer-e hilf-e] ▸ see box on p. 144

**that** *(demonstrative use)* das [das]; *(in relative clauses)* der [dehr], die [dee], das [das] ◆ *(as adjective)* dieser [deezer]

▸ who's that? wer ist das? [vehr ist das]
▸ that's right das stimmt [das shtimt]
▸ the road that goes to Bremen die Straße, die nach Bremen führt [dee shtraas-e dee naakh braymen fuurt]
▸ I'll have that one ich nehme das [ish naym-e das]

**theater** das Theater [tayaater]

▸ where is there a theater? wo gibt es ein Theater? [voh gipt ehs eyn tayaater]

**theft** der Diebstahl [deebshtaal]

▸ I'd like to report a theft ich möchte einen Diebstahl melden [ish meusht-e eynen deebshtaal mehlden]

**then** dann [dan]

▸ I'll see you then bis dann [bis dan]
▸ I'll see you at six then bis dann um sechs [bis dan um zehks]

**there** *(in that place)* dort [dort]; *(to that place)* dorthin [dort-hin]

▸ he's over there er ist dort drüben [ehr ist dort druuben]
▸ there is/are ... es gibt ... [ehs gipt]
▸ there's a problem es gibt ein Problem [ehs gipt eyn problaym]
▸ are there any restrooms near here? gibt es hier in der Nähe Toiletten? [gipt ehs heer in dehr nay-e toylehten]
▸ there you are *(handing over something)* bitte sehr [bi-te zehr]

**thermometer** das Thermometer [tehrmohmayter]

▸ do you have a thermometer? haben Sie ein Thermometer? [haaben zee eyn tehrmohmayter]
▸ the thermometer shows 18 degrees (Celsius) das Thermometer zeigt achtzehn Grad (Celsius) [das tehrmohmayter tseykt akht-tsayn graat (zehlzius)]

---

### saying thank you

▸ thank you danke [dank-e]
▸ thanks, that's very kind of you danke, das ist sehr nett von Ihnen [dank-e das ist zehr neht fon eenen]
▸ I can't thank you enough ich kann Ihnen nicht genug danken [ish kan eenen nisht genookh danken]
▸ thank you for your help danke für Ihre Hilfe [dank-e fuur eer-e hilf-e]
▸ I wanted to thank you for inviting me ich wollte mich bei Ihnen für die Einladung bedanken [ish volt-e mish bey eenen fuur dee eynlaadung bedanken]

**thin** dünn [duun]

> isn't that jacket too thin for a cold evening like this? ist diese Jacke nicht zu dünn für einen kalten Abend wie diesen? [ist deez-e yak-e nisht tsoo duun fuur eynen kalten aabent vee deezen]

**thing** *(object)* das Ding [ding]; *(idea, matter)* die Sache [zakh-e]

> what's that thing for? wofür ist das? [vohfuur ist das]
> I don't know what the best thing to do is ich weiß nicht, was man am besten machen sollte [ish veys nisht vas man am behsten makhen zolt-e]
> could you look after my things for a minute? könnten Sie für eine Minute auf meine Sachen aufpassen? [keunten zee fuur ey-ne minoot-e owf meyn-e zakhen owfpas-en]

**think** denken [dehnken]; *(believe)* glauben [glowben]

> I think (that)... ich glaube, (dass) ... [ish glowb-e (das)]
> I thought the service charge was included ich dachte, die Bedienung wäre im Preis enthalten [ish dakht-e dee bedeenung vehr-e im preys ehnt-halten]
> I don't think so ich glaube nicht [ish glowb-e nisht]

**third** dritter [drit-er] ♦ *(fraction)* das Drittel [drit-el]; *(gear)* der dritte Gang [drit-e gang]

> this is my third time in Germany dies ist mein drittes Mal in Deutschland [deez ist meyn dritez mal in doytshlant]

**thirsty** dürstig [duurstish]

> to be thirsty Durst haben [doorst haaben]
> I'm very thirsty ich habe großen Durst [ish haab-e grohsen doorst]

**three** drei [drey]

> there are three of us wir sind zu dritt [veer zint tsoo drit]

**throat** der Hals [hals]

> I have a fish bone stuck in my throat mir steckt eine Fischgräte im Hals fest [meer shtehkt ey-ne fishgrayt-e im hals fehst]

**throat lozenge** der Halsbonbon [halsbonbon]

> I'd like some throat lozenges ich hätte gerne Halsbonbons [ish heht-e gehrn-e halsbonbonz]

**thunderstorm** das Gewitter [gevit-er]

> will there be a thunderstorm? wird es ein Gewitter geben? [virt ehs eyn gevit-er gayben]

**Thursday** der Donnerstag [don-erz-taak]

> we're arriving/leaving on Thursday wir kommen am Donnerstag an/wir reisen am Donnerstag ab [veer kom-en am don-erz-taak an/veer reyzen am don-erz-taak ap]

**ticket** *(for a plane)* das Flugticket [flooktikit]; *(for a bus, a train, the subway)* die Fahrkarte [faarkart-e]; *(for a movie theater, a museum, a sports event)* die (Eintritts)Karte [(eyntrits)kart-e]

> I'd like a ticket to ... ich hätte gerne eine Fahrkarte nach ... [ish heht-e gehm-e ey-ne faarkart-e naakh] ▸ see box on p. 146

## buying tickets

Public transportation in towns (buses, trams, the subway (*U-Bahn*) and commuter trains (*S-Bahn*)) offers a wide range of ticket types. There's the regular ticket, the *Normaltarif*, which is valid for 2 hours (or the *Kurzstrecke* for short journeys), and the *Tageskarte* (daily travel card) or *Wochenkarte* (weekly card). And finally there's the *Welcome Card*, which is valid for 3 days and also gives access to discounts on cultural attractions.

- how much is a ticket to...? wie viel kostet eine Fahrkarte nach ... [vee feel kostet ey-ne faarkart-e naakh]
- a book of 10 tickets, please ein Heft mit zehn Fahrkarten, bitte [eyn hehft mit tsayn faarkarten bi-te]
- I'd like to book a ticket *(for flight)* ich möchte ein Flugticket buchen [ish meushte eyn flooktikit bookhen]
- I'd like three tickets for... ich hätte gerne drei Fahrkarten nach ... [ish heht-e gehrn-e drey faarkarten naakh]

**tide** die Gezeiten [getseyten]

- what time does the tide come in? wann setzt die Flut ein? [van zehtst dee floot eyn]

**tight** *(piece of clothing)* eng [ehng]

- these pants are too tight diese Hose ist zu eng [deez-e hohz-e ist tsoo ehng]

**time** *(gen)* die Zeit [tseyt]; *(occasion)* das Mal [mal]

- do we have time to visit the town? haben wir Zeit uns die Stadt anzusehen? [haaben veer tseyt uns dee shtat antsuzayen]
- what time is it? wie viel Uhr ist es? [vee feel oor ist ehs]
- what time do you close? um wie viel Uhr machen Sie zu? [um vee feel oor makhen zee tsoo]
- could you tell me if the train from Hamburg is on time? könnten Sie mir sagen, ob der Zug aus Hamburg pünktlich ist? [keunten zee meer zaagen op dehr tsook ows hamburk puunktlish ist]
- maybe some other time vielleicht ein andermal [feeleysht eyn andermal]
- three times dreimal [dreymal]

## telling time

The 24-hour clock is used when Germans want to be precise, but in normal circumstances they would say '2 o'clock' rather than '14 o'clock'. Be careful, because in German 'at half past one' becomes *um halb zwei* (half two).

▸ at the same time zur gleichen Zeit [tsoor gleyshen tseyt]

▸ the first time das erste Mal [das ehrst-e mal]

**timetable** der Fahrplan [faarplan]

▸ do you have local bus timetables? haben Sie Busfahrpläne für den Nahverkehr? [haaben zee busfaarplayn-e fuur dayn naafehrkehr]

**tip** *(gratuity)* das Trinkgeld [trinkgehlt] ♦ *(give a gratuity to)* Trinkgeld geben [trinkgehlt gayben]

▸ how much should I leave as a tip? wie viel Trinkgeld soll ich geben? [vee feel trinkgehlt zol ish gayben]

**tire** der Reifen [reyfen]

▸ the tire's flat der Reifen ist platt [dehr reyfen ist plat]

▸ the tire's punctured der Reifen hat ein Loch [dehr reyfen hat eyn lokh]

**tired** müde [muud-e]

▸ I'm too tired ich bin zu müde [ish bin tsoo muud-e]

**to** *(town, country, direction)* nach [naakh]; *(post office, school etc.)* zu [tsoo]; *(in telling time)* vor [for]

▸ when is the next train to Kiel? wann fährt der nächste Zug nach Kiel? [van fehrt dehr nehkst-e tsook naakh keel]

▸ it's twenty to nine es ist zwanzig vor neun [ehs ist tsvantsish for noyn]

**tobacco store** der Tabakwarenladen [tabakvaarenlaaden]

▸ where is the nearest tobacco store? wo ist der nächste Tabakwarenladen? [voh ist dehr nehkst-e tabakvaarenlaaden]

**today** heute [hoyt-e]

▸ what's today's date? welches Datum ist heute? [vehlshez daatum ist hoyt-e]

**toe** der Zeh [tsay]

▸ I think I've broken my toe ich glaube, ich habe mir den Zeh gebrochen [ish glowb-e ish haab-e meer dayn tsay gebrokhen]

**together** zusammen [tsuzam-en]

▸ let's go together gehen wir doch zusammen [gayen veer dokh tsuzam-en]

**toilet** die Toilette [toyleht-e]

▸ I need to go to the toilet ich muss auf die Toilette gehen [ish mus owf dee toyleht-e gayen]

- do you have to pay to use the toilet? kostet es etwas die Toilette zu benutzen? [kostet ehs ehtvas dee toyleht-e tsoo benutsen]

**toilet paper** das Toilettenpapier [toylehtenpapeer]
- there is no toilet paper es ist kein Toilettenpapier da [ehs ist keyn toylehtenpapeer daa]

**toll** *(for a road, a bridge)* die Maut [mowt]
- do you have to pay a toll to use the bridge? muss man eine Maut für die Brücke bezahlen? [mus man ey-ne mowt fuur dee bruuk-e betsaalen]

**toll-free** gebührenfrei [gebuurenfrey]
- there's a toll-free number you can call Sie können eine gebührenfreie Nummer anrufen [zee keunen ey-ne gebuurenfrey-e num-er anroofen]

**tomato** die Tomate [tomaat-e]
- a pound of tomatoes ein Pfund Tomaten [eyn pfunt tomaaten]

**tomato juice** der Tomatensaft [tomaatenzaft]
- I'd like a tomato juice ich hätte gerne einen Tomatensaft [ish heht-e gehrn-e eynen tomaatenzaft]

**tomorrow** morgen [morgen]
- can you hold my reservation until tomorrow? können Sie meine Buchung bis morgen aufrechterhalten? [keunen zee meyn-e bookhung bis morgen owfrehsht-ehrhalten]
- I'm leaving tomorrow morning ich reise morgen Früh ab [ish reyz-e morgen fruu ap]
- see you tomorrow night bis morgen Abend [bis morgen aabent]

**tonight**
- do you have any beds available for tonight? haben Sie für heute Nacht noch Zimmer frei? [haaben zee fuur hoyt-e nakht nokh tsim-er frey]

**too** *(also)* auch [owkh]; *(excessively)* zu [tsoo]
- enjoy your meal! – you too guten Appetit! – Ihnen auch [gooten apehteet eenen owkh]
- she's too tired to... sie ist zu müde um zu ... [zee ist tsoo muud-e um tsoo]
- it's too expensive es ist zu teuer [ehs ist tsoo toyer]
- there are too many people es sind zu viele Leute [ehs zint tsoo feel-e loyt-e]

**tooth** der Zahn [tsaan]
- I've broken a tooth ich habe mir einen Zahn abgebrochen [ish haab-e meer eynen tsaan apgebrokhen]

**toothache** die Zahnschmerzen [tsaan-shmehrtsen]
- I have a toothache ich habe Zahnschmerzen [ish haab-e tsaan-shmehrtsen]

**toothbrush** die Zahnbürste [tsaanbuurst-e]
- I forgot my toothbrush ich habe meine Zahnbürste vergessen [ish haab-e meyn-e tsaanbuurst-e fehrgehsen]

**toothpaste** die Zahnpasta [tsaanpasta]
- I'd like to buy some toothpaste ich möchte gerne Zahnpasta kaufen [ish meusht-e gehrn-e tsaanpasta kowfen]

**top** *(of a bottle)* der Verschluss [fehrshlus]; *(of a pen)* die Hülle [huul-e]; *(of a jar, a tube)* der Deckel [dehkel] ♦ *(maximum)* höchster [heukster]
- the car drove away at top speed das Auto fuhr mit Höchstgeschwindigkeit davon [das owtoh foor mit heukst-geshvindishkeyt daafon]

**tour** die Tour [toor]
- I'm planning to do a two-week tour of the country ich plane eine zweiwöchige Tour durch das Land zu machen [ish plaan-e ey-ne tsveyveushig-e toor dursh das lant tsoo makhen]

**tourist** der Tourist [toorist], die Touristin [tooristin] ♦ *(season)* Reise- [reyz-e]
- do you get many tourists here? kommen viele Touristen hierher? [kom-en feel-e tooristen heerhehr]

**tourist attraction** die Touristenattraktion [tooristen-atraktsiohn]
- what are the main tourist attractions in the area? was sind die Haupttouristen-attraktionen in der Gegend? [vas zint dee howpt-tooristen-atraktsiohnen in dehr gaygent]

**tourist class** die Touristenklasse [tooristen-klas-e]
- in tourist class, please in der Touristenklasse, bitte [in dehr tooristen-klas-e bi-te]

**tourist guide** *(book)* der Reiseführer [reyzefuurer]
- we have a good tourist guide with a lot of up-to-date information wir haben einen guten Reiseführer mit vielen aktuellen Informationen [veer haaben eynen gooten reyzefuurer mit feelen aktu-ehlen informatsiohnen]

**tourist office** das Fremdenverkehrsbüro [frehmden-fehrkehrz-buuroh]
- I'm looking for the tourist office ich suche das Fremdenverkehrsbüro [ish zookh-e das frehmden-fehrkehrz-buuroh]
- can I get a street map at the tourist office? kann ich beim Fremdenverkehrsbüro einen Stadtplan bekommen? [kan ish beym frehmden-fehrkehrz-buuroh eynen shtatplan bekom-en]

**tow** abschleppen [apshlehpen]
- could you tow me to a garage? könnten Sie mich zu einer Werkstatt abschleppen? [keunten zee mish tsoo eyner vehrkshtat apshlehpen]

**toward** *(a place)* in Richtung [in rishtung]
- we're heading toward Bremen wir fahren in Richtung Bremen [veer faaren in rishtung braymen]

**tow away** abschleppen [apshlehpen]
- my car's been towed away mein Auto ist abgeschleppt worden [meyn owtoh ist apgeshlehpt vorden]

**towel** das Handtuch [hant-tookh]
- we don't have any towels wir haben keine Handtücher [veer haaben keyn-e hant-tuusher]

- could we have more towels? könnten wir mehr Handtücher bekommen? [keunten veer mehr hant-tuusher bekom-en]

**tower** der Turm [toorm]
- can you visit the tower? kann man den Turm besichtigen? [kan man dayn toorm bezishtigen]

**town** die Stadt [shtat]
- to go into town in die Stadt gehen [in dee shtat gayen]

**town hall** das Rathaus [raat-hows]
- where is the town hall? wo ist das Rathaus? [voh ist das raat-hows]

**traffic** der Verkehr [fehrkehr]
- is there a lot of traffic on the freeway? ist viel Verkehr auf der Autobahn? [ist feel fehrkehr owf dehr owtohbaan]

**traffic circle** der Kreisverkehr [kreysfehrkehr]
- you turn right at the traffic circle biegen Sie beim Kreisverkehr links ab [beegen zee beym kreysfehrkehr links ap]

**traffic jam** der Stau [shtow]
- we got stuck in a traffic jam wir saßen in einem Stau fest [veer zaasen in eynem shtow fehst]

**traffic lights** die Ampel [ampel]
- turn left at the traffic lights biegen Sie bei der Ampel links ab [beegen zee bey dehr ampel links ap]

**trail** *(path)* der Weg [vayk]
- will this trail take us back to the parking lot? bringt uns dieser Weg zum Parkplatz zurück? [bringt uns deezer vayk tsum parkplats tsuruuk]

---

### getting around town

- which bus goes to the airport? welcher Bus fährt zum Flughafen? [vehlsh-e bus fehrt tsum flookhaafen]
- where does the bus to the station leave from? wo fährt der Bus zum Bahnhof ab? [voh fehrt dehr bus tsum baanhohf ap]
- I'd like a one-way (ticket) to ... ich hätte gerne eine einfache Fahrkarte nach ... [ish heht-e gehrn-e ey-ne eynfakh-e faarkart-e naakh]
- can I have a book of tickets, please? kann ich bitte ein Fahrkartenheft bekommen? [kan ish bi-te ey-ne faarkartenhehft bekom-en]
- could you tell me where I have to get off to go to the zoo? könnten Sie mir sagen, wo ich aussteigen muss um zum Zoo zu kommen? [keunten zee meer zaagen voh ish ows-shteygen mus um tsum tsoh tsoo kom-en]

**train** *(on the railroad)* der Zug [tsook]; *(on the subway)* die U-Bahn [oo-baan]

▸ when is the next train to Kiel? wann fährt der nächste Zug nach Kiel? [van fehrt dehr nehkst-e tsook naakh keel]

▸ I'd like a round-trip ticket for the 9 a.m. train to Berlin tomorrow, please ich hätte gerne eine Rückfahrkarte für den Neunuhrzug morgen nach Berlin, bitte [ish heht-e gehrn-e ey-ne ruukfaarkart-e fuur dayn noyn-oor-tsook morgen naakh behrleen bi-te]

▸ do you have reduced-price train tickets for seniors? haben Sie ermäßigte Zugfahrkarten für Senioren? [haaben zee ehrmaysisht-e tsookfaarkarten fuur zayniohren]

▸ which platform does the train for Stuttgart leave from? von welchem Bahnsteig fährt der Zug nach Stuttgart ab? [fon velshem baansteyk fehrt dehr tsook naakh shtutgart ap]

▸ the train was fifteen minutes late der Zug hatte fünfzehn Minuten Verspätung [dehr tsook hat-e fuunftseyn minooten fehrshpaytung]

▸ where do international trains leave from? von wo fahren die Züge ins Ausland ab? [fon voh faaren dee tsuug-e ins owslant ap]

**tram** die Straßenbahn [shtraasenbaan]

▸ can you buy tickets on the tram? kann man Fahrkarten in der Straßenbahn kaufen? [kan man faarkaarten in dehr shtraasenbaan kowfen]

▸ which tram line do we have to take? welche Straßenbahnlinie müssen wir nehmen? [vehlsh-e shtraasenbaan-leeni-e muusen veer naymen]

▸ where is the nearest tram stop? wo ist die nächste Straßenbahnhaltestelle? [voh ist dee nehkst-e shtraasenbaan-halt-e-shtehl-e]

**transfer** *(of money)* die Überweisung [uuberveyzung] ◆ *(money)* überweisen [uuberveyzen]

> ▸ I'd like to transfer some money from my savings account ich möchte Geld von meinem Sparkonto überweisen [ish meusht-e gehlt fon meynem shparkontoh uuberveyzen]

**travel** das Reisen [reyzen] ◆ *(go on a trip)* reisen [reyzen]

> ▸ I'd like a window seat facing the direction of travel ich hätte gerne einen Fensterplatz in Fahrtrichtung [ish heht-e gehrn-e eynen fehnsterplats in faartrishtung]
> ▸ I'm traveling on my own ich reise alleine [ish reyz-e aleyn-e]

**travel agency** das Reisebüro [reyzebuuroh]

> ▸ I'm looking for a travel agency ich suche ein Reisebüro [ish zookh-e eyn reyzebuuroh]

**traveler's check** der Reisescheck [reyzeshehk]

> ▸ do you take traveler's checks? nehmen Sie Reiseschecks an? [naymen zee reyzeshehks an]

**tree** der Baum [bowm]

> ▸ what type of tree is that? was für ein Baum ist das? [vas fuur eyn bowm ist das]

**trip** *(journey)* die Reise [reyz-e]

> ▸ have a good trip! gute Reise! [goot-e reyz-e]

**trouble** *(difficulty)* die Schwierigkeiten [shveerishkeyten]; *(effort)* die Mühe [muu-e]

> ▸ we didn't have any trouble finding the hotel wir hatten keine Schwierigkeiten das Hotel zu finden [veer hat-en keyn-e shveerishkeyten das hohtehl tsoo fin-den]
> ▸ I don't want to be any trouble ich will Ihnen keine Mühe machen [ish vil eenen keyn-e muu-e makhen]
> ▸ it's no trouble das mache ich gern [das makh-e ish gehrn]

**trunk** *(of a car)* der Kofferraum [kof-er-rowm]; *(piece of luggage)* der Schrankkoffer [shrank-kof-er]

> ▸ my things are in the trunk of the car meine Sachen sind im Kofferraum des Autos [meyn-e zakhen zint im kof-er-rowm dez owtohz]
> ▸ I've got two small suitcases and a large trunk ich habe zwei kleine Koffer und einen großen Schrankkoffer [ish haab-e tsvey kleyn-e kof-er unt eynen grohsen shrank-kof-er]

**try** *(attempt)* versuchen [fehrzookhen]; *(sample)* probieren [prohbeeren]

> ▸ I'd like to try the local beer ich würde gerne das heimische Bier probieren [ish wuurd-e gehrn-e das heymish-e beer prohbeeren]

**try on** *(dress, shoes)* anprobieren [anprohbeeren]

> ▸ I'd like to try on the one in the window ich würde gerne das im Schaufenster anprobieren [ish wuurd-e gehrn-e das im showfehnster anprohbeeren]

**tub** *(of ice cream)* der Becher [behsher]

> ▸ do you sell tubs of ice cream to take home? verkaufen Sie Eisbecher zum Mitnehmen? [fehrkowfen zee eysbehsher tsum mitnaymen]

**Tuesday** der Dienstag [deenstaak]

▸ we're arriving/leaving on Tuesday wir kommen am Dienstag an/wir reisen am Dienstag ab [veer kom-en am deenstaak an/veer reyzen am deenstaak ap]

**tunnel** der Tunnel [tun-el]

▸ is there a toll for using the tunnel? kostet es eine Maut durch den Tunnel zu fahren? [kostet ehs ey-ne mowt dursh dayn tun-el tsoo faaren]

**turn** *(off a road)* die Abzweigung [aptsveygung] ♦ *(change direction)* abbiegen [apbeegen]

▸ it's your turn Sie sind an der Reihe [zee zint an dehr rey-e]

▸ is this the turn for the campground? ist das die Abzweigung zum Campingplatz? [ist das dee aptsveygung tsum kehmpingplats]

▸ turn left at the lights biegen Sie an der Ampel links ab [beegen zee an dehr ampel links ap]

▸ you have to turn right Sie müssen rechts abbiegen [zee muusen rehshts apbeegen]

**turn down** *(gas)* kleiner stellen [kleyner shtehlen]; *(volume, radio)* leiser stellen [leyzer shtehlen]; *(bed)* aufschlagen [owfshlaagen]

▸ can we turn the air-conditioning down? können wir die Klimaanlage kleiner stellen? [keunen veer dee kleema-anlaag-e kleyner shtehlen]

▸ how do you turn the volume down? wie stellt man die Lautstärke leiser? [vee shtehlt man dee lowt-shtehrk-e leyzer]

▸ could you please turn down the bed for me? könnten Sie bitte das Bett für mich aufschlagen? [keunten zee bi-te das beht fuur mish owfshlaagen]

**turn off** *(light, appliance)* ausschalten [ows-shalten]; *(electricity)* abstellen [apshtehlen]; *(faucet)* zudrehen [tsoodrayen]

▸ where do you turn the light off? wo schaltet man das Licht aus? [voh shaltet man das lisht ows]

▸ my cell was turned off mein Handy war ausgeschaltet [meyn hehndi var owsgeshaltet]

**turn on** *(light, radio)* einschalten [eynshalten]; *(engine)* anlassen [anlas-en]; *(faucet)* aufdrehen [owfdrayen]

▸ where do I turn this light on? wo schalte ich diese Lampe ein? [voh shalt-e ish deez-e lamp-e eyn]

▸ can you turn on the ignition? können Sie die Zündung einschalten? [keunen zee dee tsuundung eynshalten]

**turn up** *(sound, central heating)* höher drehen [heuer drayen]

▸ how do you turn up the heating? wie dreht man die Heizung höher? [vee drayt man dee heytsung heuer]

**TV** *(system, broadcasts)* das Fernsehen [fehrnzayen]; *(set)* der Fernseher [fehrnzayer]

▸ the TV in our room is broken der Fernseher in unserem Zimmer ist kaputt [dehr fehrnzayer in unzerem tsim-er ist kaput]

**TV lounge** der Fernsehraum [fehrnzayrowm]
- is there a TV lounge? gibt es einen Fernsehraum? [gipt ehs eynen fehrnzayrowm]

**twelve** zwölf [tsveulf]
- there are twelve of us wir sind zu zwölft [veer zint tsoo tsveulft]
- it's twelve o'clock *(noon)* es ist zwölf Uhr mittags [ehs ist tsveulf oor mitaaks]; *(midnight)* es ist Mitternacht [ehs ist mit-er-nakht]

**twice** zweimal [tsveymal]
- the ferry runs twice a day die Fähre fährt zweimal pro Tag [dee fehr-e fehrt tsveymal proh taak]

**twin** *(brother)* der Zwillingsbruder [tsvilingzbrooder]; *(sister)* die Zwillingsschwester [tsvilingzshvester] ◆ Zwillings- [tsvilingz]
- twin brother Zwillingsbruder [tsvilingzbrooder]
- twin sister Zwillingsschwester [tsvilingzshvehster]

**twin beds** die Einzelbetten [eyntselbehten]
- a room with twin beds ein Zimmer mit zwei Einzelbetten [eyn tsim-er mit tsvey eyntselbehten]

**two** zwei [tsvey]
- there are two of us wir sind zu zweit [veer zint tsoo tsveyt]

# U

**umbrella** der (Regen)Schirm [(raygen)shirm]
- could you lend me an umbrella? könnten Sie mir einen Schirm leihen? [keunten zee meer eynen shirm leyen]

**unacceptable** nicht akzeptabel [nisht aktsehptaabel]
- it's completely unacceptable! das ist überhaupt nicht akzeptabel! [das ist uuberhowpt nisht aktsehptaabel]

**underpass** die Unterführung [unterfuurung]
- is the underpass safe at night? ist die Unterführung nachts sicher? [ist dee unterfuurung nakhts zisher]

**understand** verstehen [fehrshtayen]
- I can understand German, but I can't really speak it ich verstehe Deutsch, aber ich kann es nicht richtig sprechen [ish fehrshtay-e doytsh aber ish kan ehs nisht rishtish shprehshen]
- I understand a little ich verstehe ein bisschen [ish fehrshtay-e eyn bis-shen]
- I don't understand a word ich verstehe kein Wort [ish fehrshtay-e keyn vort]
- do you understand? verstehen Sie? [fehrshtayen zee]

**unit** *(of condominium complex)* die Wohnung [vohnung]

‣ we'd prefer a unit with air-conditioning wir hätten lieber eine Wohnung mit Klimaanlage [veer hehten leeber ey-ne vohnung mit kleema-anlaag-e]

### United States (of America)

‣ the United States die Vereinigten Staaten [dee fehreynishten shtaaten]
‣ I'm from the United States ich komme aus den Vereinigten Staaten [ish kom-e ows dayn fehreynishten shtaaten]
‣ I live in the United States ich lebe in den Vereinigten Staaten [ish layb-e in dayn fehreynishten shtaaten]
‣ have you ever been to the United States? waren Sie schon einmal in den Vereinigten Staaten [vaaren zee shohn eynmal in dayn fehreynishten shtaaten]

**unleaded** bleifrei [bleyfrey] ‣ das bleifreie Benzin [bleyfrey-e behntseen]
‣ do you have premium or just regular unleaded? haben Sie Super oder nur Normal bleifrei? [haaben zee zooper ohder noor normaal bleyfrey]

**until** bis [bis]
‣ I'm staying until Sunday ich bleibe bis Sonntag [ish bleyb-e bis zontaak]
‣ until noon bis zwölf Uhr mittags [bis tsveulf oor mitaaks]

**up** (to a higher position) nach oben [naakh ohben]; (in a higher position) oben [ohben] ‣ **up to** bis [bis]
‣ what's up? (what's wrong) was ist los? [vas ist lohs]; (as greeting) wie geht's? [vee gayts]
‣ what are you up to tonight? was haben Sie heute Abend vor? [vas haaben zee hoyt-e aabent for]
‣ up to now bis jetzt [bis yehtst]

**urgent** dringend [dringent]
‣ it's not urgent es ist nicht dringend [ehs ist nisht dringent]

**urgently** dringend [dringent]
‣ I have to see a dentist urgently ich muss dringend zu einem Zahnarzt [ish mus dringent tsoo eynem tsaan-artst]

---

### saying that you have understood/not understood

‣ oh, I see...! ach so, ich verstehe ...! [akh zoh ish fehrshtay-e]
‣ sorry, but I didn't understand tut mir Leid, aber ich habe es nicht verstanden [toot meer leyt aber ish haab-e ehs nisht fehrshtanden]
‣ I'm a little confused... ich bin etwas verwirrt ... [ish bin ehtvas fehrvirt]
‣ I don't understand your question ich verstehe Ihre Frage nicht [ish fehrshtay-e eer-e fraag-e nisht]
‣ sorry, but I still don't understand tut mir Leid, aber ich verstehe immer noch nicht [toot meer leyt aber ish fehrshtay-e im-er nokh nisht]

### US(A)

- the US die USA [dee oo-ehs-aa]
- I'm from the US ich bin aus den USA [ish bin ows dayn oo-ehs-aa]
- I live in the US ich lebe in den USA [ish layb-e in dayn oo-ehs-aa]
- have you ever been to the US? waren Sie schon einmal in den USA? [vaaren zee shohn eynmal in dayn oo-ehs-aa]

**use** benutzen [benutsen]

- could I use your cellphone? könnte ich Ihr Handy benutzen? [keunt-e ish eer hehndi benutsen]

**vacancy** *(room)* das (freie) Zimmer [(frey-e) tsim-er]; *(job)* die freie Stelle [frey-e shtehl-e]

- do you have any vacancies for tonight? haben Sie noch Zimmer frei für heute Nacht? [haaben zee nokh tsim-er frey fuur hoyt-e nakht]

**vacation** der Urlaub [oorlowp]

- are you here on vacation? sind Sie hier auf Urlaub? [zint zee heer owf oorlowp]
- I'm on vacation ich mache Urlaub [ish makh-e oorlowp]

**valid** gültig [guultish]

- is this ticket valid for the exhibit too? ist diese Eintrittskarte auch für die Ausstellung gültig? [ist deez-e eyntritskart-e owkh fuur dee ows-shtehlung guultish]
- how long is this ticket valid for? wie lange ist diese Karte gültig? [vee lang-e ist deez-e kart-e guultish]
- my passport is still valid mein Pass ist noch gültig [meyn pas ist nokh guultish]

**vegetable** das Gemüse [gemuuz-e]

- does it come with vegetables? gibt es dazu Gemüse? [gipt ehs daatsoo gemuuz-e]

**vegetarian** vegetarisch [vaygaytaarish] ♦ der Vegetarier [vaygaytaarier], die Vegetarierin [vaygaytaarierin]

- I'm a vegetarian ich bin Vegetarier/Vegetarierin [ish bin vaygaytaarier/vaygaytaarierin]
- do you have vegetarian dishes? haben Sie vegetarische Gerichte? [haaben zee vaygaytaarish-e gerisht-e]

**vending machine** der Automat [owtohmaat]

- the vending machine isn't working der Automat funktioniert nicht [dehr owtohmaat funktsiohneert nisht]

**vertigo** die Gleichgewichtsstörung [gleysh-gevishts-shteurung]

- I suffer from vertigo ich leide an Gleichgewichtsstörungen [ish leyd-e an gleysh-gevishts-shteurungen]

**very** sehr [zehr]
- I'm very hungry ich bin sehr hungrig [ish bin zehr hungrish]
- very much sehr [zehr]
- very near ganz nah [gants naa]

**view** der Blick [blik]
- I'd prefer a room with an ocean view ich möchte lieber ein Zimmer mit Meerblick [ish meusht-e leeber eyn tsim-er mit mehrblik]

**villa** die Villa [vila]
- we'd like to rent a villa for one week wir möchten gerne eine Villa für eine Woche mieten [veer meushten gehrn-e ey-ne vila fuur ey-ne vokh-e meeten]

**virus** der Virus [veerus]
- I must have picked up a virus ich muss mir einen Virus geholt haben [ish mus meer eynen veerus gehohlt haaben]

**visa** das Visum [veezum]
- do you need a visa? braucht man ein Visum? [browkht man eyn veezum]

**visit** der Besuch [bezookh] ◆ besuchen [bezookhen]
- is this your first visit to Berlin? ist das Ihr erster Besuch in Berlin? [ist das eer ehrster bezookh in behrleen]
- I'd like to visit the castle ich möchte das Schloss besuchen [ish meusht-e das shlos bezookhen]

**voicemail** die Voicemail [voysmayl]
- I need to check my voicemail ich muss meine Voicemail abhören [ish mus meyn-e voysmayl apheuren]

**voucher** der Gutschein [goot-sheyn]
- I haven't received the voucher ich habe den Gutschein nicht erhalten [ish haab-e dayn goot-sheyn nisht ehrhalten]

**waist** die Taille [tal-ye]
- it's a little bit tight at the waist es ist ein bisschen eng in der Taille [ehs ist eyn bis-shen ehng in dehr tal-ye]

**wait** warten [varten]
- have you been waiting long? warten Sie schon lange? [varten zee shohn lang-e]

**waiter** der Kellner [kehlner]
- waiter, could we have the check, please? Herr Ober, könnten wir bitte die Rechnung haben? [hehr ohber keunten veer bi-te dee rehshnung haaben]

**wait for** warten auf [varten owf]
- are you waiting for the bus? warten Sie auf den Bus? [varten zee owf dayn bus]
- I'm waiting for them to call back ich warte auf ihren Rückruf [ish vart-e owf eeren ruukroof]
- don't wait for me warten Sie nicht auf mich [varten zee nisht owf mish]

**waiting room** *(for train)* der Wartesaal [vart-e-zaal]; *(for a doctor)* das Wartezimmer [vart-e-tsim-er]
- is there a waiting room near the platform? gibt es in der Nähe des Bahnsteigs einen Wartesaal? [gipt ehs in dehr nay-e dehz baanshteygz eynen vart-e-zaal]

**waitress** die Kellnerin [kehlnerin]
- the waitress has already taken our order die Kellnerin hat unsere Bestellung schon aufgenommen [dee kehlnerin hat unzer-e beshtehlung shohn owfgenom-en]

**wake** (auf)wecken [(owf)vehken] ◆ aufwachen [owfvakhen]
- could you wake me at 6:45? könnten Sie mich um sechs Uhr fünfundvierzig wecken? [keunten zee mish um zehks oor fuunf-unt-feertsish vehken]
- I always wake early ich wache immer früh auf [ish vakh-e im-er fruu owf]

**wake up** (auf)wecken [(owf)vehken] ◆ aufwachen [owfvakhen]
- a noise woke me up in the middle of the night ein Geräusch hat mich mitten in der Nacht aufgeweckt [eyn geroysh hat mish mit-en in dehr nakht owfgevehkt]
- I have to wake up very early tomorrow to catch the plane ich muss morgen ganz früh aufwachen um das Flugzeug zu kriegen [ish mus morgen gants fruu owfvakhen um das flooktsoyk tsoo kreegen]

**walk** *(stroll)* der Spaziergang [shpatseergang]; *(hike)* die Wanderung [vanderung] ◆ *(go on foot)* zu Fuß gehen [tsoo foos gayen] ◆ *(person)* bringen [bringen]; *(distance)* laufen [lowfen]
- are there any interesting walks in the area? gibt es in der Gegend interessante Wanderungen? [gipt ehs in dehr gaygent interehsant-e vanderungen]
- let's go for a walk machen wir doch einen Spaziergang [makhen veer dokh eynen shpatseergang]
- how long would it take me to walk it? wie lange würde ich dafür zu Fuß brauchen? [vee lang-e wuurd-e ish daafuur tsoo foos browkhen]

**walking boots** die Wanderstiefel [vander-shteefel]
- do you need walking boots? braucht man Wanderstiefel? [browkht man vander-shteefel]

**wallet** die Brieftasche [breeftash-e]
- I've lost my wallet ich habe meine Brieftasche verloren [ish haab-e meyn-e breeftash-e fehrlohren]

**want** *(wish, desire)* wollen [vol-en]
- I wanted to buy it ich wollte es kaufen [ish volt-e ehs kowfen]
- I don't want to go there ich möchte dort nicht hin [ish meusht-e dort nisht hin]

### water

You will rarely be offered a jug of tap water (*Leitungswasser*) in a German restaurant. If you order mineral water you'll be brought sparkling water, so if you want noncarbonated water, you should specify *stilles Wasser*.

**warm** warm [varm]
- ▶ it's warm es ist warm [ehs ist varm]
- ▶ where can I buy some warm clothing for the trip? wo kann ich warme Kleidung für die Reise kaufen? [voh kan ish varm-e kleydung fuur dee reyz-e kowfen]

**warn** warnen [varnen]
- ▶ no one warned me about that! keiner hat mich davor gewarnt! [keyner hat mish daafor gevarnt]

**wash** waschen [vashen]; *(dishes)* abwaschen [apvashen] ♦ *(get washed)* sich waschen [zish vashen]
- ▶ where can I wash my hands? wo kann ich meine Hände waschen? [voh kan ish meyn-e hehnd-e vashen]

**watch** *(for arm)* die Armbanduhr [armbant-oor] ♦ *(observe)* beobachten [be-ohbakhten]; *(film, play)* sich ansehen [zish anzayen]; *(guard)* aufpassen auf [owfpassen owf]
- ▶ my watch has been stolen meine Armbanduhr ist gestohlen worden [meyn-e armbant-oor ist geshtohlen vorden]
- ▶ can you watch my bags for a minute? können Sie für eine Minute auf meine Koffer aufpassen? [keunen zee fuur ey-ne minoot-e owf meyn-e kof-er owfpas-en]

**water** das Wasser [vas-er]
- ▶ could I have some hot water, please? könnte ich bitte heißes Wasser bekommen? [keunt-e ish bi-te heysez vas-er bekom-en]
- ▶ there's no hot water es gibt kein heißes Wasser [ehs gipt keyn heysez vas-er]

**water ski** der Wasserski [vas-er-shee]
- ▶ can I rent water skis here? kann ich hier Wasserskier mieten? [kan ish heer vas-er-shee-er meeten]

**water skiing** das Wasserskilaufen [vas-er-sheelowfen]
- ▶ can I go water skiing anywhere around here? kann ich hier in der Gegend irgendwo Wasserski laufen? [kan ish heer in dehr gaygent irgentvoh vas-er-shee lowfen]

**wave** *(of water)* die Welle [vehl-e]
- ▶ the waves are very big today die Wellen sind heute sehr hoch [dee vehlen zint hoyt-e zehr hohkh]

**way** *(means, route, path)* der Weg [vayk]; *(direction)* die Richtung [rishtung]

- what's the best way of getting there? wie kommt man dort am besten hin? [vee komt man dort am behsten hin]
- which way is it to the station? wo lang geht es zum Bahnhof? [voh lang gayt ehs tsum baanhohf]
- I went the wrong way ich bin in die falsche Richtung gegangen [ish bin in dee falsh-e rishtung gegangen]
- is this the right way to the cathedral? geht es hier zum Dom? [gayt ehs heer tsum dohm]
- on the way to the hotel auf dem Weg ins Hotel [owf daym vayk ins hohtehl]
- all the way *(push)* so weit wie möglich [zoh veyt vee meuglish]
- no way! auf keinen Fall! [owf keynen fal]

**way out** der Ausgang [owsgang]

- where's the way out? wo ist der Ausgang? [voh ist dehr owsgang]

**weak** schwach [shvakh]

- I feel very weak ich fühle mich sehr schwach [ish fuul-e mish zehr shvakh]
- could I have a very weak coffee? könnte ich einen ganz schwachen Kaffee bekommen? [keunt-e ish eynen gants shvakhen kafay bekom-en]

**wear** *(piece of clothing, glasses)* tragen [traagen]

- is what I'm wearing all right? ist das in Ordnung, was ich anhabe? [ist das in ordnung vas ish anhaab-e]

**weather** das Wetter [vehter]

- what is the weather like today? wie ist das Wetter heute? [vee ist das vehter hoyt-e ]
- is the weather going to change? wird sich das Wetter ändern? [virt zish das vehter ehndern]

**weather forecast** die Wettervorhersage [vehter-forhehr-zaag-e]

- what's the weather forecast for tomorrow? was ist die Wettervorhersage für morgen? [vas ist dee vehter-forhehr-zaag-e fuur morgen]

---

### asking the way

- can you show me where we are on the map? können Sie mir auf der Karte zeigen, wo wir sind? [keunen zee meer owf dehr kart-e tseygen voh veer zint]
- excuse me, how do you get to Bahnhofstraße? Entschuldigung, wie komme ich in die Bahnhofstraße? [ehntshuldigung vee kom-e ish in dee baanhohfshtraas-e]
- is it far? ist es weit? [ist ehs weyt]
- is it within walking distance? kann man zu Fuß gehen? [kan man tsoo foos gayen]

**website address** die Websiteadresse [wehbseyt-adrehs-e]
- can you give me your website address? können Sie mir Ihre Websiteadresse geben? [keunen zee meer eer-e wehbseyt-adrehs-e gayben]

**Wednesday** der Mittwoch [mitvokh]
- we're arriving/leaving on Wednesday wir kommen am Mittwoch an/wir reisen am Mittwoch ab [veer kom-en am mitvokh an/veer reyzen am mitvokh ap]

**week** die Woche [vokh-e]
- how much is it for a week? wie viel kostet es pro Woche? [vee feel kostet ehs proh vokh-e]
- I'm leaving in a week ich reise in einer Woche ab [ish reyz-e in eyner vokh-e ap]
- two weeks zwei Wochen [tsvey vokhen]

**weekly** wöchentlich [veukhentlish]; *(newspaper)* Wochen- [vokhen]
- is there a weekly rate? gibt es einen Preis pro Woche? [gipt ehs eynen preys proh vokh-e]

**welcome** *(guest, news)* willkommen [vilkom-en] ◆ der Empfang [ehmpfang] ◆ *(person)* willkommen heißen [vilkom-en heysen]
- welcome! herzlich willkommen! [hehrtslish vilkom-en]
- you're welcome *(in reply to thanks)* bitte sehr [bi-te zehr]
- we're going for a walk. you're welcome to join us wir gehen spazieren. Sie können gerne mit uns kommen [veer gayen shpatseeren zee keunen gehrn-e mit uns kom-en]

**well** *(healthy)* gesund [gezunt] ◆ gut [goot]
- I'm very well, thank you es geht mir sehr gut, danke [ehs gayt meer zehr goot dank-e]
- get well soon! gute Besserung! [goot-e behserung]
- well played gut gespielt [goot geshpeelt]

**well done** *(steak)* gut durchgebraten [goot durshgebraaten]
- well done, please gut durchgebraten, bitte [goot durshgebraaten bi-te]

**what** *(as adjective)* welcher [vehlsher] ◆ *(as question)* was [vas]
- what? *(asking for repetition)* was? [vas]
- what is it? *(what's this thing?)* was ist das? [vas ist das]; *(what's the matter?)* was ist los? [vas ist lohs]
- what's up? *(what's wrong)* was ist los? [vas ist lohs]; *(as greeting)* wie geht's? [vee gayts]
- what's your name? wie heißen Sie? [vee heysen zee]
- what's it called? wie heißt das? [vee heyst das]
- what time is it? wie spät ist es? [vee shpayt ist ehs]
- what day is it? welcher Tag ist heute? [velsher taak ist hoyt-e]
- what desserts do you have? was für Desserts haben Sie? [vas fuur dehzehrts haaben zee]

**wheel** das Rad [raat]
- could you help me change the wheel? könnten Sie mir helfen das Rad zu wechseln? [keunten zee meer hehlfen das raat tsoo vehkseln]

**when** *(as question)* wann [van] ♦ *(at the time when)* wenn [vehn]; *(used in past tense)* als [als]
- when was it built? wann ist es gebaut worden? [van ist ehs gebowt vorden]
- when is the next train to Dresden? wann fährt der nächste Zug nach Dresden? [van fehrt dehr nehkst-e tsook naakh drayzden]

**where** wo [voh]
- where do you live? wo leben Sie? [voh layben zee]
- where are you from? woher sind Sie? [voh-hehr zint zee]
- excuse me, where is the nearest bus stop, please? Entschuldigung, wo ist bitte die nächste Bushaltestelle? [ehntshuldigung voh ist bi-te dee nehkst-e bus-halt-e-shtehl-e]

**which** welcher [vehlsher] ♦ *(in relative clauses)* der [dehr], die [dee], das [das]
- which hotel would you recommend for us? welches Hotel würden Sie uns empfehlen? [velshez hohtehl wuurden zee uns ehmpfaylen]
- which way should we go? wo lang sollen wir gehen? [voh lang zol-en veer gayen]
- which do you prefer? welches ziehen Sie vor? [vehlshez tsee-en zee for]

**while** die Weile [veyl-e]
- I'm only planning to stay for a while ich will nur eine Weile bleiben [ish vil noor ey-ne veyl-e bleyben]

**white** weiß [veys]
- I need a white T-shirt ich brauche ein weißes T-Shirt [ish browkh-e ein veysez teeshert]

**white wine** der Weißwein [veysveyn]
- a glass of white wine, please ein Glas Weißwein, bitte [eyn glaas veysveyn bi-te]

**who** *(in questions)* wer [vehr] ♦ *(in relative clauses)* der [dehr], die [dee], das [das]
- who are you? wer sind Sie? [vehr zint zee]
- who should I speak to about the heating? mit wem sollte ich wegen der Heizung sprechen? [mit vaym zolt-e ish vaygen dehr heytsung shprehshen]
- who's calling? wer ist am Apparat? [vehr ist am aparaat]

**whole** ganz [gants]
- we spent the whole day walking wir sind den ganzen Tag gelaufen [veer zint dayn gantsen taak gelowfen]
- on the whole we had a good time im Großen und Ganzen hatten wir eine schöne Zeit [im grohsen unt gantsen hat-en veer ey-ne sheun-e tseyt]

**whole-wheat** Vollkorn- [folkorn]
- I'd like some whole-wheat bread ich hätte gerne Vollkornbrot [ish heht-e gehrn-e folkornbroht]

---

### wine bars (i)

It's great to enjoy a glass of white wine in a *Weinstube*. These wine bars are common all over the country; sometimes they are called *Weinkeller*. They're perfect for having a glass of *Sekt* (sparkling wine) as an aperitif, or a *Schoppen* (glass), or maybe a *Viertel* (quarter liter), of white wine to go with a bite to eat.

---

**why** warum [varum]
- why not? warum nicht? [varum nisht]

**wide** *(river, road)* breit [breyt]
- 2 meters wide zwei Meter breit [tsvey mayter breyt]

**will** *(to express future tense)* werden [vehrden]; *(indicating willingness)* wollen [vol-en]
- I'll be arriving at six ich werde um sechs ankommen [ish vehrd-e um zehks ankom-en]

**win** gewinnen [gevin-en]
- who's winning? wer wird gewinnen? [vehr virt gevin-en]

**wind** der Wind [vint]
- there's a strong west wind es weht ein starker Westwind [ehs vayt eyn shtarker vehstvint]

**window** das Fenster [fehnster]; *(of a store)* das Schaufenster [showfehnster]; *(at a station, in a post office)* der Schalter [shalter]
- I can't open the window ich kann das Fenster nicht öffnen [ish kan das fehnster nisht eufnen]
- I'm cold: could you close your window? mir ist kalt, könnten Sie Ihr Fenster zumachen? [meer ist kalt keunten zee eer fehnster tsoomakhen]
- I'd like to see the dress in the window ich würde gerne das Kleid im Schaufenster ansehen [ish wuurd-e gehrn-e das kleyt im showfehnster anzayen]
- where's the window for buying tickets? wo ist der Fahrkartenschalter? [voh ist dehr faarkartenshalter]

**window seat** der Fensterplatz [fehnsterplats]
- I'd like a window seat if possible ich hätte gerne wenn möglich einen Fensterplatz [ish heht-e gehrn-e vehn meuglish eynen fehnsterplats]

**windshield** die Windschutzscheibe [vint-shuts-sheyb-e]
- could you clean the windshield? könnten Sie die Windschutzscheibe sauber machen? [keunten zee dee vint-shuts-sheyb-e zowber makhen]

**windsurfing** das Windsurfen [vint-surfen]
- is there anywhere around here I can go windsurfing? kann man hier in der Gegend irgendwo Windsurfen gehen? [kan man heer in dehr gaygent irgentvoh vint-surfen gayen]

## wishes and regrets

- I hope it won't be too busy **ich hoffe, es ist nicht so viel los** [ish hof-e ehs ist nisht zoh feel lohs]
- it'd be great if you stayed **es wäre toll, wenn Sie bleiben könnten** [ehs vehr-e tol vehn zee bleyben keunten]
- if only we had a car! **wenn wir nur ein Auto hätten!** [vehn veer noor eyn owtoh hehten]
- unfortunately, we couldn't get there in time **leider waren wir nicht rechtzeitig dort** [leyder varen veer nisht rehsht-tseytish dort]
- I'm really sorry you couldn't make it **es tut mir wirklich Leid, dass Sie es nicht geschafft haben** [ehs toot meer virklish leyt das zee ehs nisht geshaft haaben]

**windy** *(day)* **windig** [vindish]
- it's windy **es ist windig** [ehs ist vindish]

**wine** der **Wein** [veyn]
- this wine is not chilled enough **dieser Wein ist nicht kühl genug** [deezer veyn ist nisht kuul genookh]

**wine list** die **Weinkarte** [veynkart-e]
- can we see the wine list, please? **können wir bitte die Weinkarte haben?** [keunen veer bi-te dee veynkart-e haaben]

**wish** der **Wunsch** [vunsh] ✦ **wünschen** [vuunshen]
- best wishes! **alles Gute!** [al-es goot-e]
- we wish you good luck **wir wünschen Ihnen viel Glück** [veer vuunshen eenen feel gluuk]

**with mit** [mit]
- thanks, but I'm here with my boyfriend **danke, aber ich bin mit meinem Freund hier** [dank-e aber ish bin mit meynem froynt heer]

## wishing someone something

- Happy Birthday! **alles Gute zum Geburtstag!** [al-es goot-e tsum geburts-taak]
- Merry Christmas! **Frohe Weihnachten!** [froh-e veynakhten]
- Happy New Year! **ein gutes neues Jahr!** [eyn gootez noyez yaar]
- enjoy your vacation! **schöne Ferien!** [sheun-e fayri-en]
- enjoy your meal! **guten Appetit!** [gooten apehteet]
- good night! *(goodbye)* **guten Abend!** [gooten aabent]; *(before going to bed)* **gute Nacht!** [goot-e nakht]
- congratulations! **herzlichen Glückwunsch!** [hehrtslishen gluukvunsh]

**withdraw** *(money)* abheben [ap-hayben]
> I'd like to withdraw 100 euros ich möchte einhundert Euro abheben [ish meusht-e eynhundert oyroh ap-hayben]

**without** ohne [ohn-e]
> a chicken sandwich without mayonnaise ein Geflügelsandwich ohne Majonäse [eyn gefluugelsehntvitsh ohn-e mayoh-nayz-e]

**woman** die Frau [frow]
> where's the women's changing room? wo ist die Damenumkleidekabine? [voh ist dee daamen-umkleyd-e-kabeen-e]

**wonderful** wunderbar [vunderbar]
> that's wonderful! das ist wunderbar! [das ist vunderbar]
> the weather was wonderful das Wetter war wunderbar [das vehter var vunderbar]

**word** das Wort [vort]
> I don't know what the word is in German ich weiß nicht, was das Wort auf Deutsch heißt [ish veys nisht vas das vort owf doytsh heyst]
> I don't understand a word ich verstehe kein Wort [ish fehrshtay-e keyn vort]

**work** die Arbeit [arbeyt] ♦ *(do a job)* arbeiten [arbeyten]; *(function)* funktionieren [funktsiohneeren]
> to be out of work arbeitslos sein [arbeytslohs zeyn]
> I work in marketing ich arbeite im Marketingbereich [ish arbeyt-e im marketingbereysh]
> the heating's not working die Heizung funktioniert nicht [dee heytsung funktsiohneert nisht]
> how does the shower work? wie funktioniert die Dusche? [vee funktsiohneert dee dush-e]

**workday** der Arbeitstag [arbeytstaak]
> is tomorrow a workday? ist morgen ein Arbeitstag? [ist morgen eyn arbeytstaak]

**world** die Welt [vehlt]
> what part of the world are you from? aus welchem Teil der Welt kommen Sie? [ows vehlshem teyl dehr vehlt kom-en zee]

**worried** besorgt [bezorkt]
> I'm worried about his health ich bin wegen seiner Gesundheit besorgt [ish bin vaygen zeyner gezunt-heyt bezorkt]

**worry** sich Sorgen machen [zish zorgen makhen]
> don't worry! keine Sorge [keyn-e zorg-e]

**worth** wert [vehrt]
> how much is it worth? wie viel ist es wert? [vee feel ist ehs vehrt]
> it's well worth a visit es ist auf jeden Fall einen Besuch wert [ehs ist owf yayden fal eynen bezookh vehrt]
> what's worth seeing in this town? was gibt es Sehenswertes in dieser Stadt? [vas gipt ehs zayenz-vehrtez in deezer shtat]

**wound** die Wunde [vund-e]
- I need something for disinfecting a wound ich brauche etwas um eine Wunde zu desinfizieren [ish browkh-e ehtvas um ey-ne vund-e tsoo dehzinfitseeren]

**wrap (up)** einpacken [eynpaken]
- can you wrap it (up) for me? können Sie es für mich einpacken? [keunen zee ehs fuur mish eynpaken]

**wrist** das Handgelenk [hantgelehnk]
- I've sprained my wrist ich habe mir das Handgelenk verstaucht [ish haab-e meer das hantgelehnk fehrshtowkht]

**write** schreiben [shreyben]
- I have some letters to write ich muss ein paar Briefe schreiben [ish mus eyn par breef-e shreyben]

**wrong** *(incorrect)* falsch [falsh]; *(amiss)* nicht in Ordnung [nisht in ordnung]
- to be wrong *(person)* Unrecht haben [unrehsht haaben]; *(answer)* falsch sein [falsh zeyn]
- I'm sorry, but I think you're wrong es tut mir Leid, aber ich glaube, Sie haben Unrecht [ehs toot meer leyt aber ish glowb-e zee haaben unrehsht]
- sorry, I dialed the wrong number Entschuldigung, ich habe mich verwählt [ehntshuldigung ish haab-e mish fehrvaylt]
- you've got the wrong number Sie haben sich verwählt [zee haaben zish fehrvaylt]
- this is the wrong train dies ist der falsche Zug [deez ist dehr falsh-e tsook]
- what's wrong? was ist los? [vas ist lohs]
- there's something wrong with the switch mit dem Schalter stimmt etwas nicht [mit daym shalter shtimt ehtvas nisht]

# X, Y, Z

**X-ray** die Röntgenaufnahme [reuntgen-owfnaam-e]
- do you think I should have an X-ray? meinen Sie, ich sollte mich röntgen lassen? [meynen zee ish zolt-e mish reuntgen las-en]

**year** das Jahr [yaar]
- we came here last year wir sind im letzten Jahr hierher gekommen [veer zint im lehtsten yaar heerhehr gekom-en]
- I'm 21 years old ich bin einundzwanzig Jahre alt [ish bin eyn-unt-tsvantsish yaar-e alt]

**yellow** gelb [gehlp]
- the yellow one der Gelbe [dehr gehlb-e]

## youth hostels

There are more than 600 youth hostels (*Jugendherbergen*) in Germany. There are also *Jugendgästehäuser*, which are a bit more expensive. You need to be a member of the youth hosteling association, and there is an 11 or 12 o'clock curfew. In some of them the sexes are kept strictly apart, but some hostels do have family rooms for rent. Note that Bavarian youth hostels can only offer accommodation to people who are 26 and under.

**Yellow Pages**® die Gelben Seiten® [gehlben zeyten]
- ▸ do you have a copy of theYellow Pages®? haben Sie dieGelben Seiten®? [haaben zee dee gehlben zeyten]
- ▸ why don't you look in the Yellow Pages®? warum sehen Sie nicht in den Gelben Seiten® nach? [varum zayen zee nisht in dayn gehlben zeyten naakh]

**yes** *(in agreement)* ja [yaa]; *(in disagreement)* doch [dokh]
- ▸ yes, please ja, bitte [yaa bi-te]
- ▸ it doesn't matter – yes it does! es macht nichts – doch! [ehs makht nishts dokh]

**yet** noch [nokh]
- ▸ I haven't been there yet ich war dort bis jetzt noch nicht [ish var dort bis yehtst nokh nisht]
- ▸ are you finished yet? sind Sie schon fertig? [zint zee shohn fehrtish]

**yogurt** der Jogurt [yohgurt]
- ▸ do you have any organic yogurt? haben Sie Biojogurt? [haaben zee beeoh-yohgurt]

**young man** der junge Mann [yung-e man]
- ▸ who is that young man? wer ist der junge Mann? [vehr ist dehr yung-e man]

**young people** die jungen Leute [yungen loyt-e]
- ▸ are there any discounts for young people? gibt es Ermäßigungen für junge Leute? [gipt ehs ehrmaysigungen fuur yung-e loyt-e]

**young woman** die junge Frau [yung-e frow]
- ▸ who is the young woman he's with? wer ist die junge Frau mit ihm? [vehr ist dee yung-e frow mit eem]

**youth hostel** die Jugendherberge [yoogent-hehrbehrg-e]
- ▸ I'd like to book two beds for three nights in a youth hostel ich möchte zwei Betten für drei Nächte in einer Jugendherberge buchen [ish meusht-e tsvey behten fuur drey nehsht-e in eyner yoogent-hehrbehrg-e bookhen]

**zone** *(on public transportation)* die Zone [tsohn-e]
- ▸ I'd like a ticket for zones one to four ich möchte ein Ticket für die Zonen eins bis vier haben [ish meusht-e eyn tikit fuur dee tsohnen eyns bis feer haaben]

# German language
# and culture

## German around the world: who speaks it and where?

### German in Europe

German is spoken by more than 120 million people worldwide. Apart from being the most frequently spoken native language in Europe (with around 100 million native speakers compared to 66 million native French speakers and 64 million native English speakers), it can be found in places as diverse as Pennsylvania and Kazakhstan, Argentina and Namibia. Within Europe it is the official language of Germany, Austria and Liechtenstein, and shares official status with French and Italian in Switzerland, and with French and Luxembourgish in Luxembourg. It is also one of the three working languages of the European Union. Dialects of German are spoken in the border regions of neighboring countries including Belgium, Holland, Denmark and Italy and in the Alsace-Lorraine region of France. German-speaking communities are also to be found throughout Eastern Europe. They still survive today in Poland, the Czech Republic, Hungary, Romania, Russia and Kazakhstan but their numbers were severely depleted by the large numbers of people relocating to Germany, Switzerland and Austria after the end of the Cold War.

### Elsewhere in the world

Further afield, German speakers are to be found in Namibia which is the former German colony of German South-West Africa, and in places to which large numbers of German speakers emigrated over the 19th and 20th centuries. Foremost among these are Brazil, Venezuela and Argentina which support large numbers of German-speaking communities. In Brazil, it is estimated that over 600,000 people speak German as a first or second language.

Of course, many immigrants of German extraction made their home in the United States. The largest concentrations of German speakers can be found in Pennsylvania, Texas, Kansas, the Dakotas, Montana, Wisconsin, Ohio and Indiana, as well as in the major cities. In Pennsylvania the Amish, Hutterite and Mennonite communities speak **Pennsylvania German** which is derived from the Franconian dialect spoken in the Rhineland, and **Hutterite German** which evolved from the dialect spoken in Carinthia in Austria. Despite the slow decline of the German dialects in the US, **Pennsylvania German** is still spoken by an estimated 250,000 – 300,000 people today.

# A short history of the language and its dialects

German, English, Flemish and Dutch make up the West Germanic group of Indo-European languages and share many words and characteristics between them. A German speaker can understand a text written in Dutch or Flemish to a reasonable degree, although the understanding breaks down when these languages are spoken. The relationship between German and English is slightly more distant. The German words **Zimmer** (*room*), **Pfeife** and **Milch** have the same root as the English words *timber*, *pipe* and *milk* but demonstrate the softening of consonant sounds that took place in German after the Angles, Jutes and Saxons took their language to Britain in the mid 5th century AD.

### German dialects

The dialects from which the German spoken within the United States is derived are still alive and well within the German-speaking countries of Europe. They are so alive and well in fact that it can be very difficult for speakers of different dialects to understand one another. There are geographical reasons for this. The mountains of Austria and Switzerland, for example, used to prevent easy communication with the outside world, but there are also historical reasons. Until 1871, Germany existed as an empire of disparate city states, duchies and even kingdoms, each with their own fiercely-guarded identity. This political fragmentation influenced the language by causing the dialects to retain their individual characteristics.

### Southern dialects

German dialects fall into two general groups, those spoken in the north and in the south of the region. In the south, the dialect spoken in Bavaria and Austria is characterized by its sing-song quality, a hard rolling 'r' and the tendency to pronounce monophthongs such as 'u' as diphthongs 'u-o.' The German word **gut** (*good*) is therefore pronounced **goot** in northern Germany, but **goo-ot** in the south. The other southern dialect, Alemannic, comprises Swiss German and Swabian which is spoken in south-west Germany. Swiss German is considered to be a language in its own right, not just a dialect. Geographical isolation has led to its vowels and consonants retaining the characteristics of the language spoken in this region many hundreds of years ago. Many German speakers find Swiss German impossible to understand, not only because of its peculiarity of pronunciation but also because of the wealth of dialect words and loanwords from other languages in the Swiss Confederation. A Swiss German speaker would quite naturally thank you by saying **merci vielmals** and go for a ride on his **vélo**.

## Northern and central dialects

In the northern parts of Germany another dialect is spoken that is also regarded by some as a separate language. It is known as Low German or **Plattdeutsch** and shares an even closer similarity to English than other dialects in Germany owing to the fact that it did not undergo the same process that led to the softening of consonants. For example, the Low German word **peper** is virtually identical to *pepper* in English but has become **Pfeffer** in standard German. Similarly, the verb *to make* is **maken** in Low German as opposed to the standard German **machen**.

The central regions of Germany also have their distinct dialects including Franconian spoken around the Rhineland. Although these central regional dialects have their own flavor, they are the most accessible to all German speakers because they were the dialects closest to the Saxon chancery language on which the standard German language or **Hochdeutsch** was based. This particular written language was standardized to simplify the administration of the duchy of Saxony. The reason why it became the model for standard modern German is because it was adopted by Martin Luther in his literature and Bible translations. The advent of the printing press meant that Luther was able to reach an audience throughout the German empire and he therefore wanted to use a language which the largest number of people would understand rather than his own dialect. His influence on the age led to the language he used in his writings becoming the model for the standard language used in Germany today. This is the German which is taught as a foreign language and which is used in the media, in administration and in schools.

## Characteristics of the German language

As Mark Twain said in his famous essay *The Awful German Language* in which he describes his personal struggle to learn the language, 'it ought to be gently and reverently set aside among the dead languages, for only the dead have time to learn it.' German continues to have a reputation as a difficult language to learn. It is true that it has a relatively complex grammatical structure but this is compensated for by the fact that it is a very logical language and its spelling and pronunciation, unlike those of English, are consistent.

### Compound words

To the non-German speaker some of the most striking characteristics of German are its long words. Actually, these are compounds made up of strings of shorter words written together as one. Once broken down into their component parts they soon become less formidable. German nouns are also written with capital letters, a historical trait which continues to this day, but which, again, is consistent.

### Umlauts

The two little dots appearing above certain vowels are known as the **Umlaut** and can also look unnerving but they are simply a form of shorthand used to represent the letter **e**. They modify the vowels **a**, **o** and **u** so that they are pronounced as if combined with a following **e**. The letter **ä** corresponds to the **ai** sound in the English *air*, the letter **ö** rhymes with the **eu** sound in *chauffeur* and the letter **ü** corresponds to the vowel sound in the French word *rue*. A common vowel combination is also **äu**, which rhymes with the English *boy*, as in **Fräulein**. Another unfamiliar letter is the sharp **s** which is written **ß**. However, it is simply shorthand for double **s**, so that the word **heiß** meaning *hot* is pronounced **heiss**.

### Genders

Unlike English, German attributes different genders to its nouns. There is a choice of three, the masculine **der**, the feminine **die** and the neuter **das**. Sometimes the gender is obvious, such as in **der Mann** and **die Frau** and sometimes the ending of the noun provides a clue. Words ending in **-ung** or **-keit**, for example, are always feminine. But most of the time the student of German has no choice but to learn the gender along with the noun. It is in this area that Mark Twain perhaps had a point. However, Germans are very forgiving if a non-German native attaches the wrong gender to a noun.

## True friends and false friends

The close relationship between the English and the German languages means that there are many pairs of words that look and/or sound similar in the two languages and that do mean the same thing. These are *vrais amis* – true friends for the English native speaker who is learning German. Words such as **Haus**, **Garten**, **Schuh** or **Wein** are instantly recognizable. However, it is unwise to assume that a familiar looking word will necessarily have the same meaning in German as it has in English. Often the meaning can change over the years. **Tier**, for example, comes from the same root as the English *deer*. However, **Tier** means *animal* in German and demonstrates how the English form of the word has become very specific in meaning whereas the German has remained very general. It pays, therefore, to be wary when confronted with an apparently familiar word in German, especially since the shift in meaning of a word can be so extreme as to make it virtually unrecognizable and therefore something of a hazard.

### False friends

The close relationship between the two languages means that there are not only many helpful and familiar *vrais amis* – but also many *faux amis* or 'false friends' in German, that is, words that resemble English words but which have very different meanings. One of the more infamous ones is **Gift**, which could cause great consternation if offered to a German speaker for whom it means *poison*. Similarly, the word **Mist** on a weather report might cause alarm as it means *manure* in German. Here is a selection of other *false friends* with their real meanings:

| | |
|---|---|
| **aktuell** | *current, up-to-date* |
| **bekommen** | *to get* |
| **eventuell** | *maybe* |
| **Fabrik** | *factory* |
| **Fantasie** | *imagination* |
| **Pickel** | *pimple* |
| **sympathisch** | *nice* |

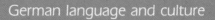

## The influence of German on the English language

As we will soon see, the influence of modern English on the German language is substantial and continues at a good pace. The same cannot be said for the influence of German on English. Only a small number of German words have been adopted into English and most of these are taken from the world of philosophy or literature, for example **weltanschauung**, **doppelgänger** or **leitmotiv**. Others come from the world of politics (**realpolitik**) or warfare: **flak**, for example, is an abbreviation of **Flugabwehrkanone** meaning *anti-aircraft gun*. The Second World War also gave the English language the terms *blitz* and *strafe*.

### The influence of English on the German language

English words have been entering the German language since the 18th century when British culture became highly popular in Germany. In these early years, many of the English words entering German had to do with fashion, for example **Smoking** or **Cape**, with food and drink (**Beefsteak** and **Pudding**), or with social life (**Klub** and **Gentleman**). Similar areas of influence were the field of commerce with **Scheck**, **Manager**, **Konzern**, politics with **Streik** and **Parlament**, industry (**Lokomotive**, **Tunnel**) and sports and entertainment (**Sport**, **Tennis**, **Match**). The continuing popularity of British and then, since the First World War, primarily American culture means that words from all of these areas of influence are still entering the German language today. English has come to dominate high-tech industry and is used as a *lingua franca* in commerce, politics and science. As a result, words such as **Computer**, **DVD**, **Internet**, **Website**, **Global player** and **Marketing** have been imported wholesale into German as they have into many languages around the world. However, the cultural influence still pervades, as a quick glance at the German pop charts, bestseller lists or movie charts will confirm. Pop groups from English-speaking countries continue to dominate in Germany, Austria and Switzerland and the lyrics of their songs remain untranslated.

### Loan translations

English words do not only enter the German language in an unchanged form. English words are often imported as loan translations, that is, a new German word is coined to convey the meaning of the English, usually by literally translating elements of the English word. One of the most obvious examples of this is *skyscraper*, which became **Wolkenkratzer** in German, a new coinage which literally means *cloud scraper*. Other examples include **Buchmacher** (*bookmaker*), **Anrufbeantworter** (*answering machine*) and **Bildschirmschoner** (*screen saver*). Sometimes a new word is a mixture of a loan translation and an adopted English word (admittedly with altered spelling) as in the case of **doppelklicken** or *to double-click*. Likewise, differences in grammar have led to the tendency for German inflections to be added onto English words as in the verbs **downloaden**, **shoppen**, **chatten** and **crashen**.

## Resistance to English

The influence of English on the German language has not been without its critics, however. In times of increased national fervor, such as during the First World War and under the Nazis, the rate of adoption of English terms slowed. In times favoring a more cosmopolitan outlook, such as during the 1920s and after the Second World War, the rate increased. Even without the influence of nationalism, attempts have been made since the 18th century to keep the German language 'pure' by discouraging the import of English words and by manufacturing loan translations in order to 'Germanify' those that did enter the language. The argument over whether something should be done to stop Anglicisms entering the German language continues. As recently as 2001 a bill was brought before the German parliament outlining measures to 'protect' the language. In 1997, the **Verein deutsche Sprache** (*German Language Society*) was formed with the express aim of promoting German and stemming the tide of English imports into the language.

## Denglisch and Germish

Not only has the import of English terms into German led to loan translations being formed, it has also resulted in the creation of *Denglisch* or *Germish* words in German, i.e. words which look like English but do not actually exist in the English language. An example is **Handy** which means *cellphone* in German, or **Dressman** which means *male model*. Sometimes this process can lead to confusion for the English speaker as a rising star is referred to in German as a **Shooting Star** and a **Freeway** is a prepaid package. Occasionally it also has rather unfortunate consequences. A *fanny pack* is known in German by the Denglisch term **Bodybag**.

## English as a marketing language

English has also had a profound influence on the language of marketing in Germany. In a bid to emphasize the international nature of their product or else to lend it and themselves an air of trendiness with which English is associated in German, companies often use English for product names and advertising slogans. The telecommunications giant, Deutsche Telekom, was criticized for introducing rates such as **CityCall** or **GermanCall** while the German railroad company, Deutsche Bahn, has renamed its customer service desks **ServicePoints**. Lufthansa, the leading German airline, used to advertise under the slogan *there's no better way to fly*. However, in the attempt to make their products sound sexy, advertisers have overestimated the English proficiency of the average German. In a recent poll, a target group of people aged between 14 and 59 was asked to say what they understood by Mitsubishi's slogan *Drive Alive*. Only 18% understood it as *drive in a way which makes you feel alive*. The other 82% though it meant *survive the drive in this car* – not an encouraging thought for a potential buyer. Similarly, the slogan used by the German perfume retailer, Douglas, was discovered in a survey in 2003 to be misunderstood by 92% of those surveyed. Most people thought that *come in and find out* was an invitation to go into the store and then find their way out again. In the face of the evidence that English slogans, far from being trendy and sexy, can actually lead to confusion and be detrimental to sales, the tendency among German advertisers is to now use German in their slogans and product names. Not only is there no danger of being misunderstood, the overuse of English has meant that using German in advertising is now seen as the latest cool trend.

## Youth slang

The new tendency for German to be considered hip and cool can also be seen in that most fertile area for English imports, youth slang. The familiarity of young people with new technology in particular has brought a huge influx of Anglicisms relating to the Internet, computing or mobile telephony into the language of German youth. Similarly, the influence of predominantly American youth culture on young Europeans in the form of music trends and leisure pursuits has brought even more English imports into the language. However, there are signs of a backlash against this trend with some German hip hop groups now choosing to sing in their native language, and the development of German replacements for English slang terms. This trend can be seen not so much as a rejection of English for its own sake, but as a normal reaction when new trends become mainstream and are rejected in favor of new alternatives. However, the move away from English is not yet widespread and German youth slang still abounds with English terms such as **cool** or **chillen**.

As with all youth slang, there has been a tendency in German to alter the meaning of an existing word. This corresponds to the shift in meaning of *wicked* in English. An example in German is the use of **geil** to mean *fantastic* in youth slang but in the standard language it still means *horny*. Other developments include the addition of prefixes such as **mega** or **hammer** to adjectives in order to intensify the meaning. A movie may be described as **megagut** or **hammergeil** for example.

## Kanakensprache

One other area in which youth slang has developed in Germany recently is in adopting the pidgin German known as **Kanakensprache** which is spoken by Turkish immigrant workers or immigrants from the former Yugoslavia. Although **Kanake** is a racist term for foreigners in general it has been embraced by many second and third generation immigrants. The pidgin **Kanakensprache** has become well-established throughout Germany, even generating dictionaries and comedy programs on television. Its general characteristics are simplified verb and adjectival endings and the use of the informal **du** form of address. So, for example, the perennial question posed by taxi drivers throughout Germany **wo wollen Sie hin?** (*where to?*) would be phrased in **Kanakensprache** as **wo du wolle?**. There is also a tendency to use the dative form **dem** as a multipurpose definite article, for example **dem ist das Problem** (*that's the problem*) rather than **das ist das Problem**, and to add the endings **-tu** or **-su** onto verbs to form questions, e.g. **raussu?** for **rauchst du?** (*do you smoke?*).

## German culture

Some of the more common stereotypes about German culture actually stem from Bavaria and Austria. It is only here that you will find men wearing the traditional **Lederhosen** and green hats decorated with a brush-like **Gamsbart** and the women wearing the low-cut and tightly-bodiced **Dirndl** dresses. Likewise **oompah** music is associated only with the south of Germany and Austria. This north/south divide has historical roots. It was not until the late 19th century that the different duchies, principalities and city states were formed into one German nation and the sense of regional pride remains strong today. This divide is also visible in terms of religion. Southern Germany and Austria are overwhelmingly Catholic, while the north of Germany and Switzerland are mostly Protestant.

### Food and drink

However, other German stereotypes, those of drinking beer and eating sausages, are truly national. In fact, German food and drink has become famous the world over. The many varieties of beer, bread and sausages created in Germany are also the result of the country's fragmented history with each area having its own specialties. Germany and Austria also have a great reputation for wines, cakes and pastries. A visit to any café in these countries will bring the visitor face to face with a mouthwatering array of cream cakes and exquisite pastries for which these countries are justly famous and which should definitely be sampled as part of any visitor's attempts to immerse himself or herself in the culture of the country.

### German influences on the arts and sciences

It is not only in terms of food and drink that the German-speaking countries have wielded international influence. They are also famous the world over for their contribution to the arts and sciences. In the field of music, great German and Austrian composers abound and German is one of the main languages of opera and song. One need only think of such names as Bach, Mozart, Schubert, Mahler, Wagner and Beethoven, to name only the most influential. Likewise, the German-speaking countries are famous for their philosophers such as Wittgenstein, Nietzsche and Hegel. In the twentieth century the United States was able to benefit more directly from German culture in the form of German émigrés from the Nazis. In this way, American architecture, music and film-making were enriched by the talents of Mies van der Rohe, Kurt Weill and Fritz Lang. But perhaps the most famous émigré from this era was the German born physicist Albert Einstein who decided not to return to his homeland while on a speaking tour to the US in 1932.

### Christmas traditions

It is also the German-speaking countries that the US has to thank for some of its Christmas traditions. Advent calendars, for example, were first printed in Germany and the Germans were the first to decorate Christmas trees. This tradition spread from Germany to Great Britain when the German Prince Albert married Queen Victoria and introduced the custom into the British royal family. It was duly copied by their subjects and by their cousins across the pond. Some features of German Christmases may not be so familiar, however. Presents are given on Christmas Eve when the family gathers in the evening to eat a traditional meal of roast goose. Likewise, Christmas cards are not as widely sent in Germany, Switzerland and Austria as they are in the US.

## German characteristics and everyday life

The Germans, Austrians and Swiss are often seen as stereotypically humorless and serious. The humorless label is perhaps a result of the fact that the German sense of humor is very different from the American. German comedies, for example, come across to the American viewer as rather farcical and relying heavily on slapstick. In particular, there is an element of irony which is missing and this also comes across in everyday conversation. A German speaker will often take an ironic statement literally which can lead to major confusion and jokes falling rather flat. Their reputation for seriousness is well deserved but this does not necessarily mean that all German speakers are dull. It is true that in the German-speaking countries even young people love to have earnest conversations about politics or culture. They do take things seriously, this cannot be denied, but this trait also means that they tend to get things done, whether it be at work, in sports, or simply in the garden at home. They approach work and pastimes with great thoroughness, energy and dedication.

## Green thinking

This hard-working culture has led to the German-speaking countries being at the forefront of many innovations. The most obvious example of this is their dedication to environmentally-friendly living and renewable energy sources. Where other countries have been slow to embrace recycling, biodegradable household products, organic farming and renewable energy and have only come to embrace them wholeheartedly when alternatives prove scarce or expensive, the Germans, Austrians and Swiss have been eager to invest in these areas right from the start, simply because it makes long-term sense to do so.

## Formal and informal modes of address

A further expression of this innate seriousness which might strike the foreign visitor is in the great formality with which German speakers address one another. In German, there are two options for translating the English *you*. The informal **du** is used between people who are on first-name terms, among young people and by older people when addressing children and teenagers. The formal **Sie** is used by children speaking to adults with whom they are not related and between adults who are not acquainted, who are superior in rank, or who do not share a close friendship. It would be considered very rude for a German to address an adult stranger as **du** but such slips are forgiven if made by foreigners. Although the use of the formal address is perhaps not as rigid as it used to be, it still persists among work colleagues. Whereas it is the norm for American co-workers to be on first-name terms right from the start of their acquaintance, Germans will still address a colleague they have worked alongside for decades as **Sie** and refer to him or her as **Herr X** or **Frau Y**.

## Shaking hands

This tendency toward greater formality also extends to the widespread practice of shaking hands which is normal between young or old whether they are acquainted or not. In a group of people it is the proper thing to go around and shake everyone's hand and introduce yourself if you are not acquainted, and it is an endearing sight to see small German children solemnly introducing themselves in this way to each member of a group.

## Working and business hours

Everyday life in the German-speaking countries has many similarities with that in the US but also striking differences. The working day starts early with schools and offices starting at 8 or even earlier, but they finish early too. Schools tend to finish around 1 or 2 p.m. and offices close at 4. Normal store business hours are from 9 a.m. to 6 p.m. and may appear restricted to the visitor from the United States. Sunday business hours are still quite rare in Germany, Austria and Switzerland. Ten years ago it was still very common for stores to close at noon on Saturdays except for one **langer Samstag** or *long Saturday* in the month. Nowadays it is more common for stores to remain open throughout the day on Saturday, particularly in the larger towns and cities, and even for stores to be open until 8 p.m. on certain days of the week. The rationale behind these restricted business hours is geared towards the rights of the store worker rather than the convenience of the customer.

## Houses and apartments

In towns and cities it is common in Germany, Austria and Switzerland for people to live in apartments. In the suburbs and in rural areas, however, the traditional large **Familienhaus** or *family house* is still a common sight. They tend to have a number of stories and the tradition is for different generations of a family to live on separate stories under the same roof. This practice is not as widespread as it used to be but is still relatively common.

## Public transportation

Even though people in the German-speaking countries enthusiastically embrace car travel, they are also able to take advantage of the sophisticated public transportation network for getting around. The majority of towns and cities in these countries have bus and streetcar networks as well as generous cycle paths and cycling is a very popular means of transportation in urban areas. Larger towns also have suburban railways or **S-Bahn** and all the countries have large railroad networks which are internationally famous for their punctuality. Public transportation is also relatively cheap and reliable and is an excellent way for the visitor to get around too.

## Sports and pastimes

The most popular sport in the German-speaking countries is undoubtedly soccer but other popular sports include handball, tennis and all forms of skiing. Many people also enjoy hiking and mountain climbing and take these pursuits with characteristic seriousness. A foreign visitor strolling along and admiring the view can expect to be passed by the natives intent on completing their hike as quickly and efficiently as possible. Large numbers of people also keep in shape by simply taking advantage of the cycle path networks and cycling everywhere they need to go.

Handicrafts are also a popular way for people in the German-speaking countries to relax. Knitting and needlework are still extremely popular, even among the younger generations. Many children will rate **Basteln** or *crafts* as their hobby and this may include model making, painting or different dyeing techniques. Gardening is also very popular with many apartment dwellers owning a **Schrebergarten** or *allotment*. Groups of these plots sometimes cover quite large areas and each one is large enough for a vegetable patch and fruit trees and a **Gartenhaus** or small cabin. People often spend whole weekends relaxing on the **Schrebergarten** and sleeping in the cabin.

### Relaxation

Other forms of relaxation include visiting health spas or beer gardens. The latter are often found in the middle of parks or attached to a particular brewery and offer a great way to spend time outdoors, sampling the local brew. All of these relaxation pursuits will be familiar to the visitor from the US. However, there is one particular pastime which will appear unusual and about which visitors should be aware. People in the German-speaking countries tend to be very uninhibited and nudism is very common and accepted as completely normal. Often areas in parks, on the side of lakes or swimming pools or on beaches are reserved for people wanting to indulge in the **Freikörperkultur** (*free body culture*) or **FKK** for short. Often whole families go in for this pursuit and the visitor who modestly remains covered up can often feel rather outnumbered and definitely overdressed when confronted with large numbers of **FKK** enthusiasts. There is no need to feel alarmed, however. Nudism, like mountain climbing, drinking beer and shaking hands, is merely one of those national characteristics which is all part of the experience of any visit to a German-speaking country.

# German–English dictionary

**ab** [ap] *prep* from ▸ ab Dortmund 12.35 Uhr departing Dortmund 12:35

**abbiegen** [apbeegen] *v* to turn off; *(road)* to bend

**Abblendlicht** [apblehndlisht] *das* dimmed headlights

**Abend** [aabent] *der* evening

**Abendessen** [aabentehsen] *das* dinner

**Abendkasse** [aabent-kas-e] *die* box office

**Abfahrt** [apfaart] *die* departure; *(on freeway)* exit; *(skiing)* descent

**Abfall** [apfal] *der* garbage

**Abfertigungsschalter** [apfehrtigungz-shalter] *der* check-in desk

**Abflug** [apflook] *der* departure; take-off

**abgelaufen** [apgelowfen] *adj (passport)* expired

**Abhang** [aphang] *der* slope

**abkühlen** [apkuulen] *v* to cool down

**ablegen** [aplaygen] *v* to take one's things off; to set sail

**abmelden** [apmehlden] ◆ **sich abmelden** *v (of hotel)* to check out

**Abreise** [apreyz-e] *die* departure

**absagen** [apzaagen] *v* to cancel

**abschalten** [apshalten] *v* to switch off

**Abschleppdienst** [apshlehpdeenst] *der* breakdown service

**abschließen** [apshleesen] *v (door)* to lock; *(task)* to finish

**Abstand** [apshtant] *der* distance; *(in time)* interval

**Abstecher** [apshtehsher] *der* detour

**abstellen** [apshtehlen] *v* to put down; *(car)* to park; to switch off

**Abstieg** [apshteek] *der* descent

**Abtei** [aptey] *die* abbey

**Abteil** [apteyl] *das* compartment

**abwärts** [apvehrts] *adv* down

**abwesend** [apvayzent] *adj* absent

**acht** [akht] *num* eight

**Achtung** [akhtung] *die* attention ▸ Achtung! watch out! ▸ Achtung Stufe! watch your step

**achtzehn** [akhtsayn] *num* eighteen

**achtzig** [akhtsish] *num* eighty

**ADAC** [aa-day-aa-tsay] *der organization equivalent to AAA*

**Adapter** [adapter] *der* adapter, adaptor

**Advent** [atvehnt] *der* Advent

**Aids** [aydz] *das* AIDS

**Alarmanlage** [alaarmanlaag-e] *die*

---

## Advent

In the four weeks leading up to Christmas, preparations are made in the traditional way. People go shopping at the Christmas market, bake their own cookies (*Plätzchen*) and make an Advent crown with its four candles. One candle is lit each Sunday until Christmas Day.

alarm system ▸ 'durch Alarmanlage gesichert' 'alarm protected'

**alkoholfrei** [alkoh-hohlfrey] *adj* alcohol-free

**alle** [al-e] *det* all; the; every ▸ alle beide both of us

**Alpen** [alpen] *pl* the Alps

**alt** [alt] *adj* old

**Alt** [alt], **Altbier** [altbeer] *das* dark beer

**Alter** [alter] *das* age

**Altglas** [altglaas] *das* glass for recycling

**Altpapier** [altpapeer] *das* waste paper

**Altstadt** [altshtat] *die* old town

**am** [am] *prep* on the ▸ am Abend in the evening ▸ am Flughafen at the airport

**Ampel** [ampel] *die* traffic lights

**Amt** [amt] *das* office

**an** [an] *prep* on; at, ▸ an dieser Stelle here ▸ an die 30 Grad about 30 degrees ▸ 'Licht an!' 'switch your lights on' ▸ an Heidelberg 22.12 Uhr arriving Heidelberg 22:12

**Andenken** [andehnken] *das* souvenir

**andere** [andere] *adj* other; another; different

**Änderung** [ehnderung] *die* change ▸ Änderungen vorbehalten subject to change

**Anfänger** [anfehnger] *der* beginner

**anfassen** [anfas-en] *v* to touch

**Angebot** [angeboht] *das* offer

**Angel** [ang-el] *die* fishing rod

**Angelschein** [ang-el-sheyn] *der* fishing permit

**Angestellte** [an-geshtehlt-e] *der, die* employee

**anhalten** [anhalten] *v* to stop; to persist

**Anhänger** [anhehnger] *der* (on car) trailer; (on suitcase) tag

**Ankleidekabine** [ankleyd-e-kabeen-e] *die* changing stall

**ankreuzen** [ankroytsen] *v* to mark with a cross

**ankündigen** [ankuundigen] *v* to announce

**Ankunft** [ankunft] *die* arrival

**Anlegestelle** [anlay-ge-shtehl-e] *die* mooring

**Anleitung** [anleytung] *die* instructions

**Anlieger** [anleeger] *der* resident ▸ 'Anlieger frei' 'residents only'

**Anmeldung** [anmehldung] *die* announcement; (of car, resident) registration; (at doctor's) appointment

**Annahme** [annaam-e] *die* acceptance ▸ 'keine Annahme von 50-Cent-Stücken' '50 cent coins not accepted'

**Anprobe** [anprohb-e] *die* fitting

**Anruf** [anroof] *der* call

**Anrufbeantworter** [anroof-be-antvorter] *der* answering machine

**anrufen** [anroofen] *v* to call, to phone

**Ansage** [anzaag-e] *die* announcement; answering machine message

**Anschlag** [anshlaak] *der* notice; attack ▸ 'bis zum Anschlag drehen' 'turn as far as it will go'

**Anschluss** [anshlus] *der* (train) connection ▸ 'kein Anschluss unter dieser Nummer!' 'the number you have dialed is no longer in service or has been disconnected'

**anschnallen** [anshnal-en] ◆ **sich anschnallen** *v* to fasten one's seat belt

**Anschrift** [anshrift] *die* address

**Ansichtskarte** [anzishtskart-e] *die* postcard

**ansteckend** [anshtehkent] *adj* infectious

**Antrag** [antraak] *der* application

**Antwort** [antvort] *die* answer

**Anwohner** [anvohner] *der* resident

**Anzahl** [antsaal] *die* number ▸ eine Anzahl an a number of

**Anzeige** [antseyg-e] *die* advertisement; *(of birth etc.)* announcement ▸ Anzeige erstatten to press charges

**Anzug** [antsook] *der* suit

**anzünden** [antsuunden] *v* to light

**Apfel** [apfel] *der* apple

**Apfelsine** [apfelzeen-e] *die* orange

**Apotheke** [apohtayk-e] *die* pharmacy

**Apparat** [aparaat] *der* device, machine

**April** [apreel] *der* April

**Arbeit** [arbeyt] *die* work

**arm** [arm] *adj* poor

**Arm** [arm] *der* arm

**Art** [aart] *die (of doing something)* way; kind, sort ▸ eine Art Musikinstrument a sort of musical instrument

**Arznei** [artsney] *die* medicine

**Arzt** [aartst] *der* doctor

**Ärztin** [ehrtstin] *die* doctor

**Asche** [ash-e] *die (of fire)* ashes; *(of cigarette)* ash ▸ 'keine heiße Asche einfüllen' 'no hot ashes'

**Aschenbecher** [ashenbehsher] *der* ashtray

**Attest** [atehst] *das* certificate

**auch** [owkh] *adv* also, too ▸ das habe ich auch nicht gewusst I didn't know that either

**auf** [owf] *prep* on ▸ auf dem Land in the country ▸ auf Englisch in English ▸ auf der Post at the post office ▸ die Tür ist auf the door is open

**aufbewahren** [owfbevaaren] *v* to keep

**aufdrehen** [owfdrayen] *v (faucet)* to turn on

**Aufenthalt** [owfehnt-halt] *der* stay; *(of train)* stop

**Aufenthaltsraum** [owfehnt-haltsrowm] *der (in hotel)* lounge

**Auffahrt** [owf-faart] *die* access road, connecting road

**Aufführung** [owf-fuurung] *die* performance

**Aufgabe** [owfgaab-e] *die* task; *(of parcel)* mailing; *(of baggage at airport)* check-in

**aufgrund** [owfgrunt] *prep* because of

**aufhängen** [owfhehngen] *v* to hang up

**aufheben** [owfhayben] *v* to raise, to lift

**aufhören** [owfheuren] *v* to stop

**aufklappen** [owfklapen] *v* to open up

**auflassen** [owflas-en] *v* to leave open

**Auflauf** [owflowf] *der* bake

**aufleuchten** [owfloyshten] *v* to light up

**auflösen** [owfleuzen] *v* to dissolve

**Aufnahme** [owfnaam-e] *die (of performance, guest)* reception; *(to hospital)* admission; photograph

**Aufruf** [owfroof] *der* call ▸ letzter Aufruf für Flug LH 404 last call for flight LH 404

**aufschließen** [owfshleesen] *v* to unlock

**Aufschnitt** [owfshnit] *der slices of cold meat and/or cheese*

**aufstehen** [owfshtayen] *v* to get up; *(door)* to be open

**auftauen** [owftowen] *v* to defrost; to thaw

**aufwärmen** [owfvehrmen] *v* to warm up

**aufwärts** [owfvehrts] *adv* up

**Aufzug** [owftsook] *der* elevator

**Auge** [owg-e] *das* eye

**August** [owgust] *der* August

**aus** [ows] *prep* from; out of; made of ♦ *adv* out; *(finished)* over ▸ er ist aus Amerika he is from America ▸ aus dem Haus gehen to go out of the house ▸ aus Plastik sein to be made of plastic

**Ausfahrt** [owsfaart] *die* exit; *(of train)* departure

**ausfallen** [owsfal-en] *v (hair, teeth)* to fall out; to be canceled

## Autobahn

With more than 10,000 km of freeways, Germany has the second biggest network in the world. Unlike in many of its neighboring countries, there is no charge for using them. There is also no speed limit but Germans usually drive responsibly.

**Ausflug** [owsflook] *der* trip

**Ausflugslokal** [owsflookslohkaal] *das country restaurant or bar popular with people on day trips*

**ausfüllen** [owsfuulen] *v* to fill out

**Ausgang** [owsgang] *der* exit

**ausgebucht** [owsgebookht] *adj* fully booked

**ausgeschildert** [owsgeshildert] *adj* to have signs showing the way

**Auskunft** [owskunft] *die* information; information desk; *(on telephone)* directory enquiries

**Auslandsschutzbrief** [owslandsshutsbreef] *der certificate of car insurance required for travel abroad*

**Auslese** [owslayz-e] *die wine made from select grapes*

**Ausreise** [owsreyz-e] *die* departure ▸ bei der Ausreise on leaving the country

**ausschalten** [ows-shalten] *v* to switch off

**ausschließlich** [ows-shleeslish] *adv* exclusively ◆ *prep* excluding

**außer** [owser] *prep* out of; except for ◆ *conj* except ▸ 'außer Betrieb' 'out of order'

**außerhalb** [owserhalp] *prep* outside

**äußerlich** [oyserlish] *adj* external; *(impression)* outward

**Aussicht** [ows-zisht] *die* view

**Aussichtsturm** [ows-zishts-toorm] *der* lookout tower

**ausspülen** [ows-shpuulen] *v* to rinse out

**aussteigen** [ows-shteygen] *v (of car)* to get out; *(of train, bus)* to get off ▸ 'Aussteigen bitte Knopf drücken' 'press button for next stop'

**Ausstellung** [ows-shtehlung] *die* exhibition

**Ausverkauf** [owsfehrkowf] *der* sale

**ausverkauft** [owsfehrkowft] *adj* sold out

**Auswahl** [owsvaal] *die* choice, selection

**auswärts** [owsvehrts] *adv* outwards; *(stay, play)* away from home ▸ auswärts essen to eat out

**Ausweis** [owsveys] *der* identity card

**Autobahn** [owtohbaan] *die* freeway

**Autobahngebühr** [owtohbaangebuur] *die* toll

**Autobahnkreuz** [owtohbaankroyts] *das* interchange

**Autofähre** [owtohfehr-e] *die* car ferry

**Autofahrer** [owtohfaarer] *der* motorist, car driver

**Automat** [owtohmaat] *der* vending machine

**Autovermietung** [owtohfehrmeetung] *die* car rental

# b

**Baby** [baybi] *das* baby

**Babysitz** [baybizits] *der* baby seat

**Baby-Wickelraum** [baybivikelrowm] *der* baby changing room

**Bach** [bakh] *der* stream

**Bäckerei** [behkerey] *die* bakery

**Backwaren** [bakvaaren] *pl* bread, cakes and pastries

**Bad** [baat] *das* bathroom; spa town ▸ ein Bad nehmen to have a bath

**Badeanzug** [baad-e-antsook] *der* swimsuit

**Badehose** [baad-e-hohz-e] *die* swimming trunks

**Bademütze** [baad-e-muuts-e] *die* swimming cap

**baden** [baaden] *v* to have a bath; to swim

**Badeort** [baad-e-ort] *der* spa

**Badetuch** [baad-e-tookh] *das* bath towel

**Badewanne** [baad-e-van-e] *die* bath (tub)

**Badezimmer** [baad-e-tsimer] *das* bathroom

**Bahn** [baan] *die* railroad; train ▸ mit der Bahn fahren to go by train

**Bahnhof** [baanhohf] *der* station

**Bahnhofsmission** [baanhohfsmisiohn] *die* room at station provided by charity organizations for care of rail travelers

**Bahnsteig** [baanshteyk] *der* platform ▸ am selben Bahnsteig gegenüber on the other side of the same platform

**Bahnübergang** [baanuubergang] *der* grade crossing ▸ unbeschrankter

Bahnübergang grade crossing without a barrier

**bald** [balt] *adv* soon

**Ball** [bal] *der* ball

**Bankleitzahl** [bankleyt-tsaal] *die* bank routing number

**Banknote** [banknoht-e] *die* banknote

**Bankverbindung** [bankfehrbindung] *die* account details

**bar** [baar] *adv* in cash

**Bär** [behr] *der* bear

**barfuß** [baarfus] *adv* barefoot

**Bargeld** [baargehlt] *das* cash

**Bauarbeiten** [bowarbeyten] *pl* construction work; roadwork ▸ wegen Bauarbeiten gesperrt closed for roadwork

**Bauchschmerzen** [bowkhshmehrtsen] *pl* stomachache

**Bauernbrot** [bowernbroht] *das* type of coarse brown bread

**Bauernfrühstück** [bowernfruuhshtuuk] *das* scrambled eggs with bacon and fried potatoes

**Bauernhof** [bowernhohf] *der* farm

**Baum** [bowm] *der* tree

**Baumwolle** [bowm-vol-e] *die* cotton

**Baustelle** [bowshtehl-e] *die* building site; roadwork site ▸ 'Vorsicht Baustelle!' (on road) 'caution: roadwork ahead'

**beachten** [be-akhten] *v (right of way)* to observe; *(instruction)* to follow

**Beanstandung** [be-anshtandung] *die* complaint

**beantworten** [be-antvorten] *v* to answer

**beaufsichtigen** [be-owfzishtigen] v to supervise

**Becken** [behken] das washbasin; (for swimming) pool

**Beckenrand** [behkenrant] der edge of the pool ▸ 'Springen vom Beckenrand nicht erlaubt!' 'no diving or jumping in from the edge of the pool'

**bedanken** [bedanken] ◆ **sich bedanken** v to say thank you

**Bedarfshaltestelle** [bedaarfs-halt-e-shtehl-e] die stop at which bus halts only by request of a dismounting or boarding passenger

**bedauern** [bedowern] v to regret

**bedeutend** [bedoytent] adj important; (in size) considerable

**Bedeutung** [bedoytung] die meaning; importance

**bedienen** [bedeenen] v to serve ▸ bedienen Sie sich! help yourself!

**Bedienung** [bedeenung] die service; waiter, waitress

**Bedienungsanleitung** [bedeenungz-anleytung] die operating instructions

**Bedingung** [bedingung] die condition

**Beet** [bayt] das (for flowers etc.) bed

**Beete** [bayt-e] die beet

**befestigen** [befehstigen] v to attach

**befinden** [befinden] ◆ **sich befinden** v to be situated ▸ 'Sie befinden sich hier' 'you are here'

**befolgen** [befolgen] v to follow

**befördern** [befeurdern] v to transport

**Beginn** [begin] der beginning

**Beglaubigung** [beglowbigung] die authentication

**begleiten** [begleyten] v to accompany

**Begleitperson** [begleytpehrzohn] die escort

**Begründung** [begruundung] die reason; (of town etc.) founding

**begrüßen** [begruusen] v to greet

**behalten** [behalten] v to keep

**Behälter** [behehlter] der container

**Behandlung** [behandlung] die treatment

**beheizt** [beheytst] adj heated

**behindert** [behindert] adj disabled

**Behörde** [beheurd-e] die authority

**bei** [bey] prep next to; at ▸ beim Signal at the signal ▸ ich habe kein Geld bei mir I don't have any money on me ▸ bei Nacht at night ▸ bei Regen in wet weather ▸ beim Fahren while driving ▸ bei Paul at Paul's house

**beide** [beyd-e] pron both

**Beifahrer** [beyfaarer] der front-seat passenger

**Beilage** [beylaag-e] die side dish; (in newspaper) supplement

**Beipackzettel** [beypak-tsehtel] der instruction leaflet

**beißen** [beysen] v to bite; (smoke) to sting

**Beitrag** [beytraak] der contribution

**bekannt** [bekant] adj well-known

**bekommen** [bekomen] v to get; (bus, train) to catch

**Beleg** [belayk] der receipt; proof

**belegt** [belaykt] adj (room) occupied; (hotel) full ▸ belegtes Brötchen/Brot open-faced roll/sandwich ▸ voll belegt full up

**Beleuchtung** [beloyshtung] die lighting

**benutzen** [benutsen] v to use

**Benutzer** [benutser] der user

**Benzin** [behntseen] das gas ▸ bleifreies Benzin unleaded gas

**bequem** [bekvaym] adj comfortable

**berechnen** [berehshnen] v to calculate; to charge

**berechtigt** [berehshtisht] adj justified

### Berliner Mauer

The symbol of a divided city, the Berlin Wall was built in 1961 in order to prevent the exodus of citizens from the East. 79 people lost their lives trying to get into West Berlin, which was situated smack in the middle of the GDR. When the Wall fell on November 9th 1989, thousands of Berliners were reunited in front of the world's cameras.

**Bereich** [bereysh] *der* area

**bereit** [bereyt] *adj* ready

**bereithalten** [bereyt-halten] *v* to have ready

**Bereitschaftsdienst** [bereytshaftsdeenst] *der* emergency service

**Berg** [behrk] *der* mountain, hill

**bergab** [behrk-ap] *adv* downhill

**bergauf** [behrk-owf] *adv* uphill

**Bergführer** [behrkfuurer] *der* mountain guide

**Berghütte** [behrk-huut-e] *die* mountain hut

**Bergsteigen** [behrkshteygen] *das* mountaineering

**Bergwacht** [behrkvakht] *die* mountain rescue service

**Bergwanderung** [behrkvanderung] *die* mountain hike

**Berliner** [behrleener] *der (inhabitant)* Berliner; jelly doughnut

**Berliner Mauer** [behrleener mower] *die* Berlin Wall

**Beruf** [beroof] *der* profession

**Beruhigungsmittel** [berooigungzmitel] *das* sedative

**berühmt** [beruumt] *adj* famous

**beschädigen** [beshaydigen] *v* to damage

**Bescheinigung** [besheynigung] *die* certificate; written confirmation; receipt

**beschlagnahmen** [beshlaaknaamen] *v* to confiscate

**Beschwerde** [beshvehrd-e] *die* complaint ▸ Beschwerden trouble, pain

**besetzt** [bezehtst] *adj (telephone line)* busy; *(toilet)* occupied; *(seat)* taken

**Besichtigung** [bezishtigung] *die* visit, tour

**Besitzer** [bezitser] *der* owner

**besondere, r, s** [bezonder-e] *adj* special

**besser** [behser] *adv* better

**Besserung** [behserung] *die* improvement ▸ gute Besserung! get well soon!

**Bestätigung** [beshtaytigung] *die* confirmation

**beste, r, s** [behst-e] *adj* best

**Besteck** [beshtehk] *das* flatware

**bestellen** [beshtehlen] *v* to order; to reserve, to book

**Bestellung** [beshtehlung] *die* order; reservation, booking

**Besuch** [bezookh] *der* visit

**Besucher** [bezookher] *der* visitor, guest ▸ 'nur für Besucher' 'guests only'

**betätigen** [betaytigen] *v* to operate

**Betrag** [betraak] *der* amount ▸ angezeigter Betrag indicated amount

**betreten** [betrayten] *v* to enter ▸ 'Betreten verboten!' 'keep out/off!'

**Betreuer** [betroyer] *der* person in charge; *(for tourists)* guide

## Bier

With more than 1,250 breweries and 5,000 types of beer, it's no surprise that the Germans are the 2nd biggest beer drinkers in the world. Since 1516, the 'edict of purity' has strictly guaranteed the high quality of German beer. In addition to the Pils that is sold throughout Germany, each region has its own specialty, such as *Altbier* in Düsseldorf, *Berliner Weiße* in Berlin, *Kölsch* in Cologne and *Weizenbier* in Bavaria.

---

**Betrieb** [betreep] *der* company; *(activity)* operation ▸ außer Betrieb out of order

**Betrüger** [betruuger] *der* conman

**betrunken** [betrunken] *adj* drunk

**Bett** [beht] *das* bed ▸ französisches Bett double bed

**Bettdecke** [behtdehk-e] *die* quilt; blanket

**Bettwäsche** [behtvehsh-e] *die* bedclothes

**Beutel** [boytel] *der* bag

**bevor** [befor] *conj* before

**bewacht** [bevakht] *adj* guarded

**Bewegung** [bevaygung] *die* movement

**bewölkt** [beveulkt] *adj* cloudy

**bezahlen** [betsaalen] *v* to pay (for)

**Bezeichnung** [betseyshnung] *die* description; marking ▸ 'genaue Bezeichnung des Inhalts' 'exact description of contents'

**BH** [bayhaa] *der* bra

**Bhf.** [baanhohf] *abbr of* Bahnhof station

**Biene** [been-e] *die* bee

**Bienenstich** [beenenshtish] *der* bee sting; *type of small cake filled with cream and topped with almonds*

**Bier** [beer] *das* beer ▸ Bier vom Fass draft beer

**Biergarten** [beergaarten] *der* beer garden

**Bild** [bilt] *das* picture; photo

**Bildhauer** [bilt-hower] *der* sculptor

**Bildschirm** [biltshirm] *der* screen ▸ 'Bildschirm berühren!' 'touch the screen'

**billig** [bilish] *adj* cheap

**Binde** [bind-e] *die* bandage; sanitary napkin

**Biokost** [beeohkost] *die* health food

**Birne** [beern-e] *die* pear; light bulb

**bis** [bis] *prep* until; by; to ▸ zwei bis drei Tage two to three days ▸ von Montag bis Freitag Monday through Friday

**bisher** [bis-hehr] *adv* until now; yet

**bitte** [bi-te] *adv* please ▸ danke! – bitte!

---

## Biergarten

In summer, in the Bavarian 'beer gardens,' the waitresses bring fresh supplies to carousing Germans by carrying four or five one-liter tankards (*Maß*) in each hand! The Munich *Hirschgarten* can accommodate up to 8,000 people. Sausages and pork shanks are sure to be on the menu, or you can take along your own picnic.

## Brot

Germany is a great place for bread, too. With over 200 different kinds, there's a type of bread to suit all tastes. For breakfast it's normal to eat *Brötchen* (little white bread rolls) or *Weißbrot* (white bread), and to have *Schwarzbrot* and *Pumpernickel* (black breads) or *Vollkornbrot* (whole wheat bread) with cold meats and cheese for supper (*Abendbrot*).

thanks! – don't mention it! ▸ **wie bitte?** pardon me?

**Blatt** [blat] *das* leaf; *(of paper)* sheet

**blau** [blow] *adj* blue

**Blaubeere** [blowbehr-e] *die* blueberry

**bleiben** [bleyben] *v* to stay

**bleifrei** [bleyfrey] *adj* unleaded

**Bleistift** [bleyshtift] *der* pencil

**Blitzlicht** [blits-lisht] *das* flash

**blühen** [bluuen] *v* to blossom

**Blume** [bloom-e] *die* flower

**Blumenkohl** [bloomenkohl] *der* cauliflower

**Bluse** [blooz-e] *die* blouse

**Blut** [bloot] *das* blood

**Blutdruck** [blootdruk] *der* blood pressure ▸ **hoher Blutdruck** high blood pressure

**bluten** [blooten] *v* to bleed

**Blutwurst** [blootvurst] *die* blood sausage

**Bockbier** [bokbeer] *das* *type of strong, dark beer*

**Bocksbeutel** [boksboytel] *der* *type of rounded bottle used for Franconian wine*

**Bockwurst** [bokvurst] *die* *type of boiled pork sausage*

**Boden** [bohden] *der* ground; soil; attic

**Bodensee** [bohdenzay] *der* Lake Constance

**Bohne** [bohn-e] *die* bean

**Boje** [bohy-e] *die* buoy

**Boot** [boht] *das* boat

**Bootsverleih** [bohtsfehrley] *der* boat rental

**Bordkarte** [bordkart-e] *die* boarding pass

**Botschaft** [boht-shaft] *die* embassy; message

**Bowle** [bohl-e] *die* punch

**Brandwunde** [brantvund-e] *die* burn

**Braten** [braaten] *der* to fry; to roast; to bake

**Brathähnchen** [braathehnshen] *das* roast chicken

**Bratkartoffeln** [braatkartofeln] *pl* fried potatoes

**Bratwurst** [braatvurst] *die* fried sausage

**brauchen** [browkhen] *v* to need; to use

**braun** [brown] *adj* brown

**BRD** [bay-ehr-day] *die* FRG

**breit** [breyt] *adj* wide

**Bremse** [brehmz-e] *die* brake

**brennen** [brehnen] *v* to burn; *(lamp)* to be on ▸ **es brennt!** fire!

**Brief** [breef] *der* letter

**Briefkasten** [breefkasten] *der* mailbox

**Briefmarke** [breefmark-e] *die* stamp

**Brille** [bril-e] *die* glasses

**bringen** [bringen] *v* to bring; to take

**Brombeere** [brombehr-e] *die* blackberry

**Brot** [broht] *das* bread; loaf of bread; sandwich

**Bundesland**

Since reunification in 1990, Germany has been divided into 16 *Länder* (regions). Largely autonomous, they each have their own constitution and make all decisions regarding, for example, education, policing and culture. However, according to the German basic law, the State has sovereignty in matters of defense, transport and communication.

**Brötchen** [breutshen] *das* (bread) roll
▸ belegtes Brötchen open-faced roll
**Brücke** [bruuk-e] *die* bridge
**Bruder** [brooder] *der* brother
**Brunnen** [brunen] *der* fountain; well
**Buch** [bookh] *das* book
**buchen** [bookhen] *v* to book
**Bücherei** [buusherey] *die* library
**Buchstabe** [bookhshtaab-e] *der* letter
▸ großer Buchstabe capital letter
**Bucht** [bukht] *die* bay
**Buchung** [bookhung] *die* booking
**bügeln** [buugeln] *v* to iron
**Bühne** [buun-e] *die* stage
**Bundeskanzler** [bundezkantsler] *der* chancellor
**Bundesland** [bundezlant] *das* federal state
**Bundesrepublik** [bundezrehpubleek] *die* federal republic ▸ Bundesrepublik

Deutschland Federal Republic of Germany
**Bundesstraße** [bundez-shtraas-e] *die* ≃ state highway
**bunt** [bunt] *adj* colorful
**Burg** [burk] *die* castle
**Bürger** [buurger] *der* citizen
**Bürgermeister** [buurgermeyster] *der* mayor
**Bürste** [buurst-e] *die* brush
**Bus** [bus] *der* bus
**Busbahnhof** [busbaanhohf] *der* bus station
**Busfahrer** [busfaarer] *der* bus driver
▸ 'Fahrscheine beim Busfahrer' 'buy tickets from driver'
**Bushaltestelle** [bus-halt-e-shtehl-e] *die* bus stop
**Butter** [buter] *die* butter
**Buttermilch** [butermilsh] *die* buttermilk

# C

**ca.** [tseerka] *abbr of* circa approx.
**Campingwagen** [kehmpingvaagen] *der* motorhome, camper
**CD-Spieler** [tsaydayshpeeler] *der* CD player
**Chip** [tship] *der* chip

**Chipkarte** [tshipkart-e] *die* smart card
**Chor** [kor] *der* choir
**Computer** [kompyooter] *der* computer
**Currywurst** [karivurst] *die* sausage served with curry sauce

# d

**da** [daa] *adv* there; here; then ▸ bleib da! stay where you are!

**Dach** [dakh] *das* roof

**dahin** [daahin] *adv* there; then ▸ bis dahin until then

**Dame** [daam-e] *die* lady

**Damenbinde** [daamenbin-de] *die* sanitary napkin

**Dämmerung** [dehmerung] *die* dawn; dusk

**Dampf** [dampf] *der* steam

**Dampfer** [dampfer] *der* steamer

**Dampfnudel** [dampfnoodel] *die dough cake served with vanilla sauce*

**danach** [daanakh] *adv* afterward

**danke** [dank-e] *excl* thank you, thanks

**dann** [dan] *adv* then

**darf** [darf] *v* may ▸ darf ich? may I?

**daran** [daaran] *adv* on it ▸ daran denken to think about it

**Darmgrippe** [darmgrip-e] *die* stomach flu

**Darsteller** [daarshtehler] *der* actor

**Darstellerin** [daarshtehlerin] *die* actress

**darüber** [daaruuber] *adv* over it ▸ darüber sprechen to talk about it

**darunter** [daarunter] *adv* under it; among them

**das** [das] *det* the

**da sein** [daa zeyn] *v* to be there

**dasselbe** [das-zehlb-e] *det* the same

**Datum** [daatum] *das* date

**Dauer** [dower] *die* duration

**dauern** [dowern] *v* to last ▸ es dauert nicht lange it won't take long

**Daumen** [dowmen] *der* thumb

**davor** [daafor] *adv* in front of it; beforehand ▸ er hat Angst davor he's scared of it

**dazu** [daatsoo] *adv* with it ▸ sie hat keine Lust dazu she doesn't feel like it

**Deck** [dehk] *das* deck

**Decke** [dehk-e] *die* ceiling; blanket; tablecloth

**Deckel** [dehkel] *der* lid

**deftig** [dehftish] *adj* (meal) substantial

**Deich** [deysh] *der* (levee) dike

**denken** [dehnken] *v* to think

**Denkmal** [dehnkmal] *das* monument

**denn** [dehn] *conj* because

**der** [dehr] *det* the

**derselbe** [dehrzehlb-e] *pron* the same

**deutsch** [doytsh] *adj* German

**Deutschland** [doytshlant] *neut* Germany

**Dezember** [daytsehmber] *der* December

**Dialekt** [dialehkt] *der* dialect ▸ see box on p. 21

**Diät** [diayt] *die* diet

**Dichter** [dishter] *der* poet; writer

**dick** [dik] *adj* fat; (book etc.) thick

**Dickmilch** [dikmilsh] *die* sour milk

**die** [dee] *det* the

**Dieb** [deep] *der* thief

**Dienstag** [deenstaak] *der* Tuesday

**diese, r, s** [deez-e] *det* this, these; that, those ◆ *pron* this one, these ones; that one, those ones

**dieselbe** [deezehlb-e] *det* the same

**diesmal** [deezmal] *adv* this time

## Dialekt

Germany has several dialects as well as *Hochdeutsch*, the standard language. The dialects are so different that a Bavarian and a Frisian (or a Mecklenburger) who could only speak their respective dialects would have to use a bit of sign language to be able to communicate.

**Dill** [dil] *der* dill

**Ding** [ding] *das* thing

**Dirigent** [dirigehnt] *der (of orchestra)* conductor

**DLRG** [day-ehl-ehr-gay] *die German Lifesaving Association (of lifeguards for pools and beaches)*

**Dom** [dohm] *der* cathedral

**Donnerstag** [donerztaak] *der* Thursday

**doof** [dohf] *adj* stupid

**Doppelbett** [dopelbeht] *das* double bed

**doppelt** [dopelt] *adj* double

**Doppelzimmer** [dopel-tsimer] *das* double room

**Dorf** [dorf] *das* village

**dort** [dort] *adv* there

**Dose** [dohz-e] *die* can; box

**Dosenmilch** [dohzenmilsh] *die* condensed milk

**Drachenfliegen** [drakhenfleegen] *das* hang-gliding

**Drahtseilbahn** [draatzeylbaan] *die* cable railway

**draußen** [drowsen] *adv* outside

**dreckig** [drehkish] *adj* dirty ▸ dreckig machen to get dirty

**drehen** [drayen] *v* to turn; to film

**drei** [drey] *num* three

**dreißig** [dreysish] *num* thirty

**dreizehn** [dreytsayn] *num* thirteen

**Dressing** [drehsing] *das* dressing

**dringend** [dringent] *adj* urgent

**drinnen** [drinen] *adv* inside

**dritte, r, s** [drit-e] *adj* third

**Drittel** [dritel] *das* third

**Drogerie** [drogeree] *die* drugstore

**Druckbuchstabe** [drukbookhshtaab-e] *der* block letter ▸ in Druckbuchstaben schreiben to print

**drücken** [druuken] *v* to press; to push

**du** [doo] *pron* you (informal)

**Düne** [duun-e] *die* dune

**dunkel** [dunkel] *adj* dark

**durch** [dursh] *prep* through; by

**Durchfahrt** [durshfaart] *die* way through; thoroughfare ▸ 'Durchfahrt verboten!' 'no outlet' ▸ auf der Durchfahrt sein to be passing through

**Durchfall** [durshfal] *der* diarrhea

**Durchgang** [durshgang] *der* passage ▸ 'Durchgang verboten!' 'passing prohibited'

**durchgebraten** [durshgebraaten] *adj* well done

**durchgehend** [durshgayent] *adj (train, flight)* direct ▸ durchgehend geöffnet open all day

**Durchsage** [durshzaag-e] *die* announcement

**durchstreichen** [dursh-shtreyshen] *v* to cross out

**Durchwahl** [durshvaal] *die (on phone)* extension

**dürfen** [duurfen] *v* to be allowed ▸ Sie dürfen gehen you may go ▸ das dürfen wir nicht vergessen we mustn't forget that

**Durst** [durst] *der* thirst ▸ ich habe Durst I'm thirsty

**Dusche** [dush-e] *die* shower

**Dutzend** [dutsent] *das* dozen

**duzen** [dootsen] *v* to address somebody using the familiar 'du' form

**DZ** [day-tseht] *das* *abbr of* **Doppelzimmer** double room

**Ebbe** [ehb-e] *die* low tide

**Ebene** [ayben-e] *die* plain; level

**echt** [ehsht] *adj* real, genuine

**Ecke** [ehk-e] *die* corner

**Edelstein** [aydelshteyn] *der* precious stone

**EDV** [ay-day-fow] *die* electronic data processing

**Ei** [ey] *das* egg ▸ ein weiches Ei a soft-boiled egg ▸ ein hart gekochtes Ei a hard-boiled egg

**Eigentümer** [eygentoomer] *der* owner

**ein, e** [eyn] *det* a, an ✦ *num* one

**einatmen** [eynaatmen] *v* to breathe in

**Einbahnstraße** [eynbaanshtraas-e] *die* one-way street

**Einbettzimmer** [eynbeht-tsimer] *das* single room

**Einbrecher** [eynbresher] *der* burglar

**Einbruch** [eynbrukh] *der* break-in ▸ bei Einbruch der Nacht at nightfall

**einchecken** [eyn-tshehken] *v* to check in

**eincremen** [eynkraymen] *v* to put cream on

**eine** [ey-ne] *det* a, an ✦ *num* one

**eineinhalb** [eyn-eyn-halp] *num* one and a half

**einfach** [eynfakh] *adj* simple; (ticket) one-way

**Einfahrt** [eynfaart] *die* arrival; entrance

▸ 'Einfahrt freihalten!' 'keep clear'

**Eingang** [eyngang] *der* entrance

**einheimisch** [eynheymish] *adj* local

**einige** [eynig-e] *det* a few, some

**Einkaufsbummel** [eynkowfsbumel] *der* shopping trip

**Einladung** [eynlaadung] *die* invitation

**einmal** [eynmal] *adv* once ▸ noch einmal once again

**einnehmen** [eyn-naymen] *v* (medication) to take

**Einreise** [eynreyz-e] *die* entry

**Einreisevisum** [eynreyz-e-veezum] *das* entry visa

**eins** [eyns] *num* one

**einsam** [eynzaam] *adj* lonely; isolated

**einschalten** [eyn-shalten] *v* to switch on

**einschließlich** [eyn-shleeslish] *prep* including

**Einschreiben** [eyn-shreyben] *das* registered letter ▸ per Einschreiben by registered mail

**Einspänner** [eyn-shpehner] *der* *black coffee topped with whipped cream*

**einsteigen** [eyn-shteygen] *v* (into car) to get in; (onto train, bus) to get on ▸ alles einsteigen! all aboard!

**Einstieg** [eyn-shteek] *der* (into car) getting in; (onto bus, train) getting on; door ▸ 'Einstieg nur vorne' 'entry only at the front'

**Einsturzgefahr** [eyn-shturtsgefaar] *die* danger of collapse ▸ Vorsicht, Einsturzgefahr! danger – building unsafe!

**Eintopf** [eyntopf] *der* stew

**eintreten** [eyn-trayten] *v* to enter

**Eintritt** [eyntrit] *der* entry ▸ Eintritt frei admission free

**Eintrittskarte** [eyntritskart-e] *die* ticket

**einwerfen** [eynvehrfen] *v* to throw in; to insert; to mail

**Einwohner** [eynvohner] *der* inhabitant

**Einwurf** [eynvurf] *der* slot

**Einzelbett** [eyntselbeht] *das* single bed

**Einzelfahrschein** [eyntselfaarsheyn] *der* one-way ticket

**Einzelzimmer** [eyntsel-tsimer] *das* single room

**einzig** [eyntsish] *adj* only

**Eis** [eys] *das* ice; ice cream

**Eisen** [eyzen] *das* iron

**Eisenbahn** [eyzenbaan] *die* railroad; train

**eisgekühlt** [eys-gekuult] *adj* chilled

**Eiswürfel** [eysvuurfel] *der* ice cube

**Eiter** [eyter] *der* pus

**Eiweiß** [eyveys] *das* egg white; protein

**Elektrogerät** [ehlehktrohgerayt] *das* electrical appliance

**elf** [ehlf] *num* eleven

**Eltern** [ehltern] *pl* parents

**Empfang** [ehmpfang] *der* reception; *(in hotel)* reception desk; *(of letter, goods)* receipt

**Empfänger** [ehmpfehnger] *der* receiver; *(of letter)* addressee

**Empfehlung** [ehmpfaylung] *die* recommendation

**Ende** [ehnd-e] *das* end

**enden** [ehnden] *v* to end

**Endstation** [ehnt-shtatsiohn] *die* terminus

**eng** [ehng] *adj* narrow; *(clothes)* tight; *(friend)* close

**Enkel** [ehnkel] *der* grandson

**entdecken** [ehntdehken] *v* to discover

**Ente** [ehnt-e] *die* duck

**entfernen** [ehntfehrnen] *v* to remove

**entfernt** [ehntfehrnt] *adj* distant ▸ weit entfernt von far away from

**Entfernung** [ehntfehrnung] *die* distance; removal

**enthalten** [ehnt-halten] *v* to contain ▸ im Preis enthalten included in the price

**entlang** [ehntlang] *prep* along

**entrahmt** [ehntraamt] *adj (milk)* skim

**Entschädigung** [ehnt-shaydigung] *die* compensation

**Entscheidung** [ehnt-sheydung] *die* decision

**Entschluss** [ehnt-shlus] *der* decision

**Entschuldigung** [ehnt-shuldigung] *die* excuse; apology ▸ Entschuldigung! sorry! ▸ Entschuldigung, haben Sie Feuer? excuse me, do you have a light?

**entspannen** [ehnt-shpanen] *v* to relax

**entsprechend** [ehnt-shprehshent] *adj* corresponding; appropriate

**entstehen** [ehnt-shtayen] *v (situation)* to arise; *(building)* to be built; *(costs)* to be incurred

**entweder** [ehntvayder] *conj* either ▸ entweder ... oder either ... or

**entwerten** [ehntvehrten] *v (ticket)* to cancel

**entwickeln** [ehntvikeln] *v* to develop

**Entzündung** [ehnt-tsuundung] *die* inflammation

**Enzian** [ehntsiaan] *der type of schnapps made from gentian*

**er** [ehr] *pron* he; it

**Erbse** [ehrps-e] *die* pea

**Erdbeere** [ehrdbehr-e] *die* strawberry

**Erdgeschoss** [ehrtgeshos] *das* first floor

**Erdnuss** [ehrdnus] *die* peanut

**Ereignis** [ehreygnis] *das* event

**erfahren** [ehrfaaren] *adj* experienced
• *v* to learn, to find out; to experience

**Erfahrung** [ehrfaarung] *die* experience

**Erfrischung** [ehrfrishung] *die* refreshment

**erfüllen** [ehrfuulen] *v (condition)* to fulfill

**erhalten** [ehrhalten] *v* to receive; *(building)* to preserve

**erhöhen** [ehrheuen] *v* to raise

**Erholung** [ehrhohlung] *die* relaxation; recovery

**Erkältung** [ehrkehltung] *die* cold

**erkennen** [ehrkehnen] *v* to recognize

**Erklärung** [ehrklehrung] *die* explanation

**erlauben** [ehrlowben] *v* to allow

**Ermäßigung** [ehrmehsigung] *die* reduction

**ermöglichen** [ehrmeuglishen] *v* to make possible

**Ernährung** [ehrnehrung] *die* food; diet

**Ernte** [ehrnt-e] *die* harvest

**Eröffnung** [ehr-eufnung] *die* opening

**erreichen** [ehreyshen] *v* to reach; *(bus, train)* to catch

**Ersatzreifen** [ehrzatsreyfen] *der* spare tire

**ersetzen** [ehrzehtzen] *v* to replace

**erst** [ehrst] *adv* only; not until; (at) first

**erste** [ehrst-e] *adj* first

**Erwachsene** [ehrvaksen-e] *der, die* adult

**erzählen** [ehrtsaylen] *v* to tell

**Erzeugnis** [ehrtsoygnis] *das* product

**es** [ehs] *pron* it • es ist kalt it's cold

**Esel** [ayzel] *der* donkey

**essen** [ehsen] *v* to eat

**Essen** [ehsen] *das* food; meal

**Essig** [ehsish] *der* vinegar

**Esslöffel** [esleufel] *der* dessert spoon

**Esszimmer** [ehs-tsimer] *das* dining room

**etwa** [ehtva] *adv* about • es kostet etwa 100 Euro it costs about 100 euros

**etwas** [ehtvas] *pron* something; *(in questions, negative statements)* anything • etwas Sahne some cream

**EU** [ay-oo] *abbr of* **Europäische Union** *die* EU

**EZ** [ay-tseht] *das abbr of* **Einzelzimmer** single room

**Fach** [fakh] *das* compartment; subject

**Fachmann** [fakhman] *der* expert

**Fachwerkhaus** [faakhvehrk-hows] *das* half-timbered house

**Fahrausweis** [faar-owsveys] *der* ticket

**Fahrbahnschäden** [faarbaanshayden] *pl* damage to road surface

**Fahrbahnverschmutzung** [faarbaan-fehrshmutsung] *die* dirt on the road

**Fähre** [fehr-e] *die* ferry

**fahren** [faaren] *v* to go; *(in car)* to drive; *(on bicycle)* to ride • der Bus fährt bald the bus is leaving soon • mit dem Zug fahren to go by train • Ski fahren to ski

**Fahrer** [faarer] *der* driver

**Fahrgast** [faargast] *der* passenger

**Fahrgeld** [faargehlt] *das* fare

**Fahrkarte** [faarkart-e] *die* ticket

**Fahrplan** [faarplan] *der* timetable

**fahrplanmäßig** [faarplanmaysish] *adj* scheduled ▸ fahrplanmäßige Abfahrt scheduled departure

**Fahrpreis** [faarpreys] *der* fare

**Fahrrad** [faar-raat] *das* bicycle ▸ mit dem Fahrrad by bicycle

**Fahrradverleih** [faar-raatfehrley] *der* cycle rental

**Fahrradweg** [faar-raatvayk] *der* cycle path

**Fahrschein** [faarsheyn] *der* ticket ▸ 'Fahrscheine hier entwerten' 'cancel tickets here'

**Fahrspur** [faarshpoor] *die* lane

**Fahrstreifen** [faarshtreyfen] *der* lane

**Fahrstuhl** [faarshtool] *der* elevator

**Fahrt** [faart] *die* journey; trip ▸ freie Fahrt auf der A3 traffic is moving freely on the A3

**fährt** [fehrt] *pres* goes; (in car) drives; (on bicycle) rides

**Fahrtantritt** [faartantritt] *der* start of the journey ▸ 'Fahrscheine vor Fahrtantritt entwerten' 'cancel ticket before starting journey'

**Fahrzeug** [faar-tsoyk] *das* vehicle

**Fahrzeugpapiere** [faar-tsoykpapeer-e] *pl* vehicle documents

**Fahrzeugschein** [faar-tsoyksheyn] *der* vehicle registration document

**Fall** [fal] *der* case

**fallen** [fal-en] *v* to fall

**falsch** [falsh] *adj* wrong, incorrect; (name) false; (passport) forged ◆ *adv* wrongly

**Familienname** [fameelien-naam-e] *der* family name, surname

**Familienstand** [fameelienshtant] *der* marital status

**Farbe** [farb-e] *die* color; paint

**Farbstoff** [farbshtof] *der* coloring

**Fasching** [fashing] *der* carnival held before Lent

**Fass** [fas] *das* barrel ▸ vom Fass draft (beer)

**Fastnacht** [fastnakht] *die* carnival held before Lent

**Februar** [faybruar] *der* February

**Federweiße** [fayderveys-e] *der* type of young white wine

**fehlen** [faylen] *v* to be missing ▸ was fehlt Ihnen/dir? what's the matter?

**Fehler** [fayler] *der* mistake

**Feier** [feyer] *die* party

**Feiertag** [feyertaak] *der* holiday

**Feind** [feynt] *der* enemy

**Feinkostgeschäft** [feynkostgeshehft] *das* delicatessen

**Feinschmecker** [feynshmehker] *der* gourmet

**Feld** [fehlt] *das* field; (on form) box

**Feldsalat** [fehltzalaat] *der* corn salad

**Felsen** [fehlzen] *der* cliff

**Fenster** [fehnster] *das* window

**Ferien** [fehrien] *pl* vacation ▸ Ferien machen to go on vacation ▸ in Ferien sein to be on vacation

**Feriengast** [fehriengast] *der* vacationer

**Ferngespräch** [fehrngeshprehsh] *das* long-distance call

**fernsehen** [fehrnzayen] *v* to watch television

**Fernsehen** [fehrnzayen] *das* television

**Fernseher** [fehrnzayer] *der* television (set)

**fertig** [fehrtish] *adj* finished

**Fertiggericht** [fehrtishgerisht] *das* frozen dinner, TV dinner

**fest** [fehst] *adj* tight; firm; fixed

**Fest** [fehst] *das* party; festival

**Festspiele** [fehst-shpeel-e] *pl* festival

**fettarm** [fehtarm] *adj* low-fat

**feucht** [foysht] *adj* damp

**Feuer** [foyer] *das* fire ▸ 'Feuer und offenes Licht verboten!' 'no open flames'

**Feuerlöscher** [foyerleusher] *der* fire extinguisher

**Feuerwehr-Zufahrt** [foyervehr-tsoofaart] *die* fire lane

**Feuerwerk** [foyervehrk] *das* fireworks

**Fieber** [feeber] *das (fever)* temperature ▸ Fieber haben to have a temperature

**Figur** [figoor] *die* figure

**finden** [finden] *v* to find

**Finger** [fing-er] *der* finger

**Fingernagel** [fing-er-naagel] *der* fingernail

**Fisch** [fish] *der* fish

**Fischer** [fisher] *der* fisherman

**Fischstäbchen** [fish-shtaypshen] *das* fish stick

**FKK-Strand** [ehf-kaa-kaa-shtrant] *der* nudist beach

**flach** [flakh] *adj* flat; shallow

**Flasche** [flash-e] *die* bottle

**Fleisch** [fleysh] *das* meat

**Fleischer** [fleysher] *der* butcher

**Fleischsalat** [fleyshzalaat] *der salad made of strips of meat and dill pickles in mayonnaise*

**Fliege** [fleeg-e] *die (insect)* fly; bow tie

**fliegen** [fleegen] *v* to fly ▸ über Frankfurt fliegen to change planes in Frankfurt

**fließen** [fleesen] *v* to flow

**Flohmarkt** [flohmarkt] *der* flea market

**Flosse** [flos-e] *die* flipper

**Flug** [flook] *der* flight ▸ der Flug nach Berlin the flight to Berlin

**Fluggast** [flookgast] *der* passenger

**Fluggepäck** [flookgepehk] *das* baggage

**Flughafen** [flookhaafen] *der* airport

**Flugplatz** [flookplats] *der* airfield

**Flugschein** [flooksheyn] *der* plane ticket

**Flugverbindung** [flookfehrbindung] *die* connecting flight

**Flugzeug** [flooktsoyk] *das* (air)plane ▸ mit dem Flugzeug fliegen to fly

**Flur** [floor] *der* hallway

**Fluss** [flus] *der* river

**Flut** [floot] *die* high tide

**folgen** [folgen] *v* to follow

**Forelle** [forehl-e] *die* trout ▸ Forelle blau poached trout ▸ Forelle Müllerinnen Art *trout fried in butter and served with parsley and lemon*

**Formular** [formulaar] *das* form ▸ ein Formular ausfüllen to fill out a form

**Fortsetzung** [fortzehtsung] *die* sequel ▸ Fortsetzung folgt to be continued

**Frage** [fraag-e] *die* question

**fragen** [fraagen] *v* to ask

**Frau** [frow] *die* woman; wife ▸ Frau Schmidt Mrs./Ms. Schmidt

**Fräulein** [froyleyn] *das* young lady ▸ Fräulein Schäfer Miss Schäfer

**frei** [frey] *adj* free ◆ *adv* freely; for free ▸ frei von free of ▸ machen Sie sich bitte frei please take your clothes off ▸ im Freien in the open air

**Freibad** [freybaat] *das* outdoor swimming pool

**Freikarte** [freykart-e] *die* free ticket

**Freilichtbühne** [freylishtbuun-e] *die* open-air theater

**Freitag** [freytaak] *der* Friday

**Freizeichen** [frey-tseyshen] *das* dial tone

**Freizeit** [freytseyt] *die* free time

**Freizeitbad** [freytseytbaat] *das* swimming pool with waterslides etc.

**Fremdenführer** [frehmdenfuurer] *der* tourist guide

**Fremdenverkehrsamt** [frehmdenfehrkehrz-amt] *das* tourist office

**Fremdenzimmer** [frehmden-tsimer] *das* (guest) room

**Freund** [froynt] *der* friend; boyfriend

**Freundin** [froyndin] *die* friend; girlfriend

**Freundschaft** [froyntshaft] *die* friendship

**Frieden** [freeden] *der* peace

**Friedhof** [freethohf] *der* cemetery

**Frikadelle** [frikadehl-e] *die small cake of seasoned, ground meat or poultry coated in breadcrumbs and egg, then fried*

**frisch** [frish] *adj* fresh ▸ sich frisch machen to freshen up ▸ 'Vorsicht, frisch gestrichen!' 'wet paint'

**Frischkäse** [frishkayz-e] *der* soft cream cheese

**Friseur** [frizeur] *der* hairdresser

**Frucht** [frukht] *die* fruit

**Fruchtsaft** [frukht-zaft] *der* fruit juice

**früh** [fruu] *adv* early ▸ zu früh too early ▸ gestern/heute/morgen Früh yesterday/this/tomorrow morning

**früher** [fruuer] *adj* former ◆ *adv* formerly

**Frühjahr** [fruuyaar] *das* spring

**Frühling** [fruuling] *der* spring

**Frühstück** [fruushtuuk] *das* breakfast

**Führer** [fuurer] *der* guide

**Führerschein** [fuurersheyn] *der* driver's license

**Führung** [fuurung] *die* guided tour

**füllen** [fuulen] *v* to fill

**Füllung** [fuulung] *die* filling

**Fundbüro** [funtbuuroh] *das* lost-and-found office

**fünf** [fuunf] *num* five

**fünfzehn** [fuunf-tsayn] *num* fifteen

**fünfzig** [fuunf-tsish] *num* fifty

**für** [fuur] *prep* for ▸ was für einen Computer haben Sie? what sort of computer do you have?

**Fuß** [foos] *der* foot

**Fußgänger** [foosgehnger] *der* pedestrian

**füttern** [fuutern] *v* to feed

**Gefahr** [gefaar] *die* danger ▸ auf eigene Gefahr at one's own risk

**Gefälle** [gefehl-e] *das* slope

**Gefängnis** [gefehngnis] *das* jail

**Geflügel** [gefluugel] *das* poultry

**gefroren** [gefroren] *adj* frozen

**Gefühl** [gefuul] *das* feeling

**gefüllt** [gefuult] *adj* stuffed

**gegen** [gaygen] *prep* against; (in time) about ▸ gegen zehn Uhr at about ten o'clock

**Gegend** [gaygent] *die* area

**Gegenstand** [gaygen-shtant] *der* object

**gegenüber** [gaygenuuber] *prep* opposite

**Gegenwart** [gaygen-vaart] *die (point in time, tense)* present

**Gegner** [gaygner] *der* opponent

**gegrillt** [gegrilt] *adj* grilled

**Geheimnummer** [geheymnumer] *die* PIN (number); (for telephone directory) unlisted number

**gehen** [gayen] *v* to go; to walk ▸ wie geht's? *(familiar form)* how are you? ▸ wie geht es Ihnen? *(polite form)* how are you? ▸ es geht mir gut I'm fine ▸ das

**geht nicht** that's not possible ▸ **geht das?** is that OK?

**Geige** [geyg-e] *die* violin

**gekocht** [gekokht] *adj* cooked

**gekühlt** [gekuult] *adj* chilled ▸ 'gekühlt mindestens haltbar bis ...' 'if refrigerated best before ...'

**Gelände** [gelehnd-e] *das* site, area

**gelb** [gehlp] *adj* yellow

**Geld** [gehlt] *das* money

**Geldeinwurf** [gehlt-eynvurf] *der* slot

**Geldrückgabe** [gehlt-ruukgaab-e] *die* coin return

**Geldschein** [gehlt-sheyn] *der* banknote

**Geldwechsel** [gehlt-vehksel] *der* office for changing currency

**Gelenk** [gelehnk] *das* ANAT joint

**gelten** [gehlten] *v* to be valid for

**Gemälde** [gemehld-e] *das* painting

**Gemeinde** [gemeynd-e] *die* municipality; community; parish

**gemeinsam** [gemeynzaam] *adj* common; *(account)* joint ◆ *adv* together

**gemischt** [gemisht] *adj* mixed

**Gemüse** [gemuuz-e] *das* vegetables

**genau** [genow] *adj* exact ▸ **genau!** exactly!

**Genehmigung** [genaymigung] *die* authorization; permit

**geöffnet** [ge-eufnet] *adj* open

**Gepäck** [gepehk] *das* baggage

**Gepäckabfertigung** [gepehk-apfehrtigung], **Gepäckannahme** [gepehk-annaam-e] *die (at station)* baggage room; *(at airport)* baggage check-in

**Gepäckaufbewahrung** [gepehk-owfbevaarung] *die* baggage room

**Gepäckaufgabe** [gepehk-owfgaab-e] *die (at station)* baggage room; *(at airport)* baggage check-in

**Gepäckausgabe** [gepehk-owsgaab-e] *die (at station)* baggage room; *(at airport)* baggage claim

**Gepäckwagen** [gepehk-vaagen] *der* baggage car

**geradeaus** [geraad-e-ows] *adv* straight ahead

**Gerät** [gerayt] *das* device, machine

**geräuchert** [geroyshert] *adj* smoked

**Geräusch** [geroysh] *das* noise

**Gericht** [gerisht] *das (institution)* court; *(of food)* dish

**gerieben** [gereeben] *adj* grated

**gern** [gehrn] *adv* ▸ **ich habe es gern** I like it ▸ **er schwimmt gern** he likes swimming ▸ **wollen Sie mitmachen? – aber gern!** do you want to join in? – I'd love to ▸ **danke – gern geschehen** thanks – you're welcome

**geröstet** [gereustet] *adj* roasted

**Geruch** [gerookh] *der* smell

**gesalzen** [gezaltsen] *adj* salted

**Geschäft** [geshehft] *das* store; business, company

**Geschäftsschluss** [geshehfts-shlus] *der* closing time

**Geschäftszeiten** [geshehfts-tseyten] *pl* store hours; *(of business, office)* business hours

**Geschenk** [geshehnk] *das* present, gift

**Geschichte** [geshisht-e] *die* story; history

**Geschirr** [geshir] *das* dishes

**Geschlecht** [geshlehsht] *das (male, female)* sex; *(of word)* gender

**geschlossen** [geshlos-en] *adj* closed

**Geschmack** [geshmak] *der* taste

**geschmort** [geshmort] *adj* braised

**Geschnetzeltes** [geshnehtselt-e] *das* pieces of chicken or veal in sauce

**geschnitten** [geshniten] *adj* sliced

**Geschwindigkeit** [geshvindishkeyt] *die* speed

**geschwollen** [geshvol-en] *adj* swollen

**Gesellschaft** [gezehlshaft] *die* society; company, business; group; *(celebration)* party ▸ jemandem Gesellschaft leisten to keep somebody company

**Gesellschaftsraum** [gezehlshafts-rowm] *der* banquet room

**Gesetz** [gezehts] *das* law

**gesetzlich** [gezehtslish] *adj* legal ▸ gesetzlicher Feiertag public holiday

**Gesicht** [gezisht] *das* face

**gesperrt** [geshpehrt] *adj (road)* closed off

**gestattet** [ge-shtatet] *adj* permitted ▸ 'Rauchen nicht gestattet' 'no smoking'

**gestern** [geh-stern] *adv* yesterday

**Gesundheit** [gezunt-heyt] *die* health ▸ Gesundheit! *(after sneezing)* bless you!

**gesundheitsschädlich** [gezunt-heytss-shaydlish] *adj* damaging to one's health

**Getränk** [getrehnk] *das* drink

**Getreide** [getreyd-e] *das* cereals, grain

**Gewicht** [gevisht] *das* weight

**gewinnen** [gevin-en] *v* to win

**Gewitter** [geviter] *das* thunderstorm

**Gewürz** [gevuurts] *das* spice

**Gewürzgurke** [gevuurtsgurk-e] *die* dill pickle

**Gezeiten** [ge-tseyten] *pl* tides

**gibt** [gipt] *pres* gives ▸ es gibt there is/are

**Gift** [gift] *das* poison

**giftig** [giftish] *adj* poisonous

**Gipfel** [gipfel] *der* summit, peak

**Glas** [glaas] *das* glass; *(for jelly)* jar

**glatt** [glat] *adj* smooth; slippery

**Glatteis** [glat-eys] *das* black ice

**glauben** [glowben] *v* to think; *(in God etc.)* to believe

**gleich** [gleysh] *adj* same ◆ *adv* right away

**Gleis** [gleys] *das* platform

**Gleitschirm** [gleyt-shirm] *der (apparatus)* paraglider

**Gletscher** [glehtsher] *der* glacier

**Glocke** [glok-e] *die* bell

**Glück** [gluuk] *das* luck; happiness ▸ viel Glück! good luck!

**glücklich** [gluuklish] *adj* happy; *(coincidence)* lucky, happy

**Glühbirne** [gluubirn-e] *die* light bulb

**Glühwein** [gluuhveyn] *der* mulled wine

**Gold** [golt] *das* gold

**Gott** [got] *der* god ▸ Grüß Gott! hello!

**Gottesdienst** [got-ez-deenst] *der (in church)* service

**Grab** [graap] *das* grave

**graben** [graaben] *v* to dig

**Graben** [graaben] *der* ditch

**Grad** [graat] *der* degree ▸ drei Grad unter/über null three degrees below/above freezing

**Gras** [graas] *das* grass

**Gräte** [grayt-e] *die* fish bone

**grau** [grow] *adj* gray

**Grenzbeamte** [grehnts-be-amt-e] *der* customs and immigration officer

**Grenze** [grehnts-e] *die* border; limit

**Grenzübergang** [grehnts-uubergang] *der* border crossing

**Griebenschmalz** [greebenshmalts] *das spread made from animal fat*

**Grieß** [grees] *der* semolina

**grillen** [gril-en] *v* to grill ◆ *v* to have a barbecue

**Grillspieß** [grilshpees] *der* barbecue skewer

**Grillteller** [gril-tehler] *der* mixed grill

**groß** [grohs] *adj* big, large; *(person)*

tall; *(letter of alphabet)* capital

**Größe** [greus-e] *die* size; height

**Großraumwagen** [grohsrowmvaagen] *der (on train)* open car, *not divided into compartments*

**grün** [gruun] *adj* green

**Grünanlage** [gruun-anlaag-e] *die* park

**Grund** [grunt] *der* reason; *(floor)* ground; *(of river, sea)* bed ▸ **aus diesem Grund** for this reason

**Grundstück** [grunt-shtuuk] *das* plot of land

**Grünkohl** [gruunkohl] *der* kale

**Gruppe** [grup-e] *die* group

**grüßen** [gruusen] *v (guest)* to greet ▸ **grüß ihn von mir** say hello to him for me ▸ **grüß dich!** hello!

**gültig** [guultish] *adj* valid

**Gummi** [gumi] *das* rubber

**günstig** [guunstish] *adj (price)* reasonable; *(conditions)* favorable

**Gurke** [gurk-e] *die* cucumber ▸ **saure Gurke** dill pickle

**Gurt** [gurt] *der* strap; seat belt

**Gürtel** [guurtel] *der* belt

**gut** [goot] *adj* good ◆ *adv* well

**Gutschein** [gootsheyn] *der* voucher

# h

**Haar** [haar] *das* hair

**haben** [haaben] *v* to have ▸ **bei sich haben** to have on one

**Hackbraten** [hakbraaten] *der* meatloaf

**Hackfleisch** [hakfleysh] *das* ground meat

**Hafen** [haafen] *der* harbor; *(larger)* port

**Hafenrundfahrt** [haafenruntfaart] *die* boat trip around the harbor

**Haferflocken** [haaferfloken] *pl* rolled oats

**Haftung** [haftung] *die* liability

**Hagel** [haagel] *der* hail

**Hähnchen** [hehnshen] *das* chicken

**Haken** [haaken] *der (on wall)* hook; *(in box on form)* tick

**halb** [halp] *adj & adv* half ▸ **halb sechs** half past five ▸ **ein halbes Kilo** half a kilo

**Halbe** [halb-e] *die, der or das (of beer)* half a liter

**halbfett** [halpfeht] *adj* low-fat

**Halbpension** [halp-penziohn] *die hotel room with breakfast and a main meal included*

**Hälfte** [hehlft-e] *die* half ▸ **die Hälfte der Flasche** half the bottle

**Halle** [hal-e] *die* hall

**Hallenbad** [halenbaat] *das* indoor swimming pool

**Hals** [hals] *der* neck; throat

**Halsschmerzen** [hals-shmehrtsen] *pl* sore throat

**Haltbarkeitsdatum** [haltbarkeytsdaatum] *das* best-before date

**halten** [halten] *v* to hold; to keep ◆ *v (vehicle)* to stop

**Haltestelle** [halt-e-shtehl-e] *die* stop

**Hammelfleisch** [hamelfleysh] *das* mutton

**Hand** [hant] *die* hand ▸ **rechter/linker Hand** on the right/left

## Hansestädte

In the Middle Ages, the *Hanse* (Hanseatic League) was a powerful association of more than 160 towns (including Hamburg, Bremen, Lübeck and Rostock) which controlled trade in the north of Germany as far as the Baltic ports. These towns, which are often fortified, are organized around the *Markt* (market) and the *Rathaus* (town hall) and are full of fine churches and gabled houses.

**Handarbeit** [hantarbeyt] *die* handmade article; needlework

**Handbremse** [hantbrehmz-e] *die* parking brake

**handeln** [handeln] *v* to act; to haggle; to trade

**Handgelenk** [hantgelehnk] *das* wrist

**handgemacht** [hantgemakht] *adj* handmade

**Handgepäck** [hantgepehk] *das* carry-on luggage

**Händler** [hehndler] *der* dealer

**Handtasche** [hant-tash-e] *die* purse

**Handtuch** [hant-tookh] *das* towel

**Handy** [hehndi] *das* cellphone

**Hansestädte** [hanz-e-shteht-e] *die* Hanseatic League

**Häppchen** [hehpshen] *das* morsel, tidbit; canapé

**Hase** [haaz-e] *der* hare

**Haselnuss** [haazelnus] *die* hazelnut

**hat** [hat] *pres* has

**Hauptbahnhof** [howptbaanhohf] *der* main station

**Hauptgericht** [howptgerisht] *das* main course

**Haus** [hows] *das* house ▸ nach Hause gehen to go home ▸ zu Hause at home

**hausgemacht** [howsgemakht] *adj* home-made

**Haushaltswaren** [hows-halts-vaaren] *pl* household goods

**Hausmannskost** [howsmanzkost] *die* plain food

**Haustier** [howsteer] *das* pet

**Haut** [howt] *die* skin

**Hbf.** *abbr of* **Hauptbahnhof** main station

**Hefe** [hayf-e] *die* yeast

**Heide** [heyd-e] *die* heath, moor

**Heidelbeere** [heydelbehr-e] *die* blueberry

**heilen** [heylen] *v* to cure

**heilig** [heylish] *adj* holy

**Heiligabend** [heylish-aabent] *der* Christmas Eve

**Heim** [heym] *das* home

**Heimatmuseum** [heymaatmoozayum] *das* museum of local history

**Heirat** [heyraat] *die* marriage

**heiß** [heys] *adj* hot ▸ mir ist heiß I feel hot

**Heizkörper** [heyts-keurper] *der* radiator

**Heizung** [heytsung] *die* heating

**helfen** [hehlfen] *v* to help

**hell** [hehl] *adj (color)* light; *(light)* bright

**Helm** [hehlm] *der* helmet

**Hemd** [hehmt] *das* shirt; undershirt

**Hendl** [hehndl] *das* roast chicken

**herb** [hehrp] *adj (taste)* sharp; *(wine)* dry

**Herbst** [hehrpst] *der* fall

**Herd** [hehrt] *der (for cooking)* stove

**Herde** [hehrd-e] *die* herd; flock

**Hering** [hehring] *der* herring; tent peg

**Herkunft** [hehrkunft] *die* origins

**Herr** [hehr] *der* gentleman ▸ Herr Rau Mr. Rau

**herstellen** [hehr-shtehlen] *v* to make, to produce

**herumdrehen** [hehrum-drayen] *v* *(page)* to turn over; *(key)* to turn

**Herz** [hehrts] *das* heart

**herzhaft** [hehrts-haft] *adj (meal)* hearty

**Heu** [hoy] *das* hay

**Heurige** [hoyrig-e] *der* new wine; *bar serving local new wine*

**Heuschnupfen** [hoyshnupfen] *der* hay fever

**heute** [hoy-te] *adv* today ▸ heute Früh/Nachmittag/Abend this morning/afternoon/evening

**hier** [heer] *adv* here

**Hilfe** [hilf-e] *die* help ▸ Hilfe! help!

**Himbeere** [himbehr-e] *die* raspberry

**Himmel** [him-el] *der* sky; heaven

**Hindernis** [hindernis] *das* obstacle

**Hinfahrt** [hinfaart] *die* journey there

**Hinflug** [hinflook] *der* outbound flight

**hinten** [hinten] *adv* at the back; on the back ▸ nach hinten durchgehen! move down to the back! ▸ dort hinten back there

**hinter** [hinter] *prep* behind

**hinterher** [hinterhehr] *adv* behind; afterward

**hinterlassen** [hinterlas-en] *v* to leave

**Hintertür** [hintertuur] *die* back door

**Hin- und Rückfahrt** [hinuntruukfaart] *die* round trip

**Hinweg** [hinvayk] *der* way there

**Hinweis** [hinveys] *der* hint; tip; instruction; sign

**Hirn** [hirn] *das* brain

**Hirsch** [hirsh] *der* deer; venison

**Hitze** [hits-e] *die* heat

**H-Milch** [haamilsh] *die* milk with a long shelf life (UHT milk)

**hoch** [hohkh] *adj* high; *(tree)* tall; *(age)* great, advanced; *(sum)* large

**hochklappen** [hohkhklap-en] *v* to fold up; *(cinema seat)* to tip up

**Hochsaison** [hohkhsayzon] *die* high season

**Hochschule** [hohkhshool-e] *die* college; university

**Hochspannung** [hohkhshpanung] *die* high voltage

**Höchstgeschwindigkeit** [heukstgeshvindishkeyt] *die* speed limit; *(of car)* top speed

**Höchstparkdauer** [heukst-paarkdower] *die (when parking)* maximum stay

**Hochwasser** [hohkh-vas-er] *das* high water ▸ Hochwasser haben to be flooded, to be in spate

**Hochzeit** [hohkhtseyt] *die* wedding

**Höhe** [heu-e] *die* height; *(of sum)* amount ▸ in 2000 m Höhe at a height of 2,000 m

**Höhle** [heul-e] *die* cave

**holen** [hohlen] *v* to fetch, to get; *(police, doctor)* to send for

**Holz** [holts] *das* wood

**Honig** [hohnish] *der* honey

**Honigmelone** [hohnishmehlohn-e] *die* honeydew melon

**hören** [heuren] *v* to hear; to listen to

**Hörer** [heurer] *der (on telephone)* receiver

**Hörnchen** [heurnshen] *das* croissant

**Hose** [hohz-e] *die* pants ▸ eine Hose a pair of pants

**Hubschrauber** [hoopshrowber] *der* helicopter

**Hügel** [huugel] *der* hill

**Huhn** [hoon] *das* chicken

**Hühnchen** [huunshen] *das* chicken
**Hummer** [hum-er] *der* lobster
**Hund** [hunt] *der* dog ▸ 'Vorsicht, bissiger Hund!' 'beware of dog'
**hundert** [hundert] *num* a hundred
**Hunger** [hung-er] *der* hunger ▸ ich habe Hunger I'm hungry

**hungrig** [hungrish] *adj* hungry ▸ hungrig sein to be hungry
**hupen** [hoopen] *v* to sound one's horn
**Husten** [husten] *der* cough
**Hütte** [huut-e] *die* hut; cottage
**Hüttenkäse** [huutenkayz-e] *der* cottage cheese

**ICE** [ee-tsay-ay] *abbr of* **InterCity Express** *der* Intercity express (train)
**ich** [ish] *pron* I ▸ ich bin's! it's me!
**IC-Zuschlag** [ee-tsay-tsooshlaak] *der extra charge for traveling aboard Intercity express train*
**ihm** [eem] *pron* him, to him; it, to it
**ihn** [een] *pron* him; it
**ihnen** [eenen] *pron* them, to them
**Ihnen** [eenen] *pron (polite form)* you, to you
**ihr** [eer] *pron (familiar plural form)* you; her, to her; it, to it
**ihr** [eer] *det* her; its; their
**Ihr** [eer] *det (polite form)* your
**ihre** [eer-e] *pron* hers; its; theirs
**Ihre** [eer-e] *pron (polite form)* yours
**im** [im] *prep* in, in the
**Imbiss** [imbis] *der* snack; snack bar

**immer** [im-er] *adv* always
**Impfstoff** [impf-shtof] *der* vaccine
**in** [in] *prep* in; into ▸ in der Schule at school ▸ in eine Kneipe gehen to go to a bar
**inbegriffen** [inbegrif-en] *adj* included
**Inhaber** [inhaaber] *der* owner; *(of passport)* holder
**Inhalt** [inhalt] *der* contents; *(of film etc.)* content
**inkl.** [inkloozeev-e] incl., including
**Inlandsflug** [inlantsflook] *der* domestic flight
**innen** [in-en] *adv* inside
**Innenstadt** [in-en-shtat] *die* downtown area
**innerhalb** [in-er-halp] *prep* within
**innerlich** [in-erlish] *adj* inner, internal
**Insektenstich** [inzehktenshtish] *der* insect bite; insect sting

## Imbissbude

On every street corner, and on main thoroughfares, these often rather ordinary-looking stands are the place to grab a quick and inexpensive meal. They sell lots of different kinds of sausages, roast chicken, fries, and sometimes soups and salads. Some of them are run by immigrants and have Arabic, Turkish or Asian dishes to offer.

**Insel** [inzel] *die* island

**insgesamt** [insgezamt] *adv* altogether

**Inszenierung** [ins-tsehneerung] *die (in theater)* production

**InterCity** [intersiti] *der* intercity train

**InterCity Express** [intersiti ehksprehs]
*der* intercity express train

**Interesse** [interehs-e] *das* interest

**inzwischen** [intsvishen] *adv* in the meantime; now

**Irrtum** [irtoom] *der* mistake

**ist** [ist] *pres* is

# j

**ja** [yaa] *excl* yes

**Jacke** [ya-ke] *die* jacket; cardigan

**Jagd** [yaakt] *die* hunt

**Jägerschnitzel** [yaygershnitsel] *das pork scallops in mushroom sauce*

**Jahr** [yaar] *das* year

**Jahreszeit** [yaares-tseyt] *die* season

**Jahrgang** [yaargang] *der (of wine)* year, vintage

**Jahrhundert** [yaarhundert] *das* century

**jährlich** [yehrlish] *adj* annual

**Jahrmarkt** [yaarmarkt] *der* fair

**Jalousie** [dzhalusee] *die* venetian blind

**Januar** [yanuar] *der* January

**Jausenstation** [yowzen-shtatsiohn] *die mountain refuge serving food and drink*

**jede, r, s** [yay-de] *det* each, every
♦ *pron* everybody; each one

**jederzeit** [yaydertseyt] *adv* at any time

**jemand** [yaymant] *pron* somebody; *(in questions)* anybody

**jetzt** [yehtst] *adv* now

**Johannisbeere** [yohanisbehr-e] *die*
▸ **rote Johannisbeere** redcurrant
▸ **schwarze Johannisbeere** blackcurrant

**jucken** [yuken] *v* to itch

**jüdisch** [yuudish] *adj* Jewish

**Jugendherberge** [yoogent-hehrbehrg-e] *die* youth hostel

**Jugendliche** [yoogentlish-e] *der, die* young person

**Jugendstil** [yoogent-shteel] *der* art nouveau

**Juli** [yooli] *der* July

**jung** [yung] *adj* young

**Junge** [yung-e] *der* boy

**Junggeselle** [yung-gezehl-e] *der* bachelor

**Juni** [yooni] *der* June

## Kaffeehaus

More refined than German cafés, the Viennese *Kaffeehaus* is an institution. People even talk about *Kaffeekultur*. You can go there to read the newspaper or reread Stefan Zweig, play cards or billiards, and at the same time enjoy a *Sachertorte* with a *Wiener Melange* (white coffee) or an *Einspänner* (black coffee with whipped cream).

# k

**Kabeljau** [kaabelyow] *der* cod

**Kabinenbahn** [kabeenenbaan] *die* cable railway

**Kabinett** [kabineht] *der high-quality German wine*

**Kaffee** [kafay] *der* coffee

**Kaffeehaus** [kafayhows] *das* coffee shop, café

**Käfig** [kayfish] *der* cage

**Kai** [key] *der* quay

**Kaiser** [keyzer] *der* emperor

**Kaiserschmarren** [keyzershmaren] *der thin strips of pancake*

**Kalb** [kalp] *das* calf; veal

**kalt** [kalt] *adj* cold ▸ mir ist kalt I'm cold

**Kälte** [kehlt-e] *die* cold, coldness

**Kamin** [kameen] *der* fireplace; chimney

**Kampf** [kampf] *der* fight; contest

**Kanal** [kanaal] *der* canal; *(on radio, TV)* channel

**kandiert** [kandeert] *adj* candied

**Kaninchen** [kaneenshen] *das* rabbit

**Kanister** [kanister] *der* can

**kann** [kan] *pres (able to)* can

**Kännchen** [kehnshen] *das (of coffee)* pot

**Kapsel** [kapsel] *die* capsule

**Kapuziner** [kaputseener] *der coffee with a small amount of milk*

**Karneval** [kaarneval] *der* carnival

**Karte** [kart-e] *die* card; ticket; menu; map ▸ 'folgende Karten werden akzeptiert:' 'we accept the following cards:' ▸ 'Karte einführen!' 'insert card' ▸ 'Karte

## Karneval

In the Rhineland, and particularly in Cologne, the carnival is not to be missed. It starts on November 11th at 11 minutes past 11, but it reaches its peak during the *Drei Tollen Tage*, the 'three days of madness' before Ash Wednesday. After you've shouted the traditional greeting of *Alaaf!* ('Forward!'), you'll stop thinking the Germans take life too seriously...

entnehmen!' 'remove card' ▸ 'Karte fehlerhaft' 'this card is faulty' ▸ 'Karte ungültig' 'this card is invalid'

**Kartenvorverkauf** [kartenforfehrkowf] *der* advance booking

**Kartoffel** [kartof-el] *die* potato

**Karussell** [karoosehl] *das* merry-go-round

**Käse** [kayz-e] *der* cheese

**Käsekuchen** [kayzekookhen] *der* cheesecake

**Kasse** [kas-e] *die* till; checkout; box office ▸ 'Kasse beim Fahrer' 'please pay the driver'

**Kassenbon** [kasenbohn] *der* receipt ▸ gegen Vorlage des Kassenbons on production of a receipt

**Kassenzettel** [kas-en-tsehtel] *der* receipt

**Kasten** [kasten] *der* box; crate; mailbox

**Kater** [kaater] *der* tomcat; hangover ▸ einen Kater haben to have a hangover

**Katze** [kats-e] *die* cat

**kaufen** [kowfen] *v* to buy

**Kaufhaus** [kowfhows] *das* department store

**Kaugummi** [kowgumi] *der or das* chewing gum

**Kefir** [kayfir] *der* kefir, *drink made from sour fermented milk*

**Kegelbahn** [kaygelbaan] *die* bowling alley

**kein** [keyn] *det* no, not a; not ... any ▸ das ist kein Hotel that's not a hotel ▸ ich habe kein Geld I don't have any money

**keine** [keyn-e] *pron* nobody; *(referring to thing)* none

**keinesfalls** [keynezfals] *adv* on no account

**Keks** [kayks] *der* cookie

**Keller** [kehler] *der* cellar

**Kellerei** [kehlerey] *die* wine cellar

**Kellner** [kehlner] *der* waiter

**Kellnerin** [kehlnerin] *die* waitress

**kennen** [kehnen] *v* to know

**Kenntnisse** [kehntnis-e] *pl* knowledge

**Kennzeichen** [kehn-tseyshen] *das* sign; license plate number ▸ 'besondere Kennzeichen' 'distinguishing features'

**Kern** [kehrn] *der (of apple)* pip; *(of peach)* pit, stone; *(of nut)* kernel

**Kernkraftwerk** [kehrnkraftvehrk] *das* nuclear power station

**Kerze** [kehrts-e] *die* candle

**Kette** [keht-e] *die* chain

**Keule** [koyl-e] *die (of meat)* leg

**Kfz-Werkstatt** [kaa-ehf-tseht-vehrksh-tat] *die (for repairing vehicles)* garage

**Kind** [kint] *das* child

**Kinn** [kin] *das* chin

**Kino** [keenoh] *das* movie theater ▸ ins Kino gehen to go to the movies

**Kirche** [kirsh-e] *die* church

**Kirsche** [kirsh-e] *die* cherry

**Kissen** [kis-en] *das* cushion; pillow

**Klage** [klaag-e] *die* complaint

**Klappbett** [klapbeht] *das* folding bed

**Klappsitz** [klapzits] *der* folding seat

**klar** [klaar] *adj* clear

**Klare** [klaar-e] *der* schnapps

**klasse** [klas-e] *adj* great

**Klasse** [klas-e] *die* class

**klatschen** [klatshen] *v* to clap

**Klavier** [klaveer] *das* piano

**kleben** [klayben] *v* to stick

**Kleid** [kleyt] *das* dress ▸ Kleider clothes

**Kleiderschrank** [kleydershrank] *der* closet, wardrobe

**Kleidung** [kleydung] *die* clothes

**klein** [kleyn] *adj* small, little

**Kleingeld** [kleyngehlt] *das (coins)* change

## Kneipe

These are bars which are open all day and which often serve snacks and light meals to have with your beer. The waiter or waitress usually serves you at your table and keeps a tab of what you order so that you can pay for everything all at once before you leave.

**Kleinkunstbühne** [kleynkunstbuun-e] *die* cabaret

**Kleinstadt** [kleynshtat] *die* small town

**klettern** [klehtern] *v* to climb

**Klimaanlage** [kleema-anlaag-e] *die* air-conditioning

**Klingel** [klingel] *die* bell

**klingeln** [klingeln] *v* to ring the bell

**Klippe** [klip-e] *die* cliff

**klopfen** [klopfen] *v* to knock

**Kloß** [klohs] *der* dumpling

**Kloster** [klohster] *das* monastery; convent

**knabbern** [knabern] *v* to nibble

**Knäckebrot** [knehkebroht] *das* crisp-bread

**Kneipe** [kneyp-e] *die* bar

**knicken** [kniken] *v* to fold

**Knie** [knee] *das* knee

**knitterfrei** [kniterfrey] *adj* crease-resistant

**Knoblauch** [knohplowkh] *der* garlic

**Knochen** [knokhen] *der* bone

**Knochenbruch** [knokhenbrukh] *der* fracture

**Knödel** [kneudel] *der* dumpling

**Knopf** [knopf] *der* button

**Knorpel** [knorpel] *der* cartilage

**Knoten** [knohten] *der* knot

**knusprig** [knusprish] *adj* crisp; crunchy

**kochen** [kokhen] *v* to cook; to boil

**koffeinfrei** [kofayeenfrey] *adj* decaffeinated

**Koffer** [kof-er] *der* suitcase

**Kofferkuli** [kof-er-kooli] *der* baggage cart ▸ 'Kofferkuli nur gegen Pfand' 'deposit required'

**Kofferraum** [kof-er-rowm] *der (of car)* trunk

**Kohl** [kohl] *der* cabbage

**Kohle** [kohl-e] *die* coal

**Kohlensäure** [kohlenzoyr-e] *die* carbon dioxide

**Kohlrabi** [kohlraabi] *der* kohlrabi

**Kohlroulade** [kohlroolaad-e] *die* stuffed cabbage leaves

**Koje** [koy-e] *die* berth

**Kölsch** [keulsh] *das* *strong lager brewed in Cologne*

**Kombi-Ticket** [kombi-tikit] *das* *ticket allowing travel on multiple modes of transportation (bus, streetcar, subway etc.)*

**kommen** [kom-en] *v* to come ▸ nach Hause kommen to get home

**Kompass** [kompas] *der* compass

**Kondensmilch** [kondehnsmilsh] *die* condensed milk

**Konditorei** [konditorey] *die* cake shop

**Kongresshalle** [kongrehs-hal-e] *die* conference center

**König** [keunish] *der* king

**Königin** [keunigin] *die* queen

**können** [keunen] *v* can, to be able to ▸ können Sie Deutsch? do you speak German? ▸ können wir gehen? can we go?

**Konservierungsstoff** [konzerveer-ungz-shtof] *der* preservative

**Kontaktlinse** [kontaktlinz-e] *die* contact lens

**Konto** [kontoh] *das* account

**Kontrollabschnitt** [kontrolapshnit] *der (in check book etc.)* stub

**Kopf** [kopf] *der* head

**Kopfkissen** [kopf-kis-en] *das* pillow

**Kopfsalat** [kopfzalaat] *der* lettuce

**Kopfschmerzen** [kopfshmehrtsen] *pl* headache ▸ Kopfschmerzen haben to have a headache

**Korb** [korp] *der* basket

**Korken** [korken] *der* cork

**Korn** [korn] *das* grain

**Korn** [korn] *der* schnapps

**Körper** [keurper] *der* body

**körperbehindert** [keurperbehindert] *adj* disabled

**Körpergewicht** [keurpergevisht] *das* weight

**körperlich** [keurperlish] *adj* physical ▸ *adv* physically

**Körperpflege** [keurper-pflay-ge] *die* personal hygiene

**Kost** [kost] *die* food

**kostbar** [kostbar] *adj* valuable

**kosten** [kosten] *v* to cost; to taste ▸ was kostet das? how much is it?

**kostenlos** [kostenlohs] *adj (ticket, admission etc.)* free

**kostenpflichtig** [kostenpflishtish] *adj (person)* liable to pay costs

**Kostprobe** [kostprohb-e] *die (of food etc.)* taste

**Krabbe** [krab-e] *die* crab; shrimp

**Kraft** [kraft] *die* strength; power ▸ in Kraft treten to come into force

**Kraftfahrzeugschein** [kraftfaar-tsoyk-sheyn] *der* vehicle registration document

**Kraftstoff** [kraftshtof] *der* fuel

**Kragen** [kraagen] *der* collar

**Krampf** [krampf] *der* cramp

**krank** [krank] *adj* ill, sick ▸ krank werden to get sick, to fall ill

**Krankenhaus** [krankenhows] *das* hospital

**Krankenschwester** [krankenshveh-ster] *die* nurse

**Krankheit** [krankheyt] *die* illness; disease

**Krapfen** [krapfen] *der* doughnut

**Kräuterbutter** [kroyterbuter] *die* herb butter

**Kräuterlikör** [kroyterlikeur] *der liqueur made from herbs*

**Kräutertee** [kroytertay] *der* herbal tea

**Krautsalat** [krowtzalaat] *der* coleslaw

**Krebs** [krayps] *der* crab; cancer

**Kreis** [kreys] *der* circle; district

**Kreislaufstörungen** [kreyslowf-shteurungen] *pl* circulatory problems

**Kreisverkehr** [kreysfehrkehr] *der* traffic circle

**Kren** [krayn] *der* horseradish

**Kresse** [krehs-e] *die* cress

**Kreuz** [kroyts] *das* cross; *(on road)* intersection; small of the back

**Kreuzung** [kroytsung] *die* crossroads

**Kriechspur** [kreesh-shpoor] *die* slow lane

**Krieg** [kreek] *der* war

**Krimi** [krimi] *der (book, movie)* thriller

**Krone** [krohn-e] *die* crown

**Krug** [krook] *der* jug; *(for beer)* mug

**Kruste** [krust-e] *die* crust

**Küche** [kuush-e] *die* kitchen ▸ die deutsche Küche German cooking, German cuisine

**Kuchen** [kookhen] *der* cake

**Kugel** [koogel] *die* ball; bullet

**Kugelschreiber** [koogelshreyber] *der* ballpoint pen

**Kuh** [koo] *die* cow

**kühl** [kuul] *adj (not warm)* cool

**Kühlschrank** [kuulshrank] *der* refrigerator

**Kühltruhe** [kuul-troo-e] *die* freezer

**Kuli** [kooli] *der* ballpoint pen

**Kümmel** [kuumel] *der* caraway seed

**kümmern** [kuumern] ◆ **sich kümmern** *v* to concern ▸ sich kümmern um *(person)* to look after; *(thing)* to see to

**Kunde** [kund-e] *der* customer

**Kundendienst** [kundendeenst] *der* customer service

**Kündigung** [kuundigung] *die (of contract, credit)* termination; *(of employee)* dismissal; *(on rented accommodation)* eviction notice

**Kunst** [kunst] *die* art

**Kunstfaser** [kunstfaazer] *die* synthetic fiber

**Kunsthandwerk** [kunst-hantvehrk] *das* craft

**Künstler** [kuunstler] *der* artist

**künstlich** [kuunstlish] *adj* artificial

**Kunststoff** [kunst-shtof] *der* plastic

**Kunstwerk** [kunstvehrk] *das* work of art

**Kupfer** [kupfer] *das* copper

**Kürbis** [kuurbis] *der* pumpkin

**Kurgast** [koorgast] *der* visitor to a spa

**Kurpark** [koorpark] *der* gardens at a spa

**Kurtaxe** [koor-taks-e] *die  tax paid by visitors to a spa*

**Kurve** [kurv-e] *die* curve

**Kurverwaltung** [koorfehrvaltung] *die* spa administration

**kurz** [kurts] *adj* short

**kürzen** [kuurtsen] *v* to shorten; to cut

**kurzfristig** [kurtsfristish] *adj* sudden; short-term ◆ *adv* on short notice

**küssen** [kuus-en] *v* to kiss

**Küste** [kuust-e] *die* coast

**Küstenwache** [kuustenvakh-e] *die* Coast Guard

**Kutsche** [kutsh-e] *die (horse-drawn)* coach

**lächeln** [lehsheln] *v* to smile

**lachen** [lakhen] *v* to laugh

**Lachs** [laks] *der* salmon

**Laden** [laaden] *der* store

**Ladendiebstahl** [laadendeepshtal] *der* shoplifting

**Ladenschlusszeiten** [laadenshlusstseyten] *pl* store closing times

**Lage** [laag-e] *die* situation, position; layer

**Lagerfeuer** [laagerfoyer] *das* campfire

**Laken** [laaken] *das* sheet

**Lakritze** [lakrits-e] *die* licorice

**Lamm** [lam] *das* lamb

**Lampe** [lamp-e] *die* lamp

**Land** [lant] *das* country; state; countryside; *(for farming etc.)* land ▸ auf dem Land in the country(side)

**Landbrot** [lantbroht] *das  type of rye bread with hard crust*

**landen** [landen] *v* to land

**Landkarte** [lantkart-e] *die* map

**Landschaftsschutzgebiet** [lantshafts-shutsgebeet] *das* nature reserve

**Landstraße** [lant-shtraas-e] *die* country road

**Landung** [landung] *die (by airplane)* landing

**Landwein** [lantveyn] *der* table wine

**Landwirtschaft** [lantvirtshaft] *die* agriculture

**lang** [lang] *adj* long ▸ vier Tage lang for four days

**lange** [lang-e] *adv* (for) a long time ▸ wie lange? how long?

**Länge** [lehng-e] *die* length

**Langeweile** [lang-e-veyl-e] *die* boredom

**langsam** [langzaam] *adj* slow ✦ *adv* slowly

**lassen** [las-en] *v* to let; to leave; to stop ▸ etwas machen lassen to have something done

**Lastwagen** [lastvaagen] *der* truck

**Lauch** [lowkh] *der* leek

**laufen** [lowfen] *v* to run; to walk; *(film)* to be on

**Laugenbrezel** [lowgenbrehtsel] *die* pretzel

**laut** [lowt] *adj* loud

**läuten** [loyten] *v* to ring

**Lautsprecher** [lowt-shprehsher] *der* loudspeaker

**Lautstärke** [lowt-shtehrk-e] *die* volume

**lauwarm** [lowvaarm] *adj* lukewarm

**Lawinengefahr** [laveenengefaar] *die* danger of avalanches

**lebendig** [lehbehndish] *adj* lively; alive

**Lebensgefahr** [laybenzgefaar] *die* ▸ 'Lebensgefahr!' 'danger' ▸ er ist in Lebensgefahr his life is at risk

**Lebensmittel** [laybenzmitel] *das* food

**Leber** [layber] *die* liver

**Leberknödel** [layberkneudel] *der* liver dumpling

**Leberpastete** [layberpastayt-e] *die* liver pâté

**Leberwurst** [laybervurst] *die* liver sausage, liverwurst

**Lebkuchen** [laypkookhen] *der* type of frosted gingerbread eaten at Christmas

**lecker** [lehker] *adj* delicious

**Leder** [layder] *das* leather

**ledig** [laydish] *adj (unmarried)* single

**leer** [lehr] *adj* empty

**Leergut** [lehrgoot] *das* empties

**Leerung** [lehrung] *die* emptying; *(of mail)* collection

**legen** [laygen] *v* to put; to lay

**Lehrer, Lehrerin** [lehrer, lehrerin] *der, die* teacher

**Lehrling** [lehrling] *der* apprentice

**leicht** [leysht] *adj* light; easy

**Leichtathletik** [leysht-atlehtik] *die* track and field

**leiden** [leyden] *v* to suffer

**leider** [leyder] *adv* unfortunately

**leihen** [leyen] *v* to borrow; to lend ▸ jemandem etwas leihen to lend somebody something ▸ ich habe mir ein Auto geliehen *(from friend etc.)* I borrowed a car; *(from rental company)* I rented a car

**Leihgebühr** [leygebuur] *die* rental fee

**Leihwagen** [leyvaagen] *der* rental car

**Leine** [leyn-e] *die (for washing)* line; *(for dog)* leash

**Leinen** [leynen] *das* linen

**leise** [leyz-e] *adj* quiet ✦ *adv* quietly

**leiten** [leyten] *v (group, team)* to lead; *(company)* to run

**Leitung** [leytung] *die (telephone)* line;

## Loveparade

You'll hear the pulsating rhythms of a veritable tide of people (up to a million in a good year) who take to the streets of Berlin every summer. The bewildered residents of Tiergarten watch the techno-heads go by in their craziest outfits, perched on carnival-type floats.

wire, cable; *(for water)* pipe; management

**Leitungswasser** [leytungz-vas-er] *das* tap water

**Lenker** [lehnker] *der* steering wheel; handlebars

**Lenkrad** [lehnkraat] *das* steering wheel

**lernen** [lehrnen] *v* to learn

**lesen** [layzen] *v* to read

**letzte, r, s** [lehtst-e] *adj* last

**Leuchtturm** [loysht-toorm] *der* lighthouse

**Leute** [loyt-e] *pl* people

**Licht** [lisht] *das* light

**Lichtschutzfaktor** [lisht-shutsfaktor] *der (of suntan lotion)* protection factor, SPF

**Lid** [leet] *das* eyelid

**lieb** [leep] *adj* kind; *(as address, in letter)* dear

**Liebe** [leeb-e] *die* love

**lieben** [leeben] *v* to love

**Lied** [leet] *das* song

**liefern** [leefern] *v* to deliver

**Liege** [leeg-e] *die (folding bed)* cot; *reclining chair for beach, garden*

**liegen** [leegen] *v (on floor, in first place etc.)* to lie; to be

**Liegesitz** [leeg-e-zits] *der* reclining seat

**Liegestuhl** [leeg-e-shtool] *der* deck chair; *reclining chair for beach, garden*

**Liegewagen** [leeg-e-vaagen] *der* sleeping car

**Lift** [lift] *der* elevator; ski lift

**Linie** [leeni-e] *die* line; *(of bus etc.)* route, line ▸ welche Linie fährt zum Rathaus? which line goes to the town hall?

**Linienflug** [leenienflook] *der* scheduled flight

**links** [links] *adv* on the left; *(to turn)* left ▸ nach links left

**Linse** [linz-e] *die* lens; lentil

**Lippe** [lip-e] *die* lip

**Loch** [lokh] *das* hole

**Löffel** [leufel] *der* spoon

**lohnen** [lohnen] *v* ▸ sich lohnen to be worth it

**Lokal** [lohkaal] *das* bar

**Los** [lohs] *das* lottery ticket

**löschen** [leushen] *v (fire)* to put out

**lösen** [leuzen] *v (ticket)* to buy; *(problem)* to solve

**losfahren** [losfaaren] *v* to set off

**losgehen** [lohsgayen] *v* to set off; to start

**löslich** [leuzlish] *adj* instant

**Lösung** [leuzung] *die* solution

**Loveparade** [levperayd] *die* love parade

**Lücke** [luuk-e] *die* gap

**Luft** [luft] *die* air

**lüften** [luuften] *v (clothes)* to air out

**Luftfahrtgesellschaft** [luftfaart-gezehlshaft] *die* airline

**Luftmatratze** [luftmatrats-e] *die* airbed
**Lunge** [lung-e] *die* lung
**Lust** [lust] *die* desire ▸ ich habe keine

**Lust** I don't feel like it
**lustig** [lustish] *adj* funny
**lutschen** [lutshen] *v* to suck

# m

**machen** [makhen] *v* to do; to make ▸ mach's gut! take care! ▸ das macht 20 Euro that comes to 20 euros ▸ das macht nichts it doesn't matter
**Mädchen** [maytshen] *das* girl
**Mädchenname** [maytshen-naam-e] *der* maiden name
**Magen** [maagen] *der* stomach
**Magengeschwür** [maagengeshvuur] *das* stomach ulcer
**mager** [maager] *adj* thin; *(meat)* lean; *(cheese)* low-fat
**Magermilch** [maagermilsh] *die* skim milk
**Mahlzeit** [maal-tseyt] *die* meal ▸ Mahlzeit! enjoy your meal!
**Mai** [mey] *der* May
**Maiskolben** [meys-kolben] *der* corn on the cob
**Majoran** [meyoraan] *der* marjoram
**Makrele** [makrayl-e] *die* mackerel
**Makrone** [makrohn-e] *die* macaroon
**Mal** [mal] *das* time ▸ letztes Mal next time
**malen** [maalen] *v* to paint
**Maler** [maaler] *der* painter
**malerisch** [maalerish] *adj* picturesque
**Malzbier** [maltsbeer] *das* malt beer
**man** [man] *pron* you ▸ man kann das hier kaufen you can buy it here
**manche** [mansh-e] *det* some; many
**Mandel** [mandel] *die* almond ▸ Mandeln tonsils

**Mann** [man] *der* man; husband
**männlich** [mehnlish] *adj* male; masculine
**Mannschaft** [manshaft] *die* team
**Mantel** [mantel] *der* coat
**Märchen** [mehrshen] *das* fairy tale
**Marille** [maril-e] *die* apricot
**Marillenknödel** [marilen-kneudel] *der* apricot dumpling
**Markierung** [markeerung] *die* marking
**Markklößchen** [mark-kleusshen] *das bone marrow dumpling eaten in soup*
**Markt** [markt] *der* market
**Marmelade** [marmelaad-e] *die* jelly
**Marmor** [marmor] *der* marble
**Marone** [marohn-e] *die* (sweet) chestnut; chestnut boletus mushroom
**März** [mehrts] *der* March
**Marzipan** [martsipan] *das* marzipan
**Masern** [maazern] *pl* measles
**Maß** [maas] *das* measurement; measure
**Maß** [maas] *die* liter (glass)
**Maßnahme** [maasnaam-e] *die* measure
**Mast** [mast] *der* mast
**Matjes** [matyes] *der* salted herring
**Matratze** [matrats-e] *die* mattress
**matt** [mat] *adj* weak; *(paint, photo)* matte
**Mauer** [mower] *die* wall
**Maus** [mows] *die* mouse
**Mautgebühr** [mowtgebuur], **Mautstelle** [mowt-shtehl-e] *die* toll

**Meer** [mehr] *das* sea

**Meeresfrüchte** [mehrez-fruusht-e] *die* seafood

**Meerrettich** [mehr-rehtish] *der* horseradish

**Mehl** [mayl] *das* flour

**mehr** [mehr] *det* more ◆ *adv* more ▸ ich sehe ihn nicht mehr I don't see him any more

**mehrere** [mehrer-e] *adj & pron* several

**Mehrfahrtenausweis** [mehrfaartenowsveys] *der* multiple-journey ticket

**Mehrheit** [mehrheyt] *die* majority

**mehrmals** [mehrmals] *adv* several times

**Mehrwertsteuer** [mehrvehrt-shtoyer] *die* sales tax

**Meinung** [meynung] *die* opinion ▸ meiner Meinung nach in my opinion

**meiste** [meyst-e] *adj* most ▸ die meisten most people

**Meister, Meisterin** [meyster, meysterin] *der, die* master; champion

**Meisterwerk** [meystervehrk] *das* masterpiece

**melden** [mehlden] *v* to report ▸ sich melden *(on telephone)* to answer; *(with police)* to register

**Mensch** [mehnsh] *der* person; human being

**merken** [mehrken] *v* to realize

**Merkmal** [mehrkmal] *das* feature

**Messer** [mehser] *das* knife

**Mettwurst** [mehtvurst] *die* spreadable smoked pork and beef sausage

**Metzgerei** [mehtzgerey] *die* butcher (shop)

**Miete** [meet-e] *die* rent; rental

**mieten** [meeten] *v* to rent

**Mieter** [meeter] *der* tenant

**Mietwagen** [meetvaagen] *der* rental car

**Mikrowellenherd** [meekroh-vehlenhehrt] *der* microwave (oven)

**Milch** [milsh] *die* milk

**mild** [milt] *adj* mild

**Minderjährige** [minderyehrig-e] *der, die* minor

**mindestens** [mindestenz] *adv* at least

**Mindesthaltbarkeit** [mindest-haltbarkeyt] *die* expiration

**minus** [meenus] *conj* minus

**Minze** [mints-e] *die* mint

**Mischbrot** [mishbroht] *das* bread made from a mixture of rye and wheat flour

**Mischung** [mishung] *die* mixture

**missachten** [misakhten] *v (instruction)* to disregard

**Missbrauch** [misbrowkh] *der* abuse

**Missverständnis** [misfehrshtehndnis] *das* misunderstanding

**mit** [mit] *prep* with ▸ mit dem Bus by bus

**Mitbewohner** [mitbevohner] *der* roommate

**mitbringen** [mitbringen] *v* to bring (with one); to bring back

**miteinander** [miteynander] *adv* with each other, together

**mitgeben** [mitgayben] *v* to give

**Mitglied** [mitgleet] *das* member

**mitnehmen** [mitnaymen] *v* to take (with one) ▸ Pizza zum Mitnehmen pizza to go

**Mitreisende** [mitreyzend-e] *der, die* fellow passenger

**Mittag** [mitaak] *der* midday ▸ gegen Mittag around midday ▸ zu Mittag essen to have lunch

**Mittagessen** [mitaak-ehsen] *das* lunch

**mittags** [mitaaks] *adv* at midday

**Mitte** [mit-e] *die* middle

**Mittel** [mitel] *das* means; medicine ▸ ein Mittel gegen Husten a cough remedy

**Mittelalter** [mitelalter] *das* middle ages

**Mittelmeer** [mitelmehr] *das* the Mediterranean

**Mittelpunkt** [mitelpunkt] *der* center

**Mittelstreifen** [mitelshtreyfen] *der* (on road) median

**Mitternacht** [miternakht] *die* midnight

**Mittwoch** [mitvokh] *der* Wednesday

**Möbel** [meubel] *das* furniture

**möchte** [meusht-e] *pres* would like ▸ ich möchte Steak I would like some steak

**Modeschmuck** [moh-de-shmuk] *der* costume jewelry

**mögen** [meugen] *v* to like

**Möglichkeit** [meuglishkeyt] *die* possibility; opportunity

**möglichst** [meuglishst] *adv* if possible ▸ möglichst schnell as fast as possible

**Mohn** [mohn] *der* poppy; poppy seeds

**Möhre** [meur-e] *die* carrot

**Mohrenkopf** [mohrenkopf] *der* chocolate-covered marshmallow

**Monat** [mohnaat] *der* month

**Mönch** [meunsh] *der* monk

**Mond** [mohnt] *der* moon

**Montag** [mohntaak] *der* Monday

**Moor** [mohr] *das* bog

**morgen** [morgen] *adv* tomorrow ▸ morgen Früh tomorrow morning ▸ bis morgen! see you tomorrow!

**Morgen** [morgen] *der* morning ▸ guten Morgen! good morning! ▸ heute Morgen this morning

**Motor** [mohtor] *der* engine ▸ 'Motor abstellen!' 'switch off engine'

**Mückenstich** [muukenshtish] *der* the midge (fly) bite

**müde** [muud-e] *adj* tired

**Mühle** [muul-e] *die* mill

**Müll** [muul] *der* garbage

**Mund** [munt] *der* mouth

**Mündung** [muyundung] *die* (of river) mouth

**Münster** [muunster] *das* cathedral

**Münze** [muunts-e] *die* coin ▸ 'nur mit Münzen zahlen' 'coins only'

**Münzeinwurf** [muunts-eynvurf] *der* coin slot ▸ 'Münzeinwurf' 'insert coins'

**Münzrückgabe** [muunts-ruukgaab-e] *die* coin return ▸ 'keine Münzrückgabe' 'no change given'

**Mus** [moos] *das* puree

**Muschel** [mushel] *die* shell; mussel

**Muskelkater** [muskelkaater] *der* sore muscles

**muss** [mus] *pres* must, have to

**müssen** [muusen] *v* must, to have to

**Mutter** [mut-er] *die* mother

**Muttersprache** [mut-er-shpraakh-e] *die* native language

**Mütze** [muuts-e] *die* (worn on head) cap

**MwSt.** *abbr of* **Mehrwertsteuer** sales tax

# n

**Nabel** [naabel] *der* navel

**nach** [naakh] *prep* to; after ▸ nach Italien fahren to go to Italy ▸ es ist zehn Minuten nach elf it's ten minutes after eleven ▸ nach unten gehen to go down

**Nachbar** [nakhbar] *der* neighbor

**Nachmittag** [naakhmitaak] *der* afternoon ▸ heute Nachmittag this afternoon

**Nachname** [naakhnaam-e] *der* surname

**Nachricht** [naakh-risht] *die* message; piece of news ▸ eine Nachricht hinterlassen to leave a message ▸ Nachrichten news

**Nachsaison** [naakh-sayzon] *die* low season

**Nachspeise** [naakh-shpeyz-e] *die* dessert

**nächste, r, s** [nehkst-e] *adj* next

**Nacht** [nakht] *die* night ▸ gute Nacht! good night!

**Nachteil** [naakhteyl] *der* disadvantage

**Nachtisch** [naakhtish] *der* dessert

**nachts** [nakhts] *adv* at night

**nachzahlen** [naakh-tsaalen] *v* to pay extra

**Nacken** [nak-en] *der* neck

**nackt** [nakt] *adj* naked

**Nacktbadestrand** [nakt-baad-e-shtrant] *der* nudist beach

**Nadel** [naadel] *die* needle

**Nagel** [naagel] *der* nail

**Nähe** [nay-e] *die* ▸ in der Nähe nearby ▸ in der Nähe von dem Hotel near the hotel ▸ aus der Nähe from close up

**nähen** [nayen] *v* to sew

**Naherholungsgebiet** [naa-ehrhoh-lungz-gebeet] *das* recreational area close to a town

**nähern** [nayern] *v* ▸ sich nähern to approach

**Nahrung** [naarung] *die* food

**Nahrungsmittel** [naarungzmitel] *das* food

**Naht** [naat] *die (in material)* seam

**Nahverkehr** [naa-fehrkehr] *der* local traffic

**Name** [naam-e] *der* name

**Narbe** [narb-e] *die* scar

**naschen** [nashen] *v* to nibble

**Nase** [naaz-e] *die* nose

**Nasenbluten** [naazenblooten] *das* nosebleed

**nass** [nas] *adj* wet

**Nässe** [nehs-e] *die* wet ▸ überfrierende Nässe icy patches ▸ 'bei Nässe' 'in wet weather'

**natürlich** [natuurlish] *adv* natural ◆ *adj* naturally

**Naturschutz** [natoorshuts] *der* conservation

**Nebel** [naybel] *der* fog

**neben** [nayben] *prep* next to

**Nebenstraße** [nayben-shtraas-e] *die* side street

**Nebenwirkung** [naybenvirkung] *die* side effect

**neblig** [nayblish] *adj* foggy

**nehmen** [naymen] *v* to take

**nein** [neyn] *adv* no

**nennen** [nehn-en] *v (by name)* to call; to name

## Nummernschild

The first part of German license plates show the vehicle's place of origin. 1 letter usually stands for a big city (B for Berlin, M for Munich), 2 for a large town (MS for Münster) and 3 for a small town (WAF for Warendorf). The second set of letters and the number are for administrative purposes only.

**nett** [neht] *adj* nice ♦ *adv* nicely

**netto** [nehtoh] *adv* net

**Netz** [nehts] *das* net

**Netzkarte** [nehtskart-e] *die ticket allowing travel throughout a particular network, such as a national train network or local transportation network*

**neu** [noy] *adj* new

**Neujahr** [noy-yaar] *das* New Year

**neun** [noyn] *num* nine

**neunzehn** [noyn-tsayn] *num* nineteen

**neunzig** [noyn-tsish] *num* ninety

**nicht** [nisht] *adv* not ♦ es ist schön, nicht wahr? it's lovely, isn't it?

**Nichtraucher** [nishtrowkher] *der* non-smoker

**nichts** [nishts] *pron* nothing; *(with questions and negatives)* anything ♦ das macht nichts it doesn't matter

**Nichtschwimmerbecken** [nisht-shvimer-behken] *das* kiddie pool

**Nichtzutreffende** [nisht-tsootrehfend-e] *das* ♦ 'Nichtzutreffendes bitte streichen' 'delete as applicable'

**nie** [nee] *adv* never

**niedrig** [needrish] *adj* low

**niemand** [neemant] *pron* nobody

**Niere** [neer-e] *die* kidney

**niesen** [neesen] *v* to sneeze

**Niete** [neet-e] *die (made of metal)* stud; losing ticket

**Nikolaus** [nikohlows] *der* Santa Claus

**noch** [nokh] *adv* still ♦ noch nicht not

yet ♦ noch langsamer even slower ♦ noch ein Bier, bitte! another beer, please

**Nordsee** [nortzay] *die* the North Sea

**Normalbenzin** [normaalbehntseen] *das* regular gasoline

**Notarzt** [noht-aartst] *der* emergency doctor

**Notausgang** [noht-owsgang] *der* emergency exit

**Notbremse** [noht-brehmz-e] *die* emergency brake

**Notdienstapotheke** [nohtdeenst-apohtayk-e] *die* emergency pharmacy

**Notfall** [nohtfal] *der* emergency

**Nothaltebucht** [noht-halt-e-bukht] *die lane used for a few minutes at a time by trucks traveling more slowly than other traffic (to let traffic pass)*

**nötig** [neutish] *adj* necessary

**Notruf** [nohtroof] *der* emergency call

**Nougat** [noogat] *der* nougat

**November** [nohfehmber] *der* November

**Nr.** *abbr of* **Nummer** No., no.

**Nudeln** [noodeln] *pl* noodles

**null** [nul] *num* zero

**Nummer** [num-er] *die* number; *(in clothes, shoes)* size

**Nummernschild** [numernshilt] *das* license plate

**nur** [noor] *adv* only

**Nuss** [nus] *die* nut

**Nussknacker** [nusknaker] *der* nutcracker

**nützlich** [nuuts-lish] *adj* useful

**ob** [op] *conj* whether, if ▸ ob es regnet oder nicht whether it rains or not

**oben** [ohben] *adv* at the top; upstairs; *(in text)* above ▸ dort oben up there ▸ nach oben up ▸ oben ohne topless

**Ober** [ohber] *der* waiter

**obere, r, s** [ohbere-e] *adj* upper

**Oberkörper** [ohberkeurper] *der* upper body

**Oberschenkel** [ohbershenkel] *der* thigh

**Oberteil** [ohberteyl] *das (clothing)* top

**Obst** [ohbst] *das* fruit

**Ochsenschwanzsuppe** [oksenshvants-zup-e] *die* oxtail soup

**oder** [ohder] *conj* or ▸ Sie sind Herr Schwarz, oder? you're Mr. Schwarz, aren't you?

**Ofen** [ohfen] *der* oven; stove

**offen** [ofen] *adj* open

**öffentlich** [eufentlish] *adj* public ◆ *adv* in public

**öffnen** [eufnen] *v* to open

**Öffnungszeiten** [eufnungz-tseyten] *pl* business hours

**oft** [oft] *adv* often ▸ wie oft? how often?

**ohne** [ohn-e] *conj* without

**ohnmächtig** [ohnmehtish] *adj* unconscious ▸ ohnmächtig werden to faint

**Ohr** [ohr] *das* ear

**Ohrring** [ohr-ring] *der* earring

**Ökoladen** [eukoh-laaden] *der* health food store, natural foods store

**Oktober** [oktohber] *der* October

**Oktoberfest** [oktohberfehst] *das* Oktoberfest

**Öl** [eul] *das* oil

**Oper** [ohper] *die* opera

**Opfer** [opfer] *das* victim; sacrifice

**Ordner** [ordner] *der (for documents)* folder; *(at stadium etc.)* manager, steward

**Ordnung** [ordnung] *die* order ▸ (geht) in Ordnung! OK!

**Orgel** [orgel] *die* MUSIC organ

**Ort** [ort] *der* place ▸ andere Orte other routes

**Ortschaft** [ortshaft] *die* village ▸ geschlossene Ortschaft built-up area

**Osten** [osten] *der* east

**Ostern** [ohstern] *neut* Easter ▸ zu Ostern at Easter

**Ostsee** [ostzay] *die* the Baltic Sea

---

### Oktoberfest

*Kolossal!* From mid-September to the 1st Sunday in October, Munich holds an enormous beer festival, with brass bands and drinking competitions. In tents that each hold 6,000 people, revellers gulp down more than 6 million liters of beer every year, not to mention the mountains of sausages and meat that they consume!

**paar** [paar] *adj* few ▸ **ein paar** a few
**Paar** [paar] *das* pair; couple ▸ **ein Paar ...** a pair of ...
**Päckchen** [pehkshen] *das* parcel
**packen** [pak-en] *v* to pack
**Packung** [pakung] *die* packet; *(of chocolates)* box
**Packungsbeilage** [pakungz-beylaag-e] *die (with medication)* enclosed information
**Paddel** [padel] *das* paddle
**paniert** [paneert] *adj* breaded, in breadcrumbs
**Pannendienst** [panendeenst] *der* breakdown service
**Papier** [papeer] *das* paper
**Pappe** [pap-e] *die* cardboard
**Paradeiser** [paradeyzer] *der* tomato
**Parkanlage** [park-anlaag-e] *die* park
**Parkdauer** [parkdower] *die (when parking)* length of stay
**Parkdeck** [parkdehk] *das* parking level
**parken** [parken] *v* to park ▸ '**Parken verboten**' 'no parking'
**Parkett** [par-keht] *das (in theater etc.)* parquet
**Parkgebühr** [parkgebuur] *die* parking fee
**Parkhaus** [parkhows] *das* parking garage
**Parkhöchstdauer** [park-heukst-dower] *die (for parking)* maximum length of stay ▸ '**Parkhöchstdauer 1 Stunde**' 'maximum length of stay: 1 hour'
**Parkplatz** [parkplats] *der* parking lot
**Parkscheibe** [parksheyb-e] *die* parking permit
**Parkschein** [parksheyn] *der (document permitting parking)* parking ticket
**Parkuhr** [parkoor] *die* parking meter
**Parkverbot** [parkfehrboht] *das* ▸ **hier herrscht Parkverbot** this is a no-parking zone
**Party** [paarti] *die* party
**Pass** [pas] *der* passport; *(through mountains)* pass
**Passbild** [pasbilt] *das* passport photo
**passend** [pasent] *adj* suitable; *(colors)* matching ▸ **haben Sie es passend?** do you have the right change?
**Passfoto** [pasfohtoh] *das* passport photo
**Passkontrolle** [paskontrol-e] *die* passport check
**Pastete** [pastayt-e] *die* pie; pâté
**Pech** [pehsh] *das* bad luck
**Pellkartoffel** [pehlkartofel] *die* unpeeled boiled potatoes
**Pension** [penziohn] *die* guesthouse ▸ see box on p. 40
**Peperoni** [pehperohni] *die* chili pepper
**Personal** [pehrzohnaal] *das* staff
**Personalausweis** [pehrzohnaal-owsveys] *der* ID card, identity card
**persönlich** [pehrzeunlish] *adj* personal ✦ *adv* personally
**Petersilie** [payterzeeli-e] *die* parsley
**Pfad** [pfaat] *der* path
**Pfand** [pfant] *das (on bottles)* deposit
**Pfandrückgabe** [pfant-ruukgaab-e] *die counter for returning bottles*
**Pfanne** [pfan-e] *die* frying pan
**Pfannengericht** [pfanen-gerisht] *das* fried dish

## Pension

*Pensions*, which are more common in towns than villages, have just a few rooms to rent. They offer a family atmosphere, are quite comfortable, and don't cost too much. You can reckon on paying between 20 and 30 euros per person or 30 to 40 euros for two people. You can also have breakfast and dinner there, and sometimes even lunch.

**Pfannkuchen** [pfankookhen] *der* pancake

**Pfeffer** [pfehfer] *der* pepper

**Pfefferkuchen** [pfehferkookhen] *der* gingerbread

**Pfefferminztee** [pfehfermints-<u>tay</u>] *der* peppermint tea

**Pfeil** [pfeyl] *der* arrow ▸ 'folgen Sie dem gelben Pfeil!' 'follow the yellow arrow'

**Pferd** [pfehrt] *das* horse

**Pfifferling** [pfiferling] *der* chanterelle mushroom

**Pfingsten** [pfingsten]Whitsun

**Pfirsich** [pfirzish] *der* peach

**Pflanze** [pflants-e] *die* plant

**Pflaster** [pflaster] *das* Band-Aid®; road surface

**Pflaume** [pflowm-e] *die* plum

**Pflicht** [pflisht] *die* duty

**pflücken** [pfluuken] *v (flowers)* to pick

**Pförtner** [pfeurtner] *der* porter

**Pfund** [pfunt] *das* pound

**Pickel** [pikel] *der* pimple, spot

**Pille** [pil-e] *die* pill

**Pils** [pils] *das* Pils, Pilsner

**Pilz** [pilts] *der* mushroom; fungal infection

**Pinzette** [pintseht-e] *die* tweezers

**Plakat** [plakaat] *das* poster

**planmäßig** [plaanmaysig] *adj* scheduled

**Planschbecken** [planshbehken] *das* kiddie pool (for back yard, etc.)

**platt** [plat] *adj (tire)* flat

**Platte** [plat-e] *die* platter; *(on stove)* ring; paving stone; *(disk)* record

**Platz** [plats] *der* the place; space, room; seat; *(in town)* square

**Platzkarte** [platskart-e] *die* seat reservation

**PLZ** *abbr of* **Postleitzahl** zip code

**Polizei** [politsey] *die* police

**Porree** [poray] *der* leek

**Porto** [portoh] *das* postage

**Postamt** [post-amt] *das* post office

**Postkarte** [postkart-e] *die* postcard

**Postleitzahl** [post-leyt-tsaal] *die* zip code

**Potsdamerplatz** [potsdamerplats] *der* Potsdamerplatz

## Potsdamerplatz

The nerve center of pre-war Berlin, this square was destroyed by bombing in the war, formed part of the no-man's-land between East and West during the Cold War, and is now the symbol of the new Berlin. In just a few years, celebrated architects such as Renzo Piano and Helmut Jahn have created an ultra-modern business and leisure district.

**Prädikat** [praydik<u>aa</u>t] *das (of film etc.)* rating

**Praline** [pral<u>ee</u>n-e] *die* chocolate

**Prater** [pr<u>aa</u>ter] *der large park and funfair in Vienna*

**Praxis** [praksis] *die (of doctor)* office

**Preis** [preys] *der* price; prize

**Preiselbeere** [pr<u>ey</u>zelbehr-e] *die* cranberry

**Preisermäßigung** [pr<u>ey</u>s-ehrmehsi-gung] *die* reduction in price

**Preislage** [pr<u>ey</u>s-laag-e] *die* price range

**preiswert** [pr<u>ey</u>svehrt] *adj* cheap

**Prellung** [prehlung] *die* bruise

**prima** [pr<u>ee</u>ma] *adj* fantastic

**Prise** [pr<u>ee</u>z-e] *die* pinch ▸ eine Prise Salz a pinch of salt

**Privatunterkunft** [priv<u>aa</u>t-unterkunft] *die* private accommodation

**pro** [proh] *prep* per ▸ pro Person per person

**Probe** [pr<u>oh</u>b-e] *die (in theater)* rehearsal

**probieren** [probeeren] *v* to try

**Produkt** [prod<u>u</u>kt] *das* product

**Promille** [prom<u>ee</u>l-e] *das* alcohol level

**prominent** [promin<u>e</u>hnt] *adj* prominent

**Proviant** [provi<u>a</u>nt] *der* provisions

**Prozent** [proh-ts<u>e</u>hnt] *das* percent

**Prüfung** [pr<u>uu</u>fung] *die* examination

**PS** [pay-ehs] *das abbr of* **Pferdestärke** hp, horse power

**Pudding** [p<u>u</u>ding] *der cold dessert similar to pudding*

**Puder** [p<u>oo</u>der] *der* powder

**Puderzucker** [p<u>oo</u>der-tsuker] *der* confectioners' sugar

**Pulli** [p<u>u</u>l-i] *der* sweater

**Pullover** [pul<u>oh</u>ver] *der* sweater

**Puls** [p<u>u</u>ls] *der (medical)* pulse

**Pulver** [p<u>u</u>lver] *das* powder

**Pumpe** [p<u>u</u>mp-e] *die* pump

**Punkt** [p<u>u</u>nkt] *der* point; dot; *(in punctuation)* period ▸ Punkt ein Uhr one o'clock exactly

**pünktlich** [p<u>uu</u>nktlish] *adj* punctual

**Pute** [p<u>oo</u>t-e] *die* turkey

**Putenschnitzel** [p<u>oo</u>ten-shnitsel] *das* turkey scallop

**putzen** [p<u>u</u>tsen] *v* to clean

# q

**Quadrat** [kvadr<u>aa</u>t] *das* square

**Qualle** [kv<u>a</u>l-e] *die* jellyfish

**Qualm** [kv<u>a</u>lm] *der* smoke

**Quark** [kv<u>a</u>rk] *der soft cheese made from skim milk*

**Quarktasche** [kv<u>a</u>rk-tash-e] *die pastry filled with quark cheese*

**Quartier** [kvart<u>ee</u>r] *das* accommodation

**Quelle** [kv<u>e</u>hl-e] *die* source; *(of water)* spring

**Quitte** [kv<u>i</u>t-e] *die* quince

**Quittung** [kv<u>i</u>tung] *die* receipt

# r

**Rabatt** [rabat] *der* discount

**Rad** [raat] *das* wheel; bike ▸ Rad fahren to ride a bike

**Radfahrer** [raatfaarer] *der* cyclist

**Radi** [raadi] *der* radish

**Radieschen** [radees-shen] *das* radish

**Radtour** [raat-toor] *die* cycling tour

**Rahm** [raam] *der* cream

**Rand** [rant] *der* edge; rim

**Randstreifen** [rant-shtreyfen] *der (of road)* berm; *(of freeway)* shoulder

**Rappen** [rap-en] *der (one hundredth of a Swiss franc)* centime

**Rasen** [raazen] *der* lawn; grass

**Rasierer** [razeerer] *der* electric shaver

**Rasierklinge** [razeer-kling-e] *die* razor blade

**Rasierschaum** [razeershowm] *der* shaving cream

**Rast** [rast] *die* rest ▸ Rast machen to have a rest

**rasten** [rasten] *v* to rest

**Rasthof** [rast-hohf] *der (on interstate)* services

**Rastplatz** [rastplats] *der* picnic area ▸ 'Rastplatz bitte sauber halten!' 'please keep picnic area tidy'

**Raststätte** [rast-shteht-e] *die (on interstate)* services

**Rat** [raat] *der* advice; council

**Rathaus** [raat-hows] *das* town hall

**Rätsel** [rehtsel] *das* puzzle

**Ratskeller** [raatskehler] *der* bar in cellar beneath town hall

**rauchen** [rowkhen] *v* to smoke ▸ 'bitte nicht rauchen' 'please do not smoke' ▸ 'Rauchen verboten' 'no smoking'

**Raucher** [rowkher] *der* smoker

**Räucherlachs** [roysherlaks] *der* smoked salmon

**Raum** [rowm] *der* room; area

**räumen** [roymen] *v (dishes etc.)* to clear away; *(apartment, hotel room)* to vacate

**Räumungsverkauf** [roymungz-fehr-kowf] *der* clearance sale

**Rebhuhn** [raybhoon] *das* partridge

**rechnen** [rehshnen] *v (math problem)* to work out ▸ auf etwas rechnen to count on something

**Rechnung** [rehshnung] *die (in restaurant)* check

**Recht** [rehsht] *das* right ▸ Recht haben to be right

**rechtlich** [rehshtlish] *adj* legal

---

## Ratskeller

Typically German, the *Ratskeller* is a restaurant that you can find in the basement of every *Rathaus* (town hall). Its décor is often historic, like a vaulted wine-cellar, and it's a popular place to eat local specialties at a very reasonable price.

## Reeperbahn

This red-light district of Hamburg, also known as *Sankt Pauli*, is a former haunt of sailors where the bars, nightclubs and local prostitutes are always to the fore. It is also where four young men in a band called the Beatles started out on their road to fame.

**rechts** [rehshts] *adv* on the right; *(to turn)* right ▸ nach rechts right

**rechtzeitig** [rehsht-tseytish] *adv* on time

**reden** [rayden] *v* to talk

**reduziert** [rehdootseert] *adj* reduced ▸ reduzierte Waren reduced-price goods

**Reederei** [rayderey] *die* shipping company

**Reeperbahn** [rayperbaan] *die street in Hamburg famous for bars and nightclubs*

**Reformhaus** [rehformhows] *das* health food store, natural food store

**Regal** [rehgaal] *das* shelves

**Regel** [raygel] *die* rule; *(menstruation)* period

**Regen** [raygen] *der* rain ▸ bei Regen in wet weather

**Regenschauer** [raygenshower] *der* rain shower

**Regenschirm** [raygenshirm] *der* umbrella

**Regierung** [rehgeeerung] *die* government

**regnen** [raygnen] *v* to rain

**regnerisch** [raygnerish] *adj* rainy

**Reh** [ray] *das* deer; venison

**Reibekuchen** [reyb-e-kookhen] *der* ≃ hash browns

**reiben** [reyben] *v* to rub; to grate

**Reiberdatschi** [reyberdatshi] *der* ≃ hash browns

**reich** [reysh] *adj* rich

**Reichstag** [reyshs-taak] *der* Reichstag, German parliament ▸ see box on p.44

**reif** [reyf] *adj* ripe; mature

**Reifen** [reyfen] *der* tire

**Reifendruck** [reyfendruk] *der* tire pressure

**Reihe** [rey-e] *die (of seats etc.)* row ▸ ich bin an der Reihe it's my turn

**Reihenfolge** [reyenfolg-e] *die* order, sequence

**rein** [reyn] *adj* clean; pure

**reinigen** [reynigen] *v* to clean

**Reinigung** [reynigung] *die* cleaning; dry cleaner's

**Reis** [reys] *der* rice

**Reise** [reyz-e] *die* journey; trip ▸ gute Reise! have a good trip!

**Reisebegleiter** [reyz-e-begleyter] *der* traveling companion

## Reformhaus

While vegetarian restaurants are still scarce in Germany (what can you expect where sausages are so popular?), health food enthusiasts can head straight for the *Reformhäuser*. These health-food stores were started in Wuppertal in 1900 and are now in evidence all over the country.

## Reichstag

The Parliament building in Berlin was built at the end of the 19th century. The Republic was proclaimed here in 1918, and the Nazis set the building on fire in 1933 and then blamed the Communists. After the war, the Red Army raised the Soviet flag over the smoking ruins of the parliament. Finally, the Reunification treaty was signed here in 1990 and the *Reichstag* was renamed the *Bundestag*.

**Reisebüro** [reyz-e-buuroh] *das* travel agency

**Reiseführer** [reyz-e-fuurer] *der* guide book; *(on trip)* guide

**Reisegepäck** [reyz-e-gepehk] *das* baggage

**Reisegesellschaft** [reyz-e-gezehlshaft] *die* group of tourists; tour operator

**Reiseleiter** [reyz-e-leyter] *der (on trip)* guide

**reisen** [reyzen] *v* to travel

**Reisende** [reyzend-e] *der, die* traveler; passenger

**Reisepass** [reyz-e-pas] *der* passport

**Reiseveranstalter** [reyz-e-fehranshtalter] *der* tour operator

**Reiseversicherung** [reyz-e-fehrzisherung] *die* travel insurance

**Reiseziel** [reyz-e-tseel] *das* destination

**reiten** [reyten] *v* to ride horseback

**Reitstall** [reyt-shtal] *der* riding stable

**Rennen** [rehnen] *das* race; racing

**Restgeld** [rehstgehlt] *das (money)* change ▸ 'kein Restgeld' 'no change given' ▸ 'Restgeld wird erstattet' 'change given'

**Rettich** [rehtish] *der* radish

**Rettungsboot** [rehtungzboht] *das* lifeboat

**Rettungsdienst** [rehtungzdeenst] *der* emergency services

**Rettungsring** [rehtungzring] *der* life belt

**Rettungswagen** [rehtungzvaagen] *der* ambulance

**Rezept** [rehtsehpt] *das* recipe; prescription

**rezeptfrei** [rehtsehptfrey] *adj* available without a prescription

**rezeptpflichtig** [rehtsehpt-pflishtish] *adj* available only by prescription

**R-Gespräch** [ehr-geshprehsh] *das* collect call

**Richtgeschwindigkeit** [risht-geshvindishkeyt] *die* recommended speed limit

**richtig** [rishtish] *adj (correct, suitable)* right; *(name, pleasure)* real

**Richtung** [rishtung] *die* direction ▸ 'alle Richtungen' 'all routes' ▸ in Richtung Dresden towards Dresden

**riechen** [reeshen] *v* to smell

**Riegel** [reegel] *der (on door)* bolt; *(of chocolate)* piece

**Riesenrad** [reezenraat] *das* Ferris wheel

**Riff** [rif] *das* reef

**Rind** [rint] *das* cow; beef

**Rinderbraten** [rinderbraaten] *der* roast beef

**Ringstraße** [ring-shtraas-e] *die* beltway

**Rippchen** [ripshen] *das lightly smoked pork rib*

**Rippe** [rip-e] *die* rib

**Risiko** [reezikoh] *das* risk ▸ auf eigenes Risiko at one's own risk

**Ritt** [rit] *der* ride

**Rock** [rok] *der* skirt

**Rodelbahn** [rohdelbaan] *die* toboggan run

**Roggen** [rog-en] *der* rye

**roh** [roh] *adj (food)* raw

**Rohkost** [rohkost] *die* raw fruit and vegetables

**Rohrzucker** [rohr-tsuker] *der* cane sugar

**Rollbraten** [rolbraaten] *der* roast

**Rollschuh** [rol-shoo] *der* roller skate

**Rollsplitt** [rol-shplit] *der* gravel

**Rollstuhl** [rol-shtool] *der* wheelchair

**Rolltreppe** [rol-trehp-e] *die* escalator

**röntgen** [reuntgen] *v to* X-ray

**Rosenkohl** [rohzen-kohl] *der* Brussels sprouts

**Rosine** [rozeen-e] *die* raisin

**Rostbratwurst** [rostbraatvurst] *die* grilled sausage

**rösten** [reusten] *v to* roast

**rot** [roht] *adj* red

**Rot** [roht] *das* red ▸ 'bei Rot hier halten' 'stop here when red light shows'

**Röteln** [reuteln] *pl* German measles

**Rotkohl** [rohtkohl] *der* red cabbage

**Rotkraut** [rohtkrowt] *das* red cabbage

**Roulade** [roolaad-e] *die* ≃ beef olive, slice of beef or veal rolled up with herbs and stuffed

**Rücken** [ruuken] *der* back

**Rückfahrkarte** [ruukfaarkart-e] *die* round-trip ticket

**Rückfahrt** [ruukfaart] *die* return journey

**Rückflug** [ruukflook] *der* return flight

**Rückgabeknopf** [ruukgaab-e-knopf] *der* coin return button

**Rückreise** [ruukreyz-e] *die* return journey

**Rucksack** [rukzak] *der* backpack

**Rückseite** [ruukzeyt-e] *die (of page etc.)* back

**Rücksicht** [ruukzisht] *die* consideration

**Rücksitz** [ruukzits] *der* back seat

**rückwärts** [ruukvehrts] *adv* backwards

**Rückweg** [ruukvayk] *der* way back

**Rückzahlung** [ruuk-tsaalung] *die* repayment

**Ruder** [rooder] *das* oar; rudder

**Ruderboot** [rooderboht] *das* rowboat

**Ruf** [roof] *der (appeal, request)* call; reputation

**Ruhe** [roo-e] *die* quiet; silence; calmness ▸ lass mich in Ruhe! leave me in peace!

**Ruhetag** [roo-e-taak] *der* closing day

**ruhig** [rooish] *adj* quiet; calm

**Rührei** [ruurey] *das* scrambled egg

**rühren** [ruuren] *v to* stir; to move

**Rummelplatz** [rumelplats] *der* fairground

**rund** [runt] *adj* round ◆ *adv* about; around

**Runde** [rund-e] *die* round; *(of track)* lap

**Rundfahrt** [runtfaart] *die* tour

**Rundflug** [runtflook] *der* sightseeing flight

**Rundfunk** [runtfunk] *der* radio

**Rundgang** [runtgang] *der* walk

**Rundreise** [runt-reyz-e] *die* tour

**rutschig** [rutshish] *adj* slippery

# S

**Saal** [zaal] *der* hall

**Sache** [sakh-e] *die* thing; *(affair)* matter
▸ Sachen things

**Sachschaden** [sakh-shaaden] *der* material damage

**Sackgasse** [zakgas-e] *die* dead end

**Saft** [zaft] *der* juice

**sagen** [zaagen] *v* to say; to tell

**Sahne** [zaan-e] *die* cream ▸ saure Sahne sour cream

**Salat** [zalaat] *der* salad; lettuce

**Salatbar** [zalaatbar] *die* salad bar

**Salbe** [zalb-e] *die* ointment

**Salz** [zalts] *das* salt

**Salzburger Festspiele** [zaltsburger-fehst-shpeel-e] *die* Salzburg festival

**Salzkartoffeln** [zaltskartofeln] *die* boiled potatoes

**Sammelfahrschein** [zamelfaarsheyn] *der* multiple journey ticket; group ticket

**sammeln** [zameln] *v* to collect

**Sammlung** [zamlung] *die* collection

**Samstag** [zamztaak] *der* Saturday

**Sandkasten** [zantkasten] *der* sandbox

**Sandstrand** [zant-shtrant] *der* sandy beach

**Sänger** [zehnger] *der* singer

**Sardelle** [zardehl-e] *die* anchovy

**satt** [zat] *adv (after eating)* full ▸ satt sein to be full

**sauber** [zowber] *adj* clean; neat

**sauer** [zower] *adj* sour; annoyed

**Sauerbraten** [zowerbraaten] *der* braised beef marinated in vinegar

**Sauerkirsche** [zowerkirsh-e] *die* sour cherry

**Sauerkraut** [zowerkrowt] *das* sauerkraut

**Sauerrahm** [zower-raam] *der* sour cream

**Sauerteig** [zowerteyk] *der* sourdough

**Säugling** [zoygling] *der* baby

**S-Bahn** [ehsbaan] *die* suburban railway

**Schaden** [shaaden] *der* damage

**Schadenersatz** [shaaden-ehrzats] *der* compensation

**Schaf** [shaaf] *das* sheep

**Schaffner** [shafner] *der (on bus, train etc.)* conductor

**Schafskäse** [shaafs-kayz-e] *der* sheep's milk cheese

**Schal** [shaal] *der* scarf

**Schalter** [shalter] *der* switch; *(in bank etc.)* counter

---

### Salzburger Festspiele

Who hasn't heard of Salzburg, the hometown of Mozart, which has organized this prestigious music festival in his honor since 1920? Tribute is also paid to one of the festival's founders, Hugo von Hofmannsthal, whose play *Jedermann* ('Everyman') is put on every year in the square in front of the cathedral.

**Schalterschluss** [shaltershlus] *der* closing time

**scharf** [sharf] *adj* sharp; hot, spicy

**Schaschlik** [shashlik] *das or der* shish kebab

**Schatten** [shat-en] *der* shadow; shade

**Schatz** [shats] *der* treasure

**Schau** [show] *die* show

**schauen** [showen] *v* to look

**Schauer** [shower] *der* (of rain) shower

**Schaufenster** [showfehnster] *das* store window

**Schaufensterbummel** [show-fehn-ster-bum-el] *der* window-shopping trip

**Schaukel** [showkel] *die* (in playground) swing

**Schaum** [showm] *der* foam

**Schaumwein** [showmveyn] *der* sparkling wine

**Schauspieler** [showshpeeler] *der* actor

**Schauspielhaus** [showshpeelhows] *das* theater

**Scheck** [shehk] *der* check ▸ einen Scheck einlösen to cash a check ▸ Schecks aller Art all checks welcome

**Scheckgebühr** [shehkgebuur] *die* charge for checks

**Scheckkarte** [shehk-kart-e] *die* check card

**Scheibe** [sheyb-e] *die* slice; window

**Scheibenwischer** [sheybenvisher] *der* windshield wiper

**Schein** [sheyn] *der* bill, banknote; certificate; (of lamp, sun) light

**scheinen** [sheynen] *v* to shine; to seem

**Scheinwerfer** [sheynvehrfer] *der* headlight; floodlight; spotlight

**Schenkel** [shehnkel] *der* thigh

**schenken** [shehnken] *v* to give (as a present)

**Schere** [shayr-e] *die* scissors

**schicken** [shik-en] *v* to send

**Schiedsrichter, Schiedsrichterin** [sheets-rishter, sheets-rishterin] *der, die* referee; umpire

**Schienbein** [sheenbeyn] *das* shin

**schießen** [shees-en] *v* to shoot

**Schiff** [shif] *das* ship; (of church) nave

**Schifffahrt** [shif-faart] *die* shipping

**Schiffskarte** [shifs-kart-e] *die* navigation chart

**Schiffsverbindung** [shifs-fehrbindung] *die* connecting boat service

**Schild** [shilt] *das* sign; label

**Schinken** [shinken] *der* ham ▸ roher/gekochter/geräucherter Schinken cured/cooked/smoked ham

**Schinkenspeck** [shinkenshpehk] *der* bacon

**Schinkenwurst** [shinkenvurst] *die* ham sausage

**Schirm** [shirm] *der* umbrella

**schlafen** [shlaafen] *v* to sleep

**Schlaflosigkeit** [shlaaflohzishkeyt] *die* insomnia

**Schlafsaal** [shlaafzaal] *der* dormitory

**Schlafsack** [shlaafzak] *der* sleeping bag

**Schlafwagen** [shlaafvaagen] *der* sleeping car, sleeper

**Schlag** [shlaak] *der* blow; (of pulse, heart) beat; electric shock

**schlagen** [shlaagen] *v* to hit, to strike; (egg, opposing team) to beat

**Schlagobers** [shlaak-ohbers] *das* whipped cream

**Schlagsahne** [shlaakzaan-e] *die* whipped cream

**Schlamm** [shlam] *der* mud

**Schlange** [shlang-e] *die* snake; (of people) line ▸ Schlange stehen to stand in line

**schlank** [shlank] *adj* slim

**Schlauchboot** [shl<u>ow</u>khboht] *das* rubber dinghy

**schlecht** [shlehsht] *adj* bad ◆ *adv* badly; *(taste)* bad ▸ schlecht werden to go bad

**Schleimhaut** [shl<u>ey</u>mhowt] *die* mucus membrane

**Schlemmerlokal** [shlehmerlohkaal] *das* gourmet restaurant

**schlendern** [shl<u>e</u>hndern] *v* to stroll

**Schlepplift** [shl<u>e</u>hplift] *der* ski tow

**Schleudergefahr** [shl<u>oy</u>dergefaar] *die* danger of skidding ▸ 'Vorsicht Schleudergefahr!' 'slippery road'

**Schleuse** [shl<u>oy</u>z-e] *die* (on canal) lock

**schließen** [shl<u>ee</u>sen] *v* to close

**Schließfach** [shl<u>ee</u>sfakh] *das* locker; safe deposit box

**Schlitten** [shl<u>i</u>t-en] *der* toboggan

**Schlittschuh** [shl<u>i</u>t-shoo] *der* ice skate ▸ Schlittschuh laufen to ice-skate

**Schloss** [shl<u>o</u>s] *das* (on door) lock; castle

**Schlucht** [shl<u>u</u>kht] *die* ravine

**schlucken** [shl<u>u</u>k-en] *v* to swallow

**Schluss** [shl<u>u</u>s] *der* end; ending

**Schlüssel** [shl<u>ü</u>sel] *der* key

**Schlussverkauf** [shl<u>u</u>s-fehr-kowf] *der* end-of-season sale

**Schmalz** [shm<u>a</u>lts] *das* lard; dripping

**Schmerz** [shm<u>e</u>hrts] *der* pain

**Schmerzmittel** [shm<u>e</u>hrts-mit-el] *das* painkiller

**schmieren** [shm<u>ee</u>ren] *v* to spread

**Schmierkäse** [shm<u>ee</u>rkayz-e] *der* cheese spread

**schminken** [shm<u>i</u>nken] *v* to make up ▸ sich schminken to put on one's makeup

**Schmorbraten** [shm<u>o</u>hrbraaten] *der* pot roast

**Schmuck** [shm<u>u</u>k] *der* the jewelry; decoration

**schmutzig** [shm<u>u</u>tsish] *adj* dirty

**Schnecke** [shn<u>e</u>hk-e] *die* snail; ≃ Danish pastry

**Schnee** [shn<u>ay</u>] *der* snow

**Schneeglätte** [shn<u>ay</u>gleht-e] *die* packed snow

**Schneekette** [shn<u>ay</u>keht-e] *die* snow chain

**Schneepflug** [shn<u>ay</u>pflook] *der* snowplow

**schneiden** [shn<u>ey</u>den] *v* to cut

**schneien** [shn<u>ey</u>en] *v* to snow

**schnell** [shn<u>e</u>hl] *adj* quick, fast ◆ *adv* quickly, fast

**Schnellstraße** [shn<u>e</u>hl-shtraas-e] *die* expressway

**Schnitte** [shn<u>i</u>t-e] *die* slice; open-faced sandwich

**Schnittkäse** [shn<u>i</u>tkayz-e] *der* sliced cheese

**Schnittlauch** [shn<u>i</u>tlowkh] *der* chives

**Schnitzel** [shn<u>i</u>tsel] *das* (meat) scallop ▸ Wiener Schnitzel veal scallop

**Schnupfen** [shn<u>u</u>pfen] *der* cold ▸ Schnupfen haben to have a cold

**Scholle** [sh<u>o</u>l-e] *die* plaice

**Schorle** [sh<u>o</u>rl-e] *die* (with wine) spritzer; *apple juice with sparkling mineral water*

**Schrank** [shr<u>a</u>nk] *der* cupboard; closet

**Schranke** [shr<u>a</u>nk-e] *die* barrier

**Schraube** [shr<u>ow</u>b-e] *die* screw

**schreiben** [shr<u>ey</u>ben] *v* to write

**Schreibwarengeschäft** [shr<u>ey</u>p-vaa-ren-geshehft] *das* stationery store

**schreien** [shr<u>ey</u>en] *v* to shout; to scream

**Schritt** [shr<u>i</u>t] *der* step ▸ 'Schritt fahren' 'go very slowly'

**Schritttempo** [shr<u>i</u>t-tehmpoh] *das* walking pace ▸ im Schritttempo at a walking pace

**Schublade** [shoob-laad-e] *die* drawer

**Schüfeli** [shuufeli] *das* smoked pork

**Schuh** [shoo] *der* shoe

**Schuld** [shult] *die* blame; guilt

**Schule** [shool-e] *die* school

**Schüler, Schülerin** [shooler, shoolerin] *der, die* pupil

**Schulferien** [shoolfehrien] *pl* school vacation

**Schulter** [shulter] *die* shoulder

**Schuppe** [shup-e] *die* (on fish) scale ▸ Schuppen dandruff

**Schuss** [shus] *der* shot; (of whisky etc.) dash

**Schüssel** [shuusel] *die* bowl

**Schutt** [shut] *der* rubble ▸ 'Schutt abladen verboten' 'no dumping'

**schütteln** [shuuteln] *v* to shake

**Schutz** [shuts] *der* protection

**Schutzbrief** [shutsbreef] *der* travel insurance certificate

**Schützenfest** [shuutsen-fehst] *das* shooting festival

**Schwamm** [shvam] *der* sponge

**schwanger** [shvanger] *adj* pregnant

**Schwangerschaft** [shvangershaft] *die* pregnancy

**schwarz** [shvarts] *adj* black

**Schwarzbrot** [shvartsbroht] *das* black bread

**schwarzfahren** [shvartsfaaren] *v* to travel without a ticket

**Schwarzwurzel** [shvartsvurtsel] *die* scorzonera

**Schwebebahn** [shvaybebaan] *die* overhead monorail

**Schwein** [shveyn] *das* pig; pork

**Schweinebraten** [shveynebraaten] *der* roast pork

**Schweinshaxe** [shveynz-haks-e] *die* fried knuckle of pork

**Schwerbehinderte** [shvehrbehinderte] *der, die* severely disabled person

**Schwester** [shvehster] *die* sister; nurse

**schwierig** [shveerish] *adj* difficult

**Schwimmbad** [shvimbaat] *das* swimming pool

**Schwimmbecken** [shvimbehken] *das* swimming pool

**schwimmen** [shvimen] *v* to swim

**Schwimmerbecken** [shvimerbehken] *das* main swimming pool

**Schwimmhalle** [shvim-hal-e] *die* indoor swimming pool

**Schwimmweste** [shvim-vehst-e] *die* life jacket

**schwül** [shvuul] *adj* (weather) muggy

**sechs** [zehks] *num* six

**sechzehn** [zehsh-tsayn] *num* sixteen

**sechzig** [zehsh-tsish] *num* sixty

**See** [zay] *der* lake

**See** [zay] *die* sea

**Seebad** [zaybaat] *das* seaside resort

**segeln** [zaygeln] *v* to sail

**sehen** [zayen] *v* to see; to look

**sehr** [zehr] *adv* very; very much, a lot

**Seide** [zeyd-e] *die* silk

**Seife** [zeyf-e] *die* soap

**Seilbahn** [zeylbaan] *die* cable railway

**sein** [zeyn] *v* to be

**sein, e** [zeyn] *det* his; its

**seit** [zeyt] *prep* since ▸ er wohnt hier seit einem Jahr he's been living here for a year

**Seite** [zeyt-e] *die* side; page

**Seitenstreifen** [zeytenshtreyfen] *der* (on freeway) shoulder ▸ 'Seitenstreifen nicht befahrbar' 'soft shoulder'

**Sekt** [zehkt] *der* sparkling wine

**Selbstbedienung** [zehlpstbedeenung] *die* self-service

## Silvester

On December 31st (known in Germany as *Silvester*) the Germans show they know how to celebrate. At midnight, fireworks fill the skies: from streets, gardens, and balconies. It is also the tradition to melt a small piece of lead and throw it into some water where it forms strange shapes that are said to predict the future.

**selbst gemacht** [zehlpst gemakht] *adj* homemade

**Selters** [zehlters] *die* or *das* sparkling mineral water

**Semmel** [zehmel] *die* bread roll

**Semmelknödel** [zehmelkneudel] *der* bread dumpling

**Senf** [zehnf] *der* mustard

**senkrecht** [zehnk-rehsht] *adj* vertical

**September** [zehptehmber] *der* September

**Sessel** [zehsel] *der* armchair

**Sessellift** [zehsel-lift] *der* chairlift

**setzen** [zehtsen] *v* to put ▸ **sich setzen** to sit (down)

**sfr.** *abbr of* **Schweizer Franken** Swiss francs

**sicher** [zisher] *adj* safe; certain, sure ▸ **aber sicher!** of course!

**Sicherheitsgurt** [zisherheytsgurt] *der* safety belt

**Sicherung** [zisherung] *die* fuse

**Sicht** [zisht] *die* view

**sichtbar** [zishtbar] *adj* visible

**sie** [zee] *pron* she; her; it; they; them

**Sie** [zee] *pron (polite form)* you

**siebzehn** [zeep-tsayn] *num* seventeen

**siebzig** [zeep-tsish] *num* seventy

**Siedlung** [zeedlung] *die* housing estate; settlement

**Sieger** [zeeger] *der* the winner

**Silber** [zilber] *das* silver

**Silvester** [zilvehster] *das* New Year's Eve

**sind** [zint] *pres* are

**singen** [zingen] *v* to sing

**Sitte** [zit-e] *die* custom

**Sitz** [zits] *der* seat

**sitzen** [zitsen] *v* to sit

**Sitzplatz** [zitsplats] *der* seat

**Skiausrüstung** [shee-owsruustung] *die* skiing equipment

**Skikurs** [shee-kurs] *der* skiing course

**Skilehrer, Skilehrerin** [shee-lehrer, shee-lehrerin] *der, die* ski instructor

**Skilift** [shee-lift] *der* ski lift

**Skistock** [shee-shtok] *der* ski pole

**sofort** [zohfort] *adv* immediately, at once

**Sohn** [zohn] *der* son

**solange** [zoh-lang-e] *conj* as long as

**sollen** [zol-en] *v* should; to be supposed to ▸ **sollen wir anfangen?** shall we begin?

**Sommer** [zom-er] *der* summer

**Sommerfahrplan** [zom-er-faarplan] *der* summer timetable

**Sonderangebot** [zonder-an-ge-boht] *das* special offer

**sondern** [zondern] *conj* but

**Sonderpreis** [zonderpreys] *der* special price

**Sonnabend** [zonaabent] *der* Saturday

**Sonne** [zon-e] *die* sun

**Sonnenaufgang** [zon-en-owfgang] *der* sunrise

**Sonnenschirm** [zon-en-shirm] *der* sunshade

**Sonnenuntergang** [zon-en-untergang] *der* sunset

**sonnig** [zon-ish] *adj* sunny

**Sonntag** [zontaak] *der* Sunday

**sonn- und feiertags** *adv* on Sundays and public holidays

**Sozialversicherung** [zohtsiaal-fehr-zisherung] *die* social security

**Spanferkel** [shpaanfehrkel] *das* suckling pig

**sparen** [shpaaren] *v* to save

**Spargel** [shpaargel] *der* asparagus

**Sparkasse** [shpaar-kas-e] *die* savings bank

**Spaßbad** [shpaasbaat] *das swimming pool with waterslides, etc.*

**spät** [shpayt] *adv* late ▸ wie spät ist es? what time is it?

**später** [shpayter] *adv* later ▸ bis später! see you later!

**spätestens** [shpaytestenz] *adv* at the latest

**Spätlese** [shpaytlayz-e] *die* late vintage

**Spätvorstellung** [shpaytforshtehlung] *die* late performance

**Spätzle** [shpehtsl-e] *pl type of noodles resembling macaroni*

**Spaziergang** [shpatseergang] *der* walk ▸ einen Spaziergang machen to go for a walk

**Speck** [shpehk] *der* bacon; fat

**Speiseeis** [shpeyz-e-eys] *das* ice cream

**Speisekarte** [shpeyz-e-kart-e] *die* menu

**Speisesaal** [shpeyz-e-zaal] *der* dining room

**Speisewagen** [shpeyz-e-vaagen] *der* dining car

**Spezi**® [shpehtsi] *das* cola and lemonade

**Spiegelei** [shpeegeley] *das* fried egg

**Spiel** [shpeel] *das* game

**spielen** [shpeelen] *v* to play

**Spieler, Spielerin** [shpeeler, shpeeler-in] *der, die* player

**Spielfilm** [shpeelfilm] *der* feature film

**Spielplatz** [shpeelplats] *der* playground

**Spieß** [shpees] *der (for meat)* spit

**Spießchen** [shpees-shen] *das* skewer

**Spinat** [shpinaat] *der* spinach

**Spirituskocher** [shpirituskokher] *der* spirit stove

**Spitze** [shpits-e] *die (of pencil, knife)* point; peak; *(of league etc.)* top

**Sporthalle** [shport-hal-e] *die* sports hall

**Sporthotel** [shport-hohtehl] *das* hotel with sports facilities

**Sportler** [shportler] *der* sportsman

**Sportlerin** [shportlerin] *die* sportswoman

**Sportplatz** [shportplats] *der* sports field

**Sprache** [shpraakh-e] *die* language

**sprechen** [shprehshen] *v* to speak, to talk

**Sprechstunde** [shprehsh-shtund-e] *die (at doctor's)* office

**springen** [shpringen] *v* to jump

**Sprudel** [shproodel] *der* sparkling mineral water

**Sprühregen** [shpruu-raygen] *der* drizzle

**Sprungbrett** [shprungbreht] *das* springboard

**Spüle** [shpuul-e] *die* sink

**Spülmaschine** [shpuulmasheen-e] *die* dishwasher

**Spülmittel** [shpuul-mit-el] *das* dishwashing liquid

**Spülung** [shpuulung] *die (of toilet)* flush handle or button

**Spur** [shpoor] *die* trace; *(on road)* lane ▸ die Spur wechseln to change lanes

## Stammtisch

Don't sit down at a table in a bar with a *Stammtisch* sign on it unless you've been invited. The sign means that it's reserved for regulars.

**Spurrillen** [shpoor-ril-en] *pl* temporary road surface

**Staat** [shtaat] *der* state; country

**Staatsangehörigkeit** [shtaats-an-ge-heurishkeyt] *die* nationality

**Stachel** [shtakhel] *der* thorn; sting

**Stachelbeere** [shtakhelbehr-e] *die* gooseberry

**Stadt** [shtat] *die* town; city

**Stadtautobahn** [shtat-owtohbaan] *die* urban freeway

**Stadtbummel** [shtat-bum-el] *der* stroll through town

**Stadtführung** [shtatfuurung] *die* city sightseeing tour

**städtisch** [shtehtish] *adj* municipal; urban

**Stadtmitte** [shtat-mit-e] *die* downtown area

**Stadtrundfahrt** [shtatrundfaart] *die* city sightseeing tour

**Stammtisch** [shtamtish] *der table in a bar reserved for regulars*

**Standlicht** [shtantlisht] *das* sidelights

**Standspur** [shtantshpoor] *die* (on freeway) shoulder

**Stangenbrot** [shtangenbroht] *das* baguette, thin loaf of French bread

**stark** [shtark] *adj* strong; (rain) heavy

**Start** [shtart] *der* start; takeoff

**statt** [shtat] *conj & prep* instead of

**stattfinden** [shtatfinden] *v* to take place

**Stau** [shtow] *der* traffic jam

**Staubsauger** [shtowpzowger] *der* vacuum cleaner

**Staudamm** [shtowdam] *der* dam

**Staugefahr** [shtowgefaar] *die* risk of traffic congestion

**Stausee** [shtowzay] *der* reservoir

**Std.** *abbr of* **Stunde** hr

**Steakhaus** [staykhows] *das* steakhouse

**Stechmücke** [shtehsh-muuk-e] *die* mosquito

**Steckdose** [shtehk-dohz-e] *die* socket

**stecken** [shtehken] *v* to put

**Stecker** [shtehker] *der* plug

**Steg** [shtayk] *der* footbridge; jetty

**Stehcafé** [shtay-kafay] *das café in which customers stand at a counter to drink*

**stehen** [shtayen] *v* to stand; to be
▸ **stehen bleiben** to stop

**Stehplatz** [shtayplats] *der* standing place

**Steigung** [shteygung] *die* gradient

**steil** [shteyl] *adj* steep

**Steilküste** [shteyl-kuust-e] *die* cliffs

**Stein** [shteyn] *der* stone

**Steinbutt** [shteynbut] *der* turbot

**Steinpilz** [shteynpilts] *der* cep (mushroom)

**Steinschlag** [shteyn-shlaak] *der* falling rocks

**stellen** [shtehlen] *v* to put; (bottle) to stand upright; (alarm clock etc.) to set

**Stempel** [shtehmpel] *der* (in passport etc.) stamp

**Stereoanlage** [shtehrehyoh-anlaag-e] *die* stereo system

**Stern** [shtehm] *der* star

**Steuer** [shtoyer] *die* tax

**Steuer** [shtoyer] *das* steering wheel

**Stiefel** [shteefel] *der* boot

**Stiel** [shteel] *der (of brush, pan)* handle

**Stier** [shteer] *der* bull

**Stift** [shtift] *der* pen; pencil

**Stimmung** [shtimung] *die* mood; atmosphere

**Stirn** [shtirn] *die* forehead

**Stock** [shtok] *der* stick; story, floor ▸ im zweiten Stock on the third floor

**Stockwerk** [shtokvehrk] *das* story, floor

**Stoff** [shtof] *der* material; substance

**Stollen** [shtol-en] *der* stollen, *type of sweet bread eaten at Christmas*

**Stöpsel** [shteupsel] *der* plug

**stören** [shteuren] *v* to disturb ▸ 'bitte nicht stören!' 'please do not disturb'

**Störung** [shteurung] *die* disturbance, interruption; *(in transmission)* interference

**Str.** [shtraas-e] *abbr of* Straße St.

**Strafe** [shtraaf-e] *die* punishment; fine

**Strafzettel** [shtraaf-tsehtel] *der (for speeding etc.)* ticket

**Strand** [shtrant] *der* beach

**Strandkorb** [shtrantkorp] *der* wicker beach chair

**Straße** [shtraas-e] *die* street; road

**Straßenbahn** [shtraasenbaan] *die* streetcar

**Straßenglätte** [shtraasen-gleht-e] *die* slippery road ▸ mit Straßenglätte muss gerechnet werden slippery road surface ahead

**Straßenschäden** [shtraasenshayden] *pl* uneven road surface

**Straßenverkehrsordnung** [shtraasen-fehrkehrz-ordnung] *die* road traffic regulations

**Strecke** [shtrehk-e] *die* route; *(of road)* stretch; *(of railroad)* line; distance

**streicheln** [shtreysheln] *v* to stroke

**streichen** [shtreyshen] *v* to paint; to spread; to cross out; to cancel

**Streichkäse** [shtreysh-kayz-e] *der* cheese spread

**Streifenkarte** [shtreyfenkart-e] *die* multiple-journey ticket

**streiken** [shtreyken] *v* to strike

**streng** [shtrehng] *adj* strict

**streuen** [shtroyen] *v* to sprinkle

**Streuselkuchen** [shtroyzelkookhen] *der type of cake with crumble topping*

**Strickwaren** [shtrikvaaren] *pl* knitwear

**Strohhalm** [shtroh-halm] *der* the straw

**Strom** [shtrohm] *der* electricity; river; *(in sea)* current ▸ es regnet in Strömen it's pouring down rain

**Stück** [shtuuk] *das* piece; *(in theater)* play

**Student, Studentin** [shtoodehnt, shtoodehntin] *der, die* student

**Stufe** [shtoof-e] *die (on stairway)* step ▸ 'Vorsicht Stufe!' 'watch your step'

**Stuhl** [shtool] *der* chair

**Stunde** [shtund-e] *die* hour; lesson

**Sturm** [shturm] *der* storm

**Sturzhelm** [shturts-hehlm] *der* crash helmet

**Stuten** [shtooten] *der white bread containing raisins and almonds*

**suchen** [zookhen] *v* to look for

**Südfrucht** [zuutfrukht] *die* exotic fruit

**Sülze** [zuults-e] *die* headcheese

**Sumpf** [zumpf] *der* swamp

**Suppe** [zup-e] *die* soup

**süß** [zuus] *adj* sweet

**süßsauer** [zuus-zower] *adj* sweet and sour

**Süßspeise** [zuus-shpeyz-e] *die* dessert

**Süßstoff** [zuus-shtof] *der* sweetener

**Süßwaren** [zuus-vaaren] *pl* candy

**Tablett** [tableht] *das* tray

**Tablette** [tableht-e] *die* tablet

**Tafelwasser** [taafel-vas-er] *das* mineral water

**Tafelwein** [taafelveyn] *der* table wine

**Tag** [taak] *der* day ▸ guten Tag! hello!

**Tage** [taag-e] *pl* (menstruation) period

**Tag der Deutschen Einheit** [taak dehr doytshen eynheyt] *der* Day of German Unity

**Tagesfahrkarte** [taagez-faarkart-e] *die* day ticket

**Tagesfahrt** [taagezfaart] *die* day trip

**Tagesgericht** [taagez-gerisht] *das* dish of the day

**Tageskarte** [taagez-kart-e] *die* day ticket; today's menu

**Tagesrückfahrkarte** [taagez-ruukfaar-kart-e] *die* round-trip day ticket

**Tageszeitung** [taagez-tseytung] *die* daily newspaper

**täglich** [tayglish] *adj* daily ▸ dreimal täglich three times a day

**Tal** [taal] *das* valley

**Talsperre** [taal-shpehr-e] *die* dam

**Tank** [tank] *der* tank

**tanken** [tanken] *v* to get some gas

**Tankstelle** [tank-shtehl-e] *die* gas station

**Tankwart** [tankvaart] *der* gas station attendant

**Tanne** [tan-e] *die* fir tree

**tanzen** [tantsen] *v* to dance

**Tasche** [tash-e] *die* bag; pocket

**Taschendieb** [tashendeep] *der* pickpocket ▸ 'vor Taschendieben wird gewarnt' 'beware of pickpockets'

**Taste** [tast-e] *die* (on keyboard) key

**Taube** [towb-e] *die* pigeon; dove

**tauchen** [towkhen] *v* to dive

**tauen** [towen] *v* to melt

**taufen** [towfen] *v* to baptize

**tauschen** [towshen] *v* to swap

**tausend** [towzent] *num* a thousand

**Taxirufsäule** [taksi-roofzoyl-e] *die* public telephone for ordering taxis

**Taxistand** [taksi-shtant] *der* taxi stand

**Tee** [tay] *der* tea ▸ schwarzer Tee black tea

**Teebeutel** [tayboytel] *der* tea bag

**Teich** [teysh] *der* pond

**Teig** [teyk] *der* dough

**Teigwaren** [teykvaaren] *pl* pasta

**Teil** [teyl] *der* part

**teilnehmen** [teylnaymen] *v* to take part

**Teller** [tehler] *der* plate

**Tellerfleisch** [tehlerfleysh] *das* roast beef with horseradish and boiled potatoes

**Tempolimit** [tehmpoh-limit] *das* speed limit

**Tennisplatz** [tehnisplats] *der* tennis court

**Tennisschläger** [tehnis-shlayger] *der* tennis racket

**Teppich** [tehpish] *der* carpet; rug

**Termin** [tehrmeen] *der* date; appointment

**teuer** [toyer] *adj* expensive

**Teufel** [toyfel] *der* devil

**Theaterkarte** [tayaater-kart-e] *die* theater ticket

### Trafik

This has nothing to do with any illegal activity, or there wouldn't be so many of them in Austria! It's a type of tobacco store where they sell stamps, postcards and tickets for public transportation.

---

**Theaterstück** [tayaater-shtuuk] *das* play

**Theatervorstellung** [tayaater-forshtehlung] *die* performance

**Theke** [tay-ke] *die (in bar)* bar; *(in store)* counter

**Thermalbad** [tehrmaalbaat] *das* thermal bath (in hot springs)

**Thunfisch** [toonfish], **Tunfisch** [toonfish] *der* tuna

**tief** [teef] *adj* deep; *(temperature)* low

**Tiefe** [teef-e] *die* depth

**Tiefgarage** [teefgaraazh-e] *die* underground parking lot

**tiefgefroren** [teefgefroren] *adj* frozen

**tiefgekühlt** [teefgekuult] *adj* frozen

**Tiefkühltruhe** [teefkuul-troo-e] *die* freezer

**Tier** [teer] *das* animal

**Tierheim** [teerheym] *das* animal shelter

**Tinte** [tint-e] *die* ink

**Tintenfisch** [tintenfish] *der* octopus; squid; cuttlefish

**Tipp** [tip] *der (hint, advice)* tip

**Tisch** [tish] *der* table

**Tochter** [tokhter] *die* daughter

**Tod** [toht] *der* death

**tödlich** [teutlish] *adj* fatal

**toll** [tol] *adj* fantastic

**Tollwut** [tolvoot] *die* rabies

**Ton** [tohn] *der (musical)* note; *(of television)* sound; tone

**Tonne** [ton-e] *die* metric ton; barrel

**Topfen** [topfen] *der* cottage cheese

**Tor** [tor] *das* gate; door; *(in sport)* goal

**Torte** [tort-e] *die* gateau, torte, fancy cake

**tot** [toht] *adj* dead

**töten** [teuten] *v* to kill

**Tracht** [trakht] *die* traditional costume

**Trachtenfest** [trakhtenfehst] *das* event at which traditional costumes are worn

**Trafik** [trafik] *die* tobacconist

**tragen** [traagen] *v* to carry; to wear

**Tragetasche** [traag-e-tash-e] *die* plastic or paper shopping bag

**Transportmittel** [transportmitel] *das* means of transportation

**Traube** [trowb-e] *die* grape

**Traubenzucker** [trowben-tsuker] *der* glucose

**Traum** [trowm] *der* dream

**traurig** [trowrish] *adj* sad

**treffen** [trehfen] *v* to meet; *(target)* to hit ▸ **sich treffen** to meet

**Treffpunkt** [trehfpunkt] *der* meeting place

**Treibstoff** [treypshtof] *der* fuel

**trennen** [trehnen] *v* to separate; to divide

**Treppe** [trehp-e] *die* stairs

**Treppenhaus** [trehpenhows] *das* stairwell

**Tresen** [trayzen] *der (in store)* counter

**Tretboot** [traytboht] *das* paddle boat

**treten** [trayten] *v* to kick; *(brake)* to step on

**Trickfilm** [trikfilm] *der* cartoon

**Trimm-dich-Pfad** [trimdishpfaat] *der* fitness trail

**trinkbar** [trinkbar] *adj* drinkable

**trinken** [trinken] *v* to drink

**Trinkgeld** [trinkgehlt] *das (gratuity)* tip

**Trinkhalle** [trink-hal-e] *die* concession stand; *(in spa)* pump room

**Trinkhalm** [trinkhalm] *der* drinking straw

**Trinkwasser** [trink-vas-er] *das* drinking water

**trocken** [trok-en] *adj* dry

**trocknen** [troknen] *v* to dry

**Trödelmarkt** [treudelmarkt] *der* flea market

**Tropfen** [tropfen] *der* drop

**Tropfsteinhöhle** [tropf-shteyn-heul-e] *die* cave with stalactites and stalagmites

**trotz** [trots] *prep* in spite of

**trüb** [truup] *adj* cloudy

**Trüffel** [truufel] *der (mushroom)* truffle

**Truthahn** [troot-haan] *der* turkey

**Tuch** [tookh] *das* cloth; scarf

**tun** [toon] *v* to do; to put

**Tür** [tuur] *die* door

**Turm** [turm] *der* tower

**Turnhalle** [turn-hal-e] *die* gymnasium

**Turnier** [turneer] *das* tournament

**Turnschuh** [turnshoo] *der* sneaker

**Tüte** [tuut-e] *die* bag

# U

**U-Bahn** [oo-baan] *die* subway

**Übelkeit** [uubelkeyt] *die* nausea

**üben** [uuben] *v* to practice

**über** [uuber] *prep* over; above; via ◆ *adv* over ▸ ein Buch über Deutschland a book about Germany ▸ eine Rechnung über 149,50 Euro a bill for 149.50 euros ▸ über Ostern over Easter ▸ über Nacht bleiben to stay overnight

**überall** [uuberal] *adv* everywhere

**überbacken** [uuberbaken] *v* to bake or grill with a cheese topping

**überbucht** [uuberbookht] *adj* overbooked

**Überfahrt** [uuberfaart] *die* crossing

**überfüllt** [uuberfuult] *adj* overcrowded

**Übergewicht** [uubergevisht] *das* excess weight ▸ er hat Übergewicht he is overweight

**überholen** [uuberhohlen] *v* to overtake

**Überholverbot** [uuberhohlfehrboht] *das* ban on overtaking

**übermorgen** [uubermorgen] *adv* the day after tomorrow

**Übernachtung** [uubernakhtung] *die* overnight stay

**Überschwemmung** [uubershvehmung] *die* flood

**Übersetzung** [uuberzehtsung] *die* translation

**Übersichtskarte** [uuberzishtskart-e] *die* general map

**überwachen** [uubervakhen] *v* to monitor

**überweisen** [uuberveyzen] *v (money)* to transfer ▸ jemanden ins Krankenhaus überweisen to have somebody admitted to the hospital

**Ufer** [oofer] *das (of river)* bank; shore

### Umweltbewusstsein

This is a long word meaning 'environmental awareness.' In fact, the Germans are pioneers as far as ecology is concerned and the Greens (*Die Grünen*) are a strong political force here.

**Uhr** [oor] *die* clock; watch ▸ um 3 Uhr at 3 o'clock ▸ um wie viel Uhr? what time? ▸ wie viel Uhr ist es? what time is it?

**Uhrzeit** [oortseyt] *die* time

**UKW** [oo-kaa-vay] *die* FM

**um** [um] *prep* around; *(time)* at ◆ *conj* (in order) to ▸ um etwas bitten to ask for something ▸ um die 100 Euro about 100 euros ▸ um 10% steigen to increase by 10% ▸ um Ostern herum around Easter ▸ um zu in order to

**umbuchen** [umbookhen] *v* to change one's reservation for

**umdrehen** [umdrayen] *v* to turn; to turn around ▸ sich umdrehen to turn around

**Umgebung** [umgaybung] *die* surroundings

**Umgehungsstraße** [umgayungzshtraas-e] *die* bypass

**umgekehrt** [umgekehrt] *adj* opposite; reverse ◆ *adv* the other way around

**umkehren** [umkehren] *v* to turn around

**Umkleideraum** [umkleyd-e-rowm] *der* changing room

**Umleitung** [umleytung] *die* diversion

**Umrechnungskurs** [umrehshnungzkurs] *der* conversion table

**Umschlag** [umshlaak] *der* envelope

**umsonst** [umzonst] *adj* in vain; free

**Umsteigebahnhof** [umshteyg-e-baanhohf] *der* subway station where it is possible to change to a different line

**umsteigen** [umshteygen] *v* to change

▸ in den Intercity umsteigen to change to the intercity train

**Umtausch** [umtowsh] *der* exchange ▸ 'vom Umtausch ausgeschlossen' 'no refunds or exchanges'

**Umweg** [umvayk] *der* detour

**Umweltbewusstsein** [umvehltbevustzeyn] *das* environmental awareness

**Unbefugte** [unbefookt-e] *der* unauthorized person

**unbekannt** [unbekant] *adj* unknown

**unberechtigt** [unberehshtisht] *adj* unauthorized; unjustified ◆ *adv* without authorization ▸ unberechtigt parkende Fahrzeuge illegally parked vehicles

**und** [unt] *conj* and

**unerlaubt** [unehrlowpt] *adj* unauthorized

**Unfall** [unfal] *der* accident

**Unfallstation** [unfal-shtatsiohn] *die* emergency room

**ungefähr** [ungefehr] *adv* approximately, about

**ungültig** [unguultish] *adj* invalid

**Unkostenbeitrag** [unkostenbeytraak] *der* contribution towards expenses

**Unrecht** [unrehsht] *das* wrong

**unregelmäßig** [unraygelmaysish] *adj* irregular ◆ *adv* irregularly

**unser, e** [unzer] *det* our

**unten** [unten] *adv* at the bottom; downstairs ▸ nach unten down ▸ von unten from below

**unter** [unter] *prep* under; among; below

**Unterbrechung** [unterbrehshung] *die* interruption

**Unterbringung** [unterbringung] *die* accommodation

**Unterführung** [unterfuurung] *die* underpass

**Unterhaltung** [unterhaltung] *die* conversation; entertainment

**Unterkunft** [unterkunft] *die* accommodations

**unternehmen** [unternaymen] *v* to do; *(attempt, journey)* to make

**Unterricht** [unterisht] *der* lessons

**unterschiedlich** [untersheedlish] *adj* different

**unterschreiben** [untershreyben] *v* to sign

**Unterschrift** [untershrift] *die* signature

**unterstreichen** [untershtreyshen] *v* to underline

**Untersuchung** [unterzookhung] *die (medical)* examination; investigation

**Unterwäsche** [unter-vehsh-e] *die* underwear

**unterwegs** [untervayks] *adv* on the way

**unverbindlich** [unfehrbindlish] *adj* not binding

**unverbleit** [unfehrbleyt] *adj* unleaded

**Unwetter** [unvehter] *das* storm

**Uraufführung** [oor-owf-fuurung] *die* premiere

**Urlaub** [oorlowp] *der* vacation

**Urlauber** [oorlowber] *der* vacationer

**Ursache** [oorzakh-e] *die* cause

**usw.** [untzohveyter] *abbr of* **und so weiter** etc.

**Vater** [faater] *der* father

**Ventil** [vehnteel] *das* valve

**Verabredung** [fehr-apraydung] *die* appointment; *(rendezvous)* date ▸ eine Verabredung haben to have arranged to meet somebody

**Veranstaltung** [fehr-anshtaltung] *die* event; organization

**Verantwortung** [fehr-antvortung] *die* responsibility

**Verband** [fehr-bant] *der* association; bandage

**verbieten** [fehr-beeten] *v* to forbid

**verbilligt** [fehr-bilikt] *adj* reduced

**verbleit** [fehr-bleyt] *adj* leaded

**verboten** [fehr-bohten] *adj* forbidden

**Verbrauch** [fehr-browkh] *der* consumption

**Verbrennung** [fehr-brehnung] *die (injury)* burn

**verbringen** [fehr-bringen] *v (time)* to spend

**verdorben** [fehr-dorben] *adj (expired, rotten)* bad

**Verein** [fehr-eyn] *der* association, society

**vereist** [fehr-eyzt] *adj* icy

**Verfallsdatum** [fehrfalz-daatum] *das* expiration date

**Verfügung** [fehr-fuugung] *die* ▸ zur Verfügung stehen to be available ▸ zur Verfügung haben to have at one's disposal

**vergangen** [fehr-gangen] *adj* last

**vergessen** [fehr-gehs-en] *v* to forget

**Vergnügen** [fehr-gnuugen] *das* pleasure

**Vergnügungspark** [fehr-gnuugungzpark] *der* funfair

**vergoldet** [fehr-goldet] *adj* gilded

**verheiratet** [fehr-heyraatet] *adj* married

**verkaufen** [fehr-kowfen] *v* to sell

**Verkäufer, Verkäuferin** [fehr-koyfer, fehr-koyferin] *der, die* sales clerk

**verkehrsberuhigt** [fehr-kehrz-berooikt] *adj (street)* with speed reduction measures

**Verkehrsführung** [fehr-kehrz-fuurung] *die* road signs ▸ Verkehrsführung beachten follow road signs

**Verkehrsverein** [fehr-kehrz-fehreyn] *der* tourist office

**verlängern** [fehr-lehng-ern] *v* to extend; *(passport)* to renew

**verlassen** [fehr-las-en] *v* to leave

**Verleih** [fehr-ley] *der* rental store; rental company

**verleihen** [fehr-leyen] *v* to rent (out)

**verlieren** [fehr-leeren] *v* to lose

**Verlosung** [fehr-lohzung] *die* prize drawing

**Verlust** [fehr-lust] *der* loss

**vermieten** [fehr-meeten] *v* to rent (out) ▸ 'zu vermieten!' 'for rent'

**Vermieter** [fehr-meeter] *der* landlord

**Verpackung** [fehr-pakung] *die* packaging

**verpassen** [fehr-pas-en] *v* to miss

**Verpflegung** [fehr-pflaygung] *die* food

**versammeln** [fehr-zameln] *v* to gather

**verschenken** [fehr-shehnken] *v* to give away

**verschieben** [fehr-sheeben] *v* to postpone

**verschieden** [fehr-sheeden] *adj* different

**verschlechtern** [fehr-shlehshtern] *v* to make worse

**verschließen** [fehr-shlees-en] *v* to lock; to seal

**Verschluss** [fehr-shlus] *der* fastener; *(of bottle)* top

**verschneit** [fehr-shneyt] *adj* snow-covered

**verschreiben** [fehr-shreyben] *v* to prescribe

**verschreibungspflichtig** [fehr-shreybungz-pflishtish] *adj* available only by prescription

**versichert** [fehr-zishert] *adj* insured

**Versicherung** [fehr-zisherung] *die* insurance; insurance company

**versilbert** [fehr-zilbert] *adj* silver-plated

**Verspätung** [fehr-shpaytung] *die* delay ▸ eine Stunde Verspätung haben to be an hour late

**verstehen** [fehr-shtayen] *v* to understand ▸ sich verstehen to get along ▸ es versteht sich von selbst that goes without saying

**verteilen** [fehr-teylen] *v* to distribute ▸ sich verteilen to spread out

**Vertrag** [fehr-traak] *der* contract

**vertreten** [fehr-trayten] *v* to represent

**Vertretung** [fehr-traytung] *die* representation; representative

**verursachen** [fehr-oor-zakhen] *v* to cause

**Verwaltung** [fehr-valtung] *die* administration

**verwenden** [fehr-vehnden] *v* to use

**Verzeihung** [fehr-tseyung] *die* forgiveness ▸ Verzeihung! sorry!

**verzichten** [fehr-tsishten] *v* to do without

**Verzögerung** [fehr-tseugerung] *die* delay

**verzollen** [fehr-tsol-en] *v (at customs)* to declare

**viel** [feel] *adj* all the ◆ *det* a lot of, much; many ◆ *adv* a lot ▸ zu viel too much ▸ viel zu viel much too much

**vielleicht** [fileysht] *adv* perhaps; really

**vier** [feer] *num* four

**vierspurig** [feer-shpoorish] *adj* four-lane

**Viertel** [feertel] *das* quarter ▸ Viertel vor quarter to ▸ Viertel nach quarter after

**Viertelstunde** [feertel-shtund-e] *die* quarter of an hour

**vierzehn** [feer-tsayn] *num* fourteen

**vierzig** [feer-tsish] *num* forty

**Visum** [veezum] *das* visa

**Vogel** [fohgel] *der* bird

**Volksfest** [folkzfehst] *das* festival

**Volkstanz** [folkztants] *der* folk dance

**voll** [fol] *adj* full

**volljährig** [fol-yehrish] *adj* of age

**Vollkaskoversicherung** [fol-kaskoh-fehrzisherung] *die* comprehensive insurance

**Vollkornbrot** [fol-korn-broht] *das* wholemeal bread

**Vollmilch** [fol-milsh] *die* whole milk

**Vollpension** [fol-pehnziohn] *die* hotel room with all meals included

**Vollwertkost** [vol-vehrt-kost] *die* natural foods

**von** [fon] *prep* from; of ▸ sie wurde von einem Auto überfahren she was hit by a car ▸ von hier aus from here

**vor** [for] *prep* in front of; before ▸ vor drei Jahren three years ago ▸ fünf vor zwölf five to twelve

**voraus** [for-ows] *adv* in front; ahead ▸ im Voraus in advance

**Voraussetzung** [for-ows-zehtsung] *die* requirement

**vorbei** [for-bey] *adj* past, by; *(in time)* past, over ▸ vorbei sein to be over

**Vorbereitung** [for-bereytung] *die* preparation

**Vorbestellung** [for-beshtehlung] *die* advance reservation

**vorbeugen** [forboygen] *v* to prevent

▸ sich vorbeugen to lean forwards

**Vorbild** [forbilt] *das* role model

**vordere, r, s** [for-de-re] *adj* front

**Vorfahrt** [forfaart] *die* right of way ▸ 'Vorfahrt gewähren' 'yield' ▸ 'Vorfahrt geändert' 'altered right of way'

**Vorführung** [forfuurung] *die* performance

**vorgesehen** [for-gezayen] *adj* intended

**Vorhang** [forhang] *der* curtain

**Vorhängeschloss** [forhehng-e-shlos] *das* padlock

**vorher** [forhehr] *adv* beforehand

**Vorhersage** [forhehr-zaag-e] *die* forecast

**vorläufig** [forloyfish] *adj* provisional

**Vormittag** [formitaak] *der* morning

**vorn** [forn] *adv* at the front ▸ da vorn over there

**Vorname** [fornaam-e] *der* first name

**Vorort** [for-ort] *der* suburb

**Vorrat** [for-raat] *der* supply, stock ▸ solange der Vorrat reicht while supplies last

**Vorsaison** [for-sayzon] *die* pre-season

**Vorschlag** [forshlaak] *der* suggestion

**Vorschrift** [forshrift] *die* regulation

**Vorsicht** [forzisht] *die* care ▸ Vorsicht! look out!

**vorsichtig** [forzishtish] *adj* careful

**Vorspeise** [forshpeyz-e] *die* starter

**Vorstellung** [forshtehlung] *die* idea; *(in cinema, theater)* performance

**Vorteil** [forteyl] *der* advantage

**Vortrag** [fortraak] *der* talk

**Vor- und Zuname** [for-unt-tsoo-naam-e] *der* first name and last name

**Vorverkauf** [forfehrkowf] *der* advance reservation

**Vorwahl** [forvaal] *die (telephone)* area code

**waagerecht** [vaagerehsht] *adj* horizontal

**wach** [vakh] *adj* awake ▸ wach werden to wake up

**Wacholder** [vakholder] *der* juniper

**wachsen** [vaksen] *v* to grow

**Wachtel** [vakhtel] *die* quail

**Wächter** [vehshter] *der* guard

**Wackelpeter** [vakelpayter] *der* Jell-O®

**Waffe** [vaf-e] *die* weapon

**Waffel** [vafel] *die* waffle

**Wagen** [vaagen] *der* car ▸ 'Wagen hält' 'bus stopping'

**Wahl** [vaal] *die* choice; election

**wählen** [vaylen] *v* to choose; *(telephone number)* to dial

**während** [vehrent] *prep* during

**Wald** [valt] *der* wood, forest

**Waldlehrpfad** [valtlehrpfaat] *der* nature trail

**Waldorfsalat** [valdorfzalaat] *der* Waldorf salad

**Waldweg** [valtvayk] *der* forest path

**Walnuss** [valnus] *die* walnut

**Walzer** [valtser] *der* waltz

**Wand** [vant] *die* wall

**Wanderkarte** [vanderkart-e] *die* walking map

**wandern** [vandern] *v* to go walking

**Wanderweg** [vandervayk] *der* trail

**wann** [van] *adv* when

**Ware** [vaar-e] *die* product

**Warenhaus** [vaarenhows] *das* department store

**warm** [varm] *adj* warm ▸ es ist warm it's warm

**warnen** [varnen] *v* to warn ▸ vor ... wird gewarnt beware of ...

**warten** [varten] *v* to wait ▸ 'hier warten' 'wait here'

**warum** [varum] *adv* why

**was** [vas] *pron* what; which, that ▸ was für what kind of

**Wäsche** [vehsh-e] *die* washing, laundry; underwear

**waschen** [vashen] *v* to wash ▸ Waschen und Fönen shampoo and blow-dry

**Waschmittel** [vash-mit-el] *das* detergent

**Wasser** [vas-er] *das* water ▸ stilles Wasser flat water, uncarbonated water

**wasserdicht** [vas-er-disht] *adj* waterproof

**Wasserfall** [vas-er-fal] *der* waterfall

**Wasserhahn** [vas-er-haan] *der* faucet

**wasserlöslich** [vas-er-leuzlish] *adj* soluble in water

**Wassermelone** [vas-er-mehlohn-e] *die* watermelon

**Watte** [vat-e] *die* absorbent cotton

**Wechselgeld** [vehkselgehlt] *das* change

**wechseln** [vehkseln] *v (money, subject)* to change; to exchange

**Wechselstube** [vehksel-shtoob-e] *die* office for changing currency

**wecken** [vehken] *v* to wake

**Wecker** [vehker] *der* alarm clock

**weg** [vehk] *adv* away ▸ er ist schon weg he's already gone

## Weihnachtsmarkt

Christmas markets have a long tradition in Germany's big towns, with the most famous one being held in Nuremberg. For the whole of the month of December, stands that look like little chalets are crammed with handicrafts. Foods such as spiced bread (*Lebkuchen*) and tasty mulled wine made with cinnamon (*Glühwein*) are also for sale.

**Weg** [vayk] *der* path; way ▸ dem ausgeschilderten Weg folgen follow the path that has the signs

**wegen** [vaygen] *prep* because of

**Wegweiser** [vaykveyser] *der* signpost

**wegwerfen** [vehkvehrfen] *v* to throw away

**weiblich** [veyblish] *adj* female; feminine

**weich** [veysh] *adj* soft

**weich gekocht** [veysh gekokht] *adj* soft-boiled

**Weichkäse** [veyshkayz-e] *der* soft cheese

**Weihnachten** [veynakhten] Christmas ▸ frohe Weihnachten! Merry Christmas!

**Weihnachtsabend** [veynakhtsaabent] *der* Christmas Eve

**Weihnachtsmann** [veynakhtsman] *der* Santa Claus

**Weihnachtsmarkt** [veynakhtsmarkt] *der* Christmas market

**Weihnachtstag** [veynakhtstaak] *der* Christmas Day ▸ erster/zweiter Weihnachtstag Christmas/Boxing Day

**weil** [veyl] *conj* because

**Wein** [veyn] *der* wine; vine

**Weinberg** [veynbehrk] *der* vineyard

**Weinbergschnecke** [veynbehrkshnehk-e] *die* snail

**Weinbrand** [veynbrant] *der* brandy

**weinen** [veynen] *v* to cry

**Weinlese** [veynlayz-e] *die* grape harvest

**Weinprobe** [veynprohb-e] *die* wine tasting

**Weinstube** [veyn-shtoob-e] *die* wine bar

**Weintraube** [veyntrowb-e] *die* grape

**weiß** [veys] *adj* white

**Weißbier** [veysbeer] *das* wheat beer

**Weiße** [veys-e] *die* wheat beer

**Weißkohl** [veyskohl] *der* white cabbage

**Weißwurst** [veysvurst] *die* veal sausage

## Wein

White wine makes up 90% of German wine production. Grown in several regions (in the Rhineland, the Moselle, Franconia, the Elbe valley and the Bade region), they are similar to the French wines from Alsace. There are three categories: *Tafelwein* (table wine), *QBA* (quality of guaranteed origin) and *QMP* (vintage).

**weit** [veyt] *adj* wide; long ♦ *adv* far, a long way

**weiter** [veyter] *adv* further

**weiterfahren** [veyterfaaren] *v* to drive on

**Weizen** [veytsen] *der* wheat

**Weizenbier** [veytsenbeer] *das* wheat beer

**welche, r, s** [vehlsh-e] *det* which ♦ *pron (in a question)* which one

**Wellenbad** [vehlenbaat] *das* wave pool

**Welt** [vehlt] *die* world

**wem** [vaym] *pron* (to) who

**wen** [vayn] *pron* who

**Wendemöglichkeit** [vehnd-e-meu-glishkeyt] *die* ▸ keine Wendemöglichkeit no turning

**wenden** [vehnden] *v* to turn

**wenig** [vaynish] *det* little; a few

**weniger** [vayniger] *adv* less

**wenigstens** [vaynikztenz] *adv* at least

**wenn** [vehn] *conj* when; if

**wer** [vehr] *pron* who

**Werbung** [vehrbung] *die* advertising

**werden** [vehrden] *v* to become ♦ *v* to get ▸ wir werden sehen we will see

**werfen** [vehrfen] *v* to throw

**Werk** [vehrk] *das (of art)* work; plant, works

**Werkstatt** [vehrkshtat] *die* workshop; *(for repairing cars)* garage

**Werktag** [vehrktaak] *der* weekday

**Wert** [vehrt] *der* value

**wertlos** [vehrtlohs] *adj* worthless

**Wertsachen** [vehrtzakhen] *pl* valuables

**wertvoll** [vehrtfol] *adj* valuable

**weshalb** [vehs-halp] *adv* why

**Wespe** [vehsp-e] *die* wasp

**Westen** [vehsten] *der* west

**Wettbewerb** [vehtbevehrp] *der* competition

**Wette** [veht-e] *die* bet

**Wetter** [vehter] *das* weather ▸ bei gutem/schlechtem Wetter if the weather is good/bad

**Wettkampf** [vehtkampf] *der* contest

**wichtig** [vishtish] *adj & adv* important

**Wickelraum** [vikelrowm] *der* baby changing room

**widerrechtlich** [vider-rehshtlish] *adj* illegal ♦ *adv* illegally ▸ widerrechtlich abgestellte Fahrzeuge illegally parked vehicles

**wie** [vee] *adv* how ♦ *conj* like; as ▸ wie spät ist es? what time is it? ▸ wie lange how long ▸ wie oft how often

**wieder** [veeder] *adv* again

**Wiederhören** [veederheuren] *das* ▸ auf Wiederhören! goodbye!

**wiederkommen** [veeder-kom-en] *v* to come back

**Wiedersehen** [veederzayen] *das* reunion ▸ auf Wiedersehen! goodbye!

**Wiedervereinigung** [veeder-fehreyni-gung] *die* reunification

**wiegen** [veegen] *v* to weigh

**Wiese** [veez-e] *die* meadow

**wie viel** [vee feel] *pron* how much ▸ wie viel Uhr ist es? what time is it?

**wild** [vilt] *adj* wild

**Wild** [vilt] *das (for hunting, eating)* game

**Wildleder** [viltlayder] *das* suede

**Wildschwein** [viltshveyn] *das* wild boar

**Wildwasser** [vilt-vas-er] *das* white water

**willkommen** [vil-kom-en] *adj* welcome

**Wimper** [vimper] *die* eyelash

**Wind** [vint] *der* wind ▸ böiger Wind gusty wind

**Windbeutel** [vintboytel] *der* ≃ cream puff

**Windel** [vindel] *die* diaper

**windig** [vindish] *adj* windy

**Windpocken** [vintpoken] *pl* chickenpox

**Winter** [vinter] *der* winter

**Winterfahrplan** [vinterfaarplan] *der (for trains, etc.)* winter schedule

**Winterreifen** [vinter-reyfen] *der* winter tire

**Wintersport** [vintershport] *der* winter sport

**wir** [veer] *pron* we

**Wirkung** [virkung] *die* effect

**Wirsing** [virzing] *der* savoy cabbage

**Wirt** [virt] *der* landlord

**Wirtin** [virtin] *die* landlady

**Wirtschaft** [virt-shaft] *die* economy; bar

**Wirtshaus** [virts-hows] *das* public bar, *often with accommodation*

**wischen** [vishen] *v* to wipe

**wissen** [vis-en] *v* to know

**Wissenschaft** [vis-en-shaft] *die* science

**Witz** [vits] *der* joke

**wo** [voh] *pron* where ▸ bis wo where to ▸ von wo where from

**Woche** [vokh-e] *die* week

**Wochenende** [vokhen-ehnd-e] *das* weekend

**Wochenkarte** [vokhenkart-e] *die* weekly ticket

**wöchentlich** [veushentlich] *adj & adv* weekly

**woher** [voh-hehr] *pron* from where ▸ woher kommen Sie? where do you come from?

**wohin** [voh-hin] *pron* where

**wohnen** [vohnen] *v* to live; to stay

**wohnhaft** [vohnhaft] *adj* resident ▸ wohnhaft in ... resident at

**Wohnmobil** [vohnmohbeel] *das* motorhome

**Wohnort** [vohnort] *der* place of residence

**Wohnsitz** [vohnzits] *der* place of residence

**Wohnung** [vohnung] *die* apartment

**Wohnwagen** [vohnvaagen] *der* trailer

**Wolke** [volk-e] *die* cloud

**Wolle** [vol-e] *die* wool

**wollen** [vol-en] *v* to want

**Wort** [vort] *das* word

**Wunde** [vund-e] *die* wound

**Wunsch** [vunsh] *der* wish ▸ nach Wunsch as desired

**wünschen** [vuunshen] *v* to wish

**Würfel** [vuurfel] *der* cube; dice

**Würfelzucker** [vuurfel-tsuker] *der* sugar cubes

**Wurm** [vurm] *der* worm

**Wurst** [vurst] *die* sausage; cold meats

**Würstchen** [vuurst-shen] *das* sausage

**Wurstwaren** [vurstvaaren] *pl* sausages and cold meats

**Wurzel** [vurtsel] *die* root

**würzig** [vuurtsish] *adj* spicy

**Würzmischung** [vuurtsmishung] *die* spice mix

# Z

**Zahl** [tsaal] *die* number

**zahlen** [tsaalen] *v* to pay; to pay for ▸ zahlen, bitte! check please!

**zählen** [tsaylen] *v* to count

**zahlreich** [tsaalreysh] *adj* numerous

**Zahlung** [tsaalung] *die* payment

**Zahn** [tsaan] *der* tooth

**Zäpfchen** [tsehpfshen] *das* suppository

**zart** [tsart] *adj (meat)* tender

**Zaun** [tsown] *der* fence

**Zebrastreifen** [tsaybra-shtreyfen] *der* crosswalk

**zehn** [tsayn] *num* ten

**Zehnerkarte** [tsaynerkart-e] *die* book of ten tickets

**Zeichen** [tseyshen] *das* sign; symbol

**Zeichenerklärung** [tseyshen-ehrkleh-rung] *die (to symbols)* key

**Zeichentrickfilm** [tseyshentrikfilm] *der* cartoon

**zeichnen** [tseyshnen] *v* to draw

**zeigen** [tseygen] *v* to show

**Zeit** [tseyt] *die* time ▸ sich Zeit lassen to take one's time ▸ zurzeit at the moment

**Zeitschrift** [tseytshrift] *die* magazine

**Zeitung** [tseytung] *die* newspaper

**Zelt** [tsehlt] *das* tent

**zelten** [tsehlten] *v* to camp

**Zeltplatz** [tsehltplats] *der* campsite

**Zettel** [tsehtel] *der* piece of paper; *(written)* note

**Ziege** [tseeg-e] *die* goat

**Ziegenkäse** [tseegenkayz-e] *der* goat cheese

**ziehen** [tsee-en] *v* to pull

**Ziel** [tseel] *das* destination; aim, goal

**Ziffer** [tsif-er] *die (number)* figure

**Zimmer** [tsim-er] *das* room ▸ 'Zimmer frei' 'vacancies' ▸ Zimmer mit Bad room with bathroom ▸ Zimmer mit Frühstück bed and breakfast

**Zimmerkellner** [tsim-er-kehlner] *der* room-service waiter

**Zimmermädchen** [tsim-er-maydshen] *das* chambermaid

**Zimmerschlüssel** [tsim-er-shluusel] *der* room key

**Zimt** [tsimt] *der* cinnamon

**zirka** [tsirka] *adv* approximately

**ZOB** *abbr of* **Zentraler Omnibus-bahnhof** central bus station

**Zollabfertigung** [tsol-apfehrtigung] *die* customs clearance

**Zollbeamte** [tsol-be-amt-e] *der* customs officer

**Zollerklärung** [tsol-ehrklehrung] *die* customs declaration

**zollfrei** [tsolfrey] *adj* duty-free

**zollpflichtig** [tsol-pflishtish] *adj* liable for duty

**Zopf** [tsopf] *der* braid

**zu** [tsoo] *prep* to; at ◆ *conj (with infinitive)* to ▸ zu Hause at home ▸ zu Fuß on foot ▸ 5 Kilo zu 20 Euro 5 kilos for 20 euros

**Zubringer** [tsoobringer] *der (onto free-way)* ramp

**Zucchini** [tsukeeni] *die* zucchini

**Zucker** [tsuk-er] *der* sugar

**zuckerkrank** [tsuk-er-krank] *adj* diabetic

**Zuckerwatte** [tsuk-er-vat-e] *die* cotton candy

**Zuckerzusatz** [tsuk-er-tsoozats] *der*

added sugar ▸ 'ohne Zuckerzusatz' 'no added sugar'

**zudrehen** [tsoodrayen] *v (faucet)* to turn off

**zuerst** [tsooehrst] *adv* first; at first

**Zufahrtsstraße** [tsoofaarts-shtraas-e] *die* access road

**zufrieden** [tsufreeden] *adj* satisfied

**Zug** [tsook] *der* train

**Zugabteil** [tsookapteyl] *das* compartment

**Zugang** [tsoogang] *der* access

**Zugauskunft** [tsook-owskunft] *die* train information

**Zugführer** [tsookfuurer] *der* senior conductor

**Zugschaffner** [tsookshafner] *der (on train)* conductor

**Zugverbindung** [tsookfehrbindung] *die* (train )connection

**Zukunft** [tsookunft] *die* future

**zuletzt** [tsulehtst] *adv* lastly; finally

**zumachen** [tsoomakhen] *v* to close

**Zuname** [tsoonaam-e] *der* last name

**Zündschlüssel** [tsuunt-shluusel] *der* ignition key

**Zunge** [tsung-e] *die* tongue

**zurück** [tsuruuk] *adv* back ▸ der Weg zurück the way back ▸ zurück sein to be back

**zurückbekommen** [tsuruuk-bekom-en] *v* to get back ▸ Sie bekommen noch 3 Euro zurück you get three euros in change

**zurückfahren** [tsuruukfaaren] *v* to go back; to drive back

**zurückgeben** [tsuruukgayben] *v* to give back

**zurückrufen** [tsuruukroofen] *v* to call back

**zurücktreten** [tsuruuktrayten] *v* to step back

**zurückzahlen** [tsuruuk-tsaalen] *v* to pay back

**Zusage** [tsoozaag-e] *die* acceptance

**zusammen** [tsu-zam-en] *adv* together; altogether

**Zusammensetzung** [tsu-zamen-zeht-sung] *die* composition

**Zusatz** [tsoozats] *der* additive

**zusätzlich** [tsoozehtslish] *adj* extra ◆ *adv* in addition

**zuschauen** [tsooshowen] *v* to watch

**Zuschauer** [tsooshower] *der* member of the audience; spectator

**Zuschlag** [tsooshlaak] *der* extra charge

**zuschlagpflichtig** [tsooshlaakpflishtish] *adj* subject to an extra charge

**zuschließen** [tsooshleesen] *v* to lock

**zusehen** [tsoozayen] *v* to watch

**Zustand** [tsooshtant] *der* state, condition

**zusteigen** [tsooshteygen] *v (bus, train)* to get on

**zutreffen** [tsootrehfen] *v* to apply

**zwanzig** [tsvan-tsish] *num* twenty

**Zweck** [tsvek] *der* purpose

**zwei** [tsvey] *num* two

**Zweibettzimmer** [tsveybeht-tsim-er] *das* twin room

**Zwetsche** [tsvetsh-e] *die* plum

**Zwieback** [tsveebak] *der* zwieback

**Zwiebel** [tsveebel] *die* onion

**zwingen** [tsvingen] *v* to force

**zwischen** [tsvishen] *prep* between

**Zwischenfall** [tsvishenfal] *der* incident

**Zwischenlandung** [tsvishenlandung] *die* layover

**Zwischenstopp** [tsvishenshtop] *der* stop

**Zwischenzeit** [tsvishen-tseyt] *die* ▸ in der Zwischenzeit in the meantime

**zwölf** [tsveulf] *num* twelve